Routledge Revivals

English Prisons Under Local Government

English Prisons Under Local Government

Sidney and Beatrice Webb

With a Preface by Bernard Shaw

Routledge
Taylor & Francis Group

First published in 1922 by Longmans Green & Co.

This edition first published in 2018 by Routledge
2 Park Square, Milton Park, Abingdon, Oxon, OX14 4RN
and by Routledge
52 Vanderbilt Avenue, New York, NY 10017, USA

Routledge is an imprint of the Taylor & Francis Group, an informa business

© 1963 by Taylor and Francis

Publisher's Note
The publisher has gone to great lengths to ensure the quality of this reprint but points out that some imperfections in the original copies may be apparent.

Disclaimer
The publisher has made every effort to trace copyright holders and welcomes correspondence from those they have been unable to contact.
A Library of Congress record exists under ISBN:

ISBN 13: 978-0-367-11049-9 (hbk)
ISBN 13: 978-0-367-11052-9 (pbk)
ISBN 13: 978-0-429-02449-8 (ebk)

ENGLISH LOCAL GOVERNMENT

ENGLISH PRISONS UNDER
LOCAL GOVERNMENT

ENGLISH LOCAL GOVERNMENT

A series of eleven volumes on the growth
and structure of English Local Government
by SIDNEY and BEATRICE WEBB

*Volumes 10 and 11 were originally published separately, but are now
included to make the scope of the work more comprehensive.

ENGLISH LOCAL GOVERNMENT VOLUME 6

English Prisons Under Local Government

SIDNEY and BEATRICE
WEBB

With a Preface by Bernard Shaw

With a new Introduction by
LEON RADZINOWICZ

*Wolfson Professor of Criminology
in the University of Cambridge*

FRANK CASS AND CO. LTD.
1963

First published by Longmans Green & Co. in 1922

This edition published by FRANK CASS & Co., 10, Woburn Walk, London, W.C.1., by the kind permission of the Trustees of the Passfield Estate.

First published   1922
Reprinted   1963

Printed in Great Britain by Charles Birchall & Sons Ltd., Liverpool
and bound by Thomas Nelson and Sons Ltd, Edinburgh

CONTENTS

CONTENTS *(continued)*

INTRODUCTION

On the 31st December, 1800, Parliament passed an enactment which authorised, for the first time, a census of population in England. The objection that it would involve an unjustifiable interference on the part of the State was overruled. This step has been described by the social historian, Kirkman Gray, as the " first official recognition of the duty of the State to *know* in detail the vital, cultural and economic condition of the whole nation." Once a state has assumed the duties of knowing, he concludes, it accepts an obligation to act upon that knowledge, to initiate many forms of social service.

The principle of state intervention had been given its first recognition, but in practice it still meant very little. For a long time the starkest of social evils created by the industrial revolution went unperceived, and when perceived they were handled in a way which bore no relation to their magnitude and complexity. " For fifty years ", to quote Dr. Trevelyan, " that great change was left uncontrolled by the community which it was transforming. So new was the experience, that for a while the wisest were as much at fault as the most foolish. Burke for all his powers of prophecy, Pitt for all his study of Adam Smith, Fox for all his welcome to the new democracy, no more understood the English economic revolution, and no more dreamt of controlling it for the common good, than George III himself."

As long as social standards were not raised, it was vain to expect advances in the penal system. Penal standards depend largely upon the prevailing level of social conditions and the pace of penal reform is largely determined by progress in social reform. To trace this interaction in detail would be beyond the scope of an introduction, but some of the more significant links may be touched upon. Whilst the human effects of economic change were ignored in the community of large it was not surprising that prisons remained much as John Howard had found them in 1777. In his memorable survey, the 518 gaols in England and Wales, nominally belonging to the Crown, but in practice under a variety of authorities, were condemned as hot-beds of corruption, nurseries of crime and havens of vice, constituting a living scandal and a challenge to conscience. Gaol keeping had often been a business, out of which the gaoler, a private individual, earned a living. Otherwise such places of confinement were under the charge, lax or extortionate, of the justices of the peace.

And just as neither the administration of the poor law nor the doling out of private charity discriminated between the varying needs and natures of the poor, tending to reduce all to a degraded mass, so in the prisons we find the same lack of imagination, with a demoralisation even harder to escape. In only twenty-three of the five hundred and eighteen gaols were the inmates classified according to regulations. In fifty-nine there was no segregation whatever, even according to sex ; in a hundred and thirty-six there was but one division, and in nearly four-fifths there was no employment of any kind. Prison reform, conceived on the most modest scale, seemed to defeat even Peel's administrative vision and determination.

Into these conditions were thrust offenders and suspected offenders of all ages. In 1816, when the population of London was a little less than a million and a half, its prisons contained over three thousand offenders below twenty years of age, half of whom were under seventeen. How could attention be spared for children in prison when it was not until 1833 that the first measures were taken to inspect the conditions of those in factories ? The first Inspectors of Prisons were appointed two years later.

By that time, however, the social scene was changing rapidly. A series of parliamentary enquiries, altogether remarkable for the thoroughness and fairness of their reports, was set on foot. They revealed an appalling state of affairs in public health, in education, in industry, in living conditions and in municipal government. Disraeli's famous picture of " The Two Nations " was well authenticated. Yet within thirty years the " Condition of the Working Class in England ", which Frederick Engels had described in 1844 as an inevitable and permanent characteristic of a capitalist system, had been re-shaped on so large a scale that it already belonged to past history.

But in dealing with anti-social strata the state has always adhered to, though seldom openly professed, the principle of less eligibility. The standards of those coming within the scope of the poor law were to be kept well below those of the worst paid labourer in employment. And offenders were to be deterred by separate confinement and useless drudgery, whether as a preliminary to transportation or as a punishment in itself.

A belief in the reforming effect of solitary confine-ment had influenced the Quakers of Philadelphia in the construction of their town prison ; the success claimed for their experiment converted the penal authorities on the Continent as well as in England. Charles Dickens stood aloof from the general en-thusiasm for the miracles alleged to be wrought by isolation in a cell : although a deterrent effect might be conceded, reformation under those conditions was chimerical. He traced the consecutive phases from the initial shock, through depression, over-sensibility, detachment from reality, placid adjustment, down to the helpless mental state of dissolved responsi-bility on the final day of discharge. But his was a lone voice of dissent. Treadwheel and crank—the soul-destroying invention of unproductive labour—were the ideal adjuncts of this unnatural regime. " I should . . . use no other secondary punishment than the treadmill ", wrote Sydney Smith, in the *Edinburgh Review*, " varying in all degrees from a day to a life . . . This punishment would be economical, certain, well-administered, little liable to abuse, capable of infinite division, a perpetual example before the eyes of those who want it, affecting the imagination only with horror and disgust, and affording great ease to the government."

In the second half of the nineteenth century, the intervention of the state continued in general to be regarded as a last resort, needed to remedy only the gravest social evils and to meet the most obvious abuses and deficiencies. Yet during that time an administrative machinery was being built up through which the welfare state of the future could operate, and private effort was stirring the public conscience about the fate of some of those caught in the remorseless machines of the poor law and penal systems.

The Webbs have well described the stages, culminating in the great Prison Act of 1877, by which a national penal system, based on imprisonment and penal servitude, was built up. The English state, no longer relying on the elimination of its offenders by the threat of capital punishment or the regular flow of transportation, had assumed responsibility for dealing with them as part of its normal social arrangements.

Two-thirds of the corrupt and antiquated prisons hitherto under local control were closed. New penitentiaries were erected, and the whole administration was transferred to the Secretary of State for the Home Office. In Whitehall, a central body of prison administrators, not exceeding five, was set up to direct what had at last become a prison system. In no other branch of English public administration had a local service thus been transferred *en bloc* to the control of the central government.

Through the vast improvement in the regimen, the rates of mortality, of sickness and of suicide were reduced ; fair standards in living quarters, in clothing, in diet, in disciplinary measures, were established ; greater care was taken in recruiting the prison staff and a vigilant supervision from the centre was exercised to secure uniformity in all the details of the policy.

INTRODUCTION

The system of punishment was still largely based on retribution and deterrence, which were to be secured by meting out penalties proportionate to the intrinsic gravity of the offence. An underlying belief in human equality produced, in the penal sphere, the assumption that every individual has the same powers of resisting temptation, deserves the same punishment for the same crime, and will react in the same way to punishment. In the words of James Stuart Mill, the punishment " should be determined by its adaptation to the crime ".

But the first exceptions were already appearing with respect of young offenders and first offenders. In 1854 an Act was passed by which offenders under 16 years of age were recognised as a distinct class, to be sent to reformatory schools for the purposes of corrective training. Its effect was far-reaching : in 1850 there were still 15,000 juveniles detained in prisons, but by the end of the nineteenth century the number had dropped to 2,000. The Probation of First Offenders Act of 1887, " permitting the conditional release of first offenders in certain cases," marked another significant encroachment on the traditional principle of deterrence and the mechanical apportionment of punishment to crime. In using their discretionary power, the courts were expected to take into account not only the nature of the offence but the " youth, character and antecedents of the offender and any extenuating circumstances ". And, to quote the Act again, they were to release the offender on probation of good conduct when this course of action appeared to them " to be expedient." The retributory doctrine of punishment is not based on expediency.

These were, however, but isolated advances. It was not until 1894 that a major attempt was made to review penal legislation and administration critically and fundamentally, and to see whether the time had not come to endow the country with a system much more in harmony with the new consciousness of social responsibility which was then developing. This task was discharged by the Gladstone Committee, and their report of 1895 stands out as one of the most forcible and imaginative statements produced by this or any other country on the subject of penal treatment.

" While sentences may, roughly speaking, be the measure of particular offences," the report stated, " they are not the measure of the character of the offenders."   And, in accordance with this new individualised approach in penal theory and practice, the Committee recommended the replacement of the traditional system of punishments varying only in degree by new methods of treatment for certain classes of offenders, such as the habitual criminal, the young adult or the mentally defective. They refused to accept the pessimistic view that the prison system, by its very nature and effect, made the reformation of the individual impossible, and that " punish " and " reform " were, and ever would be, two contradictory and irreconcilable terms.

Once again penal history was reflecting a changed outlook on social responsibility in the community at large. State intervention was penetrating further and further in to the various spheres of communal and individual life.   Social legislation was being promoted to better the lot of the mass of the people. The evolution of the welfare state could not fail to exercise a profound influence on attitudes towards penal administration. The tenor of the new approach was captured by Winston Churchill when he was Home Secretary at that very period, more than fifty years ago : " The mood and temper of the public with regard to the treatment of crime and criminals is one of the most unfailing tests of any country. A calm, dispassionate recognition of the rights of the accused ; a constant heart-searching by all charged with the duty of punishment ; a desire and eagerness to rehabilitate in the world of industry those who have paid their due in the hard coinage of punishment ; tireless efforts towards the discovery of curative and regenerative processes ; unfailing faith that there is a treasure, if you can only find it, in the heart of every man ; these are the symbols which, in the treatment of crime and the criminal, mark and measure the stored-up strength of a nation and are sign and proof of the living virtue in it."

When the preoccupation of domestic policies is to raise the general level of economic, social and cultural standards, delinquency itself tends to be seen as part of the texture of society or as a symptom of individual maladjustment. There is a search for constructive remedial measures, with emphasis on prevention and treatment. The Probation of Offenders Act of 1907, the Children's Acts of 1908 and 1933, the Prevention of Crime Act of 1908, which introduced not only prolonged detention for persistent offenders but borstal training for young adults, the Mental Deficiency Acts of 1913 and 1927, and the Acts of 1914 and 1935 which allowed time to pay fines, thus reducing imprisonment in default, mark subsequent stages in this new approach to crime and punishment. Indeed it is the rapid restriction of imprisonment which is perhaps the most significant development. " So far as can be seen at present ", to quote the Webb's own aphorism, " the most practical and the most hopeful of prison reforms is to keep people out of prison altogether."

At the end of the nineteenth century detention in penal institutions had still been the mainstay of the entire system. The annual number of offenders received in prison in 1904 was as high as one hundred and ninety thousand, at least two-thirds of whom were undergoing short sentences of two weeks or less, whilst not even one per cent of the total were serving sentences of over twelve months. Before the second world war the number had been thinned out to under thirty thousand. And even today, in spite of the great increase in crime, it does not exceed forty-one thousand. The use of short-term imprisonment, especially for first offenders, continues to be strongly discouraged and recent legislation has abolished prison sentences, except in the gravest cases, for young offenders up to the age of twenty-one. In broad terms, the statistics of the treatment of criminals as now prevailing may thus be summed up : out of every hundred convicted of indictable offences only fourteen are sentenced to imprisonment, corrective training and preventive detention ; thirty-eight are fined ; twenty-one are put on probation ; nineteen are absolutely or conditionally discharged, and seven are sent to borstals, detention centres or approved schools.

In 1948 the gradual but far-reaching process of penal reconstruction culminated in the passing of the Criminal Justice Act. Everything that matters in the penal sphere was brought within its scope, but it is much more than a measure of consolidation and amendment. It is much more than a statute : it is a code of penal treatment. It is a product of the penal experience of more than half a century ; of the increased knowledge of the nature of crime and its prevention promoted by advances in the psychological and social sciences ; of the continued influence of philanthropic and humanitarian forces ; and of the new social attitude of which the Welfare State itself is both a manifestation and a cause.

The Act did not weaken the authority of criminal law, nor did it question the necessity of maintaining public order by the threat and imposition of effective penal sanctions. It is true that corporal punishment was done away with and the distinction between penal servitude and imprisonment abolished ; but corporal punishment had virtually fallen into disuse before the Bill was drawn up, while the differentiation between the two kinds of detention had lost all practical meaning many years earlier. Nor should it be ignored that under the statute much more drastic measures were provided to deal with persistent and habitual offenders, that probation was more clearly distinguished from discharge, and that valuable new provisions were added to counteract the delinquency of young offenders. It was not intended to make our penal system softer and more lenient, but to increase its effectiveness by rendering it more diversified and elastic. The possibilities of diversity between institutions and of elasticity in treatment, where it was inevitable that offenders should be kept in custody, were foremost in the minds of the Webbs. In their eyes these, rather than uniformity or economy, were the true benefits accruing from a centralised administration of the prison system, much as they distrusted it in some other respects.

" Penal reform " is often taken to mean something soft, sentimental, idealistic to the point of becoming unrealistic. It may imply this, but alternatively it may imply a concerted, well-thought-out effort to overcome the limitations of a particular penal system and thus render it more effective in the prevention of crime. When crime is increasing, there is a tendency to think of penal reform exclusively in the first, and distorted, sense.

Getting rid of old-fashioned and obstructive buildings, erecting new penal institutions so that thousands of offenders need no longer live three to a cell, providing observation centres, finding useful and constructive work for prisoners, strengthening after-care—these bestow no luxury upon the criminal. They are essential if we are to launch an exacting and rational regime of corrective detention.

To John Howard prison reform was an " important national concern." To the Webbs, places of confinement, if we had to have them, must be " such as the conscience of the nation can approve." " Penal Practice in a Changing Society ", the first long-term plan for coming to grips with the problem of penal administration, has its roots in both those beliefs.

We have been fortunate in that successive Chairmen of the Prison Commission have felt it almost part of their duty to leave accounts of the periods of administration for which they were responsible.

INTRODUCTION

Outstanding has been the book by Sir Edmund du Cane, the iron man of prison history for sixteen years. To him fell the task of consolidating the system of penal servitude established in the middle of the Victorian Period, when it had ceased to be possible to transport offenders overseas and means had to be devised for dealing with them in this country. His survey appeared in 1885 under the title of " The Punishment and Prevention of Crime ". Next came Sir Evelyn Ruggles-Brise, whose book, " The English Prison System ", was published in 1921. Under his régime solitary confinement was disappearing, together with many other negative provisions, whilst the conception of training was given prominence in the development of borstals. Closer to our own day there is Sir Lionel Fox, Chairman of the Commission from 1942 to 1960. His " English Prison and Borstal Systems " shows how far the new approaches have been extended, even though this extension has now been overshadowed and hampered by the great post-war increase in crime.

These contemporary accounts have, on the whole, been trustworthy, and it would be unfair to stigmatize them, especially the last, as uncritical. But they were inevitably infected with some of the dryness and lifelessness of an official history. For this reason the book written in 1922 by S. Hobhouse and A. Fenner Brockway on " English Prisons Today ", which reflected the state of our penal establishments from the inside at that stage in their evolution, is also of considerable importance and significance. It was characteristic of the high standards which the Webbs always set themselves that they looked upon their own book as merely a convenient historical introduction to this " elaborate monograph ". In fact it has established itself as a worthy part of their great analytical survey of local government.

A prison system is largely the product of history, a coral reef which can grow only by the building of the new upon the old. No contemporary descriptions could take full account of this process of accretion.

INTRODUCTION

It was here that the Webbs stepped in to fill the gap. Their book was first published forty years ago, and naturally some facets of the subject could gain by being explored in greater depth, particularly at the local level. But the main outlines of their study will continue to stand the test of time. No one can claim to understand English penology today without having read and reflected upon this book, for it imparts not only knowledge but perspective.

L. R.

INSTITUTE OF CRIMINOLOGY,
   UNIVERSITY OF CAMBRIDGE.

August, 1962

PREFACE

By BERNARD SHAW

THE SPIRIT IN WHICH TO READ THIS BOOK.

IMPRISONMENT as it exists to-day, and as it is described hereafter in these two volumes: *English Prisons under Local Government* and *English Prisons To-day*, is a worse crime than any of those committed by its victims ; for no single criminal can be as powerful for evil, or as unrestrained in its exercise, as an organized nation. Therefore, if any person is addressing himself to the perusal of these dreadful books in the spirit of a philanthropist bent on reforming a necessary and beneficent public institution, I beg him to put it down and go about some other business. It is just such reformers who have in the past made the neglect, oppression, corruption, and physical torture of the old common gaol the pretext for transforming it into that diabolical den of torment, mischief, and damnation, the modern model prison.

If, on the contrary, the reader comes to the books as a repentant sinner, let him read on.

THE OBSTACLE OF VINDICTIVENESS.

The difficulty in finding repentant sinners when this crime is in question has two roots. The first is that we are all brought up to believe that we may inflict injuries on anyone against whom we can make out a case of moral inferiority. We have this thrashed into us in our childhood by the infliction on ourselves of such injuries by our parents and teachers, or indeed by any elder who happens to be in charge of us. The second is that we are all brought up to believe, not now that the king can do no wrong, because kings have been unable to keep up that pretence, but that society can do no wrong. Now not only does society commit more frightful crimes than any individual, king or commoner : it legalizes its crimes, and forges certificates of righteousness for them, besides torturing anyone who dares expose their true character. A society like ours, which will, without remorse, ruin a boy body and soul for life for trying to sell newspapers in a railway station, is not likely to be very tender to people who venture to tell it that its laws would shock the Prince of Darkness himself if he had not been taught from his earliest childhood to respect as well as fear them.

Consequently these two volumes go to a desperately sophisticated public, as well as to a quite frankly vindictive one. Judges spend their lives consigning their fellow creatures to prison ; and when some whisper reaches them that prisons are horribly cruel and destructive places, and that no creature fit to live should be sent there, they only remark calmly that prisons are not meant to be comfortable, which is no doubt the consideration that reconciled Pontius Pilate to the practice of crucifixion.

THE OBSTACLE OF STUPIDITY.

Another difficulty is the sort of stupidity that comes from lack of imagination. When I tell people that I have seen with these eyes a man (no less a man than Richard Wagner, by the way) who once met a crowd going to see a soldier broken on the wheel by the crueller of the two legalized methods of carrying out that hideous sentence, they shudder, and are amazed to hear that what they call medieval torture was used in civilized Europe so recently. They forget that the punishment of half-hanging, unmentionably mutilating, drawing and quartering, was on the British statute book within my own memory. The same people will read of a burglar being sentenced to ten years' penal servitude without turning a hair. They are like Ibsen's Peer Gynt, who was greatly reassured when he was told that the pains of hell are mental : he thought they could not be so very bad if there was no actual burning brimstone. When such people are terrified by an outburst of robbery with violence, or Sadistically excited by reports of the White Slave traffic, they clamor to have sentences of two years' hard labor supplemented by a flogging, which is a joke by comparison. They will try to lynch a criminal who illtreats a child in some sensationally cruel manner ; but on the most trifling provocation they will inflict on the child the prison demoralization and the prison stigma which condemn it to crime for the rest of its life as the only employment open to a prison child. The public conscience would be far more active if the punishment of imprisonment were abolished, and we went back to the rack, the stake, the pillory, and the lash at the cart's tail.

BLOOD SPORTS DISGUISED AS PUNISHMENT ARE LESS CRUEL THAN IMPRISONMENT BUT MORE DEMORALIZING TO THE PUBLIC.

The objection to retrogression is not that such punishments are more cruel than imprisonment. They are less cruel, and far less permanently injurious. The decisive objection to them is that they are sports in disguise. The pleasure to the spectators, and not the pain to the criminal, condemns them. People will go to see Titus Oates flogged or Joan of Arc burnt with equal zest as an entertainment. They will pay high prices for a good view. They will reluctantly admit that they must not torture one another as long as certain rules are observed ; but they will hail a breach of the rules with delight as an excuse for a bout of cruelty. Yet they can be shamed at last into recognizing that such exhibitions are degrading and demoralizing ; that the executioner is a wretch whose hand no decent person cares to take ; and that the enjoyment of the spectators is fiendish. We have then to find some form of torment which can give no sensual satisfaction to the tormentor, and which is hidden from public view. That is how imprisonment, being just such a torment, became the normal penalty. The fact that it may be worse for the criminal is not taken into account. The public is seeking its own salvation, not that of the lawbreaker. It would be far better for him to suffer in the public eye ; for among the crowd of sightseers there might be a Victor Hugo or a Dickens, able and willing to make the sightseers think of what they are doing and ashamed of it. The prisoner has no such chance. He envies the unfortunate animals in the Zoo, watched daily by thousands of disinterested observers who never try to convert a tiger into a Quaker by solitary confinement, and would set up a resounding agitation in the papers if even the most ferocious man-eater were made to suffer what the most docile convict suffers. Not only has the convict no such protection : the secrecy of his prison makes it hard to convince the public that he is suffering at all.

HOW WE ALL BECOME INURED TO IMPRISONMENT.

There is another reason for this incredulity. The vast majority of our city populations are inured to imprisonment from their childhood. The school is a prison. The office and the factory are prisons. The home is a prison. To the young who have the misfortune to be what is called well brought up it is sometimes a prison of inhuman severity. The children of John Howard, as far as their liberty was concerned, were treated very much as he insisted criminals should be treated, with the result that his children were morally disabled, like criminals. This imprisonment in the home, the school, the office, and the factory is kept up by browbeating, scolding, bullying, punishing, disbelief of the prisoner's statements and acceptance of those of the official, essentially as in a criminal prison. The freedom given by the adult's right to walk out of his prison is only a freedom to go into another or starve : he can choose the prison where he is best treated : that is all. On

the other hand, the imprisoned criminal is free from
care as to his board, lodging, and clothing : he pays
no taxes, and has no responsibilities. Nobody
expects him to work as an unconvicted man must
work if he is to keep his job : nobody expects him
to do his work well, or cares twopence whether it is
well done or not.

Under such circumstances it is very hard to convince the ordinary citizen that the criminal is not
better off than he deserves to be, and indeed on the
verge of being positively pampered. Judges, magistrates, and Home Secretaries are so commonly under
the same delusion that people who have ascertained
the truth about prisons have been driven to declare
that the most urgent necessity of the situation is that
every judge, magistrate and Home Secretary should
serve a six months' sentence incognito ; so that when
he is dealing out and enforcing sentences he should
at least know what he is doing.

COMPETITION IN EVIL BETWEEN PRISON AND SLUM.

When we get down to the poorest and most
oppressed of our population we find the conditions
of their life so wretched that it would be impossible
to conduct a prison humanely without making the lot
of the criminal more eligible than that of many free
citizens. If the prison does not underbid the slum
in human misery, the slum will empty and the prison
will fill. This does in fact take place to a small
extent at present, because slum life at its worst is so
atrocious that its victims, when they are intelligent
enough to study alternatives instead of taking their
lot blindly, conclude that prison is the most comfortable place to spend the winter in, and qualify themselves accordingly by committing an offence for which
they will get six months. But this consideration
affects only those people whose condition is not defended by any responsible publicist : the remedy is
admittedly not to make the prison worse but the
slum better. Unfortunately the admitted claims of

the poor on life are pitifully modest. The moment
the treatment of the criminal is decent and merciful
enough to give him a chance of moral recovery, or,
in incorrigible cases, to avoid making bad worse, the
official descriptions of his lot become so rosy that a
clamor arises against thieves and murderers being
better off than honest and kindly men ; for the official
reports tell us only of the care that is taken of the
prisoner and the advantages he enjoys, or can earn
by good conduct, never of his sufferings ; and the
public is not imaginative or thoughtful enough to
supply the deficiency.

What sane man, I ask the clamorers, would accept
an offer of free board, lodging, clothing, waiters in
attendance at a touch of the bell, medical treatment,
spiritual advice, scientific ventilation and sanitation,
technical instruction, liberal education, and the use
of a carefully selected library, with regular exercise
daily and sacred music at frequent intervals, even at
the Ritz Hotel, if the conditions were that he should
never speak, never sing, never laugh, never see a
newspaper, and write only one sternly censored letter
and have one miserable interview at long intervals
through the bars of a cage under the eye of a warder ?
And when the prison is not the Ritz Hotel, when the
lodging, the food, the bed, are all deliberately made
so uncomfortable as to be instruments of torture,
when the clothes are rags promiscuously worn by all
your fellow prisoners in turn with yourself, when the
exercise is that of a turnspit, when the ventilation and
sanitation are noisome, when the instruction is a
sham, the education a fraud, when the doctor is a
bully to whom your ailments are all malingerings,
and the chaplain a moral snob with no time for anything but the distribution of unreadable books, when
the waiters are bound by penalties not to speak to
you except to give you an order or a rebuke, and then
to address you as you would not dream of addressing
your dog, when the manager holds over your head a
continual threat of starvation and confinement in a
punishment cell (as if your own cell were not punish-

ment enough), then what man in his senses would voluntarily exchange even the most harassed freedom for such a life, much less wallow luxuriously in it, as the *Punch* burglar always does on paper the moment anyone suggests the slightest alleviation of the pain of imprisonment?

GIVING THEM HELL.

Yet people cannot be brought to see this. They ask, first, what right the convict has to complain when he brought it on himself by his own misconduct, and second, what he has to complain of. You reply that his grievances are silence, solitude, idleness, waste of time, and irresponsibility. The retort is, " Why call that torture, as if it were boiling oil or red hot irons or something like that ? Why, I have taken a cottage in the country for the sake of silence and solitude ; and I should be only too glad to get rid of my responsibilities and waste my time in idleness like a real gentleman. A jolly sight too well off, the fellows are. I should give them hell."

Thus imprisonment is at once the most cruel of punishments and the one that those who inflict it without having ever experienced it cannot believe to be cruel. A country gentleman with a big hunting stable will indignantly discharge a groom and refuse him a reference for cruelly thrashing a horse. But it never occurs to him that his stables are horse prisons, and the stall a cell in which it is quite unnatural for the horse to be immured. In my youth I saw the great Italian actress Ristori play Mary Stuart ; and nothing in her performance remains more vividly with me than her representation of the relief of Mary at finding herself in the open air after months of imprisonment. When I first saw a stud of hunters turned out to grass, they reminded me so strongly of Ristori that I at once understood that they had been prisoners in their stables, a fact which, obvious as it was, I had not thought of before. And this sort of thoughtlessness, being continuous and unconscious, inflicts more suffering than all the malice and passion in the world. In prison you get one piled on the other : to the cruelty that is intended and contrived, that grudges you even the inevitable relief of sleep and tries to make that a misery by plank beds and the like, is added the worse cruelty that is not intended as cruelty, and, when its perpetrators can be made conscious of it at all, deludes them by a ghastly semblance of pampered indulgence.

THE THREE OFFICIAL AIMS OF IMPRISONMENT.

And now comes a further complication. When people are at last compelled to think about what they are doing to our unfortunate convicts, they think so unsuccessfully and confusedly that they only make matters worse. Take for example the official list of the results aimed at by the Prison Commissioners. First, imprisonment must be " retributory " (the word vindictive is not in official use). Second, it must be deterrent. Third, it must be reformative.

THE RETRIBUTION MUDDLE.

Now if you are to punish a man retributively, you must injure him. If you are to reform him, you must improve him. And men are not improved by injuries. To propose to punish and reform people by the same operation is exactly as if you were to take a man suffering from pneumonia, and attempt to combine punitive and curative treatment. Arguing that a man with pneumonia is a danger to the community, and that he need not catch it if he takes proper care of his health, you resolve that he shall have a severe lesson, both to punish him for his negligence and pulmonary weakness and to deter others from following his example. You therefore strip him naked, and in that condition stand him all night in the snow. But as you admit the duty of restoring him to health if possible, and discharging him with sound lungs, you engage a doctor to superintend the punishment and administer cough lozenges, made as unpleasant to the taste as possible so as not to pamper the culprit.

A Board of Commissioners ordering such treatment would prove thereby that either they were imbeciles or else they were hotly in earnest about punishing the patient and not in the least in earnest about curing him.

When our Prison Commissioners pretend to combine punishment with moral reformation they are in the same dilemma. We are told that the reformation of the criminal is kept constantly in view ; yet the destruction of the prisoner's self-respect by systematic humiliation is deliberately ordered and practised, and we learn from a chaplain that he " does not think it is good to give opportunity for the exercise of Christian and social virtues one towards another " among prisoners. The only consolation for such contradictions is their demonstration that, as the tormentor instinctively feels that he must be a liar and a hypocrite on the subject, his conscience cannot be very easy about the torment. The contradictions are obvious enough here, because I put them on the same page. The Prison Commissioners keep them a few pages apart ; and the average reader's memory, it seems, is not long enough to span the gap when his personal interests are not at stake.

PLAUSIBILITY OF THE DETERRENCE DELUSION.

Deterrence, which is the real object of the courts, has much more to be said for it, because it is neither simply and directly wicked like retribution, nor a false excuse for wickedness like reformation. It is an unquestionable fact that, by making rules and forcing those who break them to suffer so severely that others like them become afraid to break them, discipline can be maintained to a certain extent among creatures without sense enough to understand its necessity, or, if they do understand it, without conscience enough to refrain from violating it. This is the crude basis of all our disciplines, home discipline, school discipline, factory discipline, army and navy discipline, as well as prison discipline and the whole fabric of criminal law. It is imposed not only by cruel rulers, but by unquestionably humane ones, the only difference being that the cruel rulers impose it with alacrity and gloat over its execution, and the humane rulers are driven to it reluctantly by the failure of their appeals to the conscience of people who have no conscience. Thus we find Mahomet, a conspicuously humane and conscientious Arab, keeping his fierce staff in order, not by unusual punishments, but by threats of a hell after death which he invented for the purpose in revolting detail of a kind which suggests that Mahomet had perhaps too much of the woman and the artist in him to know what would frighten a Bedouin most. Wellington, a general so humane that he sacrificed the exercise of a military genius of the first order to his moral horror of war and his freedom from its illusions, nevertheless hanged and flogged his soldiers mercilessly because he had learnt from experience that, as he put it, nothing is worse than impunity. All revolutions have been the work of men who, like Robespierre, were sentimental humanitarians and conscientious objectors to capital punishment and the severities of military and prison discipline ; yet all the revolutions have after a very brief practical experience been driven to Terrorism (the proper name of Deterrence) as ruthless as the Counter-Revolutionary Terror of Sulla, the latest example being that of the Russian revolution now in progress. Whether it is Sulla, Robespierre, Trotsky, or the fighting mate of a sailing ship with a crew of loafers and wastrels, the result is the same : there are people to be dealt with who will not obey the law unless they are afraid to disobey it, and whose disobedience means disaster.

CRIME CANNOT BE KILLED BY KINDNESS.

It is useless for humanitarians to shirk this hard fact, and proclaim their conviction that all lawbreakers can be cured by kindness. That may be true of most cases, provided you can find a very gifted practitioner to take the worst ones in hand, with unlimited time and means to treat them. But if these conditions are not available, and a policeman and an executioner who will disable the wrongdoer instantaneously are available, the police remedy is the only practicable one, even for rulers filled with the spirit of the Sermon on the Mount. The late G. V. Foote, a strong humanitarian, once had to persuade a very intimate friend of his, a much smaller and weaker man, to allow himself to be taken to an asylum for lunatics. It took four hours of humanitarian persuasion to get the patient from the first floor of his house to the cab door. Foote told me that he not only recognized at once that no asylum attendant, with several patients to attend to, could possibly spend four hours in getting each of them downstairs, but found his temper so intolerably strained by the unnatural tax on his patience that if the breaking point had been reached, as it certainly would have been in the case of a warder or asylum attendant, he would have been far more violent, not to say savage, than if he had resorted to force at once, and finished the job in five minutes.

From taking this rational and practically compulsory use of kindly physical coercion to making it so painful that the victim will be afraid to give any trouble next time is a pretty certain step. In prisons, the warders have to protect themselves against violence from prisoners, of which there is a constant risk and very well founded dread, as there are always ungovernably savage criminals who have little more power of refraining from furious assaults than some animals, including quite carefully bred dogs and horses, have of refraining from biting and savaging. The official punishment is flogging and putting in irons for months. But the immediate rescue of the assaulted warder has to be effected by the whole body of warders within reach ; and whoever supposes that the prisoner suffers nothing more at their hands than the minimum of force necessary to restrain him knows nothing of prison life and less of human nature.

Any criticism of the deterrent theory of our prison system which ignores the existence of ungovernable savages will be discredited by the citation of actual cases. I should be dismissed as a sentimentalist if I lost sight of them for a moment. On any other subject I could dispose of the matter by reminding my critics that hard cases make bad law. On this subject I recognize that the hard cases are of such a nature that provision must be made for them. Indeed hard cases may be said to be the whole subject matter of criminal law ; for the normal human case is not that of the criminal, but of the law-abiding person on whose collar the grip of the policeman never closes. Only, it does not follow that the hardest cases should dictate the treatment of the relatively soft ones.

THE SEAMY SIDE OF DETERRENCE.

Let us now see what are the objections to the Deterrent or Terrorist system.

I. It necessarily leaves the interests of the victim wholly out of account. It injures and degrades him ; destroys the reputation without which he cannot get employment ; and when the punishment is imprisonment under our system, atrophies his powers of fending for himself in the world. Now this would not materially hurt anyone but himself if, when he had been duly made an example of, he were killed like a vivisected dog. But he is not killed. He is, at the expiration of his sentence, flung out of the prison into the streets to earn his living in a labor market where nobody will employ an ex-prisoner, betraying himself at every turn by his ignorance of the common news of the months or years he has passed without newspapers, lamed in speech, and terrified at the unaccustomed task of providing food and lodging for himself. There is only one lucrative occupation available for him ; and that is crime. He has no compunction as to society : why should he have any ? Society, for its own selfish protection, having done its worst to him, he has no feeling about it except a desire to get a bit of his own back. He seeks the only company in which he is welcome: the society of criminals; and sooner or later, according to his luck, he finds himself in prison again. The figures of recidivism shew that the exceptions to this routine are so few as to be negligible for the purposes of this argument. The criminal, far from being deterred from crime, is forced into it ; and the citizen whom his punishment was meant to protect suffers from his depredations.

OUR PLAGUE OF UNRESTRAINED CRIME.

It is, in fact, admitted that the deterrent system does not deter the convicted criminal. Its real efficacy is sought in the deterrent effect on the free citizens who would commit crimes but for their fear of punishment. The Terrorist can point to the wide range of evil-doing which, not being punished by law, is rampant among us ; for though a man can get himself hanged for a momentary lapse of self-control under intolerable provocation by a nagging woman, or into prison for putting the precepts of Christ above the orders of a Competent Military Authority, he can be a quite infernal scoundrel without breaking any penal law. If it be true, as it certainly is, that it is conscience and not the fear of punishment that makes civilized life possible, and that Dr. Johnson's

How small, of all that human hearts endure
That part that laws or kings can cause or cure !

is as applicable to crime as to human activity in general, it is none the less true that commercial civilization presents an appalling spectacle of pillage and parasitism, of corruption in the press and in the pulpit, of lying advertisements which make people buy rank poisons in the belief that they are health restorers, of traps to catch the provision for the widow and the fatherless and divert it to the pockets of company promoting rogues, of villainous oppression of the poor and cruelty to the defenceless ; and it is arguable that most of this could, like burglary and forgery, be kept within bearable bounds if its perpetrators were dealt with as burglars and forgers are dealt with to-day. It is, of course, equally arguable that if we can afford to leave so much villainy unpunished we can afford to leave all villainy unpunished. Unfortunately, we cannot afford it : our toleration is threatening our civilization. The prosperity that consists in the wicked flourishing like a green bay tree, and the humble and contrite hearts being thoroughly despised, is a commercial delusion. Facts must be looked in the face, rascals told what they are, and all men called on to justify their ways to God and Man up to the point at which the full discharge of their social duties leaves them free to exercise their individual fancies. Restraint from evil-doing is within the rights as well as within the powers of organized society over its members ; and it cannot be denied that the execution of these powers, as far as it could be made inevitable, would incidentally deter from crime a certain number of people with a marginal conscience or none at all, and that their codification would create fresh social conscience by enlarging the list of things which law-abiding people make it a point of honor not to do, besides calling the attention of the community to grave matters in which they have hitherto erred through thoughtlessness.

DETERRENCE A FUNCTION OF CERTAINTY, NOT OF SEVERITY.

But there is all the difference in the world between deterrence as an incident of the operation of criminal law, and deterrence as its sole object and justification. In a purely deterrent system, for instance, it matters not a jot who is punished provided somebody is punished and the public persuaded that he is guilty. The effect of hanging or imprisoning the wrong man is as deterrent as hanging or imprisoning the right one. This is the fundamental explanation of the extreme and apparently fiendish reluctance of the Home Office to release a prisoner when, as in the Beck case, the evidence on which he was convicted has become discredited to a point at which no jury would maintain its verdict of guilty. The reluctance is not to confess that an innocent man is being punished, but to proclaim that a guilty man has escaped. For if escape is possible, deterrence shrinks almost to nothing. There is no better established rule of criminology than that it is not the severity of punishment that deters, but its certainty. And the flaw in the case for Terrorism is that it is impossible to obtain enough certainty to deter. The police are compelled to confess every year, when they publish their statistics, that against the list of crimes reported to them they can set only a percentage of detections and convictions. And the list of reported crimes can form only a percentage, how large or small it is impossible to say, but probably small, of the crimes actually committed ; for it is the greatest mistake to suppose that everyone who is robbed runs to the police : on the contrary, only foolish and ignorant or very angry people do so without very serious consideration and great reluctance. In most cases it costs nothing to let the thief off, and a good deal to prosecute him. The burglar in Heartbreak House, who makes his living by robbing people, and then blackmailing them by threatening to give himself up to the police and put them to the expense and discomfort of attending his trial and giving evidence after enduring all the worry of the police enquiries, is not a joke : he is a comic dramatization of a process that is going on every day. As to the black sheep of respectable families who blackmail them by offering them the alternative of making good their thefts and frauds or having the family name disgraced, ask any experienced family solicitor.

I doubt whether the chances of acquittal count for very much except with very attractive women ; but it is worth mentioning that juries will snatch at the flimsiest pretexts for refusing to send people who engage their sympathy to the gallows or to penal servitude, even on evidence of murder or theft which would make short work of a repulsive person.

SOME PERSONAL EXPERIENCES.

Take my own experience as probably common enough. Fifty years ago a friend of mine, hearing that a legacy had been left him, lent himself the expected sum out of his employers' cash ; concealed the defalcation by falsifying his accounts ; and was detected before he could repay. His employers naturally resented the fraud, and had no desire to spare the culprit. But a public exposure of the affair would have involved shock to their clients' sense of security, loss of time and consequently of money, and the unpleasantness of attendance in court at the trial. All this put any recourse to the police out of the question ; and the delinquent obtained another post after a very brief interval during which he supported himself as a church organist. This, by the way, was a quite desirable conclusion, as he was for most practical purposes an honest man. It would have been pure mischief to make him a criminal ; but that is not the present point. He serves here as an illustration of the fact that our criminal law, far from inviting prosecution, attaches serious losses and inconveniences to it.

It may be said that whatever the losses and inconveniences may be, it is a public duty to prosecute. But is it ? Is it not a Christian duty not to prosecute? A man stole £500 from me by a trick. He speculated in my character with subtlety and success ; and yet he ran risks of detection which no quite sensible man would have ventured on. It was assumed that I would resort to the police. I asked why. The answer was that he should be punished to deter others from similar crimes. I naturally said, " You have been punishing people cruelly for more than a century for this kind of fraud ; and the result is that I am robbed of £500. Evidently your deterrence does not deter. What it does do is to torment the swindler for years, and then throw him back, a worse man in every respect, upon society with no other employment open to him except that of fresh swindling. However, your elaborate arrangements to deter me from prosecuting are convincing and effective. I could earn £500 by useful work in the time it would take me to prosecute this man vindictively and worse than uselessly. So I wish him joy of his booty, and invite him to swindle me again if he can." Now this was not sentimentality. I am not a bit fonder of being swindled than other people ; and if society would treat swindlers properly I should denounce them without the slightest remorse, and not grudge a reasonable expenditure of time and energy in the business. But to throw good money after bad in setting to work a wicked and mischievous process like the one described in this book would be to stamp myself as a worse man than the swindler, who earned the money more energetically, and appropriated it no more unjustly, than I earn and appropriate my dividends.

I must however warn our thieves that I can promise them no immunity from police pursuit if they rob me. Some time after the operation just recorded, an uninvited guest came to a luncheon party in my house. He (or she) got away with an overcoat and a pocketful of my wife's best table silver. But instead of selecting my overcoat, he took the best overcoat, which was that of one of my guests. My guest was insured against theft ; the insurance company had to buy him a new overcoat ; and the matter thus passed out of my hands into those of the police. But the result, as far as the thief was concerned, was the same. He was not captured ; and he had the social satisfaction of providing employment for others in converting into a strongly fortified obstacle the flimsy gate through which he had effected an entrance, thereby giving my flat the appearance of a private madhouse.

On another occasion a drunken woman obtained admission by presenting an authentic letter from a soft hearted member of the House of Lords. I had no guests at the moment ; and as she, too, wanted an overcoat, she took mine, and actually interviewed me with it most perfunctorily concealed under her jacket. When I called her attention to it, she handed

it back to me effusively; begged me to shake hands
with her ; and went her way.

Now these things occur by the dozen every day,
in spite of the severity with which they are punished
when the thief is captured by the police. I daresay
all my readers, if not too young to have completed a
representative experience, could add two or three
similar stories. What do they go to prove? Just
that detection is so uncertain that its consequences
have no really effective deterrence for the potential
offender, whilst the unpleasant and expensive consequences of prosecution, being absolutely certain,
have a very strong deterrent effect indeed on the
prosecutor. In short, all the hideous cruelty practised by us for the sake of deterrence is wasted : we
are damning our souls at great expense and trouble
for nothing.

JUDICIAL VENGEANCE AS AN ALTERNATIVE TO LYNCH LAW.

Thus we see that of the three official objects of our
prison system : vengeance, deterrence, and reformation of the criminal, only one is achieved ; and that
is the one which is nakedly abominable. But there
is a plea for it which must be taken into account, and
which brings us to the root of the matter in our own
characters. It is said, and it is in a certain degree
true, that if the Government does not lawfully
organize and regulate popular vengeance, the popu-
lace will rise up and execute this vengeance lawlessly
for itself. The standard defence of the Inquisition
is that without it no heretic's life would have been
safe. In Texas to-day the people are not satisfied
with the prospect of knowing that a murderer and ra-
visher will be electrocuted inside a jail if a jury can
resist the defence put up by his lawyer. They tear
him from the hands of the sheriff ; pour lamp oil
over him ; and burn him alive. Now the burning
of human beings is not only an expression of outraged
public morality : it is also a sport for which a taste
can be acquired much more easily and rapidly than

a taste for coursing hares, just as a taste for drink can be acquired from brandy and cocktails more easily and rapidly than from beer or sauterne. Lynching mobs begin with negro ravishers and murderers ; but they presently go on to any sort of delinquent, provided he is black. Later on, as a white man will burn as amusingly as a black one, and a white woman react to tarring and feathering as thrillingly as a negress, the color line is effaced by what professes to be a rising wave of virtuous indignation, but is in fact an epidemic of Sadism. The defenders of our penal system take advantage of it to assure us that if they did not torment and ruin a boy guilty of sleeping in the open air, the British public would rise and tear that boy limb from limb.

Now the reply to such a plea, from the point of view of civilized law, cannot be too sweeping. The government which cannot restrain a mob from taking the law into its own hands is no government at all. If Landru can go to the guillotine unmolested in France, and his British prototype who drowned all his wives in their baths can be peaceably hanged in England, Texas can protect its criminals by simply bringing its civilization up to the French and British level. But indeed the besetting sin of the mob is a morbid hero worship of great criminals rather than a ferocious abhorrence of them. In any case nobody will have the effrontery to pretend that the number of criminals who excite popular feeling enough to risk lynching is more than a negligible percentage of the whole. The theory that the problem of crime is only one of organizing, regulating, and executing the vengeance of the mob will not bear plain statement, much less discussion. It is only the retributive theory over again in its weakest form.

THE HARD CASES THAT MAKE BAD LAW.

Having now disposed of all the official theories as the trash they are, let us return to the facts, and deal with the hard ones first. Everyone who has any extensive experience of domesticated animals, human

or other, knows that there are negatively bad speci-
mens who have no conscience, and positively bad
ones who are incurably ferocious. The negative
ones are often very agreeable and even charming
companions ; but they beg, borrow, steal, defraud
and seduce almost by reflex action : they cannot
resist the most trifling temptation. They are indulged and spared to the extreme limit of endurance ;
but in the end they have to be deprived of their
liberty in some way. The positive ones enjoy no
such tolerance. Unless they are physically restrained
they break people's bones, knock out their eyes,
rupture their organs, or kill them.

Then there are the cruel people, not necessarily
unable to control their tempers, nor fraudulent, nor
in any other way disqualified for ordinary social
activity or liberty, possibly even with conspicuous
virtues. But by a horrible involution, they lust
after the spectacle of suffering, mental and physical,
as normal men lust after love. Torture is to them a
pleasure except when it is inflicted on themselves.
In scores of ways, from the habitual utterance of
wounding speeches, and the contriving of sly injuries
and humiliations for which they cannot be brought to
book legally, to thrashing their wives and children
or, as bachelors, paying prostitutes of the hardier
sort to submit to floggings, they seek the satisfaction
of their desire wherever and however they can.

POSSIBILITIES OF THERAPEUTIC TREAT-MENT.

Now in the present state of our knowledge it is
folly to talk of reforming these people. By this I do
not mean that even now they are all quite incurable.
The cases of no conscience are sometimes cases of
unawakened conscience. Violent and quarrelsome
people are often only energetic people who are under-
worked : I have known a man cured of wife-beating
by setting him to beat the drum in a village band ;
and the quarrels that make country life so very
unarcadian are picked mostly because the quarrelers

have not enough friction in their lives to keep them good humored.

Psycho-analysis, too, which is not all quackery and pornography, might conceivably cure a case of Sadism as it might cure any of the phobias. And psychoanalysis is a mere fancy compared to the knowledge we have been gathering recently as to the functions of our glands in relation to our conduct. In the nineteenth century this knowledge was pursued barbarously by crude vivisectors whose notion of finding out what a gland was for was to cut it violently out and see what would happen to the victim, meanwhile trying to bribe the public to tolerate such horrors by promising to make old debauchees young again. This was rightly felt to be a villainous business ; besides, who could suppose that the men who did these things would hesitate to lie about the results when there was plenty of money to be made by representing them as cures for dreaded diseases ? But to-day we are not asked to infer that because something has happened to a horribly mutilated dog it will happen also to an unmutilated human being. We can now make authentic pictures of internal organs by means of rays to which flesh is transparent. This makes it possible to take a criminal and say authoritatively that he is a case, not of original sin, but of an inefficient, or excessively efficient, thyroid gland, or pituitary gland, or adrenal gland, as the case may be. This of course does not help the police in dealing with a criminal : they must apprehend and bring him to trial all the same. But if the prison doctor were able to say " Put some iodine in this man's skilly, and his character will change," then the notion of punishing instead of curing him would become ridiculous. Of course the matter is not so simple as that ; but a considerable case can be made out for at least a conjecture that many cases which are now incurable may be disposed of in the not very remote future by either inducing the patient to produce more thyroxin or pituitrin or adrenalin or what not, or else administering them to him as thyroxin is at present administered in cases of myxoedema. Yet the reports of the work of our prison medical officers suggest that hardly any of them has ever heard of these discoveries, or regards a convict as anything more interesting scientifically than a malingering rascal.

THE INCORRIGIBLE VILLAINS.

It will be seen that I am prepared to go to lengths which still seem fantastic as to the possibility of changing a criminal into an honest man. But I cannot add too emphatically that the people who imagine that criminals can be reformed by setting chaplains to preach at them, by giving them pious books and tracts to read, by separating them from their companions in crime and locking them up in solitude to reflect on their sins and repent, are far worse enemies both to the criminal and to society than those who face the fact that these are merely additional cruelties which make their victims worse, or even than those who frankly use them as a means of " giving them hell." But when this is recognized, and the silly reformers with their sermons, their tracts, their horrors of separation, silence, and solitude to avoid contamination, are bundled out of our prisons as nuisances, the problem remains, how are you to deal with your incorrigibles ? Here you have a man who supports himself by gaining the confidence and affection of lonely women ; seducing them ; spending all their money ; and then burning them in a stove or drowning them in a bath. He is quite an attractive fellow, with a genuine taste for women and no taste at all for murder, which is only his way of getting rid of them when their money is spent and they are in the way of the next woman. There is no more malice or Sadism about the final operation than there is about tearing up a letter when it is done with, and throwing it into the waste paper basket. You hang him or chop his head off. But presently you have to deal with a man who lives in exactly the same way, but has not executive force or courage enough to commit murder. He only abandons his victims and turns up in a fresh place with a fresh name. He generally marries them, as it is easier to seduce them so.

Alongside him you have a married couple united by a passion for cruelty. They amuse themselves by tying their children to the bedstead ; thrashing them with straps; and branding them with red hot pokers. You also have to deal with a man who on the slightest irritation flings his wife under a dray, or throws a lighted paraffin lamp into her face. He has been in prison again and again for outbursts of this kind ; and always, within a week of his release, or within a few hours of it, he has done it again.

Now you cannot get rid of these monsters by simply cataloguing them as subthyroidics and superadrenals or the like. At present you torment them for a fixed period, at the end of which they are set free to resume their operations with a savage grudge against the community which has tormented them. That is stupid. Nothing is gained by punishing people who cannot help themselves, and on whom deterrence is thrown away. Releasing them is like releasing the tigers from the Zoo to find their next meal in the children's playing ground in Regent's Park.

THE LETHAL CHAMBER.

The most obvious course is to kill them. Some of the popular objections to this may be considered for a moment. Death, it is said, is irrevocable ; and after all, they may turn out to be innocent. But really you cannot handle criminals on the assumption that they may be innocent. You are not supposed to handle them at all until you have convinced yourself by an elaborate trial that they are guilty. Besides, imprisonment is as irrevocable as hanging. Each is a method of taking a criminal's life ; and when he prefers hanging or suicide to imprisonment for life, as he sometimes does, he says, in effect, that he had rather you took his life all at once, painlessly, than minute by minute by long drawn out torture.

You can give a prisoner a pardon ; but you cannot give him back a moment of his imprisonment. He may accept a reprieve willingly in the hope of a pardon or an escape or a revolution or an earthquake or what not ; but as you do not mean him to evade his sentence in any way whatever, it is not for you to take such clutchings at straws into account.

Another argument against the death penalty for anything short of murder is the practical one of the policeman and the householder, who plead that if you hang burglars they will shoot to avoid capture on the plea that they may as well be hanged for a sheep as for a lamb. But this can be disposed of by pointing out, first, that even under existing circumstances the burglar occasionally shoots, and, second, that recommendations to mercy, verdicts of manslaughter, successful pleas of insanity and so forth, already make the death penalty so uncertain that even red-handed murderers shoot no oftener than burglars—less often, in fact. This uncertainty would be actually increased if the death sentence were, as it should be, made applicable to other criminals than those convicted of wilful murder, and no longer made compulsory in any case.

THE SACREDNESS OF HUMAN LIFE FROM THE WARDER'S SIDE.

Then comes the plea for the sacredness of human life. The State should not set the example of killing, or of clubbing a rioter with a policeman's baton, or of dropping bombs on a sleeping city, or of doing many things that States nevertheless have to do. But let us take the plea on its own ground, which is, fundamentally, that life is the most precious of all things, and its waste the worst of crimes. We have already seen that imprisonment does not spare the life of the criminal : it takes it and wastes it in the most cruel way. But there are others to be considered besides the criminal and the citizens who fear him so much that they cannot sleep in peace unless he is locked up. There are the people who have to lock him up, and fetch him his food, and watch him. Why are their lives to be wasted? Warders, and especially wardresses, are almost as much tied to the prison by their occupation, and by their pensions, which they dare not forfeit by seeking other employment, as the criminals are. If I had to choose between a spell under preventive detention among hardened criminals in Camp Hill and one as warder in an ordinary prison, I think I should vote for Camp Hill. Warders suffer in body and mind from their employment ; and if it be true, as our examination seems to·prove, that they are doing no good to society, but very active harm, their lives are wasted more completely than those of the criminals ; for most criminals are discharged after a few weeks or months ; but the warder never escapes until he is superannuated, by which time he is an older gaolbird than any Lifer in the cells.

THE PRICE OF LIFE IN COMMUNITIES.

How then does the case stand with your incurable pathological case of crime ? If you treat the life of the criminal as sacred, you find yourself not only taking his life but sacrificing the lives of innocent men and women to keep him locked up. There is no sort of sense or humanity in such a course. The moment we face it frankly we are driven to the conclusion that the community has a right to put a price on the right to live in it. That price must be sufficient self-control to live without wasting and destroying the lives of others, whether by direct attack like a tiger, parasitic exploitation like a leech, or having to be held in a leash with another person at the end of it. Persons lacking such self-control have, in America, been thrust out into the sage-brush to wander there until they die of thirst, a cruel and cowardly way of killing them. We in England could drive them into the sea, if we were equally feckless. This dread of clean and wilful killing leads to far more cruel evasions of the commandment " Thou shalt not kill." It has never been possible to obey it, either with men or with animals ; and the attempts to keep the letter of it have led to burying vestal virgins and nuns alive, crushing men to death in the press-yard, handing heretics over to the secular arm, and the like, instead of killing them humanely and without any evasion of the heavy responsibility involved. It was a horrible thing to build a vestal virgin into a wall with food and water enough for a day ; but to build her into a prison for years as we do with just enough loathsome food to prevent her from dying is more than horrible : it is diabolical. If no better alternatives to death can be found than these, then who will not vote for death ? If people are fit to live, let them live under decent human conditions. If they are not fit to live, kill them in a decent human way. Is it any wonder that some of us are driven to prescribe the lethal chamber as the solution for the hard cases which are at present made the excuse for dragging all the other cases down to their level, and the only one that will create a sense of full social responsibility in modern populations ?

THE SIXTH COMMANDMENT.

The slaughtering of incorrigibly dangerous persons, as distinguished from the punitive execution of murderers who have violated the commandment not to kill, cannot be established summarily by these practical considerations. In spite of their cogency we have not only individuals who are resolutely and uncompromisingly opposed to slaying under any provocation whatever, we have nations who have abolished the death penalty, and who regard our retention of it as barbarous. Wider than any nation we have the Roman Catholic Church, which insists literally on absolute obedience to the commandment, and condemns as murder even the killing of an unborn child to save the mother's life. In practice this obligation has been evaded so grossly—by the Inquisition, for example, which refused to slay the heretic, but handed him over to the secular arm with a formal recommendation to mercy, knowing that the secular arm would immediately burn him—that the case of the Church might be cited to illustrate the uselessness of barring the death penalty. But it also illustrates the persistence and antiquity of a point of conscience which still defies all arguments from expediency. That point of conscience may be called a superstition because it is as old as Buddhism or the story of Cain and older, and because it is difficult to find any rational basis for it. But there is something to be said for it all the same.

Killing is a dangerously cheap way out of a difficulty.   " Stone dead hath no fellow " was a handy formula for Cromwell's troops in dealing with the Irish ; still, that precedent is not very reassuring. All the social problems of all the countries can be got rid of by extirpating the inhabitants ; but to get rid of a problem is not to solve it.   It may be argued that if society were to forgo its power of slaying, and also its practice of punishment, it would have a strong incentive to find out how to correct the apparently incorrigible.   It is true that whenever it has renounced its power to slay it has substituted a horribly rigorous and indeed virtually lethal imprisonment ; but this does not apply to homicidal lunatics, our comparatively lenient treatment of whom at Broadmoor could obviously be extended to sane murderers.   Besides, the proposal to slay the incorrigibly dangerous is not peculiar to murder.   It has nothing to do with capital punishment as at present practised : indeed it implies that executions of murderers, traitors, pirates, ravishers, incendiaries and vitriol throwers under existing laws may be a stupid waste of useful human life.   The *Oxford Dictionary* owes several of its pages to a homicide who was detained at Broadmoor (the English Asylum for Criminal Lunatics) during the pleasure of the Crown.   The really hard cases are those which might, if not disposed of by the lethal method, involve caging men as tigers are caged pending the discovery of some method of taming them.   Granted that it is questionable whether the public conscience which tolerates such caging is really more sensitive or thoughtful than that which demands the lethal solution, and that at the present time executions, and even floggings, do not harden the authorities and lower the standard of humanity all through our penal system as continuing penalties do, yet the reluctance remains. The moment it is pointed out that if we kill incurable criminals we may as well also kill incurable invalids, people realize with a shock that the urge of horror, hatred, and vengeance is needed to nerve them—or unnerve them—to slay. The moment I force humane people to face its consideration as I am doing now, I produce a terrified impression that I want to hang everybody. In vain do I protest that I am dealing with a very small class of human monsters, and that as far as crime is concerned our indiscriminate hanging of wilful murderers and traitors slays more in one year than dispassionate lethal treatment would be likely to slay in ten. I am asked at once who is to be trusted with the appalling responsibility of deciding whether a man is to live or die, and what government could be trusted not to kill its enemies under the pretence that they are enemies of society.

GOVERNMENTS MUST PRESUME OR ABDICATE.

The reply is obvious. Such responsibilities must be taken, whether we are fit for them or not, if civilized society is to be organized. No unofficial person denies that they are abused : the whole effect of this book is to shew that they are horribly abused. I can say for my own part as a vehement critic and opponent of all the Governments of which I have had any experience that I am the last person to forget that Governments use the criminal law to suppress and exterminate their opponents whenever the opposition becomes really acute, and that the more virtuous the revolutionist and the more vicious the Government, the more likely it is to kill him, and to do so under pretence of his being one of the dangerous persons for whom the lethal treatment would be reserved. It has been pointed out again and again that it is in the very nature of power to corrupt those to whom it is entrusted, and that to God alone belongs the awful prerogative of dismissing the soul from the body. Tolstoy has exhausted the persuasions of literary art in exhorting us that we resist not evil ; and men have suffered abominable persecutions sooner than accept military service with its chief commandment, Thou shalt kill.

All this leaves the problem just where it was. The irresponsible humanitarian citizen may indulge his pity and sympathy to his heart's content, knowing that there, but for the grace of God, goes he whenever a criminal passes to his doom ; but he who has to govern finds that he must either abdicate, and that promptly, or else take on himself as best he can many of the attributes of God. He must decide what is good and what evil ; he must force men to do certain things and refrain from doing certain other things whether their consciences approve or not ; he must resist evil resolutely and continually, possibly and preferably without malice or revenge, but certainly with the effect of disarming it, preventing it, stamping it out, and creating public opinion against it. In short, he must do all sorts of things which he is manifestly not ideally fit to do, and, let us hope, does with becoming misgiving ; but they must be done, all the same, well or ill, somehow and by somebody. If I were to ignore this, everyone who has had any experience of government would throw these pages aside as those of an inexperienced sentimentalist or an Impossibilist Anarchist.

Nevertheless, certain lines have to be drawn limiting the activities of governments, and allowing the individual to be a law unto himself. For instance, we are obliged (if we are wise) to tolerate sedition and blasphemy to a considerable extent because sedition and blasphemy are nothing more than the advocacy of changes in the established forms of government, morals, and religion ; and without such changes

there can be no social evolution. But as governments are not always wise, it is difficult enough to
secure this intellectual anarchy, or as we call it,
freedom of speech and conscience ; and anyone who
proposed to extend it to such actions as are contemplated by the advocates of lethal treatment would be
dismissed as insane. No country at peace will tolerate
murder, whether it is done on principle or in sin.
What is more, no country at war will tolerate a refusal
to murder the enemy. Thus, whether the powers of
the country are being exercised for good or evil, they
are exercised ; and whoever proposes to set to those
powers the limit of an absolute obedience to the commandment Thou shalt not kill, must do so quite
arbitrarily. He cannot give any reason that I can
discover for saying that it is wickeder to break a
man's neck than to cage him for life : he can only
say that his instinct places an overwhelming ban on
the one and not on the other ; and he must depend
on the existence of a similar instinct in the community for his success in having slaying legally ruled out.

THE RUTHLESSNESS OF THE PURE HEART.

In this he will have little difficulty as long as the
slaying is an act of revenge and expiation, as it is at
present : that is why capital punishment has been
abolished in some countries, and why its abolition is
agitated for in the countries which still practise it. But
if these sinful elements be discarded, and the slaying is
made a matter of pure expediency, the criminal being
pitied as sincerely as a mad dog is pitied, the most
ardent present advocate of the abolition of capital
punishment may not only consent to the slaying as
he does in the case of the mad dog, but even demand
it to put an end to an unendurable danger and horror.
Malice and fear are narrow things, and carry with
them a thousand inhibitions and terrors and scruples.
A heart and brain purified of them gain an enormous
freedom ; and this freedom is shewn not only in the
many civilized activities that are tabooed in the
savage tribe, but also in the ruthlessness with which

the civilized man destroys things that the savage prays to and propitiates. The attempt to reform an incurably dangerous criminal may come to be classed with the attempt to propitiate a sacred rattlesnake ; and a higher civilization does not make still greater sacrifices to the snake : it kills it.

I am driven to conclude, that though, if voluntary custodians can be found for dangerous incorrigibles, as they doubtless can by attaching compensating advantages to their employment, it is quite possible to proceed with slaying absolutely barred, there is not enough likelihood of this renunciation by the State of the powers of life and death to justify me in leaving lethal treatment out of the question. In any case it would be impossible to obtain any clear thinking on the question unless its possibilities were frankly faced and to some extent explored. I have faced them frankly and explored them as far as seems necessary ; and at that I must leave it. Nothing that I have to say about the other sorts of criminals will be in the least invalidated if it should be decided that killing is to be ruled out. I think it quite likely that it may be ruled out on sentimental grounds exactly as it is practised on sentimental grounds. By the time we have reached solid ground the shock of reintroducing it (though this has been effected and even clamored for in some countries) may be too great to be faced under normal conditions. Also, as far as what we call crime is concerned, the matter is not one of the first importance. I should be surprised if, even in so large a population as ours, it would ever be thought necessary to extirpate one criminal as utterly unmanageable every year ; and this means, of course, that if we decide to cage such people, the cage need not be a very large one.

I am not myself writing as an advocate one way or the other. I have to deal with European and American civilization, which, having no longer than a century ago executed people for offences now punished by a few months or even weeks imprisonment, has advanced to a point at which less than half a dozen crimes are punishable by death : murder, piracy, rape, arson, and (in Scotland) vitriol throwing. The opponents of capital punishment usually believe, naturally enough, that the effect of abandoning the notion of punishment altogether as sinful (which it is) will sweep away the scaffold from these crimes also, and thus make an end of the death penalty. No doubt it will ; but I foresee that it will reintroduce the idea of killing dangerous people simply because they are dangerous, without the least desire to punish them, and without specific reference to the actions which have called attention to their dangerousness. That extremity may be met with an absolute veto, or it may not. I cannot foresee which side I should take : a wise man does not ford a stream til he gets to it. But I am so sure that the situation will arise, that I have to deal with it here as impersonally as may be, without committing myself or anyone else one way or the other.

THE SOFT CASES THAT WE TURN INTO HARD ONES.

Now let us look at the other end of the scale, where the soft cases are. Here we are confronted with the staggering fact that many of our prisoners have not been convicted of any offence at all. They are awaiting their trial, and are too poor and friendless to find bail ; whilst others have been convicted of mere breaches of bye-laws of which they were ignorant, and which they could not have guessed by their sense of right and wrong ; for many bye-laws have no ethical character whatever. For example, a boy sells a newspaper on the premises of a railway company, and thereby infringes a bye-law the object of which is to protect the commercial monopoly of the newsagents who have paid the company for the right to have a bookstall on the platform. The boy's brother jostles a passenger who is burdened with hand luggage, and says "Carry your bag, sir?" These perfectly innocent lads are sent to prison, though the warders themselves admit that a sentence of imprisonment is so ruinous to a boy's morals that they would rather see their own sons dead than in prison.

But let us take the guilty. The great majority of them have been convicted of petty frauds compared to which the common practices of the commercial world are serious crimes. Herbert Spencer's essays on the laxity of the morals of trade have called no trader successfully to repentance. It is not too much to say that any contractor in Europe or America who does not secure business by tenders and estimates and specifications for work and materials which he has not the smallest intention of doing or putting in, and who does not resort to bribery to have the work and materials he actually does do and put in passed by anybody whose duty it is to check them, is an exceptional man. The usage is so much a matter of course, and competition has made it so compulsory, that conscience is awakened only when the fraud is carried to some unusual length. I can remember two cases which illustrate what I mean very well. A builder of high commercial standing contracted to put up a public building. When the work began, he found that the clerk of the works, whose business it was to check the work on behalf of the purchaser, lived opposite the building site. The contractor immediately protested that this was not part of the bargain, and that his estimate had been obtained on false pretences. The other is the case of the omnibus conductors of London when the alarum punch was invented and introduced. They immediately struck for higher wages, and got them, frankly on the ground that the punch had cut off the percentage they had been accustomed to add to their wages by peculation, and that it should be made up to them.

Both these cases prove that dishonesty does not pay when it becomes general. The contractor might just as well estimate for the work he really does and the material he actually uses; for, after all, since his object is to tempt the purchaser by keeping prices down, he has to give him the benefit of the fraud. If the purchaser finds him out and says, for example, " You estimated for galvanized pipes and you have put in plain ones," the contractor can reply, " If I had put in galvanized pipes I should have had to charge you more." In the same way, the bus conductors might just as well have struck for an increase of wage as stolen it : the event proved they could have got it. But they thought they could secure employment more easily by asking for a low wage and making it up to their needs surreptitiously. It is one of the grievances of clerks in many businesses that they have to connive at dishonest practices as part of the regular routine of the office ; but neither they nor their employers are any the richer, because business always finally settles down to the facts, and is conducted in terms not of the pretence but of the reality.

MOST PRISONERS NO WORSE THAN OURSELVES.

We may take it, then, that the thief who is in prison is not necessarily more dishonest than his fellows at large, but mostly only one who, through ignorance or stupidity, steals in a way that is not customary. He snatches a loaf from the baker's counter and is promptly run into gaol. Another man snatches bread from the tables of hundreds of widows and orphans and simple credulous souls who do not know the ways of company promoters ; and, as likely as not, he is run into Parliament. You may say that the remedy for this is not to spare the lesser offender but to punish the greater ; but there you miss my present point, which is, that as the great majority of prisoners are not a bit more dishonest naturally than thousands of people who are not only at liberty, but highly pampered, it is no use telling me that society will fall into anarchic dissolution if these unlucky prisoners are treated with common humanity. On the contrary, when we see the outrageous extent to which the most shamelessly selfish rogues and rascals can be granted not only impunity but encouragement and magnificent remuneration, we are tempted to ask ourselves have we any right to restrain anyone at all from doing his worst to us.   The first prison I ever saw had inscribed on it CEASE TO DO EVIL : LEARN TO DO WELL ; but as the inscription was on the outside, the prisoners could not read it. It should have been addressed to the self-righteous free spectator in the street, and should have run ALL HAVE SINNED, AND FALLEN SHORT OF THE GLORY OF GOD.

We must get out of the habit of painting human character in soot and whitewash.   It is not true that men can be divided into absolutely honest persons and absolutely dishonest ones.   Our honesty varies with the strain put on it : this is proved by the fact that every additional penny of income tax brings in less than the penny preceding.   The purchaser of a horse or motor-car has to beware much more carefully than the purchaser of an article worth five shillings.   If you take Landru at one extreme, and at the other the prisoner whose crime is sleeping out : that is to say whose crime is no crime at all, you can place every sane human being, from the monarch to the tramp, somewhere on the scale between them.   Not one of them has a blank page in the books of the recording angel.   From the people who tell white lies about their ages, social positions, and incomes, to those who grind the faces of the poor, or marry whilst suffering from contagious disease, or buy valuable properties from inexperienced owners for a tenth of their value, or sell worthless shares for the whole of a widow's savings, or obtain vast sums on false pretences held forth by lying advertisements, to say nothing of bullying and beating in their homes, and drinking and debauching in their bachelorhood, you could at any moment find dozens of people who have never been imprisoned and never will be, and are yet worse citizens than any but the very worst of our convicts. Much of the difference between the bond and the free is a difference in circumstances only : if a man is not hungry, and his children are ailing only because they are too well fed, nobody can tell whether he would

steal a loaf if his children were crying for bread and
he himself had not tasted a mouthful for twenty-four
hours. Therefore, if you are in an attitude of moral
superiority to our convicts : if you are one of the
Serve Them Right and Give Them Hell brigade, you
may justly be invited, in your own vernacular, either to
Come Off It, or else Go Inside and take the measure
you are meting out to others no worse than yourself.

GOOD SOLDIERS OFTEN BAD CITIZENS, AND BAD CITIZENS GOOD PRISONERS.

The distinction between the people the criminal
law need deal with and those it may safely leave at
large is not a distinction between depravity and good
nature : it is a distinction between people who cannot, as they themselves put it, go straight except
in leading strings, and those who can. Incurable
criminals make wellbehaved soldiers and prisoners.
The war of 1914-18 almost emptied our prisons of
ablebodied men ; and in the leading strings of military discipline these men ceased to be criminals.
Some soldiers who were discharged with not only
first-rate certificates of their good conduct as soldiers,
but with the Victoria Cross " For Valor," were no
sooner cast adrift into ordinary civil life than they
were presently found in the dock pleading their military services and good character as soldiers in mitigation of sentences of imprisonment for frauds and
thefts of the meanest sort. When we consider how
completely a soldier is enslaved by military discipline,
and how abhorrent military service consequently
is to civically capable people, we cannot doubt, even
if there were no firsthand testimony on the subject,
that many men enlist voluntarily, not because they
want to lead a drunken and dissolute life (the reason
given by the Iron Duke), or because they are under
any of the romantic illusions on which the recruiting
sergeant is supposed to practise, but because they
know themselves to be unfit for full moral responsibility, and conclude that they had better have their

lives ordered for them than face the effort (intolerably difficult for them) of ordering it themselves.

This effort is not made easier by our civilization. A man who treated his children as every laborer treated them as a matter of course a hundred years ago would now be imprisoned for neglecting them and keeping them away from school. The statute book is crammed with offences unknown to our grandfathers and unintelligible to uneducated men ; and the list needs startling extension ; for, as Mr. H. G. Wells has pointed out, its fundamental items date from the Mosaic period, when modern Capitalism, which involves a new morality, was unknown. In more obvious matters we notice how the standard of dress, manners, and lodging which qualifies a man socially for employment as a factory hand or mechanic has risen since the days when no person of any refinement could travel, as everybody now travels, third-class.

REMEDIES IN THE ROUGH.

We may now begin to arrange our problem comprehensively. The people who have to be dealt with specially by the government because for one reason or another they cannot deal satisfactorily with themselves may be roughly divided into three sections. First, the small number of dangerous or incorrigibly mischievous human animals. With them should be associated all hopeless defectives, from the idiots at Darenth to the worst homicidal maniacs at Broadmoor. Second, a body of people who cannot provide for or order their lives for themselves, but who, under discipline and tutelage, with their board and lodging and clothing provided for them, as in the case of soldiers, are normally happy, wellbehaved, useful citizens. (There would be several degrees of tutelage through which they might be promoted if they were fit and willing.) Third, all normal persons who have trespassed in some way during one of those lapses of self-discipline which are as common as colds, and who have been unlucky enough to fall into the hands of the police in consequence. These last should never be imprisoned. They should be required to compensate the State for the injury done to the body politic by their misdeeds, and, when possible, to compensate the victims, as well as pay the costs of bringing them to justice. Until they have done this they cannot complain if they find themselves distrained upon; harassed by frequent compulsory appearances in court to excuse themselves; and threatened with consignment to the second class as defectives. It is quite easy to make carelessness and selfishness, petty violence and dishonesty, unremunerative and disagreeable, without resorting to imprisonment. In the cases where the offender has fallen into bad habits and bad company, the stupidest course to take is to force him into the worst of all habits and the worst of all company : that is, prison habits and prison company. The proper remedies are good habits and good company. If these are not available, then the offender must be put into the second class, and kept straight under tutelage until he is fit for freedom.

DIFFICULTY OF THE UNDISCIPLINED.

The difficulty lies, it will be seen, in devising a means of dealing with the second class. The first is easy : too easy, in fact. You kill or you cage : that is all. In the third class, summoning and fining and admonishing are easy and not mischievous : you may worry a man considerably by badgering him about his conduct and dunning him for money in a police court occasionally ; but you do not permanently disable him morally and physically thereby. It is the offender of the second class, too good to be killed or caged, and not good enough for normal liberty, whose treatment bothers us.

THE INDETERMINATE SENTENCE.

Any proposal to place men under compulsory tutelage immediately raises the vexed question of what is called "the indeterminate sentence." Parliament has never been prevailed on to create a possibility of a criminal being "detained preventively" for life : it has set a limit of ten years to that condition. This is inevitable as long as the tutelage is primarily not a tutelage but a punishment. We have a law under which a drunkard, politely called an inebriate, can voluntarily sentence himself to a term of detention for the sake of being restrained from yielding to a temptation which he is unable to resist when left to himself. Under existing circumstances nobody is likely to do that twice, or even once if he has any knowledge of how the inebriates are treated. The only system of detention we know is the prison system ; and the only sort of prisoner we have any practice in dealing with is the criminal, with his dismal routine of punishment in the first place, deterrence in the second place, and reform in the very remote third place. The inebriate volunteer prisoner very soon finds that he is being treated as a criminal, and tries in vain to revoke his renunciation of his liberty.

Otherwise, say the authorities very truly, we should be overwhelmed with volunteers. This reminds us of the Westminster Abbey verger who charged a French gentleman with brawling in church. The magistrate, enquiring what, exactly, the foreigner had done, was told that he had knelt in prayer. "But," said the magistrate, "is not that what a church is for?" The verger was scandalized. "If we allowed that," he said, "we should have people praying all over the place." The Prison Commissioners know that if prisons were made reasonably happy places, and thrown open to volunteers like the army, they might speedily be overcrowded. And this, with its implied threat of an enormous aggravation of the Budget, seems a conclusive objection.

THE ECONOMIC ASPECT.

But if its effect would be to convert a large mass of more or less dishonest, unproductive or half productive, unsatisfactory, feckless, nervous, anxious, wretched people into good citizens, it is absurd to object to it as costly. It would be unbearably costly, of course, if the life and labor of its subjects were as stupidly wasted as they are in our prisons ; but any scheme into which the conditions of our present system are read will stand condemned at once. Whether the labor of the subject be organized by the State, as in Government dockyards, postoffices, municipal industries and services and so forth, or by private employers obtaining labor service from the authorities, organized and used productively it must be ; and anyone who maintains that such organization and production costs the nation more than wasting the labor power of ablebodied men and women either by imprisonment or by throwing criminals on the streets to prey on society and on themselves, is maintaining a monstrous capitalistic paradox. Obviously it will not cost the nation anything at all : it will enrich it and protect it. The real commercial objection to it is that it would reduce the supply of sweatable labor available for unscrupulous private employers. But so much the better if it does. Sweating may make profits for private persons here and there ; but their neighbors have to pay through the nose for these profits in poor rates, police rates, public health rates (mostly disease rates), and all the rest of the gigantic expenditure, all pure waste and mischief, which falls on the ratepayer and taxpayer in his constant struggle with the fruits of the poverty which he is nevertheless invited to maintain for the sake of making two or three of his neighbors unwholesomely and unjustly rich.

It is not altogether desirable that State tutelage should be available without limit for all who may volunteer for it. We can imagine a magistrate's court as a place in which men clamoring to be literally " taken in charge " are opposed by Crown lawyers and court officials determined to prove, if possible, that these importunate volunteers are quite well able to take care of themselves if they choose. Evidence of defective character would be sternly demanded ; and if these were manufactured (as in the not uncommon case of a poor woman charging her son with theft to get him taken off her hands and sent to a reformatory) the offender would be ruthlessly consigned to my third division, consisting of offenders who are not to be taken in charge at all, but simply harried and bothered and attached and sold up until they pay the damages of their offences.

But as a matter of experience men do not seek the avowed tutelage of conditions which imply deficiency of character. Most of them resent any sort of tutelage unless they are brought up to it and therefore do not feel it as an infringement of their individuality. The army and navy are not overcrowded, though the army has always been the refuge of the sort of imbecile called a ne'er-do-well. Indeed the great obstacle to the realization of the Socialist dream of a perfectly organized and highly prosperous community, without poverty or overwork or idleness, is the intense repugnance of the average man to the degree of public regulation of his life which it would involve. This repugnance is certainly not weaker in England than elsewhere. Englishmen are born Anarchists ; and as complete Anarchism is practically impossible, they seek the minimum of public interference with their personal initiative, and overshoot the mark so excessively that it is no exaggeration to say that civilization is perishing of Anarchism. If civilization is to be saved for the first time in history it will have to be by a much greater extension of public regulation and organization than any community has hitherto been willing to submit to. When this extension takes place, it will provide the discipline of public service for large masses of the population who now look after themselves very indifferently, and are only nominally free to control their own destinies ; and in this way many people of the sort that now finds itself in prison will be kept straight automatically. But in any case there is no danger of a tutelary system being swamped by a rush of volunteers qualifying themselves for it by hurling stones through shop windows or the like.

All this does not mean that we must have indeterminate sentences of tutelage. The mischief of the present system is not that the criminal under preventive detention must be released at the end of ten years, but that if he relapses he is sent to penal servitude instead of being simply and sensibly returned to Camp Hill. What it does mean is that if the tutelage be made humane and profitable, the criminal, far from demanding his discharge, will rather threaten the authorities with a repetition of his crime if they turn him out of doors. The change that is needed is to add to the present power of the detaining authorities to release the prisoner at any time if they consider him fit for self-responsibility, the power of the prisoner to remain if he finds himself more comfortable and safe under tutelage, as voluntary soldiers feel themselves more comfortable in the army, or nuns in a convent (sometimes a very strict prison), than cast on the world on his own resources.

WHITHER THE FACTS ARE DRIVING US.

So much for the difficulty of the indeterminate sentence, which is quite manageable. Its discussion has led us to the discovery that in spite of the unchristian spirit of our criminal law, and the cruelty of its administration, the mere logic of facts is driving us to humane solutions. Already it is a fact that no judge or magistrate is obliged to pass any sentence whatever for a first offence except when dealing with a few extraordinary crimes which have affected our imagination so strongly that we feel bound to mark our abhorrence of them by special rigor not only to those convicted of them, but, very illogically and unjustly, to those accused of them : for example, persons accused of high treason were formerly not allowed the help of counsel in defending themselves. And when the account of our system of preventive detention at Camp Hill is studied in connection with the remarkable series of experiments now being made in America, it will be seen that nothing stands between us and humanity and decency but our cruelty, vindictiveness, terror, and thoughtless indifference.

CRIME AS DISEASE.

It must not be imagined that any system will reach every anti-social deed that is committed. I have already shewn that most crime goes undetected, unreported, and even unforbidden ; and I have suggested that if our system of dealing with crime were one with which any humane and thoughtful person could conscientiously co-operate, if we compensated injured persons for bringing criminals to justice instead of, as at present, making the process expensive and extremely disagreeable and even terrifying to them, and if we revised our penal laws by striking out of their list of criminal acts a few which ought not to be there and adding a good many which ought to be there, we might have a good many more delinquents to deal with than at present unless we concurrently improved the education and condition of the masses sufficiently to do away with the large part of lawbreaking which is merely one of the symptoms of poverty, and would disappear with it. But in any case we should diligently read Samuel Butler's *Erewhon*, and accustom ourselves to regard crime as pathological, and the criminal as an invalid, curable or incurable. There is, in fact, hardly an argument that can be advanced for the stern suppression of crime by penal methods that does not apply equally to the suppression of disease ; and we have already an elaborate sanitary code under which persons neglecting certain precautions against disease are not only prosecuted but in some instances (sometimes quite mistaken ones, as the history of vaccination has proved) persecuted very cruelly. We actually force parents to subject their children to surgical operations, some of which are both dangerous and highly questionable. But we have so far stopped short of making it a punishable offence to be attacked by smallpox or typhus fever, though no legal assumption is more certain than that both diseases can be extinguished by sanitation more completely than crime by education. Yet there would be no greater injustice in such punishment than there is in the imprisonment of any thief ; and the judge in *Erewhon* who sentenced a man for phthisis in a sanctimonious speech in which he recapitulated the career of crime which began with an accident in childhood, and ended with pulmonary tuberculosis, was not a whit more ridiculous than the similar speeches made at every sessions by our own judges. Why a man who is punished for having an inefficient conscience should be privileged to have an inefficient lung is a debatable question. If one is sent to prison and the other to hospital, why make the prison so different from the hospital ?

But I make the parallel here because it brings out the significance of the fact that we admit without protest that we have to put up with a good deal of illness in the world, and to treat the sufferers with special indulgence and consideration, instead of turning on them like a herd of buffaloes and goring them to death, as we do in the case of our moral invalids. We even punish people very severely for neglecting their invalids or treating them in such a way as to make them worse instead of better : that is, for doing to them exactly what we should do ourselves if instead of going wrong in body and losing health they had gone wrong in mind and stolen a handkerchief. There are people in the world so incredibly foolish that they expect their children to be always perfectly truthful and perfectly obedient ; but even these idiots do not expect their children to be perfectly well always, nor thrash them if they catch cold. In short, if crime were not punished at all, the world would not come to an end any more than it does now that disease is not punished at all. The real gist of the distinction we make is that the consequences of crime, if unpunished, are pleasant,

whereas the consequences of catching a chill are its
own punishment ; but this will not bear examination.
A bad conscience is quite as uncomfortable as a bad
cold ; and though there are people so hardily constituted in this respect that they can behave very
selfishly without turning a hair, so are there people
of such hardy physical constitution that they can
abuse their bodies with impunity to an extent that
would be fatal to ordinary persons. Anyhow, it is
not proposed that abnormal subjects should be
unrestrained.

On the other hand avoidable illnesses are just like
avoidable crimes in respect of being the result of
some form of indulgence, positive or negative. For
all practical purposes the parallel between the physical and moral invalid holds good ; only, we may
have to reconsider the absolute sacredness of the
physical invalid's life. I shall not here attempt to
prejudge the result of that consideration, but it is
clear that if we decide that this sacredness must be
maintained at all costs, and that the idiot in Darenth, who lies there having food poured into it
so that its heart may continue to beat and its.
lungs to breathe automatically (for it can do nothing voluntarily), must be preserved from death
much more laboriously than Einstein, then we
must hold the criminal equally fetish unless we
are to keep the whole subject in its present disastrous confusion.

REFORMING OUR CONSCIENCES.

The change in the public conscience which is
necessary before these considerations can take effect
in abolishing our villainous system of dealing with
crime will never be induced by sympathy with the
criminal or even disgust at the prison. The proportion of the population directly concerned is too
small : to the great majority, imprisonment is
something so unlikely to occur—indeed, so certain
statistically never to occur—that they cannot be
persuaded to take any interest in the matter. As

long as the question is only one of the comfort of the
prisoner, nothing will be done, because as long as the
principle of punishment is admitted, and the Sermon
on the Mount ridiculed as an unpractical outburst
of anarchism and sentimentality, the public will
always be reassured by learning from the judges
(none of whom, by the way, seems to know what
really happens to a prisoner after he leaves the dock)
that our prisons are admirable institutions, and by
the romances of Prison Commissioners like Du Cane
and Sir Evelyn Ruggles-Brise, who arrange prisons
as children build houses with toy bricks, and finally
become so pleased with their arrangements that they
describe them in terms which make us wonder that
they do not commit crimes themselves to qualify
themselves for residence in their pet paradises. I
must therefore attack the punitive position at another
angle by dealing with its psychological effect on the
criminal.

EXPIATION AND MORAL ACCOUNTANCY.

No ordinary criminal will agree with me for a
moment that punishment is a mistake and a sin.
His opinions on that point are precisely those of the
policeman who arrests him ; and if I were to preach
this gospel of mine to the convicts in a prison I
should be dismissed as a hopeless crank far more
summarily than if I were to interview the Chief
Commissioner at Scotland Yard about it.

Punishment is not a simple idea : it is a very complex one. Far from being merely some injury that
an innocent person inflicts on a guilty one, and that
the guilty one evades by every means in his power,
it is a balancing of accounts with the soul. People
who feel guilty are apt to inflict it on themselves if
nobody will take the job off their hands. Con-
fessions, though less common than they would be if
the penalties were not so soul-destroying, are received
without surprise. From the criminals' point of view
punishment is expiation; and their bitterest complaints of injustice refer, not to their sentences, but to

the dishonesty with which society, having exacted the price of the crime, still treats the criminal as a defaulter. Even so sophisticated a man of the world as Oscar Wilde claimed that by his two years' imprisonment he had settled accounts with the world and was entitled to begin again with a clean slate. But the world persisted in ostracizing him as if it had not punished him at all.

This was inevitable ; but it was dishonest. If we are absurd enough to engage in a retributive trade in crime, we should at least trade fairly and give clean receipts when we are paid. If we did, we should soon find that the trade is impracticable and ridiculous ; for neither party can deliver the goods. No discharge that the authorities can give can procure the ex-prisoner an eligible situation ; and no atonement that a thief or murderer can make in suffering can make him any the less a thief or murderer. And nobody shirks this demonstration as much as the thief himself. Human self-respect wants so desperately to have its sins washed away, however purgatorially, that we are willing to go through the most fantastic ceremonies, conjurations, and ordeals to have our scarlet souls made whiter than snow. We naturally prefer to lay our sins on scapegoats or on the Cross, if our neighbors will let us off so easily ; but when they will not, then we will cleanse ourselves by suffering a penalty sooner than be worried by our consciences. This is the real foundation of the criminal law in human superstition. This is why, when we refuse to employ a discharged prisoner, he invariably pleads that what he did is paid for, and that we have no right to bring it against him after he has suffered the appointed penalty.

As we cannot admit the plea, we should consider whether we should exact the penalty. I am not arguing that the plea should be admitted : I am arguing that the bargain should never have been made. I am more merciless than the criminal law, because I would destroy the evildoer's delusion that there can be any forgiveness of sin. What is done cannot be undone ; and the man who steals must remain a thief until he becomes another man, no matter what reparation or expiation he may make or suffer. A punishment system means a pardon system : the two go together inseparably. Once admit that if I do something wicked to you we are quits when you do something equally wicked to me, and you are bound to admit also that the two blacks make a white. Our criminal system is an organized attempt to produce white by two blacks. Common sense should doggedly refuse to believe that evil can be abolished by duplicating it. But common sense is not so logical ; and thus we get the present grotesque spectacle of a judge committing thousands of horrible crimes in order that thousands of criminals may feel that they have balanced their moral accounts.

FAMILIAR FRAUDS OF THE TRADE IN SIN.

It is a game at which there is plenty of cheating. The prisoner pleads Not Guilty, and tries his best to get off, or to have as light a sentence as possible. The commercial brigand, fining himself for his plunderings by subscribing to charities, never subscribes as much as he stole. But through all the folly and absurdity of the business, and the dense mental confusion caused by the fact that it is never frankly faced and clearly stated, there shines the fact that conscience is part of the equipment of the normal man, and that it never fails in its work. It is retributive because it makes him uncomfortable ; it is deterrent because detection and retribution are absolutely certain ; and it is reformative because reformation is the only way of escape. That is to say, it does to perfection by divine methods what the Prison Commissioners are trying to do by diabolical methods without hope or even possibility of success.

REVENGE THE DESTROYER OF CONSCIENCE.

The effect of revenge, or retribution from without, is to destroy the conscience of the aggressor instantly. If I stand on the corn of a man in the street, and he winces or cries out, I am all remorse, and overwhelm him with heartfelt apologies. But if he sets about me with his fists, the first blow he lands changes my mind completely ; and I bend all my energies on doing intentionally to his eyes and nose and jaw what I did unintentionally to his toes. Vengeance is mine, saith the Lord ; and that means that it is not the Lord Chief Justice's. A violent punishing, such as a flogging, carries no sense of expiation with it : whilst its effect lasts, which is fortunately not very long, its victim is in a savage fury in which he would burn down the gaol and roast the warders and the governor and the justices alive in it with intense satisfaction if he could.

Imprisonment, on the other hand, gives the conscience a false satisfaction. The criminal feels that he is working off his crime, though he is doing it involuntarily, and would escape at any moment if he could. He preserves his sense of solvency without ceasing to be a thief, as a gambler preserves it by paying his losses without ceasing to be a gambler.

THE SENTIMENTALITY OF REVENGE.

There is a psychological limit to punishment. We dare not kill a hopelessly diseased or dangerous man by way of punishment for any offence short of murder as we would chloroform a hopelessly diseased or dangerous dog by way of kindness. Until we have purged our souls of malice, which is pure sentiment, we cannot get rid of sentimentality ; and the sentimentality which makes us abominably cruel in one direction makes us foolishly and superstitiously afraid to act sternly in others. Homicidal lunatics say in their asylums " They cannot hang *us*." I could give here, but refrain for obvious reasons, simple instructions by carrying out which any person can commit a murder with the certainty of being sent to Broadmoor instead of to the gallows. Now the killing of a sane murderer requires a great deal of consideration, and should never be a matter of course. There are murders which raise no convincing presumption that those who commit them are exceptionally likely to commit another. But about a chronically homicidal lunatic there should be no hesitation whatever as long as we practise judicial killing at all ; and there would not be if we simply considered without malice the question of his fitness to live in society. We spare him because the gallows is a punishment, and we feel that we have no right to punish a lunatic. When we realize that we have no right to punish anybody, the problem of disposing of impossible people will put itself on its proper footing. We shall drop our moral airs ; but unless we rule killing out absolutely, persons who give more trouble than they are worth will run the risk of being apologetically, sympathetically, painlessly, but effectually returned to the dust from which they sprung.

MAN IN SOCIETY MUST JUSTIFY HIS EXISTENCE.

This would at least create a sense of moral responsibility in our citizens. We are all too apt in take our lives as a matter of course. In a civilized community life is not a matter of course : it can be maintained only on complicated artificial conditions ; and whoever enlarges his life by violating these conditions enlarges it at the expense of the lives of others. The extent to which we tolerate such vital embezzlement at present is quite outrageous : we have whole classes of persons who waste, squander, and luxuriate in the hard earned income of the nation without even a pretence of social service or contribution of any kind ; and instead of sternly calling on them to justify their existence or go to the scrap heap, we encourage and honor them, and indeed conduct the whole business of the country as if its object were to produce and pamper them. How can a prison chaplain appeal with any effect to the conscience of a professional criminal who knows quite well that his illegal and impecunious modes of preying on society are no worse morally, and enormously less mischievous materially, than the self-legalized plutocratic modes practised by the chaplain's most honored friends with the chaplain's full approval ? The moment we cease asking whether men are good or bad, and ascertain simply whether they are pulling their weight in the social boat, our persistent evil doers may have a very unpleasant surprise. Far from having an easy time under a government of softhearted and softheaded sentimentalists, cooing that " to understand everything is to pardon everything," they may find themselves disciplined to an extent at present undreamed of by the average man-about-town.

CIVILIZED MAN IS NOT BORN FREE.

And here it will occur to some of my readers that a book about imprisonment should be also a book about freedom. Rousseau said that Man is born free. Rousseau was wrong. No government of a civilized state can possibly regard its citizens as born free. On the contrary, it must regard them as born in debt, and as necessarily incurring fresh debt every day they live ; and its most pressing duty is to hold them to that debt and see that they pay it. Not until it is paid can any freedom begin for the individual. When he cannot walk a hundred yards without using such a very expensive manufactured article as a street, care must be taken that he produces his share of its cost. When he has paid scot and lot his leisure begins, and with it his liberty. He can then say boldly, " Having given unto Cæsar the things that are Cæsar's I shall now, under no tutelage or compulsion except that of my conscience, give to God the things that are God's." That is the only possible basis for civil liberty ; and we are unable to attain it because our governments corruptly shirk the duties of Cæsar ; usurp the attributes of God ; and make an unholy mess of which this horrible prison system of ours is only one symptom.

OUR NATURE NOT SO BAD AS OUR PRISON SYSTEM.

We must, however, be on our guard against ascrib-

ing all the villainy of our system to our cruelty and
selfish terrors. That would be inconsistent with the
fact that, as I have pointed out, the operation of the
criminal law is made very uncertain, and therefore
loses the deterrence it aims at, by the reluctance of
sympathetic people to hand over offenders to the
police. Vindictive and frivolous as we are, we are
not downright fiends, as we should be if our modern
prison system had been deliberately invented and
constructed by us all in one piece. It has grown upon
us, and grown evilly, having evil roots ; but its worst
developments have been well meant ; for the road to
hell is paved with good intentions, not with bad ones.
The history of it will be found in the body of this
book; but a word or two of it is needed here to save
the reader from closing the volume in despair of
human nature.

THE HISTORY OF OUR PRISONS.

Imprisonment was not originally a punishment
any more than chaining up a dog, cruel as that practice is, is a punishment. It was simply a method of
detention. The officer responsible for the custody
of an offender had to lock or chain him up somewhere to prevent him from running away, and to be
able to lay his hand on him on the day of trial
or execution. This was regarded as the officer's
own affair : the law looked to him for the delivery of
the offender, and did not concern itself as to how it
was effected. This seems strange nowadays ; but
I can remember a case of a lunatic on a battleship,
who had one man told off to act as his keeper.
The lunatic was violent and troublesome, and gave
his keeper plenty of severe exercise ; but the rest of
the crew looked on with the keenest enjoyment
of the spectacle, and gave the lunatic the strictest
fair play by letting his keeper fight it out with
him unaided. And that is what the law did mostly
in England until well into the nineteenth century.
To this day there is no prison in some of the
Virgin Islands. The prisoner is tied by the leg to

a tree, and plays cards with the constable who guards
him.

The result was that the provision of lock-ups became a private commercial speculation, undertaken
and conducted for the sake of what could be made out
of it by the speculator. There was no need for these
places to be lock-ups : the accused could be chained
up or gyved or manacled if no safe prison was available ; and when lock-ups came to be provided as a
matter of business, the practice of chaining was continued as a matter of tradition, and formed a very
simple method of extorting money from prisoners by
torture. No food was provided by the State : what
the prisoner ate was charged against him as if he were
in a hotel ; and it often happened that when he was
acquitted he was taken back to prison as security for
his bill and kept there until he had paid it.

Under these circumstances the prison was only a
building into which all classes and sorts of detained
persons were thrown indiscriminately. The rich
could buy a private room, like Mr. Pickwick in the
Fleet ; but the general herd of poor criminals, old
and young, innocent and hardened, virgin and prostitute, mad and sane, clean and verminous, diseased
and whole, pigged together in indescribable promiscuity. I repeat : nobody invented this. Nobody
intended it. Nobody defended it except the people
who made money by it. Nobody else except the
prisoners knew about it : they were as innocent as
Mr. Pickwick of what went on inside the prison walls.
And, as usual in England, nobody bothered about it,
because people with money could avoid its grossest
discomforts on the negligibly rare occasions when
they fell into the hands of the officers of the law.
It was by the mere accident of being pricked for sheriff
that John Howard learnt what the inside of a gaol
was like.

HOWARD'S GOOD INTENTIONS.

As a result of Howard's agitation prisons are now
State prisons : the State accepts full responsibility

for the prisoner from the moment of his arrest. So far, so good. But in the meantime imprisonment, instead of being a means of detention, has become not only a punishment, but, for the reasons given at the outset of this preface, *the* punishment. And official shallowness, prevailing against the poet Crabbe's depth, has made it an infernal punishment. Howard saw that the prisoners in the old gaol contaminated one another ; and his remedy was to give them separate cells in which they could meditate on their crimes and repent. When prisons with separate cells were built accordingly, the prison officials soon found that it saved trouble to keep the prisoners locked up in them ; and the philanthropists out-Howarded Howard in their efforts to reform criminals by silence, separation, and the wearing of masks, lest they should contaminate one another by the expression of their faces. Until about eighteen months ago, the convicts in Belgian prisons wore iron masks. Our own convicts wore cloth masks for some time, and would probably be wearing them still had not our solicitude for their salvation killed and driven them mad in such numbers that we were forced to admit that thorough segregation, though no doubt correct in principle (which is just where it is fatally incorrect) does not work. Frightful things in the way of solitude, separation, and silence were done in American prisons, and are still being done there.

The reader will find as much as he can stand in the body of this book, and a good deal more in *English Prisons To-day*, edited by Stephen Hobhouse and Fenner Brockway, in which the system is described from the prison cells, not by common criminals, but by educated and thoughtful men and women who, as agitators for Women's Suffrage or as Conscientious Objectors to military service, have been condemned to imprisonment of late years. Our horror at the disclosure must not blind us to my immediate point, which is, that our prison system is a horrible accidental growth and not a deliberate human invention, and that its worst features have been produced with the intention, not of making it worse, but of making it better. Howard is not responsible: he warned us that "absolute solitude is more than human nature can bear without the hazard of distraction and despair." Elizabeth Fry saw nothing but mischief in prison silence and prison solitude. Their followers were fools : that is all. We can still plead that though we have been ignorant and thoughtless we meant well. We can claim the epitaph of the wife-beating father of Dickens's blacksmith in *Great Expectations* :

> For whatsome'er the failings on his part,
> Remember, reader, he were that good in his heart.

THE SO-CALLED CRIMINAL TYPE.

Perhaps the most far-reaching service done by the Brockway-Hobhouse report is the light it throws on the alleged phenomenon of a Criminal Type. The belief in this has gone through several vicissitudes. At first a criminal was supposed to be a beetle-browed, bulldog-jawed person for whom no treatment could be too bad. This suited the prison authorities, as nothing is so troublesome to them as waves of public sympathy with criminals, founded on imaginative idealizations of them. But the authorities changed their note when a scientific version of the type was put forward by Lombroso and a body of investigators calling themselves psychiatrists. These gentlemen found that criminals had asymmetrical features and other stigmata (an effective word). They contended that the criminals were the victims of these congenital peculiarities, and could not help themselves. As the obvious conclusion was that they were not morally responsible for their actions, and therefore should not be punished for them, the prison authorities saw their occupation threatened, and denied that there was any criminal type, always excepting the beetle-brows and bulldog-jaws which the criminal was assumed to have imposed on his naturally Grecian features by a life of villainy. It was soon noticed that everybody had

asymmetrical features, and that the stigmata of the
Lombrosic criminal were as characteristic of the
Church, the Stock Exchange, the Bench, and the
Legislature as of Portland and Dartmoor. That
settled the matter for the moment. The criminal
type was off.

But nobody who has ever visited a prison has any
doubt that there is a prison type, and a very marked
one at that. And if he is saturated with the teach-
ings of the Natural Selectionists, according to which
changes of type are the result of the slow accumulation of minute variations, and therefore cannot be
visibly produced in less than, say, a million years,
he will conclude, like Lombroso, that the criminal is
a natural species, and therefore incorrigible.

HOW TYPES ARE MANUFACTURED.

But twentieth century observation has lately been
knocking nineteenth century science into a cocked
hat. I have in my hand number seventy-four of the
privately printed opuscula issued by the Society
which calls itself the Set of Odd Volumes. It is
entitled *The Influence Which Our Surroundings
Exert On Us*, and is the work of Sir William Arbuthnot Lane, one of our most distinguished surgeons.
In it he shews that by keeping a man at work as a
deal porter, a coal trimmer, a shoemaker or what not,
you can, within a period no longer than that spent
in prison by typical criminals, produce a typical deal
porter, coal trimmer and so on, the changes involved
being visible grotesque skeletal changes for which
Huxley or Owen would have demanded a whole
evolutionary epoch. No Bolshevik has yet written
so revolutionary a pamphlet as this little record of
a recent after-dinner speech.

What it means is that the criminal type is an artificial type, manufactured in prison by the prison
system. It means that the type is not one of the
accidents of the system, but must be produced by imprisonment no matter how normal the victim is at the
beginning, or how anxious the authorities are to keep

him so. The simple truth is that the typical criminal is a normal man when he first enters a prison,
and develops the type during his imprisonment.
Hitherto the Darwinian criminologists have declined
to believe this, like Molière's doctor who asserted
that the coachman must be alive because he had
been ill only three days, whereas Hippocrates
describes his disease as proving fatal at the end of
six weeks. It is Sir William Arbuthnot Lane who
now comes forward with the modern equivalent of the
famous *mot* " Hippocrates may say what he likes ;
but the coachman is dead." And as the official
world will believe a surgeon baronet when they will
believe nobody else in heaven or on earth, I call
him to witness accordingly.

PSYCHIATRISTS AND ENDOCRINISTS.

This does not mean that no other types are to be
noted in prison. By all means let the endocrinists
go on dividing abnormal people, in prison and out,
into hyper and sub pituitaries and thyroidics and
adrenals. They need not, as the habit of the scientific world is, quarrel furiously with me for remarking
that another type can be externally imposed on their
pituitaries and thyroidics and adrenals impartially.
The fact that a man has an excessive adrenal secre-
tion may be a reason for trying to check it instead
of punishing him. It does not alter the fact that
if you keep one adrenal in penal servitude and another
in the House of Lords for ten years, the one will
shew the stigmata of a typical convict, and the other
of a typical peer, in addition to the stigmata of adren-
alism.

To realize the importance of this, we must recall
the discredit into which Lombroso fell when it was
pointed out that by his diagnosis everybody was more
or less a criminal. I suggest that this was not quite
so complete a reductio-ad-absurdum as it seemed.
I have already accounted for the curious insensibility
of the public to the misery they are inflicting on
their prisoners by the fact that some of the most

mischievous and unhappy conditions of prison life are imposed on all respectably brought up children as a matter of course. It is arguable that what Lombroso took to be criminal stigmata were genuine prison stigmata, and that their prevalence among respectable people is due to the prison conditions to which respectable people are subjected for the first twenty years of their life.

THE CASE OF QUEEN VICTORIA.

I take up another much discussed and most readable modern book : *Queen Victoria*, by Lytton Strachey. It contains some shocking pages, made bearable by the comedic power of the author, but still ghastly reading. Queen Victoria was very carefully brought up. When she was eighteen they came to her and told her that she was queen of England. She asked whether she could really do what she liked ; and when this was reluctantly admitted by her careful mother, Victoria considered what wonderful and hitherto impossible happiness she could confer on herself by her new powers. And she could think of nothing more delightful than an hour of separate solitary confinement. She had never been alone before, never been unwatched by people whose business it was to see that she behaved herself, and to rebuke her and punish her if she did anything they disapproved of. In short, she had been treated as a dangerous criminal, unfit to be trusted with any initiative or moral responsibility.

It would carry me too far to trace the effects of this monstrous bringing-up on the course of history. The book should be given to every prisoner who finds his solitary confinement every day from half-past four in the afternoon to next morning more than he can bear. He will find that there are worse things than solitude when the only company available is that of the warders and governor. And he will understand why the next thing the queen did was to turn her mother practically out of the house. She was, as the prisoner would say, getting a bit of her own

back. He will, if he is an intellectually curious
prisoner, and has not been long enough in prison to
have his intellect atrophied, make a list of the
miseries that are common to the lot of our little
Queen Victorias and their brothers out of prison and
the thieves and murderers in prison. Confinement,
obedience, silence at associated work, continual
supervision by hostile guardians reporting every
infraction of rule for punishment, regulation of every
moment of one's life from outside, compulsory exercise instead of play, systematic extirpation of initiative and responsibility, uncongenial and sometimes
impossible tasks, and a normal assumption that every
original and undictated action will be a wrong action.
That is the lot of the well-brought-up child : whether
heiress to a throne or heir to a country rector, like
Samuel Butler, who was beaten until he acquired
and retained until his death some of the stigmata of
a chained dog.

PREVALENCE OF CRIMINAL CHARACTERIS-
TICS IN POLITE SOCIETY.

Butler, a man of exceptionally strong character
which reacted violently against his training, would
have been what the Prison Commissioners call a bad
prisoner, and therefore does not illustrate the normal
social effect of the system. Even Queen Victoria,
with all her characteristic prison transitions from
tyranny to tutelage, and her inability to understand
or tolerate any other condition, was too energetic,
uneducated, and original, not to react vigorously
against her circumstances. It is when we look at
modern civilization in bulk that we are forced to
admit that child training (or rather taming) as we
practise it produces moral imbecility. About a
dozen millions of persons, on whose education enormous sums had been spent publicly and privately,
have gone like sheep to the slaughter lately ; and
the survivors are making elaborate arrangements to
go again. A glance at the newspapers which cater
specially for the classes which go through the full

routine of preparatory school, public school, and university, will shew that the ideals of those classes, their points of honor, their glories, their boasts, their anticipations of future exploits, are precisely those of criminals. They always are ready (Steady, boys, steady) to fight and to conquer again and again. Ned Kelly, Charles Peace, Dick Turpin and Claude Duval, the Black Prince, Harry the Fifth, Robin Hood, Paul Jones, Clive, Nelson and Captain Kidd, Cortez and Lord Roberts, were not all on the side of the law ; but their morality was the same : they all held that pugnacity, the will to conquer, and the sort of courage that makes pugnacity and the will to conquer effective, are virtues so splendid that they sanctify plunder, devastation, and murder in direct proportion to the magnitude of these operations. The relaxations of the operators are love affairs and luxurious banquets. Now pray what else is the romance of the thieves' kitchen and of the surreptitious conversations of the prison exercise ring and associated labor shop ? The difference is no more essential than that between whiskey and champagne, between an ounce of shag and a box of Havanas, between a burglary and a bombardment, between a jemmy and a bayonet, between a chloroformed pad and a gas shell, between a Browning pistol bought at a pawnbroker's and a service revolver. Gild the reputable end of it as thickly as we like with the cant of chivalry, patriotism, national prestige, national security, duty, and all the rest of it : smudge the other end with all the vituperation that the utmost transports of virtuous indignation can inspire ; and how is the divine judgment, by which all mankind must finally stand or fall, to distinguish between the victims of these two bragging predatory insects, the criminal and the gentleman ?

The most obvious reply is " By their number." For the depredations of the criminal are negligibly small compared to the military holocausts and ravaged areas, the civic slums, the hospitals, the cemeteries crowded with the prematurely dead, the labor markets in which men and women are exposed for sale for all purposes, honorable and dishonorable, which are the products of criminal ideals imposed on the entire population. The common thief and burglar, miserably sweated by the receiver to whom he has to sell his plunder, steals a few spoons or diamonds at a monstrous risk, and gets less than a tenth of their value from a rascal who runs no risk worth considering ; and the poor wretch is content with the trumpery debauch his hard earned percentage brings him. The gentleman steals a whole country, or a perpetual income for himself and his descendants, and is never satisfied until he has more conquests and more riches to boast of. What is more, the illicit thief does not defend his conduct ethically. He may cry " To hell with the parsons and with honesty and white-livered respectability!" and so forth ; but he does so as a defier of God, a public enemy, a Satanic hero. The gentleman really believes that he is an instrument of national honor, a defender of the faith, a pillar of society ; and with this conviction to strengthen him he is utterly unscrupulous in his misplaced pride and honor, and plays the wholesaler in evil to the criminal's petty retail enterprises.

THE ROOT OF THE EVIL.

And what is at the bottom of it all ? Just the belief that virtue is something to be imposed on us from without, like the tricks taught to a performing animal, by the whip. Such manufactured virtue has no ethical value whatever, as appears promptly enough when the whip is removed. All communities must live finally by their ethical values : that is, by their genuine virtues. Living virtuously is an art that can be learnt only by living in full responsibility for our own actions ; and as the process is one of trial and error as well as of accepting the guidance of others' experience, society must, whether it likes it or not, put up with a certain burden of individual error. The man who has never made a mistake will never make anything ; and the man who has never done any harm will never do any good. The disastrous people are the indelicate and conceited busybodies who want to reform criminals and mould children's characters by external pressure and mutilation. The cowards who refuse to accept the inevitable risks of human society, and would have everybody handcuffed if they could lest they should have their pockets picked or their heads punched, are bad enough ; and the flagellomaniacs who are for ever shrieking the exploded falsehood that garotting was put down by flogging, and that all crimes, especially the sexually exciting ones, can be put down by more flogging, are worse ; but such obvious cases of phobia and libido soon make themselves ridiculous if they are given a free platform. It is the busybody, the quack, the pseudo God Almighty, the Dr. Moreau of Mr. H. G. Wells's ghastliest romance, continually lusting to lay hands on living creatures and by reckless violation of their souls and bodies abort them into some monster representing their ideal of a Good Man, or a Model Citizen, or a Perfect Wife and Mother : he is the irreconcilable enemy, the ubiquitous and iniquitous nuisance, and the most difficult to get rid of because he has imposed his moral pretensions on public opinion, and is accepted as just the sort of philanthropist our prisons and criminals should be left to, whereas he (or she) is really the only sort of person who should never be admitted to any part of a prison except the gallows on which so many less mischievous egotists have expired. No one who has not a profound instinctive respect for the right of all living creatures to moral and religious liberty : that is, to liberty of moral and religious experiment on themselves, limited only by their obligations not to become unduly burdensome to others, should be let come within ten miles of a child, a criminal, or any other person in a condition of tutelage. Indelicacy on this point is the most conclusive of social disqualifications. When it is ignorant and shortsighted it produces criminals. When it is worldly-wise and pompous it produces prison commissioners.

RECAPITULATION.

For the sake of mental convenience, I recapitulate the contentions presented in this preface.

1. Modern imprisonment : that is, imprisonment practised as a punishment as well as a means of detention, is extremely cruel and mischievous, and therefore extremely wicked. The word extremely is used because our system was pushed to a degree at which prison mortality and prison insanity forced it back to the point at which it is barely endurable, which point may therefore be regarded as the practicable extreme.

2. Although public vindictiveness and public dread are largely responsible for this wickedness, some of the most cruel features of the prison system are not understood by the public, and have not been deliberately invented and contrived for the purpose of increasing the prisoner's torment. The worst of them are (a) unsuccessful attempts at reform, (b) successful attempts to make the working of the prison cheaper for the State and easier for the officials, or (c) accidents of the evolution of the old privately owned detention prison into the new punitive State prison.

3. The prison authorities profess three objects : (a) Retribution (a euphemism for vengeance), (b) Deterrence (a euphemism for Terrorism), and (c) Reform of the prisoner. They achieve the first atrociously. They fail in the second through lack of the necessary certainty of detection and prosecution, partly because their methods are too cruel and mischievous to secure the co-operation of the public, partly because the prosecutor is put to such inconvenience and loss of time that he feels that he is throwing good money after bad, partly because most people desire to avoid an unquestionable family disgrace much more than to secure a very questionable justice, and partly because the proportion of

6

avowedly undetected crimes is high enough to hold
out reasonable hopes to the criminal that he will never
be called to account. The third is irreconcilable with
the first; and the figures of recidivism, and the discovery that the so-called Criminal Type is really a
prison type, prove that the process is one of quite
uncompensated deterioration.

4. The cardinal vice of the system is the anti-
Christian vice of vengeance, or the intentional dupli-
cation of malicious injuries in compliance with the
expiatory superstition that two blacks make a white.
The criminal accepts this, but claims that punishment absolves him if the injuries seem fairly equivalent; and so, when absolution is necessarily denied
him, and he is forced back into crime by the refusal
to employ him, he feels that he is entitled to revenge
this injustice by becoming an enemy of society. No
beneficial reform of our treatment of criminals is
possible unless and until this essentially sentimental
vice of vengeance is unconditionally eradicated.

5. Society claims a right of self-defence, extending
to the destruction or restraint of lawbreakers. This
right is separable from the right to revenge or punish :
it need have no more to do with punishment or
revenge than the caging or shooting of a man-eating
tiger. It arises from the occurrence of (A) intolerably mischievous human beings, and (B) persons
defective in the self-control needed for free life in
modern society, but well behaved and contented
under tutelage and discipline. Class A can be painlessly killed or permanently restrained. The requisite
tutelage and discipline can be provided for Class B
without rancor or insult. The rest can be treated not
as criminals but as civil defendants, and made to pay
for their depredations in the same manner. At present many persons guilty of conduct much viler than
that for which poor men are sent to prison suffer
nothing worse than civil actions for damages.

6. The principle to be kept before the minds of the
citizens is that as civilized society is a very costly
arrangement necessary to their subsistence and

security they must justify their existence in it by contributing their share to the cost, and giving no more than their share of trouble, subject to every possible provision by insurance against innocent disability; and that this is a condition precedent to freedom, and might on extreme provocation be enforced to the full extent of removing cases of incurable noxious disability by simply putting an end to their existence.

7. An unconquerable repugnance to resort to killing having led to the abolition of capital punishment in several countries, and to its reservation for specially dangerous or abhorrent crimes in all the others, it is possible that the right to kill may be renounced by all civilized States. This repugnance may be intensified by the removal of the distinction between sin and infirmity, or, in prison language, between crime and disease, because it leads to the extirpation of the incurable invalid as well as to that of the incurable criminal.

On the other hand, the opposite temperament, which is not squeamish about making short work of hard cases, may be reinforced by the abandonment of ethical pretentiousness, vengeance, malice, and all uncharitableness in the matter, and may become less scrupulous than at present in advocating euthanasia for incurables.

Whichever party may prevail, capital punishment as such is likely to disappear, and with it the earmarking of certain offences as calling for specially deterrent severities. But it does not follow that lethal treatment of extreme cases will be barred. On the contrary, it may be extended to criminals of all sorts. All that can be said at present is that if it be absolutely barred, sufficient restraint must be effected, not as a punishment but as a necessity for public safety. But there will be no excuse for making it more unpleasant than it need be.

8. In all cases where detention and restraint are called for, the criminal's right to contact with all the spiritual influences of his day should be respected.

Conversation, access to books and pictures and music, unfettered scientific, philosophic, and religious activity, change of scene and occupation, the free formation of friendships and acquaintances, marriage and parentage : in short, all the normal methods of creation and recreation, must be available for criminals as for other persons, partly because deprivation of these things is severely punitive, and partly because it is destructive to the victim, and produces what we call the criminal type, making a cure impossible. Any specific liberty which the criminal's specific defects lead him to abuse will, no doubt, be taken from him ; but his right to live must be accepted in the fullest sense, and not, as at present, as merely a right to breathe and circulate his blood. In short, a criminal must be treated, not as a man who has forfeited all normal rights and liberties by the breaking of a single law, but as one who, through some specific weakness or weaknesses is incapable of exercising some specific liberty or liberties.

9. The main difficulty in applying this concept of individual freedom to the criminal arises from the fact that the concept itself is as yet unformed. We do not apply it to children, at home or at school, nor to employees, nor to persons of any class or age who are in the power of other persons. Like Queen Victoria, we conceive Man as being either in authority or as being subject to authority, each person doing only what he is expressly permitted to do, or what the example of the rest of his class encourages him to consider as permitted. The concept of the free man, who does everything he likes and everything he can unless there are express prohibitions to which he is politically a consenting party, is still unusual, and consequently terrifying, in spite of all the individualist pamphlets of the eighteenth and nineteenth centuries. It will be found that those who are most scandalized by the liberties I am claiming for the convict, would be equally scandalized if I claimed them for their own sons.

The conclusion is that imprisonment cannot be fully understood by those who do not understand freedom.

Ayot St. Lawrence,
    Dec.-Jan., 1921-22.

AUTHORS' NOTE

THE reader will find in the following pages an attempt at an historical account of the administration of prisons in England and Wales from the seventeenth to the twentieth century. It was begun as a part of the study of English Local Government, to which we turned in 1899, and of which the most considerable instalments (except for a *History of Liquor Licensing in England*, 1903) were published as *The Parish and the County* in 1907 and *The Manor and the Borough* in 1908. The subject had then to be put aside for five years under stress of more urgent work ; but in 1913 we were able to publish *The Story of the King's Highway*. Then came the interruption of the Great War. If, at the beginning of 1922, we issue *English Prisons under Local Government*, it is in order to provide a convenient historical introduction to a more important work, in which we have taken great interest, without having been able to share in the labour that its production has involved. In the book entitled *English Prisons To-day, being the Report of the Prison System Enquiry Committee*, by Stephen Hobhouse and A. Fenner Brockway (Longmans), to be published simultaneously with this volume, the student will find an authentic detailed description of the English prison system of to-day. That elaborate monograph, to which a vast amount of care and thought has been devoted, will, it is hoped, serve as the starting point of further reform of prison administration. For such an analytic description the present volume may supply a convenient historical background. We have sought to avoid encroaching on the field of the larger work ;

AUTHORS' NOTE

but we have added, as an epilogue, some of the reflections and tentative suggestions to which we have been led by our historical survey.

In dealing with the material from 1835 onward, we had, for the better part of a year, the assistance of Mr. Felix Crosse, to whom we are indebted, very largely, for Chapter IX. We also owe thanks to Miss Ivy Schmidt for much unstinted labour in the preparation of the book, and the whole production of the index.

SIDNEY AND BEATRICE WEBB.

41, Grosvenor Road,
    Westminster.
        December, 1921.

English Prisons under Local Government

CHAPTER I

THE MAINTENANCE OF PRISONS IN THE SIXTEENTH, SEVENTEENTH, AND EIGHTEENTH CENTURIES

IN English law, the prison has always been the King's; yet through all the centuries prior to 1877 it has to be dealt with as a part of Local Government. Though all prisons were, in legal theory, those of the monarch, and though from time immemorial the King's Courts at Westminster had special prisons of their own,[1] up and down the country were other prisons for the maintenance and government of which neither the King, nor any branch of the Central Administration, made any provision or admitted any responsibility.[2]

---

[1] To these National Prisons must be added that of the old Savoy Palace, long used as a prison for soldiers. The Tower of London, a prison for political offenders, was rarely so employed after 1715, but prior to 1914 its last inmate as a prisoner was Thistlewood, as late as 1820. During the Great War 1914-8, it was again used, both as the place of custody, trial and execution of enemy spies, and as a place of detention for persons arrested by the Provost Marshal of the London Military District. The King's Bench, Marshalsea, and Fleet Prisons were chiefly for debtors, but their inmates included persons committed for contempt of court, piracy, etc. The Fleet and Marshalsea Prisons were closed in 1842, being merged in the old King's Bench Prison, thenceforth called the Queen's Bench Prison. When this was closed, after 1869, as a debtors' prison, it was for some years used as a place of temporary reception for convicts on discharge. See *The London Prisons*, by W. Hepworth Dixon, 1850; *Her Majesty's Tower*, by the same, 4 vols., 1869-71; *Memorials of the Savoy*, by W. J. Loftie, 1878. Of life in the Marshalsea Prison, an inimitable picture is given in *Little Dorrit*, by Charles Dickens.

[2] We make no pretence of supplying a bibliography. In spite of a whole

For the safe custody of a person apprehended, the constable or other apprehending person was himself responsible, and it had always been left to the decision of the parochial or manorial authorities in each place whether or not they would provide a " cage,"[1] watch-house, or temporary " lock-up." Once brought before a Justice of the Peace, the person apprehended had (if not liberated on bail) to be either discharged or committed to some lawful place of detention, to which the parish constable had to convey him. These lawful places of detention were, down to the sixteenth century, only the common gaols.[2] From 1557 and 1576 onwards there existed also an increasing number of prisons bearing another name, and maintained under different statutes, known as houses of correction or bridewells.

century of controversy as to prison administration and the widespread interest in the subject, we have found nothing that can be called a history of English prisons or their administration. The elaborate descriptions of John Howard (1777-1791), James Neild (1812), and Sir Thomas Fowell Buxton (1818), together with the extensive Parliamentary inquiries into Penitentiary Houses, Police and Prisons, between 1811 and 1835, still afford the most useful material prior to 1835, as the voluminous Parliamentary papers and Home Office reports do after that date. Much, too, is to be gained from the abundant pamphlet literature, which is specially prolific between 1780 and 1830, and again between 1844 and 1865. The manuscript minutes of Quarter Sessions and Municipal Corporations between the seventeenth century and 1877, so far as we have been able to consult them (see *The Parish and the County* and *The Manor and the Borough*) are, with the exception of those of Gloucestershire and, to a lesser extent, Middlesex, disappointingly meagre as to prisons. The publications of the Society for the Improvement of Prison Discipline are important between 1816 and 1824. On the whole, the nearest approach to a history of English prison administration is afforded by the two works entitled *The Prison Chaplain : a Memoir of the Rev. John Clay*, by W. L. Clay, 1861, which contains extensive extracts from the reports, between 1825 and 1856, of the ablest of prison chaplains, and *Our Convict System* by the same author, 1862. These can now be supplemented by *The English Prison System*, by Sir Evelyn Ruggles-Brise, 1921, a semi-official but fairly candid and extremely instructive *apologia*. The principal books and pamphlets are cited in the footnotes.

[1] At the Deptford Vestry, in 1808, it is " agreed that as there appears to be an actual necessity for a place of confinement within the Manor of Hatcham, the Churchwardens are hereby authorized to cause a proper place to be erected in such convenient spot as they shall choose, at the expense of this parish." (MS. Vestry Minutes, Deptford, December 14th, 1808.)

[2] It had been expressly provided by 5 Henry IV, c. 10, that all felons should be imprisoned in the common gaol, and not elsewhere ; but the privileges of existing franchise gaols were not interfered with.

(a) *The Common Gaol*

Of common gaols, as distinguished from houses of correction, there seem to have existed, in the sixteenth, seventeenth, and eighteenth centuries, up and down the country, something like a couple of hundred, provided, owned and maintained by many diverse authorities. It is characteristic that no complete list of such gaols existed, and it cannot be stated exactly how many places of lawful detention there were. " The gaol itself is the King's," say the old law books, " but the keeping thereof is incident to the office of sheriff, and inseparable from it."[1]
But the gaol of which the County Sheriff had the keeping was only the county gaol. The towns which were counties in themselves had their own gaols under the exclusive jurisdiction of their own corporation officers. Not only these exceptional towns, but practically every municipal corporation, however small, might have its own gaol, in the keeping of the mayor or bailiffs, or of some other officer named in the charter, or of the corporation itself. Many liberties, franchises, or other parts of counties had separate gaols from which the sheriff of the county was equally excluded. Private gaols still existed in the hands of bishops and other ecclesiastical potentates, of manorial lords and other territorial dignitaries, who clung to them as income-yielding properties.[2] All these were in theory the King's prisons,

---

[1] *The Justice of the Peace*, by R. Burn (Vol. II, p. 127 of edition of 1758) ; citing Coke's *Institutes*, Vol. II, p. 589.

[2] Thus, at Ely, the gaol belonged to the Bishop, as lord of the franchise of the Isle of Ely ; it was so insecure in 1764 that the gaoler ironed his prisoners to the floor lying on their backs. The foreman of the Grand Jury, one James Collier, complained to the King, and the Privy Council directed the Bishop to be proceeded against for not maintaining his gaol. This led to its being somewhat improved. (MS. *Acts of the Privy Council*, George III, Vol. IV, pp. 172-298 ; Vol. V, p. 173, etc., March 29th and May 24th, 1765 ; January 13th and April 2nd, 1767. *John Howard*, by Hepworth Dixon, 1849, p. 151.)
The Westminster Gatehouse prison was the property of the Dean and Chapter (Howard's *State of the Prisons*, 2nd edn. 1780, p. 203). The Bury St. Edmunds Gaol belonged to Sir Charles Danvers (*ibid.*, p. 203). The King himself owned the Windsor Castle prison for debtors, and George II fixed the fees in 1728 (*ibid.*, p. 301). Between Howard's first and second visits to this royal prison the gaoler had been murdered by his turbulent

and those who " kept " them were responsible to the
law as keepers of common gaols.

We must, however, rid our minds of the modern
conception of a prison. The common gaol of the
sixteenth, seventeenth or eighteenth century in no
way resembled the gigantic, specially erected, semi-
castellated buildings with which we are now familiar,
containing hundreds of convicted criminals undergoing punishment. It was, to begin with, theoreti-
cally, a place of detention only, not of punishment.[1]
The ancient punishment for felony was death, and
that for misdemeanours the stocks or the pillory, fine
or whipping. Hence the gaol, as a place of detention
in safe custody, was hardly ever a building specially
erected for the purpose. It was part of an ancient
castle, as at York and Lancaster ; or a few rooms in
an old tower or municipal gatehouse, as at Canterbury and Lincoln ; or, as at Kidderminster, two or
three dark "dungeons" under the market-house,
court-house or other public building ; or even, as at
Reading, "three rooms in a public-house belonging
to the town," and kept as a perquisite by the eldest
sergeant-at-mace.[2]

and disorderly prisoners. The common gaol at Exeter belonged to J. R.
Walter, to whom the gaoler paid £22 a year for his post (ibid., p. 344) ;
whilst a vile den used as a prison at Penzance belonged to Lord Arundel as
lord of the Hundred of Penwith (ibid., p. 354). Penrhyn debtors' prison
was the property of the Earl of Godolphin, to whom it yielded £4 a year.
Lostwithiel debtors' prison belonged to the King as Duke of Cornwall (ibid.,
p. 335), as did Chester Gaol to His Majesty as Earl of Chester (ibid., p. 400).
It was the Bishop of Durham who owned the County Gaol at Durham
(ibid., p. 378). The Duke of Leeds got £24 a year from the profits of
Halifax prison (ibid., p. 377) ; the Duke of Norfolk something out of those
of Sheffield prison (ibid., p. 374), and the Duke of Devonshire out of the
Knaresborough debtors' prison (ibid., p. 372). Lord Derby made £13 a
year out of the Macclesfield prison (ibid., p. 407) ; and the Earl of Chol-
mondeley something out of two or three other small prisons in Cheshire
(ibid., pp. 408-9). The two prisons at Ripon belonged to the Archbishop
of York and the Dean and Chapter of Ripon respectively (ibid., p. 371),
whilst the Dean of York had his own prison yielding him £4 a year for the
175 parishes of the "Liberty of St. Peter" (ibid., p. 369).

[1] " In the first view of gaols they are certainly to be considered only as
places of security, where the bodies of prisoners may be kept till released
by due course of law." (A letter by the Rev. S. M. Lowder . . . respecting
Cardiff Gaol (Cardiff, 1789). See also Observations on the State of the English
Prisons, by Alexander Wedderburn, successively Lord Loughborough, and
the Earl of Rosslyn, 1793.)

[2] The State of the Prisons, by John Howard, 2nd edn., 1780, p. 300.
Even in 1812 the Aston Common Gaol (Warwickshire) was " two dark and

From the standpoint of the modern administrator, the most remarkable feature of the administration of all these common gaols is the fact that they were carried on as private profit-making concerns of the gaolers.[1] So completely was it assumed and accepted that the keeping of a gaol was a profitable business that it was exceptional for any salary to be attached to the post ; and, down to 1730, this unsalaried office was even made the subject of purchase and sale.[2] The gaoler avowedly lived by the fees which he extracted from the prisoners committed to his custody. These fees, originally authorized by no statute, varied from gaol to gaol, and rested on ancient custom, which had usually been embodied in a detailed table, authorized or ratified by the local Justices in Quarter Sessions.[3] Every incident in the prison life, from admission to discharge, was made the occasion for a fee. " For arresting any freeman of this town inhabitant within the watch " was, by the gaoler at Kingston-on-Thames, charged sixpence.[4] But this was cheap. At the ancient Southwark prison, where the fees in 1748 " remain yet unsettled, for want whereof divers impositions may accrue to the poor prisoners therein," the Lord Mayor and Recorder settled in that year that the

damp dungeons sunk ten steps underground . . . within the backyard of an alehouse " (*The State of the Prisons*, by James Neild, 1812, pp. 48-9).

[1] The House of Lords, in 1701, refused to pass a Bill for " regulating " the overcrowded King's Bench and Fleet prisons, expressly on the ground that if there were a diminution in the number of prisoners " the profits thereby accruing will not be a proportional recompense to the officers to attend the Courts, so that the King's four Courts at Westminster will be without prisons and without officers to assist them " (*House of Commons Journals*, May 15th, 1701).

[2] The Warden of the Fleet prison was even held to be a corporation sole, having perpetual succession. The House of Commons Committee, in 1729, found that the office had been sold by the late occupant to the then holder for £5,000. The purchase of the office of gaoler was forbidden by 3 Geo. I, c. 15, Sec. 10 (1730).

[3] Howard, between 1773 and 1780, made a point of recording such tables of fees, and his book contains over sixty examples of various dates from 1603 to 1779. In many cases he records " no table of fees " ; and in many others the table had apparently not been formally authorized until after 1729. " In July, 1775, the (Middlesex) Justices thought fit to raise the gaolers' fees at the Clerkenwell prison " (Howard's *State of the Prisons*, 2nd ed., 1780, p. 195).

[4] This was according to a table of fees dated 1603 (*ibid.*, p. 238).

payments merely " for the admission of every
prisoner " should be eleven shillings and fourpence.[1]
Other charges would be made for the privilege of
detention in this or that part of the prison ; for a
separate room or share thereof ; for a bed ; " for a
flock, dust or other ordinary mattress ; for lodging
every night in a feather bed " ; for the use of bedclothes ; for a copy of the commitment or warrant ;
for signing the certificate to obtain a supersedeas ;
" for the benefit of the rules," enabling prisoners to
enjoy a wider ambit of liberty ;[2] and " to the smith,
for ironing and taking off."[3]   These fees were sometimes at different rates for " knights, esquires, or
gentlemen," on the one hand, and " yeomen, artificers
and labourers " on the other ;[4] or at different rates
for felons, misdemeanants and debtors respectively.[5]
Even when the prisoner had been acquitted, or had
completed his sentence, or had paid his fine or debt,
he could not obtain his release until he had paid not
only all the fees already due but also a special fee
for his discharge.   The mere " turning the key " had
to be paid for, at the New Prison, Clerkenwell, to the
extent of one shilling.[6]   " Gaol fees for discharge of
every prisoner " were, at the Leicester County Gaol,
thirteen and fourpence and two shillings for the
turn key.[7]   In 1729 the judges solemnly decided
that, if a man was committed on more than one
suit, he was liable to pay separate fees for each
of them, so that one and the same prisoner had on

---

[1] *Ibid.*, p. 215.

[2] At Newcastle-on-Tyne, for instance (*ibid.*, p. 382), though the best-
known instances of " rules " were those of the London prisons of the Fleet,
King's Bench and Marshalsea.   De Foe remarked that " The King's Bench
is in Southwark, its rules are more extensive than those of the Fleet, having
all St. George's Fields to walk in, but the prison-house is not so good.   By
a Habeas Corpus you may remove yourself from one prison to the other ;
and some of those gentlemen that are in for vast sums, and probably for
life, choose the one for their summer, the other for their winter habitation ;
and, indeed, both are but the show and name of prisons " [for those having
pecuniary resources, that is].   (De Foe's *Tour through the whole Island of
Great Britain ; The London Prisons*, by Hepworth Dixon, 1850.)

[3] As at Stamford.   (Howard's *State of the Prisons*, 2nd edn., 1780,
p. 238.)

[4] As at the Durham County Gaol (*ibid.*, p. 380).

[5] As at the Shropshire County Gaol (*ibid.*, p. 315).

[6] *Ibid.*, p. 195.   [7] *Ibid.*, p. 271.

this ruling to pay two, four, or six admission fees, ironing fees, rules fees and discharge fees.[1] These lawful fees were, however, only part of the gaoler's profits. The fact that he exercised uncontrolled power over his prisoners gave him practically unlimited opportunities for extortion. Whatever allowance was made by the Justices for the provision of bread for the convicted felons was " farmed " by the gaoler, with the consequent shrinkage of the loaf. Charitable bequests and donations for the relief of poor debtors suffered taxation as they passed through his hands, and were distributed according to his caprice. In every gaol, moreover, there were degrees of discomfort, pain and risk of death, from the overcrowded, fever-haunted common dungeon, to the comfortable bedroom in the gaoler's private apartments ; from the positive physical torture of heavy and tightly fastened irons[2] to the liberty of residing outside the prison itself but " within the rules " ; from the minimum of bread and water provided by charity or the county allowance up to a diet limited only by the prisoner's ability to pay for it ; from the unendurable mental anguish of solitary confinement in a dark cell or the indescribable promiscuity of " the common side " up to the occupancy with wife and family of a private suite of apartments. For every gradation of comfort in these various respects, the prisoner was made to pay whatever he or his friends could afford. Finally, we have to note that the gaoler almost always catered, with an exorbitant profit to himself, for the prisoner's needs and luxuries. He supplied the food, the lights, the firing, the bedding, and the furniture bought by the prisoners ; he admitted friends and allowed social

---

[1] *House of Commons Journals*, March 20th, 1770. At the Batley Gaol it was humanely provided, in 1776, that " but one fee shall be taken by the gaoler for any prisoner's discharge, though there has been more than one action against him or her, which fee shall be 17s. 4d., and to the turnkey 1s." (Howard's *State of the Prisons*, 2nd edn., p. 376.)
[2] " If they have money to pay, their irons are knocked off, for fettering is a trade by which some gaolers derive considerable emolument." (*State of the Gaols in London, Westminster, and Borough of Southwark*, by William Smith, M.D., 1776, p. 12.)

intercourse ; he provided, for a fee, such games as skittles, and the means of gambling of every kind ; and there was in almost every prison, with or without the Justices' licence, a. most profitable " tap " or bar for the sale of alcoholic drinks.[1]

Out of the gaoler's receipts, lawful or unlawful, he had usually to pay such taxes as might be levied on the gaol, as for instance, window duty, which the Worcester gaoler said " brought him under the disagreeable necessity of stopping up some windows."[2] Whether he ever provided the prisoners or any of them with food at his own expense we cannot discover,[3] but it is clear that, for the most part, the

[1] The grant of a licence for the sale of spirits in a prison was not forbidden until 1751 (24 George II, c. 40), whilst the grant of an alehouse licence and the sale of beer does not seem to have been forbidden by statute until 1784 (24 George III, c. 54, Sec. 22).

The " tapster " of the Fleet prison bought, at public auction in 1775, the remainder of a lease, not only of the beer and wine cellars, but also of fifteen rooms for prisoners, which he let to such as could pay. This abuse had lasted continuously for a century, notwithstanding its exposure by the House of Commons Committee in 1729. (Howard's *State of the Prisons*, 2nd edn., 1780, p. 178.)

An eye-witness in 1776 tells us that " there have been no less than 30 gin-shops at one time in the King's Bench, and I have been credibly informed by very attentive observers that upwards of two hogsheads or 120 gallons of gin . . . sold weekly, besides other spirits. . . . The beer consumed on an average amounts, by calculation, to eight butts a week." (*State of the Gaols in London, Westminster, and Borough of Southwark*, by William Smith, M.D., 1776, p. 49.)

Notwithstanding all statutes, beer continued openly to be sold in prisons. At the King's Bench, for instance, the " tap " went on right down to its closing in 1842, yielding a profit of over £800 a year. (Report of the House of Commons Committee on the King's Bench, Fleet and Marshalsea Prisons, 1815, p. 16 ; *The London Prisons*, by Hepworth Dixon, 1850, p. 115.)

And nearly everywhere the bringing of ale and beer into the prison was expressly permitted.

At. the county bridewell at Leicester, Howard found painted up, in 1779 : " By Order of the Court at Easter Sessions, 1779, that there shall be no ale or beer brought into this prison on a Sunday, nor after seven o'clock in the evening on a week-day." (*State of the Prisons*, 2nd edn., 1780, p. 272.)

That much of the ill-health of prisoners was directly caused by excessive drinking in prison was expressly stated in *A Dissertation on the Diseases of Prisons and Poorhouses*, by Dr. J. M. Good, 1795, pp. 29-32, 68-70.

[2] Howard's *State of the Prisons*, 2nd edn., 1780, p. 308. So also at Bodmin, *ibid.*, p. 353. He naturally paid for his own alehouse licence. He paid also the water rate, where such a rate existed, as at the New Prison, Clerkenwell, and the Tothill Fields Bridewell, both in London (*ibid.*, pp. 198, 202).

[3] As the sort of exception which indicates what was the rule, we find that at the Wilts County Bridewell at Marlborough, used also as a gaol, the keeper's salary had, in 1779, been lately " raised from £20 to £50 to supply the prisoners with bread." (Howard's *State of the Prisons*, 2nd edn., 1780, p. 339.)

prisoners had to keep themselves, with the aid of such charity as they could get, supplemented in some cases by the meagre and partially distributed "county bread" or "county allowance," a varying sum, given in money or food out of the county funds for the maintenance of convicted felons.[1] For the repair of the structure of the prison, the gaoler was under no responsibility and went to no expense. His sole obligation was to prevent the prisoners from escaping. This was the legal excuse for chains and irons. But the keeping of the prison involved, in all but the smallest gaols, some turnkeys or assistants, whom the gaoler engaged and, in so far as they did not pay themselves by their own special fees and minor extortions, himself paid out of his pocket. All this was incident to his well-recognized and profitable business of keeping a gaol, with which nobody thought of interfering.

[1] This "county allowance," made under 14 Elizabeth, c. 5, was originally in all cases confined to convicted felons, and in many gaols Howard still found it confined to this class. It seems that, originally, no provision was made for the maintenance of other classes of prisoners, such as debtors, or "fines," convicted misdemeanants, or persons committed for failure to find sureties, or persons simply awaiting trial. "By the Common Law," the Law Officers unhesitatingly report to the Privy Council in 1765, "no prisoners, being in prison on suspicion of having committed an offence, have any legal right to support and maintenance from the Sheriff or gaoler." (MS. *Acts of the Privy Council*, George III, Vol. IV, p. 172, March 29th, 1765.)

Such prisoners were assumed to provide for themselves by working, gifts from friends, or begging. Hence the occasional small legacies for the relief of prisoners, and charitable gifts. In Leicestershire the Grand Jury and clergy made a systematic annual collection for the poor prisoners (Howard's *State of the Prisons*, 2nd edn., 1780, p. 271). In Derbyshire a collector went round to gentlemen's houses once a year (*ibid.*, p. 280). At the Whitechapel debtors' prison " they hang out a begging box . . . in the front of the house and attend it in turn. It brings them only a few pence a day, and of this pittance none partake but those who at entrance have paid the keeper 2s. 6d. and treated the prisoners with half a gallon of beer " (*ibid.*, p. 198). At the Kent County Gaol at Maidstone " the baker who serves the felons sells thirteen loaves to the dozen ; and debtors have amongst them every thirteenth loaf " (*ibid.*, p. 225). Outside the Wilts County Gaol at Fisherton Anger might be seen, in 1779, two men fastened at either end of a chain running though a staple fixed in the wall. " Padlocked by the leg," they stood all day, " offering to those who pass by, nets, laces, purses, etc., made in the prison. . . . At Christmas, felons chained together are permitted to go about, one of them carrying a sack or basket for food : another a box for money " (*ibid.*, p. 337 ; so at Exeter also, p. 345). Throughout the eighteenth century a " prisoners' basket carrier " was at Canterbury appointed by the Corporation to collect victuals for the poor prisoners. As late as March, 1806, he was provided with a new hat and coat. (*Canterbury in the Olden Times*, by John Brent, 1879, pp. 112-3.)

The question inevitably arises how far the Justices of the Peace were responsible for the manner in which the prisoners were treated in the gaols to which they committed them. For such common gaols as belonged to the county (omitting, therefore, those attached to municipal corporations, lords of the manor or special franchises) the Justices in Quarter Sessions had, by statute, a certain measure of responsibility. Not to mention various statutes of the sixteenth century, under which the Justices had power to build gaols,[1] they had, in 1700, been expressly authorized afresh to repair or rebuild at the cost of the county any such gaol as had been " presented " by the grand jury as insufficient or inconvenient.[2] During the first half of the eighteenth century they seem to have made hardly any use of this power, and they cannot, therefore, be accounted irresponsible for the insecurity, insanitation and overcrowding of the county gaols and, indirectly, for the cruelty and disease caused by these defects.[3] Nor were they quite without power and responsibility in the matter of the maintenance of the prisoners. By a statute of 1572 the Justices could levy a sum not exceeding sixpence or eightpence a week on each parish in the county, and with the proceeds provide food for the poor prisoners.[4] This was the well-known " county allowance," usually taking the form of two pennyworth of bread

[1] 23 Henry VIII, c. 2 (1531), 33 Henry VIII, c. 17, 37 Henry VIII, c. 23, 1 Mary, Sec. 2, c. 14, 5 Elizabeth, c. 24, 13 Elizabeth, c. 25. " That Act," said Coke of the 1531 statute, " had little effect, for that the justices did little or nothing." (*Institutes*, Vol. II, p. 705.) ' A good survey of the statutes as to prisons from 1340 to 1815 is given in *A Letter to the* . . . *Marquis of Buckingham*, etc., by Sir Edmund Carrington. (1818.)

[2] 11 & 12 William III, c. 19 (1700). An attempt to amend this Act in 1722 did not become law. (*House of Commons Journals*, Feb. 18th and March 29th, 1723.)

[3] In 1736 the Justices of Kent, and in 1753 those of Devonshire, got Local Acts specially empowering them to build new gaols, though it does not appear that any consideration for the health or comfort of the prisoners instigated their action. (*House of Commons Journals*, Feb. 16th and 24th, 1736, and Feb. 23rd and March 5th, 1753.) When the ruinous condition of the Suffolk County Bridewell at Lavenham was demonstrated to the Justices by the escape of successive prisoners, what they did was to send the keeper " some thumbscrews to secure the rest "! (*Appendix to State of the Prisons*, by John Howard, 1780, p. 207.)

[4] 14 Elizabeth, c. 5 (1572).

per day, but varying from gaol to gaol.[1] The Justices might also, under an Act of 1667, levy a further sum, not exceeding sixpence per week, on each parish for the purpose of providing a stock of materials on which to set the poor prisoners to work ; the profits being devoted to their relief.[2] This provision remained, we believed, inoperative, as we have found no mention of the prisoners in the gaols (as distinguished from the houses of correction) ever being set to work. Beyond these two permissive statutes and the general obligation to keep the gaols in repair, we cannot find that the Justices of the Peace had any legal duty in the matter. Even more undefined by common law or statute were the responsibilities of the legal owner and nominal keeper of the common gaols of the county, the high sheriff himself, and of the municipal corporations or officers, the lords of manors or franchises, and the various ecclesiastical

[1] Howard found every variety of practice with regard to the provision of the prisoners' maintenance out of county funds. Usually the debtors got nothing but what they could beg in charity, with, occasionally, the proceeds of small legacies. But if certified to be poor by the officers of their parishes they might be allowed to come in with the criminals. The "felons" (including, we infer, all persons awaiting trial, and misdemeanants of all kinds) always got the "county bread" as it was called. This might be (as at the Monmouth County Gaol) only a penny per day or (at the Dorset, Surrey, Hants and Herefordshire County Gaols) a penny-halfpenny a day ; or (as at the Lincolnshire County Gaol) eight pennyworth of bread and two pennyworth of meat weekly. More usually, at Howard's visits, it was twopence per day or a shilling a week, given either in money or bread. At the Norfolk County Gaol the prisoners got, in addition, 14 lb. of cheese a week for the whole lot of them. At the Derbyshire County Gaol they got eighteen pennyworth of bread a week each ; at the Gloucester, Berks and Worcester County Gaols three pennyworth of bread a day ; at the Staffordshire County Gaol, fifteen pennyworth of bread and nine pennyworth of cheese per week ; whilst at the Northumberland County Gaol they got two pennyworth of bread and two pennyworth of meat daily, or four times as much as at Monmouth. In view of the variations in the price of corn, it is extraordinary that the allowance should have been fixed at a money rate, involving semi-starvation in years of dearth. Yet the practice was still continued at Bristol in 1818. In Howard's time many gaols were changing to a fixed weight of bread. The Herts County Gaol gave 16 oz., the Devon County Gaol 22 oz. daily, the Warwick County Gaol 24 oz., the Bedford County Gaol two half-peck loaves a week, the Hunts County Gaol only two quartern peck loaves a week. The Essex and Kent County Gaols gave, in addition, a quart of small beer a day : and at the Bucks County Gaol both debtors and felons got a pound of bread a day and two hot dinners a week.

[2] 19 Charles II, c. 4. The total neglect of this statute and the failure of the Justices to make provision for the maintenance of other than convicted felons is described in the *Letter to the Right Hon. Robert Peel . . . on Prison Labour*, by John Headlam, 1823, pp. 5-13.'

or other dignitaries, who found themselves in possession of ancient prisons. In practice, so far as we can ascertain, every real or nominal keeper of a prison did exactly as he pleased. Right down to the third quarter of the eighteenth century at any rate, neither the Justices of the Peace nor anyone else ever thought of visiting the gaols, or taking any thought for their administration.[1]

(b) *The House of Correction*

When we turn from the common gaol to the House of Correction we find ourselves confronted with an entirely different code of law, from which, in the absence of other evidence, we might have inferred an administration on a diametrically opposite principle. Instead of the prison being, as in the case of the common gaol, the private concern of the gaoler, the various Bridewells or Houses of Correction were professedly under the direct administration of the Justices of the Peace. These institutions, of which from first to last there may have been a couple of hundred, were established, by virtue of an Act of 1576, on the model of the Bridewell organized in the City of London between 1552 and 1557,[2] not as part of the prison administration, but as an adjunct of the

[1] Writing in 1777, Howard remarks as follows : " I have often enquired of gaolers whether the sheriffs, Justices or town magistrates inspected their gaols. Many of the oldest have answered, ' None of those gentlemen ever looked into the dungeons or even the wards of my gaol.' Others have said, ' Those gentlemen think that if they came into my gaol they should soon be in their graves.' Others, ' The Justices think the inside of my house too close for them : they satisfy themselves with viewing the outside.' Now, if magistrates continue thus negligent of their duty, a general, thorough reformation of our prisons must be despaired of." (*State of the Prisons*, by John Howard, 1777, p. 379.)

[2] For this, the model for all places subsequently called after its name, see *Solitude in Imprisonment*, etc., by Jonas Hanway, 1776, chs. II and III ; *Bridewell Royal Hospital, Past and Present*, by A. J. Copeland, 1888 ; *The London Prisons*, by Hepworth Dixon, 1850, ch. XIII, pp. 265-73 ; the fourth plate of Hogarth's " Harlot's Progress," which depicts a scene in the interior of this prison. Ned Ward's *London Spy*, 1703, gives a vivid description of the life of its inmates at that date, whilst the pamphlets of the Rev. Thomas Bowen, entitled *Extracts from the Records and Court Books of Bridewell Hospital, with remarks*, 1798, and *Remarks upon the Report of a Select Committee on Bridewell Hospital*, 1799, afford some idea of its later administration. It ceased to be used as a place of confinement in 1860.

relief of destitution.[1] They had as their object, not the punishment of criminals, but very nearly what it was afterwards sought to effect by the ordinary Poor Law workhouse, namely, the elimination of the able-bodied idler, vagrant or unemployed from the recipients of what would nowadays be called outdoor relief. The House of Correction was, in fact, originally a place in which persons wantonly idle or disorderly might be compulsorily set to work, partly in order to produce their keep, partly with a view to their reformation of character, and partly with the intention of thereby deterring others from idleness and disorder. Under the statute of 1576, and all the subsequent amending Acts, it was the Justices in Quarter Sessions who had the entire responsibility for these bridewells, as they were often called, alike with regard to erection, maintenance, staffing, regimen and discipline. They appointed and paid the master or governor, made whatever arrangements they chose as to feeding, working and correcting the prisoners, and were by law, in all respects, the owners and managers of the institutions. So little at the outset were these places regarded as places of punishment, and so much as means of finding employment for the unemployed poor, that it was evidently not unusual, about the middle of the seventeenth century, to give the inmates regular wages in return for their work. In the North Riding of Yorkshire the Justices even stipulated, in the contract which they made with the governor of their House of Correction at

---

[1] Thus, in 1637, the reason for the erection of a House of Correction at Whitby was stated by the North Riding Justices as being " that the trade of fishing doth in these parts increase a multitude of poor, who in winter time, when the said trade faileth, are either driven to beg or wander, or else cast upon the charges of the several parishes, which without some means of correcting and setting them to work, are no way able to relieve so great a multitude." (*North Riding Quarter Sessions Records*, Vol. IV, p. 55.)

In 1655, when the County Bridewell, which the Middlesex Justices had built in 1618, was repaired, the following inscription was set over the gateway : " Here are several sorts of work for the poor of this parish of St. Margarets, Westminster, and also the county, according to law, and for such as will beg and live idly in this City of Westminster." (*The London Prisons*, by Hepworth Dixon, 1850, p. 249 ; *The Criminal Prisons of London*, by H. Mayhew and J. Binny, 1852, p. 362.)

Thirsk, " that he shall allow unto the people to be employed as aforesaid, for their said work and labour, the several salaries hereafter agreed on and set down, that is to say, as shall be set down by Justices of the Peace in pursuance of the statute made for servants' and laborers' wages in the time of King James "— the inmates of the House of Correction thus being secured constant employment at the full rates current in the district for free labour.[1] We cannot unravel the economic complications of these seventeenth century bridewells, with their beating of hemp and picking of oakum, their spinning of yarn and making of cloth. So far as reformatory influence is concerned, there is a certain amount of evidence that for that first generation of their existence, the local bridewells, like their London prototype, achieved a fair measure of success, and that the Justices of the Peace were diligent in their administration, with the result that Lord Coke could sharply distinguish between them and the common gaols. " Few or none," said he, " are committed to the common gaol . . . but they come out worse than they went in. And few are committed to the House of Correction or Working House but they come out better."[2] It is, however, clear that, by the end of the seventeenth century, these distinctive features had almost entirely disappeared. The Houses of Correction had by that time lost all real connection with the Poor Law and had become places of punishment of minor offenders of all sorts. The Justices no longer concerned themselves with the provision of work for the unemployed poor, or of disciplinary employment for sturdy rogues and vagabonds. They merely handed over to the master a power to exact from his prisoners whatever labour he chose, partly as a means of relieving the county from the expense of maintaining them,[3] partly as punishment, but in the main as the

---

[1] See the *North Riding Quarter Sessions Records*, Vol. V, p. 107, for the contract in full, dated April 27th, 1652.

[2] Coke's *Institutes*, II, 729.

[3] It had always been assumed that no charge would be thrown on the county funds for the prisoners' maintenance. The Act of 1609 (7 James I,

master's own perquisite by way of supplement to a small salary. Once the master appointed and his salary fixed, on the understanding that there was to be no other expense thrown on the rates, the Justices, at any rate after the Restoration, seem usually to have given no more thought or attention to the House of Correction than they did to the county gaol. Both institutions were, in effect, run as private ventures of their masters or keepers. This gradual assimilation of the bridewell and the common gaol was fostered by converging tendencies. The practice of merely " passing " vagrants, with or without a whipping, instead of committing them to the local bridewell, and the habit of farming the whole poor to a contractor who set up his own workhouse, must have diminished the use of the Houses of Correction by the classes for which they had been originally intended.[1] On the other hand, the Justices not un-

c. 4) expressly directed " that the said rogues, vagabonds and idle persons during such time as they shall continue and remain in the said house of correction shall in no sorts be chargeable to the county for any allowance, either at their bringing in or going forth, or during the time of their abode there, but shall have such and so much allowance as they shall deserve by their own labour and work." When the Middlesex Justices, in 1615, opened their new house of correction they appointed a governor at an inclusive salary of £200 a year, out of which he was directed to pay a matron, a chaplain, a porter and sufficient servants. As for the prisoners, it was ordered that " every person committed thither shall be set to labour and have no other nurture than that he or she shall get with their labor, except they be sick." They were to have " fresh straw every month and warm pottage thrice a week . . . and their linen (if any they have) be washed," all, together with " help " in sickness, at the master's expense. (*Middlesex County Records*, Vol. II, pp. 117-20.) In the North Riding, the Justices, in 1620, appointed as " maister or governor " one " G. S., of Leeds, clothier . . . he . . . finding a sufficient stock to be employed in the said house " and also " bedding and maintenance of meat and drink, and such like necessaries to those who happen to be committed." He was to be paid an inclusive sum of £60 the first year and £50 a year afterwards. The Justices found " loomes and yrons, for imploying and ruling," and if at any time the county was called upon to find " stock " (i.e., materials) the master " shall abate out of his yearly pay £10 for every £100 that shall be so put into his hands." (*North Riding Quarter Sessions Records*, Vol. II, p. 229.) The latter proviso came into force in 1622, when the governor too up £100 for additional stock and abated £10 a year " of his yearly wages (*Ibid.*, Vol. III, p. 134.)

[1] These offenders were not only those committed for short terms. In Middlesex, in 1615, one T. T., having already been branded on the left shoulder with the letter R as " a rogue incorrigible," without reformatory results, was sent to the House of Correction for life (*in perpetuum*). (*Middlesex County Records*, Vol. II, p. 140.) Even more remarkable is the sentence on one J. R., who, in 1626, was " committed to the House of Correction to

naturally thought it preferable on many grounds to
commit minor offenders to the House of Correction,
where they were supposed to be set to work, rather
than to the demoralizing common gaol. Already, in
1609, this tendency had been marked by an Act
expressly authorizing penal discipline instead of
mere reformatory treatment, in the Houses of
Correction.[1] The practical identity of the two kinds
of prison was recognized by statute in 1720, when the
Justices were expressly authorized to commit vagrants and other minor offenders, as well as persons
unable to find sureties, either to the common gaol
or to the House of Correction, as they might think
proper.[2] As the difficulty of profitably employing
the prisoners' labour increased, the master of the
House of Correction, like his colleague the gaoler,
evidently strove to increase his income by fees[3] and
extortions. He naturally objected both to any
falling off in numbers and also to being restricted
to only the poorest kind of prisoners. We find him
desiring to have the sheriff entrust him with the
charge of debtors (which was not statutorily authorized until 1865) and the Justices commit felons into
his custody. In the early part of the eighteenth
century it became, in fact, in most counties, difficult

be there flogged and there detained until it shall appear to the Court that
the female bastard, begotten by him of the body of Ann M., is dead.
(*Ibid.*, Vol. III.)

[1] 7 James I, c. 4. In 1617, the Middlesex Justices try to arrange that
" servants, apprentices and other unruly and disordered persons," sent to
the House of Correction merely " to receive correction for the better
humbling of them to their duties," should be kept apart from the " rogues "
and criminals. (*Middlesex County Records*, Vol. II, p. 130.)

[2] 6 George I, c. 19.

[3] Though the exaction of fees characterizes the common gaol rather than
the House of Correction, they were not unknown in the latter. Thus,
already in 1607, we find the North Riding Justices ordering, for the Thirsk
House of Correction, that prisoners " upon their delivery or discharge . . .
shall give for their fees . . . five shillings as they shall be able, otherwise
three and fourpence." (*North Riding Quarter Sessions Records*, Vol. I,
p. 75.) Even at the City of London Bridewell, we hear, in 1703, of prisoners
being detained solely for non-payment of fees. (*The London Spy*, by Ned
Ward, 1703.) Howard mentioned the charging of fees in 1773-80 at many
Houses of Correction (apart from those which were combined with the gaols),
e.g., Kingston-upon-Hull Bridewell (p. 374), York City Bridewell (p. 369).
North Riding Bridewell at Thirsk (p. 366), East Riding Bridewell at
Beverley (p. 366), Bristol City Bridewell (p. 360), Somerset County Bride-
well at Taunton (p. 357), Cornwall County Bridewell at Bodmin (p. 352).

to discover any practical distinction between the
House of Correction and the common gaol,[1] whether
in administration, discipline or the character of the
inmates.[2] In many cases the gaol and the House of
Correction were one and the same. In many others,
though the two institutions were nominally distinct,
they were kept in the same or adjacent buildings,
under one and the same officer.[3]

But the sheriff had no control over the House of
Correction, whilst the Justices had only concurrent
jurisdiction over the gaol. In strict law, a debtor
could be committed only to a gaol, a vagrant only
to a House of Correction. Not until the Prisons Act
of 1865 were they made by statute identical under
the name of Local Prison.

[1] As with the exaction of fees so also with the allowance of the " county
bread " ; by 1773, Howard found nearly half the bridewells assimilated
in this respect to the common gaols, the prisoners receiving from a penny
to fourpence per day each, in money or bread. In about half the bridewells,
however, the prisoners still had no allowance, and received what they
earned, or begged or received from friends.

[2] Henry Fielding, in 1751, said that magistrates shrank from committing
offenders to the bridewells for fear of thereby completing their demoralization. In Fielding's view these places were quite as contaminating as gaols.
(*Enquiry into the Causes of the Increase of Robbers*, 1751, p. 64.)

[3] On the other hand, at a few places, the Poor Law origin and primary
purpose of the House of Correction are recalled by its becoming closely
associated with the workhouse ; as at Thame (Oxfordshire), where a
building given to the custody in 1708 for a bridewell was used also as the
parish workhouse, the keeper, in 1779, farming the whole of the poor at
the lump sum of £480 a year. (Howard's *State of the Prisons*, 2nd edn.,
1780, pp. 304-5.) A similar engrafting of the parish poorhouse on a county
bridewell was found at Wrexham in Denbighshire (*ibid.*, p. 414). The
Warrington Borough Bridewell consisted merely of two rooms in the workhouse yard, under the workhouse master ; so also at Poole, in Dorsetshire
(*ibid.*, pp. 343, 399).

CHAPTER II

THE STATE OF THE PRISONS, 1700-1773

THE Political Science student has nowadays no
difficulty in seeing that the appalling condition of
the prisons in the eighteenth century, and the long
drawn-out tragedy of prison life is to be ascribed less
to any culpable neglect of the sheriffs and the Justices,
in the discharge of duties which had never been
precisely defined or even explicitly imposed on them,
than to the amazing administrative device, at that
time almost universally adopted, of converting the
keeping of a prison into a profit-making private
business. We can now realize that, so long as the
keeper of the gaol was permitted to make a profit
out of the prisoners committed to his charge, it was
quite impracticable to secure conditions of health
or decency, or even of common humanity—let alone
uniformity or reformative treatment.[1] The absence
of an adequate salary and the opportunities for
exaction had attracted to the office of gaoler, as was
bitterly remarked, none but " low-bred, mercenary
and oppressive, barbarous fellows, who think of
nothing but enriching themselves by the most cruel
extortion, and who have less regard for the life of a
poor prisoner than for the life of a brute."[2] The

---

[1] It would be instructive to analyse and compare the results on the
public service of a like conversion into profit-making ventures, characteristic of the eighteenth century, of such public offices as the superintendence
of a poorhouse or workhouse, the management of a market, the head-
mastership of an endowed school, the keeping of a private lunatic asylum,
and the " farming out " of the upkeep of a road or the collection of tolls.
It is to be noted that, even at the beginning of the nineteenth century, so
wise a man as Jeremy Bentham was seriously proposing, as the basis of his
" panopticon," letting the management by contract to the highest bidder.
A hundred years later there were still economists who wished to farm out
road maintenance.

[2] *Gentleman's Magazine*, July, 1767.

first concern of the eighteenth century gaoler was
naturally to avoid incurring any expense. Hence the
use of irons and chains for safe custody, instead of
walls and warders ; the immuring in underground
dungeons and windowless garrets, and the herding together in roofless yards, of prisoners of
both sexes and all ages, healthy and sick, innocent
and guilty ; hence also the indescribable lack of
sanitary accommodation, the scarcity of water and
the non-provision of food, clothes or firing. "The
felons in this country," said a writer in 1767, "lie
worse than dogs or swine, and are kept much more
uncleanly than those animals are in kennels or sties.
. . . The stench and nastiness are so nauseous . . .
that no person enters there without the risk of his
health and life."[1] We give, as one of many samples,
a description by a medical man, of what he saw with
his own eyes in two of the important prisons under
the Middlesex Justices. "Vagrants and disorderly
women of the very lowest and most wretched class
of human beings, almost naked, with only a few
filthy rags almost alive and in motion with vermin,
their bodies rotting with the bad distemper, and
covered with itch, scorbutic and venereal ulcers ;
and being unable to treat the constable even with
a pot of beer to let them escape, are drove in shoals
to gaols, particularly to the two Clerkenwells and
Tothill Fields ; there thirty, and sometimes near
forty of these unhappy wretches are crowded or
crammed together in one ward where, in the dark,
they bruise and beat each other in a most shocking
fashion. In the morning . . . the different wards
. . . are more like the Black Hole in Calcutta than
places of confinement in a Christian country."[2] From
all this filth and contamination arose the notorious
" gaol fever "—a malignant form of typhus, apparently unknown, as we must with shame confess, in
the prisons of other countries—which, it was con-

[1] *Gentleman's Magazine,* July, 1767.
[2] *State of the Gaols in London, Westminster, and Borough of Southwark,* etc.,
by William Smith, M.D., 1776, pp. 9-10.

stantly asserted, killed off more of the prison inmates than were either hanged or transported, and chose its victims, it is needless to say, without regard to the verdicts of the juries. The constant presence of contagious fever in the gaol served as a full excuse for the neglect of the sheriff to enter its portals, and frequently also for the non-residence of the gaoler. Now and again a malignant outburst of gaol fever would stretch, like the arm of an avenger, from the prison house to the court of justice, and sweep away, in a few days, judges and advocates, jurymen and witnesses alike.[1] The constant prevalence of disease, and the extent of the mortality among the prison population, was known to every reader. In the sonorous language, possibly of Dr. Johnson himself, the widely read *Gentleman's Magazine* declared, in 1759, that " the corrosion of resentment, the heaviness of sorrow, the corruption of confined air, the want of exercise, and sometimes of food, the contagion of diseases from which there is no retreat, and the severity of tyrants against whom there can be no resistance, and all the complicated horrors of a

---

[1] At the Lent assize in Taunton, 1730, some prisoners who were brought thither from Ivelchester (Ilchester) gaol infected the court, and Lord Chief Baron Pengelly, Sir James Shepherd, sergeant, John Pigot, Esq., sheriff, and some hundreds besides, died of the gaol distemper. At Axminster, a little town in Devonshire, a prisoner, discharged from Exeter gaol in 1755, infected his family with that disease, of which two of them died, and many others in that town afterwards. (*State of the Prisons*, by John Howard, p. 12 of 2nd edn., 1780.) The same results must have followed in innumerable unrecorded cases, from the notorious " Black Assize " at Oxford, in 1577, down to Howard's own day. In 1743, as we learn incidentally from a letter in *The Champion*, March 3rd, 5th and 8th, quoted in the *Gentleman's Magazine* of March, 1743, p. 141, the distress among the woollen workers of Somerset and Devon had " filled the gaols and prisons of the county so as to create a gaol pestilence, of which 100 died at Exeter in one prison in the space of a year, and which killed thousands in the country . . . between Taunton and Exeter, particularly at Tiverton, in which town 1,700 died in about fifteen months, and the parish was at the expense of 1,500 coffins. In October, 1750, occurred the well-known " Black Sessions " at the Old Bailey, when " the foul steams of the Bail Dock, and of two rooms opening into the Court in which the prisoners were the whole day crowded together," were specially noticed. Nearly everyone in court was taken ill, and of six judges on the bench " four died, together with two or three of the counsel, one of the under sheriffs, several of the Middlesex jury and others present, to the number of forty." (*Gentleman's Magazine*, January, 1753.) The assizes for Hampshire had to be adjourned for ten weeks in 1767 on account of the outbreak of malignant fever in Winchester Gaol (*ibid.*, July, 1767).

prison, put an end every year to the life of one in four of those that are shut up from the common comforts of human life. Thus perish yearly five thousand men, overborne with sorrow, consumed by famine or putrified by filth, many of them in the most vigorous and useful part of life."[1]

Mere parsimony could not, however, make the gaol yield a profit, and many eighteenth century gaolers accordingly varied the squalid misery of prison life by deliberate torture for the purpose of extortion, and the systematic encouragement of drunkenness and vice. We need not follow the revelations made by a House of Commons Committee in 1729 of the fiendish cruelty of the tyrants who governed the Fleet and Marshalsea Prisons. There is abundant evidence that, even if the persistency and extravagance in cruelty of Bambridge and his associates was abnormal, a whole system of skilful extortion under the pressure of wanton discomfort and physical pain, and of the sale of licentious indulgence to those who consented to pay, prevailed in the majority of the contemporary prisons. " A prison," said a writer in 1726, " is a place fitter to make a rogue than reform him. Bolts and chains are used as bugbears to extort money from those who are supposed to have it, while such as pay readily are indulged in the greatest freedom and excesses, be their crimes of what nature so ever."[2] " Every capital prison," said Jonas Hanway, " is a public house."[3] " To advance the rent thereof," the House of Commons expressly declared, in 1729, " and to consume the liquors there vended, they not only encourage riot and drunkenness, but also prevent the needy prisoner from being supplied with the

[1] *Gentleman's Magazine*, January, 1759. " In the *Idler* (No. 38), Johnson estimates that one in four of the prisoners dies every year." (Birkbeck Hill's edition of Boswell's *Life of Johnson*, Vol. I, p. 348, note.)

[2] *London Journal*, March 19th, 1726.

[3] He adds, " Though spirituous liquors, commonly so called, are prohibited, yet under the name of cordials they pass, while by the force of wine and malt liquor all the bad effects of intoxication are continued in their full force." (*Distributive Justice and Mercy*, etc., by Jonas Hanway, 1781, p. 80.)

mere necessaries of life in order to increase an exorbitant gain to their tenants."[1] " Gaolers who hold or let the tap," remarked Howard half a century later, " find their account in not only conniving at and promoting drunkenness and midnight revels. What profligate and debauched company of both sexes do we see let into our gaols that the tap may be kept running."[2] We must spare even the student some of the contemporary descriptions of the prisons. Here, as one sample, is a picture which the *Gentleman's Magazine* gave to its readers in 1757. " Clerkenwell Bridewell, though originally intended only to punish idleness by labor, has, by the interest of the keeper, been made the receptacle of felons, and is thus become the seminary of wickedness in all its branches. The idle apprentice, as soon as he is committed to this house of correction, becomes the associate of highwaymen, housebreakers, pickpockets and strolling prostitutes, the witness of the most horrid impiety and the most abandoned lewdness, and generally leaves whatever good quality he brought in, together with his health, behind him. The men and women prisoners are all together till they are locked up at night, and have perpetual opportunities of retiring to the dark cells as often as they please : the women, indeed, are generally such as do not need much solicitation to this commerce ; but as the county allowance is no more than a pennyworth of bread and some water in twenty-four hours, and many of them are totally destitute both of money and friends, they would have no alternative but to become prostitutes for subsistence or to perish with hunger. When the time of confinement limited by the sentence is expired, the prisoner, though she may be detained for her fees, is not entitled to the county allowance ; so that some have been kept a fortnight in this prison without any food at all besides what they could procure either from charity or from lust.

[1] House of Commons Committee, 1729: see *Prison Discipline*, by J. Field, 1856, p. 7.
[2] *State of the Prisons*, by John Howard (Warrington, 1777), p. 31.

But this is not all, the gatekeepers and other petty officers of the prison consider all the women prisoners as their seraglio, and indulge themselves in the promiscuous use of as many of them as they please. There are also two wards called the bawdy houses, in which the locker, for a shilling, will at any time lock up a man and woman together for the night, and he is so solicitous to encourage this practice for the sake of his fee that he addressed the author of the ' Reasons,' after he had been three days in custody, in these terms : ' When you have a mind to have one of these girls that you fancy lie with you all night you may have her ; the custom is to pay for her bed and tip me a shilling.' But this lewdness is not only practised by one prisoner with another, but by people that go thither on purpose, so that the place may be considered as a great brothel, kept under the protection of the law for the emolument of its ministers. Many dissolute persons resort thither, especially on Sunday, and after having singled out a girl, and treated her in the tap-house, they are conducted by the locker, under pretence of shewing them the prison, to a private place, where they remain undisturbed as long as they please. It is also a mart where those who subsist by keeping prostitutes in their houses, come to supply themselves with the number they want. It is common for the keeper of a bagnio or his servant to come to this place, call for a bottle or two of wine, look over the girls, enquire when their times are out, and, having made choice of such as they think fit for their purpose, they pay their fees and take them home.''[1]

The anomalous relationship between the gaoler and his prisoners does not, of course, exhaust the tragic ironies of the prison life of that time. The

[1] *Gentleman's Magazine,* June, 1757, quoting from and reviewing the pamphlet entitled *Reasons for the Reformation of the House of Correction at Clerkenwell,* 1757. The pamphlet, which was by Jacob Ilive, himself a prisoner in the House of Correction, contains 56 pages of revolting detail. Another by the same author, *A Scheme for the Employment of all persons sent as disorderly to the House of Correction in Clerkenwell,* 1759, affords further information as to the contemporary prison administration.

modern reader finds it difficult to realize the amazing heterogeneity of the prisoners themselves. In one and the same herd, exposed practically to identical treatment, were often to be found, not only convicted felons and mere misdemeanants, but also untried persons arrested on suspicion of every grade of guilt ; individuals detained merely for non-payment of fines, fees or costs ; poor men committed in default of finding sureties for their appearance to answer for trumped-up charges, and even unequivocally innocent witnesses put in prison only to ensure their being on hand when wanted.[1] Along with all these would be the perennial crowd of mere debtors— persons arrested on civil process for simple inability to discharge their real or alleged liabilities to their creditors. These prisoners, herded together day and night in lawless promiscuity, necessarily lived in the closest association. The jovial debtor possessed of unsuspected resources, the professional thief liberally provisioned by his " pals," even the convicted felon with his right to the " county bread," were actually better off than the untried prisoner, innocent witness or destitute debtor, who, if friendless, were within measurable distance of starvation. In the community of prison life, those who had food shared it with those who had none. Thus, in the relations of gratitude and good fellowship which inevitably sprang up between hardened profligates and inno- cent novices, the very virtues of the prison house increased its moral contamination. In each of the larger prisons the community evolved for itself a whole code of rules at which the gaoler connived, even if they pressed with cruelty on the poorest and weakest of the inmates. Thus the immemorial abuse of "garnish," which existed in all prisons of any size, compelled every newcomer to pay a stated sum, to

---

[1] We have it on the testimony of an ex-Lord Chancellor that, as late as 1793, mere witnesses, " merely because they are poor, and unknown, perhaps without a suspicion of crime . . . are bound over to give evidence, and having no person to answer for them, are committed to secure their testimony." (*Observations on the State of the English Prisons*, etc., by A. Wedderburn, successively Lord Loughborough and Earl of Rosslyn, 1793, p. 28.)

be spent by the whole community in drink. If the unfortunate victim was unable or unwilling to pay, he was stripped of his clothing or made to run the gauntlet.[1]

That this state of affairs should have remained practically unmitigated down to the last quarter of the eighteenth century, is but another proof of the administrative indifference and incapacity of Hanoverian England. " There is nothing more scandalous in the history of England in the eighteenth century," says Lecky, " than the neglect by legislators and statesmen of these abuses."[2] It was in vain that a diligent member of Parliament, named Pocklington, brought before the House of Commons in 1696 the iniquities that were going on in the Fleet Prison, and even succeeded in getting them exposed by a Select Committee. This inquiry led, in 1697, to the abolition of the immemorial privilege of sanctuary at Whitefriars and the Savoy, but effected nothing for the reform of the gaols.[3] It was in vain that, on

---

[1] Howard describes the custom of garnish as existing in 1773-80 in nearly all prisons. At the Essex County Gaol at Chelmsford, " in the taproom there hung a paper on which, among other things, was written ' Prisoners to pay garnish or run the gauntlet.' " It was also exacted by written rule at the Whitechapel Debtors' Prison and the Derby Town Gaol. At the Richmond Gaol (North Riding) the exaction had been officially sanctioned in a table of fees approved by two justices in 1671. At the Shropshire County Gaol at Shrewsbury the Justices, in 1774, expressly prohibited it. (*The State of the Prisons*, 2nd edn, 1780, pp. 199, 220, 277, 314, 371.) But the greatest place for garnish was Newgate, where the cruel rigour of its exaction was described in Steele's comedy, *The Lying Lover*, Gay's *Beggar's Opera*, and the anonymous *History of the Press Yard*, 1717. It was also specially characteristic of the large debtors' prisons in London, where it was described as early as 1618. " Thy chamber fellows come upon thee for a garnish, which if thou deny them, or hast no money, then exit cloak from thy shoulders." (*Certaine Characters and Essays of Prison and Prisoners*, by Geoffrey Mynshal, 1618.) In 1752 we read that " the sheriffs of London and Middlesex have ordered that no debtor in going into any of the gaols of London or Middlesex shall, for the future, pay any garnish, it having been found for many years a great oppression." (*Gentleman's Magazine*, 1752, p. 239.) Howard, however, found it still in full force in 1779. (*State of the Prisons*, 2nd edn., 1780, p. 173.) It still continued in Newgate in 1815 ; and in the great London debtors' prisons we suspect that it lasted down to the very end (see the Report of the House of Commons Committee on the King's Bench, Fleet and Marshalsea Prisons, 1815). (See also *The Old Bailey and Newgate*, by Charles Gordon, 1902, p. 117; and *Chronicles of Newgate*, by Arthur Griffiths, 1875.)

[2] *History of England*, by W. E. H. Lecky, 1887, Vol. VI, p. 249.

[3] *House of Commons Journals*, 1697 ; *The Prison Chaplain*, by W. L. Clay, 1861, p. 26 ; *History of England*, by Lord Macaulay, Vol. II, pp. 616-7, of edition of 1877.

the formation of the Society for the Promotion of Christian Knowledge in 1699, that militant ecclesiastic, Bishop Compton, noticed the state of the prisons, and got appointed a small committee, which visited Newgate and the Marshalsea ; and produced, under Dr. Thomas Bray, an admirable manuscript report on prison reform which remained quite unheeded. Though the Society continued occasionally to concern itself with prison administration during the ensuing decade, we cannot discover that its praiseworthy efforts had the slightest result.[1] It was equally in vain that the most appalling cruelties in the Fleet and Marshalsea Prisons were laid bare by the House of Commons Committee of 1729, under General Oglethorpe, in a lengthy Report which is one of the most horrifying of prison documents. The criminal prosecutions then undertaken against Huggins, Bambridge, Acton and Barnes, the principal culprits, all eventually miscarried ; and the investigation was not continued, partly, as Smollett hints, for political reasons.[2] It was not that the subject was allowed to remain absolutely unnoticed. The House of Lords had its own Committee in 1729, on the state of imprisoned debtors.[3] A few years later, William Hay,

[1] See, for this long-forgotten episode, *Howard and the Prison World*, by W. Hepworth Dixon, 1849, when the report of 1702 was for the first time printed ; *Memoirs of the Life of Robert Nelson*, by Charles Frederick Secretan, 1860, p. 102, etc. ; *The Life of John Howard*, by John Field, 1850, pp. 91-2, 484 ; *Prison Discipline*, by the same, 1848, pp. 2-3, 119 ; *The Prison Chaplain*, by W. L. Clay, 1861, p. 27.

[2] For the horrors brought to light by this investigation, see *House of Commons Journals*, Vol. XXI, p. 274, etc., 1729, for Report of House of Commons Committee of 1729 ; *The Tryal of William Acton . . . upon an Indictment for the murder of T. Bliss*, 1729 (see British Museum, Volume 6056, b. 74) ; the long reports of the prosecutions in Howell's *State Trials*, Vol. IX ; *History of England*, by T. Smollett, Vol. II, ch. xv, p. 267, of 1848 edition ; Maitland's *History of London*, Vol. II, p. 990 ; *The London Prisons*, by Hepworth Dixon, 1850, p. 116 ; *Life of John Howard*, by J. Field, 1850, pp. 92-100 ; *The Prison Chaplain*, by W. L. Clay, 1861. The oppressions of the Fleet Prison had long been known ; see *The Œconomy of the Fleete, or an Apologetic answer of Alexander Harris unto 19 articles set forth against him by the Prisoners*, 1600, reprinted by the Camden Society in their Vol. XXV, 1879. Later pamphlets are *An Oration on the Oppression of Jailers which was spoken in the Fleet Prison* (n. d. about 1730) and *The Humours of the Fleet, written by a Gentleman of the College*, by W. Paget, 1749.

[3] This led, after two years' delay, to a small Act intended to mitigate some of the worst hardships of debtors (2 George II, c. 22) ; which failed, however, to get put into practice.

M.P., whose labours for Poor Law Reform deserve
more recognition than has been accorded to them,
and who presided over another committee in 1735,
introduced Bill after Bill for the erection of new local
prisons and their supervision by inspectors appointed
by the Lord Chancellor.[1] The veteran philanthropist,
General Oglethorpe, who had been instrumental in
getting the inquiry into the Fleet Prison in 1729,
obtained another committee on the King's Bench
Prison in 1754, which revealed a continuance of the
well-known evils of promiscuity, extortion, drunkenness and every kind of irregularity.[2] All that Parliament or the local authorities could bring themselves to do was now and again to propound some
futile expedient to palliate a particular evil. Thus
the agonized petitions of poor distressed debtors,
starving and dying of fever for no crime except that
of poverty,[3] were occasionally met by the illogical
device of particular Insolvent Acts, whereby all
debtors who happened to be in durance on a certain
day were released. In 1759 Parliament went so far
as to provide, in the well-known "Lords' Act," that
creditors putting their debtors in prison might be
required to allow them fourpence a day for maintenance.[4] But the legal delays and complications
involved in putting this Act into force were so great
and so expensive that Howard, twenty years later,
found that scarcely any debtors succeeded in obtaining their "groats."[5] Parliament at the same

[1] See the Report of the Committee on the Reform of the Poor Law,
House of Commons Journals, 1735 ; and the *Works* of William Hay.

[2] *House of Commons Journals*, 1754 ; see also *The Extraordinary Case of
William Penrice . . . being a Key to the King's Bench Prison*, 1768 (British
Museum, Volume 6056, b. 74). This inquiry led to the resumption by the
Crown of the office of marshal, and the erection of a new building.

[3] There are examples of such petitions in the British Museum, dated
1622, 1641, 1655, 1678, and 1690 ; others, undated, referred to about 1700 ;
others dated 1705, 1714, 1724, 1725, and 1737. See also *Legal and other
Reasons why the Subjects of England should not be imprisoned for Debt*, by
William Cole, 1680 ; *The Cry of the Oppressed*, by Moses Pitt, 1691 ; *Some
necessary Observations on an Act of the Last Session . . . for the Relief of
Insolvent Debtors*, by Roderick Mackenzie, 1725 ; and the anonymous
Thoughts on Imprisonment for Debt, 1761.

[4] 32 George II, c. 28.

[5] "I did not find in all England and Wales (except the Counties of
Middlesex and Surrey) twelve debtors who had obtained from their creditors

time ordered the Justices in Quarter Sessions to
fix a scale of fees to be exacted from the debtors,
but it neither limited their amount, nor took any
steps to see that its injunction was carried out.
All the common gaols and Houses of Correction in
the country were, as we have seen, according to the
meanest standards of health and decency, imperfectly constructed, and many of them were so ruinous
and dilapidated that escapes and rescues were not
infrequent. Beyond passing in 1700, and again in
1711, futile Acts, limited in duration, permitting the
Justices, for a brief period and under impracticable
limitations and conditions to levy a rate for the repair
and building of county gaols,[1] the only remedy that
Parliament could devise was to add the crime of
rescue or connivance at a prisoner's escape to the
ever-growing number of capital offences.[2] The disastrous results of converting the keeping of a prison
into a private profit-making concern, made glaringly
obvious in 1729 by the scandals of the Fleet and
Marshalsea Prisons, were met only by such naïve
injunctions as forbidding the purchase and sale of
the gaoler's office, prohibiting the sale in prisons of

the fourpence a day to which they had a right by that Act ; the means of
procuring it being out of their reach." (State of the Prisons, by John
Howard, 2nd edn., 1780, p. 6). Things had not changed in this respect in
1812 (State of the Prisons, by James Neild).

[1] 11 & 12 William III, c. 19 (1700) ; 10 Anne, c. 14 (1711). Quarter
Sessions could act only after " the insufficiency and inconvenience of their
gaol had been formally presented by the grand jury ; and it was expressly
stipulated (sec. 4) " that this Act be not in any wise hurtful or prejudicial
to any person or persons having any common gaol by inheritance, for term
of life, or for years ; but that they shall have and enjoy the said gaols, and
the profits, fees and commodities of the same, as they had or might lawfully have had before making this Act, and as if this Act had never been
made." When counties found themselves eventually driven to rebuild
their gaols, they nearly always thought it necessary to obtain a Local
Act.

[2] " Evidence came before the old Parliamentary Commission (1727-9)
showing that the warders (of the Fleet Prison) were in the regular habit of
selling the ' right of escape ' to such (debtors) as could afford their terms."
(The London Prisons, by Hepworth Dixon, 1850, p. 116.) The Act against
accomplices in escapes was 16 George II, c. 31 (1743). An armed gang of
a score of violent robbers attacked the Westminster Gatehouse Prison and
forcibly rescued a notorious highwayman. As several " other offenders
who have been taken into custody have of late, with forced violence, been
rescued and set at liberty by great numbers of armed persons," the King
offers a reward of £100 for the apprehension of any highway robber.
(London Gazette, January 30th, 1749.)

spirituous liquors as distinguished from beer, commanding that no prisoner should be taken by an officer to any "tavern . . . without his consent," nor charged "for liquor or other things other than such as he shall freely and particularly call for."[1] In 1744 the House of Commons inserted in a general Vagrancy Act a clause ordering Quarter Sessions to appoint two Justices to visit and report on the county Houses of Correction.[2] In 1759 it went so far as to hide away, in the body of a statute relating to the effects of debtors, a provision requiring Quarter Sessions to draw up rules and orders "for the better government of their respective gaols," to be submitted to the judges of assize for their approval, and to be forwarded "to the gaoler or keeper of each prison, to be kept hung up in some public room." The Justices, it is clear, remained unconscious that any direct responsibility rested on them for seeing that the gaols were properly kept, nor can we find that the House of Correction, any more than the gaol, was actually visited and inspected by them.[3] The root of the failure to get these reforms carried out, even when enacted by Parliament, is to be found in the complete absence of administrative machinery, and of anything in the nature of Political Science to point to the necessary conditions of administrative reform. Parliament might pass a law, but it was nobody's business even to communicate the fact to such local authorities as existed. It was no part of the duty of the Secretary of State, nominally charged with Home Affairs, to know what the local authorities were doing. He received from them no annual or other reports. He had no inspectors to find out what was happening. He regarded it as beyond his function even to remonstrate with any local authority in the execution of its duty, let

---

[1] 32 George II, c. 28 (1759).   [2] 17 George II, c. 5 (1744).

[3] As late as 1779 Howard records that the Suffolk County Bridewell at Clare, which was so ruinous that the prisoners had to be chained to the floor to prevent their escape, had not been once visited by any magistrate for fifteen years. (*State of the Prisons*, by John Howard, 2nd edn., 1780, p. 262.)

alone intervene authoritatively to get the laws
carried out. Moreover, he had, almost invariably,
no legal power to order the local authorities to
do, or to abstain from doing, anything. It was
characteristic of the eighteenth century constitution
of England (as it seems to be of the nineteenth and
twentieth century constitution of the United States)
that, generally speaking, only the Courts of Law
could enforce the execution of a statute, and then
only in particular cases brought before them.[1]

When any local personage intervened at all in
prison administration it seems to have been regarded
as an extraordinary event, worthy of special praise
or requiring exceptional explanation. Thus, we are
told by the proud biographer of a Lord Mayor named
Brown, that he forbade the detention in Newgate of
acquitted prisoners merely because they could not
pay the gaoler's fees—a reform which does not seem
to have outlasted his own administration.[2] And
when, at a specially virulent outbreak of gaol fever
at the Old Bailey in 1750, the Lord Mayor, two
judges, one alderman, two or three counsel, several
jurymen, and the under-sheriff all died of the gaol
fever brought by the prisoners from Newgate to the
Court,[3] a public spirited sheriff thought it his " indispensable duty " to remove the " apprehensions "
of the bench and the bar, by ordering Newgate to be
cleansed, and the prisoners to be washed before being
brought into Court.[4] The " dangerous nuisance "

[1] The student of the relations between the English Home Office and the
local authorities throughout the nineteenth century, notably as regards
roads, local byelaws, police, and even the Children Act of 1908 (in special
contrast with the central departments which have since developed into the
Ministries of Education and Health), cannot fail to note the long-continued
retention of the eighteenth century standpoint.

[2] *Life and Character of Mr. Alderman Brown*, 1741, quoted in Place,
Add. MSS. 27826-42.

[3] *Crown Law*, by Sir M. Foster, p. 74 ; *State of the Prisons*, by John
Howard, 2nd edn. (Warrington, 1780), p. 12 ; *Gentleman's Magazine*,
January, 1753 ; *Letter to Sir Robert Ladbroke*, by S. Denne, 1771, pp. 14-15.

[4] *Gentleman's Magazine*, May, 1750, p. 235 ; January, 1764, p. 16. Some
particulars of Alderman Janssen's energetic action when sheriff are given
in *The Right Method of Maintaining Security in Person and Property*, by
Philonomos, 1751, pp. 52-7. At the instance of Dr. Stephen Hales, a windmill ventilator was constructed at Newgate, but it was soon disused ; see
Denne's *Letter to Sir Robert Ladbroke*, etc., 1771, p. 7.

of Newgate, as a permanent centre of infection, continued to create spasmodic panics of fear in the Metropolis ; and in 1767 Parliament brought itself to command the City Corporation to provide a new building—a command not yet obeyed,[1] in 1780, when the Lord George Gordon rioters burnt the old prison to the ground. But except for such occasional and quite ineffectual injunctions, Parliament and the local authorities did but reflect, for the first seventy years of the eighteenth century, the attitude of the ordinary prosperous citizens described by Howard, who " when they are told of the misery which our prisoners suffer, content themselves with saying, ' Let them take care to keep out.' "[2] The appalling visions of horror incidentally given in the plays and novels of Gay and Smollett and Fielding, like the revelations before the House of Commons Committee in 1729, seem to have been taken by contemporaries as matters of course. Even to such exceptional citizens as John Wesley and Samuel Johnson—even to an active-minded, reforming administrator like Henry Fielding—the state of the prisons seemed an evil for which there was no remedy.[3]

[1] The first stone of the new building had been laid in 1770, but the work had been proceeded with very slowly. Not until the actual destruction of the old building was the new one energetically taken in hand and completed.

[2] *The State of the Prisons*, by John Howard (Warrington, 1777).

[3] It is but fair to add that the total number of persons in prison at any one time was, prior to the end of the eighteenth century, comparatively small. What with the pillory and whipping, and transporting, and hanging, and the burning in the hand of those obtaining the " benefit of clergy," the persons in prison were kept down to (a) debtors, (b) those awaiting trial for felony, (c) those awaiting trial or sentenced to terms of hard labour for misdemeanours, including mere vagrancy, and (d) those committed on failure to find sureties, etc. Howard estimates the average total number in 1779 at 4,375, of whom nearly half were debtors. (This, however, whilst a smaller proportion of the population than was in prison during most of the nineteenth century, is a larger proportion than is in prison in 1921.) The only prisons having more than 90 inmates were the King's Bench, 498 (debtors only) ; Newgate, 292 ; the Fleet, 184 (debtors only) ; Clerkenwell Bridewell, 171 ; the Savoy (soldiers), 98 ; and the Marshalsea (debtors only), 92—all in London. The only provincial prisons having as many as 50 inmates were York County Gaol, 89 ; Lancaster County Gaol, 83 ; Bristol Gaol, 56 ; the Stafford County Gaol, 54 ; the Cumberland County Gaol at Carlisle, 53 ; the Norfolk County Gaol at Norwich, 53 ; and the Warwick County Gaol, 50. No fewer than 130 of the gaols and bridewells had, in 1779, under ten inmates of all classes.

Chapter III

JOHN HOWARD

How long this state of unconcern in the many, and
of mingled acquiescence and hopelessness in the few,
would have persisted, if there had not intervened
an exceptional personality, it is useless to discuss.
John Howard (1726-1790)[1] was inspired by the same
faith and belonged to the same set as the little knot
of social reformers who were destined, a few years
later, to start the national movement for a Reformation of Manners that we have elsewhere described.[2]
Like Wilberforce, Zouch and Jonas Hanway, he was
a fervent Evangelical of the peculiar philanthropist
type, believing in " grace," but determined to save
men's souls by subjecting them to the discipline of

[1] Though there have been almost innumerable accounts of Howard,
these have nearly always been written " for edification," and it cannot be
said that there exists any adequate biography of him, or any scientific
study of his work. Of the contemporary appreciations, that by his friend
Dr. John Aikin, entitled *A View of the Character and Public Services of the
late John Howard*, 1792, is perhaps the most interesting ; whilst of the
biographies, the *Memoirs of John Howard*, by James Baldwin Brown, 1823,
and *The Life of John Howard*, by Rev. John Field, 1850, contain the fullest
information. *Howard and the Prison World*, by W. Hepworth Dixon, 1849,
and *Howard and his friends*, by John Stoughton, 1884, are specially useful.
The proceedings of the International Penitentiary Congress at St. Petersburg
in 1889 were largely devoted to commemoration and appreciation of
Howard. Other works include *Memoirs of Howard*, by T. Taylor, 1836 ;
Correspondence of John Howard, by J. Field, 1855 ; *Prisons and Reformatories at Home and Abroad*, by R. W. Bellows, 1872 ; *The Condition of
Gaols as described by John Howard*, by J. B. Bailey, 1884 ; *The Experiences
and Opinions of John Howard on the Health of Prisoners*, by R. D. R.
Sweeting, 1884 ; *History of England*, by W. E. H. Lecky, 1887, Vol. VI,
pp. 255-7 ; *Through the Prison Bars*, by W. H. Render, 1894 ; *John Howard*,
by E. C. S. Gibson, 1901 ; *John Howard, the Prisoners' Friend*, by L. O.
Cooper, 1904 ; *Life of John Howard the Philanthropist*, by H. H. Scullard,
1911. The work entitled *Howard Letters and Memories*, by W. Tallack,
1905, is not about Howard. For his position in county organization, see
The Parish and the County, by S. and B. Webb, 1907.
[2] *History of Liquor Licensing in England*, 1903.

continuous work, physical abstemiousness and religious exercises—a regimen to which he unhesitatingly subjected his family and himself. Like so many of these religious-minded social reformers, he belonged by birth to the commercial world, but had become a landed proprietor enjoying easy access to the governing class. But Howard had remarkable qualities of his own, which peculiarly fitted him for the task of starting a new era in prison administration. Endowed with no special intellectual capacity, and very imperfectly educated, he had a curiously childlike simplicity of thought and directness of aim, combined with absolute fearlessness and an indomitable persistency of will. His whole life was marked by purity of motive, and an ever-present impulse to relieve human suffering. He had almost a passion for travelling, for observing details and for noting them down in precise language. Like a child, or an unsophisticated visitor from another world, he seems to have had no prepossessions, and to have taken nothing for granted. Every assertion of fact he tested by personal observation. Every obligation he took literally and to its fullest extent. Every instance of human suffering that came under his eyes he challenged as an evil which could, ought and must, forthwith be remedied.[1]

We are not concerned to tell here the story of Howard's life ; his casual upbringing, his desultory foreign travel, his outbursts of self-examination and simple piety, his domestic happiness and sorrow, and his admirable efforts as a country squire to raise the material condition and reform the habits of his dependents and neighbours. By a fortunate accident he was, in 1773, " pricked " for the office of sheriff of Bedfordshire. It was characteristic of the man that he accepted the position without demur or protest, notwithstanding that, as a conscientious

[1] " A man," says Carlyle, " full of English accuracy. English veracity, solidity, simplicity, by whom this universal gaol commission, not to be paid for in money but far otherwise, is set about with all the slow energy, the patience, practicality, sedulity and sagacity common to the best English commissioners paid in money and not expressly otherwise."

Nonconformist, he could not take the sacramental test required by law, and ran the risk of being proceeded against and fined. Once installed, he set himself to carry out, with an unaccustomed literalness, all the duties of the post. He went calmly through the usual ceremonies, paraded in his carriage, preceded by the antiquated javelin men, and followed by a long retinue of the gentlemen of the county, to meet the judges of assize, escort them to their lodgings and attend them in court. But unlike all previous sheriffs he did not stop at the ceremonial part of his office. He unquestioningly assumed that he was, really as well as legally, the keeper of the county gaol. Whilst sitting in court he observed the miserable appearance of the prisoners, and had noted that " some, who by the verdict of the juries were declared not guilty ; some on whom the grand jury did not find such an appearance of guilt as subjected them to trial ; and some whose prosecutors did not appear against them, after having been confined for months," were dragged back to gaol.[1] He followed his prisoners into their confinement, inspected the building, its cells, and its sanitation, and inquired into the system of management for which he was nominally responsible. We do not gather that the common gaol of Bedford was worse than others, but Howard saw enough to determine him on reform. To his simple mind it seemed obvious that the root of all the evils of prison management was the fact that it was allowed to be a profit-making business. He startled the Justices with the proposal that all fees should be abolished, that the gaoler should be paid a fixed salary, and that the gaol should come directly under the administration of Quarter Sessions. "The bench," he tells us, "were properly affected with the grievance, and willing to grant the relief desired, but they wanted a precedent for charging the county with the expense." "I therefore rode," he continues simply, "into several neighbouring counties in search of one, but I soon

---

[1] The opening words of his *State of the Prisons*, 1777.

learned that the same injustice was practised in them, and looking into the prisons, beheld scenes of calamity which I grew daily more and more anxious to alleviate."[1] In the course of the ensuing twelve months John Howard travelled all over England, presently including in his inspection the bridewells, or Houses of Correction. By the end of that year he had, at the age of about forty-eight, at last found his special vocation, that of an investigator or unofficial inspector of places of detention. From this time onward his biography consists of an almost continuous series of sixteen years of voyages of discovery, not only into all parts of the United Kingdom, but also throughout the countries of Europe. The outcome of this unique peregrination was the publication, in four successive volumes, between 1777 and 1791, of what was practically one continuous series of extracts from his notebook, affording in its wealth of dry detail a convincing description of the horrors of nearly all the prisons of England and Wales, and many of those in other countries.[2]

Meanwhile the question of prison administration had been independently raised in Parliament. In February, 1773, Popham, member for Taunton, introduced a Bill for authorizing the payment, out

[1] *Ibid.*, p. 1.

[2] *The State of the Prisons in England and Wales, with Preliminary Observations and an Account of some Foreign Prisons* (Warrington, 1777).

Appendix to the State of the Prisons in England and Wales . . . containing a further Account of Foreign Prisons and Hospitals, with additional Remarks on the Prisons of this Country (Warrington, 1780). (A second edition of *The State of the Prisons*, in 1800, published in 1780, incorporates most of the matter of the *Appendix* of that year. In 1784 a second and much enlarged edition of the *State of the Prisons*, in which nearly all the matter was incorporated.)

An Account of the Principal Lazarettos in Europe, with various papers relative to the Plague, together with further Observations on some Foreign Prisons and Hospitals ; and additional Remarks on the present state of those in Great Britain and Ireland (Warrington, 1789).

Appendix containing Observations concerning Foreign Prisons and Hospitals collected by Mr. Howard in his concluding Tour. Together with two letters to Mr. Howard from John Haygarth, M.D. (Warrington, 1791).

A fourth edition of the *State of the Prisons* was published in 1792, after Howard's death, which contained, for English prisons, nearly all the facts given in all the preceding works. Howard's statements as to the superior healthiness of the foreign prisons, and the absence of gaol fever there, are confirmed by the *Account of the Prisons and Hospitals in Russia, Sweden and Denmark*, etc., by William Coxe, 1781.

of the county rate, of the gaol fees of prisoners who
were acquitted or otherwise discharged. This measure, like so many others before it, miscarried, owing
to the apathy or hostility of the members.[1] But
before the opening of the next session, a rumour of
the eccentric conduct of the High Sheriff of Bedfordshire had got abroad, and Popham wisely arranged
to call him as a witness in support of his resuscitated
measure, now enlarged into two separate Bills.[2] The
instantaneous change of tone in the House of Commons which Howard's examination brought about,
was, we think, largely due to the novelty both of the
motive and of the method of his activity. To the
typical eighteenth century member of Parliament,
usually himself a Justice of the Peace, it was a startling fact that any gentleman should take literally
his official obligations as sheriff, and should further,
at his own cost, and at the risk of his life, extend his
inspection to the fever-haunted interiors of the gaols
of other counties. Howard's somewhat naïve use
of the method of statistical enumeration seems to
have brought home to the matter-of-fact mind of the
eighteenth century legislator both the truth and the
importance of his allegations. Instead of sensational
denunciation of oppression and cruelty, disease and
promiscuity, Howard laid before the committee a
detailed statement, with regard to each prison that
he had visited, of the exact fees taken by the gaolers,
the cubic contents, window space or depth below
ground of each apartment, the number, sex, age and
grade of the prisoners confined together or apart, the
exact kinds of chain or irons used, the amount and
quality of the food (or the absence of food) of the
prisoners, and the state of the sewers and water
supply. To this diagnosis of evil he added a number
of practical suggestions for reform. These sugges-

[1] *House of Commons Journals*, Vol. XXXIV, pp. 138, 142, 288 ; Almon's
Debates and Proceedings of the House of Commons, Vol. VIII, p. 215.
[2] *House of Commons Journals*, Vol. XXXIV, p. 535, March 4th, 1774 ;
Memoirs of the Life of John Howard, by J. Baldwin Brown (1823), p. 133 ;
Life of Howard, by J. Field (1850), pp. 116-18 ; *John Howard and the
Prison World*, by W. Hepworth Dixon (1849), pp. 155-7.

tions resolve themselves, omitting unnecessary detail, into four cardinal principles of gaol administration, the provision of structurally secure, roomy and sanitary prisons ;[1] the transformation of the gaoler or master from an independent profit-maker into a salaried servant of the public authority ; the subjection of all prisoners to a reformatory regimen of diet, work and religious exercises ; and the systematic inspection of every part of the prison by some outside public authority. From 1774 to 1791 we see Parliament, in bungling, piecemeal fashion, trying to get these principles embodied in statute law, whilst here and there, up and down the country, philanthropic and enterprising Justices of the Peace strive to induce their fellow Justices at Quarter Sessions to put them into practice.

[1] The general accuracy of Howard's inferences and suggestions with regard to site, construction, cubic space, ventilation, cleanliness, drainage, clothing, food, etc., and the extent to which his rough common sense anticipated the scientific conclusions of Parkes and Corfield at the end of the nineteenth century, are well shown in *The Experiences and Opinions of John Howard on the Health of Prisoners*, by R. D. R. Sweeting, 1884. See also for a useful summary *The Condition of Gaols, Hospitals and other Institutions as described by John Howard*, by J. B. Bailey, 1884.

CHAPTER IV

PARLIAMENTARY ACTION, 1774-1791

THE first legislative result of Howard's investigation was the passing, in 1774, of Popham's two Bills. The more important of these, " An Act for preserving the health of prisoners in gaol and preventing the gaol distemper,"[1] directed the prisons to be periodically cleansed, the prisoners to be washed, separate sick rooms to be provided, and a prison doctor to be appointed, who was to report to Quarter Sessions every three months on the health of the prisoners generally. The other, " An Act for the relief of prisoners who shall be acquitted or discharged," directed that such prisoners should be immediately set at large in open court, and peremptorily forbade the exaction from them of any discharge fees, in lieu of which the county treasurer was to pay the gaoler a sum not exceeding thirteen and fourpence for each case.[2]

Meanwhile the intellectual lead in prison reform had been taken by men of larger outlook than Howard, chief among them Sir William Blackstone, then at the height of his influence ; and Sir William Eden, afterwards Lord Auckland.[3] Taking for granted, as the basis of decent prison administration, Howard's

[1] 14 George III, c. 59. [2] 14 George III, c. 20.
[3] Paul mentions also Sir Charles Bunbury and Sir Gilbert Elliott (*Address . . . to the Magistrates,* etc., by Sir G. O. Paul, Bart., 2nd edn., Gloucester, 1808, p. 14). Blackstone's *Commentaries on the Laws of England*, first published between 1765 and 1769, and running rapidly through successive editions, contained in some of them (see for instance, Vol. IV of the 9th, 10th, and 11th editions, Ch. xx, p. 371) a recommendation of the proposed new penitentiaries. For Sir William Eden, afterwards the first Baron Auckland, see his *Journal and Correspondence*, edited by the Bishop of Bath and Wells, 4 vols., 1861-2.

four principles of secure and sanitary structure, systematic inspection, abolition of fees and reformatory regimen, Blackstone and Eden drafted a comprehensive Bill, laying down, in connection with the proposed erection of one or more national penitentiaries (made necessary by the sudden arrest of transportation to North America by the American War of Independence, 1776-83), a highly developed system of prison discipline. This discipline involved the adoption of certain administrative devices, each of which was destined, in after years, to become the subject of controversy, sometimes as to its intrinsic utility, sometimes as to the relative scope to be given to it. The most novel was the principle of non-intercourse among the prisoners themselves, to be secured by solitary cellular confinement at night and when not at work, and, so far as practicable, by continuous supervision during associated labour and exercise. With this went the exaction from every prisoner of labour of " the hardest and most servile kind in which drudgery is chiefly required."   On the other hand, it was contemplated that this labour should be profitable, it being expressly provided that both officers and convicts should be stimulated by sharing in the profits. Moreover, the severity both of the confinement and of the labour was to be graduated, not according to the offence of the prisoner, but according to his good behaviour in prison, and to the term for which he was committed. A definite regimen intended to secure the maximum of health and the minimum of pleasure was settled for all, including the regular supply of coarse but nutritious food, perfect cleanliness, a fixed daily routine, prison clothing and the total exclusion of luxuries and amusements. With this regimen went the enforced attendance at frequent religious services. Finally, we have the highly praiseworthy innovation of an organized attempt to provide employment and encouragement for the convict on his discharge.

This elaborate code of prison discipline, passed

into law in the session of 1779, did not, in respect of
its immediate purpose, ever become operative. Not
one of the national penitentiaries therein proposed
was actually erected, and, even as a Government
project this Act was superseded, twenty years later,
by the celebrated contract with Jeremy Bentham
for a monster "panopticon"—a scheme which was in
its turn to prove abortive. But the labour which
Blackstone and Eden had spent on the 1779 Act was
not thrown away. It is easy to trace the principles
of this measure, and sometimes even its phraseology,
in the legislation of the next twelve years. General
statutes of 1782 and 1784, relating to Houses of
Correction, and one of 1784, relating to local gaols,
embodied some of its ideas.[1]   Even more important
in their influences were the Local Acts which half a
dozen progressive counties obtained between 1785
and 1788 for the rebuilding and reorganizing of their
prisons.[2] In these Acts, notably in the first of them,
that promoted by the Gloucestershire Quarter Sessions, the clauses drafted by Blackstone and Eden
were, to a large extent, incorporated. Encouraged
by this support, the prison reformers in Parliament
succeeded, in 1791, in passing what may be described
as the first general Prisons Act, applying the principles of the projected national penitentiary to all
places of confinement in England and Wales.[3]   With
the effort to carry this measure through Parliament,
all the impetus given by Howard's revelations seems
to have come abruptly to an end, and for twenty

---

[1] 22 George III, c. 64 (1782) ; 24 George III, c. 55 (1784) ; 24 George III,
c. 54 (1784). The two former Acts were to some extent the outcome of a
House of Commons Committee of 1776 on the whole subject of poor relief
and the treatment of vagrancy. This committee obtained elaborate
statistical returns as to the Houses of Correction, which were presented in
1776, with the suggestion that the information therein contained afforded
a basis for legislation regulating all these institutions. (*Second Report of
Committee on the Poor Laws*, etc., 1776.)

[2] 25 George III, c. 10 (Gloucestershire) ; 26 George III, c. 24 (Shropshire);
26 George III, c. 55 (Middlesex) ; 27 George III, c. 58 (Sussex) ; 27 George
III, c. 60 (Staffordshire) ; 28 George III, c. 82 (Cheshire).

[3] 31 George III, c. 46 (1891). This Act, which was until 1823 the main
code applying to all places of confinement, was brought in by Powis, M.P.
for Northampton, and largely based on the Gloucestershire Local Act of
1786. (*Address . . . to the Magistrates*, etc., by Sir G. O. Paul, Bart., 2nd
edn., 1808, p. 22.)

years—most of them fully occupied by the war with France — Parliament practically let the subject alone.

The Act of 1791 represents a high-water mark in the conception of prison discipline, which was, we think, not again reached until the Act of 1835. But, like all the other legislation of this period, it had two fundamental defects. The Parliamentary draftsmen of these years were apparently incapable of inventing forms of procedure easily capable of application by different localities. The difficulties and complications of action under the 1791 statute were so great that it often proved impossible to put it in force, and reforming Justices continued to apply to Parliament for Local Acts. A more fatal flaw was the permissive character of nearly all the clauses.[1] An eighteenth century Parliament could not bring itself to command the Justices to erect new buildings, however deficient might be the accommodation ; nor, when the Justices did build, even to insist on the prisoners being given separate sleeping apartments. It could not decide to make the gaoler simply the salaried servant of the Justices, and, because it shrank from explicitly commanding the levy of a rate, it failed to abolish his fees, or the profit-making character of his post. It could not even make up its mind to order the Justices to provide food for all inmates of their prisons. Even where the clauses were mandatory in their terms, there was no penalty or other sanction to secure compliance, and, as we need hardly remind the Political Science student, no machinery by which negligent or contumacious local authorities could be required to obey the law, or by which their neglect could be brought to the knowledge of Parliament or the National Government. In short, the legislation of 1774-91 left the County Justices and Municipal Corporations, the

---

[1] " The great defect of this (1791) Act as well as of all the former Acts on the subject is that they rather counsel than command." (*Observations on the State of the English Prisons*, by Alexander Wedderburn, successively Lord Loughborough and Earl of Rosslyn, 1793, p. 24 ; see *The Religious Improvement of Prisons*, by John Brewster, 1808, Appendix.)

lords of manors and owners of franchises practically as free as before to neglect or maladminister the three or four hundred places of lawful confinement under their several jurisdictions.

CHAPTER V

NATIONAL PRISONS (THE HULKS AND MILL-
BANK)

WE must here interpose, in our account of *English
Prisons under Local Government,* a description of the
partial assumption by the National Government
from 1779 onwards, of the duty of maintaining places
of confinement and punishment for certain classes
of convicted criminals.[1] For nearly another century the maintenance of the prisons continued to
be the duty of the local authorities ; and it was no
alteration in theory that led to the establishment of
a few national prisons. But sheer necessity first
compelled the Government to supplement the local
prisons by some directly under its own management ;
and the experience of these government prisons—
still more the persistent controversy as to the effect
of this experience—was destined to have a marked
effect on the course of prison administration, so that
the story cannot be made clear without some description of this episode.

The assumption by the National Government of
the duty of establishing and maintaining prisons
arose, as we have mentioned in Chapter IV, from the
sudden stoppage of the transportation of criminals
to North America by the outbreak of the American

---

[1] As already explained, the King's Courts at Westminster had, from
time immemorial, their own prisons of the King's Bench, Marshalsea and
the Fleet, almost entirely for debtors and others, confined as the result of
civil process or for contempt of Court. The Tower of London, little used
after 1715, was for political offenders ; and that of the Savoy Palace for
soldiers. (*The London Prisons,* by W. Hepworth Dixon, 1850 ; *His
Majesty's Tower,* by the same, 4 vols., 1869-71 ; *Memorials of the Savoy,*
by W. J. Loftie, 1878.)

War in 1776. At that date something like a thousand criminals were being got rid of annually by transportation;[1] and as the Justices utterly failed to

[1] We leave on one side the whole subject of transportation, as to which the literature is voluminous. Beginning in the seventeenth century (the earliest case in 1619)—apart from the mediæval expedient of simple banishment—as a mere arbitrary shipment " to the plantations " of undesirable citizens, it grew, after the Civil War, when local castles were no longer kept up as fortresses (*Observations on the State of English Prisons*, by Alexander Wedderburn, Earl of Rosslyn, 1793, p. 5), into a systematic disposal of felons whom it was thought better not to hang. It became, in fact, virtually a branch of the slave trade, of the nature of which some impression may be formed from the incidental references in the memoirs entitled, *A Young Squire of the Seventeenth Century*, by Cordy Jeaffreson (1878). Curiously enough, Lecky regards it as having been " remarkably successful " (*History of England*, by W. E. H. Lecky, 1887, Vol. VI, p. 253). It first received legislative sanction in various Acts of Charles II (13 and 14 Car. II, c. 12 ; 16 Car. II, c. 4 ; 18 Car. II, c. 3). An Act of 1718 (4 George I, c. 2), professing concern for the ill-stocked labour market of the plantations, authorized the infliction of transportation as a sentence for various crimes ; and both assize judges and Quarter Sessions made extensive use of this power, which saved the expense of keeping felons in gaol. With the growth of the African slave trade, the shipment of English felons became unprofitable to the contractors who undertook the transportation. This led to other proposals. Not altogether ironically, Mandeville suggested that, instead of transporting our felons to the American plantations, where they depraved their companions, the negro slaves, we should offer them as slaves to " the several powers of Barbary," in redemption of their English captives, and thus exchange " lazy, cowardly thieves and incorrigible rogues for brave, laborious and useful people." (*An Enquiry into the Causes of the Frequent Executions at Tyburn . . . to which is added A Discourse on Transportation*, etc., by B. Mandeville, 1725, pp. 48-51.) An anonymous pamphleteer of 1754 proposed to allot them as slaves to the herring fishery, five to each fishing smack, " by which true policy we might soon be enabled to undersell the Dutch in foreign markets." (*Proposals to the Legislature for preventing the frequent executions and exportations of Convicts in a letter to . . . Henry Pelham*, 1754.) But the difficulty was got over by the Justices paying the contractors a bounty, usually of £5 per head, to take the convicts away. The Government was paying a similar sum in 1740, in respect of convicts sentenced in the Home Circuit, the contractor having to ship them to some part of North America, and having (under 4 George I, c. 2) the right to sell or assign them for any sort of labour for the period of the sentence, usually seven or fourteen years. More than one-third usually died on the voyage. Those who survived were put up for sale by the regular slave auctioneers, and Francis Place has preserved the " account sales " of such convicts at Charlestown in 1740, and at Potomac River, Annapolis and Rappahanoc in 1744, showing that seventeen of them realized £1,224 in the depreciated local currency, equal to about £80 sterling. (Place MSS. 27826-45.) The later establishment of a penal colony at Botany Bay, and the subsequent developments at Van Diemen's Land and Norfolk Island, and finally at the Swan River, are well known. It is, however, less familiar that the Justices continued, right into the nineteenth century, to ship off by private contract the convicts whom they sentenced at Quarter Sessions. (Such contracts were specifically authorized in the MS. Minutes, Quarter Sessions, Wiltshire, Michælmas, 1804.) Credit must be given to the Roman Catholic clergy for the first outspoken and persistent denunciation of the system, see *The Horrors of Transportation unfolded to the People*, and *The Catholic Mission to Australia*, by W. (afterwards Archbishop) Ullathorne,

comply with the request of Parliament that the local prisons should be enlarged so as to accommodate such a number, something had to be done. In this emergency the Government obtained power to confine the " transports " temporarily in hulks ; and two old vessels at Woolwich were hastily converted into places in which these convicts could be kept in safety, whilst they were employed on public works connected with the arsenal and the dockyard. This temporary expedient was continued for more than eighty years, additional hulks being used in the Thames and the Medway, and in Portsmouth Harbour.[1]

Of all the places of confinement that British history records, the hulks were apparently the most brutal-

1836. See, on the whole subject, *Transportation and Colonization*, by John Dunmore Land, 1837 ; the *Report of the House of Commons Committee on Transportation* (by Sir William Molesworth), 1838 ; *Our Convict System*, by W. L. Clay, 1862 ; *Colonial Policy*, by Earl Grey, 1853 ; *A Letter to the People of Great Britain and Ireland on Transportation, showing the effects of irresponsible power on the physical and moral condition of the convicts*, by John Frost, 1857 ; *Étude sur la Colonisation par les transportés Anglais*, by E. Campion, 1901 ; *History of Penal Methods*, by George Ives, 1914, pp. 127-70 ; *Memorials of Millbank*, by Arthur Griffiths, 1875 ; *A Colonial Autocracy*, by Marion Phillips (and other records of Australia) ; *Incidents of the Convict System in Australasia*, by Eric Gibb, 1895 ; *Convict Life in New South Wales and Van Diemen's Land*, by Charles White, 1889 ; *The Convict Ship*, 1844, and *England's Exiles*, 1842, both by Dr. Browning ; *Old Convict Days*, by L. Becke, 1889.

No student of the subject can dispense with perusal of the terribly graphic description in the novel of Marcus Clarke, *For the Term of His Natural Life*, 1875 ; see also his *Stories of Australia in the Early Days*, 1897.

[1] For details as to the hulks, see 16 George III, c. 43 ; 18 George II, c. 62 ; 19 George III, c. 74 ; 24 George III, c. 56 ; 28 George III, c. 24 ; 34 George III, c. 60 ; the 28th Report of the Committee on Finance, 1789 ; Three Reports of the House of Commons Committee on the Laws relating to Penitentiary Houses, 1811 (especially the third report) ; *The State of the Prisons in England, Scotland and Wales*, by James Neild, 1812 ; Report on Hulks to the House of Commons, by A. Graham, in 1814 ; *Memoirs*, by J. H. Vaux, 1827 ; Report and Minutes of Evidence on the Hulks at Woolwich, 1847 ; the various Reports of the Directors of Convict Prisons on the Discipline and Management of the Hulk Establishment, 1854, etc. ; *Report from the Select Committee on Secondary Punishments . . . with Notes and Appendix* (1833), pp. 17-22 ; *London Prisons*, by Hepworth Dixon, 1850 ; *The Criminal Prisons of London*, by H. Mayhew and J. Binny, 1862, pp. 198-231 ; *Our Convict System*, by W. L. Clay, 1862, p. 10 ; *Memorials of Millbank*, by Arthur Griffiths, 1875, Ch. V ; *The Punishment and Prevention of Crime*, by Sir Edmund Du Cane, 1885, pp. 117-22 ; *History of Penal Methods*, by George Ives, 1914, pp. 124-6. The hulks were not finally given up in England until 1858. One was established at Bermuda in 1824 ; and one at Gibraltar, established in 1842, lasted until 1875.

izing, the most demoralizing and the most horrible. The death rate was appalling, even for the prisons of the period. Though the convicts had the advantage of working in the open air, the cruelties to which they were subjected by day, and the horrors of their association by night, make the record one of the very blackest, which (as having nothing to do with prisons under Local Government) the reader may here be spared.

What the Government intended was to erect, under the Act of 1779, one or more penitentiaries on the most approved lines, in which the convicts who could no longer be transported to America might be put to hard labour, and—the most important point— kept for long terms from molesting English society. Unforeseen difficulties in the extraordinarily incompetent administration of those days, prevented any of the penitentiaries under the Act of 1779 from being built.[1] Meanwhile, the urgency passed away when it was decided to transport the convicts to the newly discovered continent of Australia. During the next three-quarters of a century this transportation to Australia continued. On the accession of Queen Victoria there were about 45,000 in confinement there, or on licence. From the first shipment in 1787 (to New South Wales) down to the last in

[1] The Penitentiary Act, 19 George III, c. 74 (1779), extended by successive continuing Acts, authorized the appointment of three "supervisors" to select a site. The three appointed—one being Howard himself, another his Quaker friend Dr. Fothergill, and the third a " professional philanthropist " named Whatley—obstinately refused to agree on any one site. (See *Correspondence of John Howard*, by J. Field, 1855, pp. 61-7, for the letters that passed.) Howard wanted a site at Islington, not far off that eventually chosen for Pentonville Prison ; whereas Whatley insisted on a site at Limehouse. Three others were appointed in 1781 (Acts of Privy Council, George III, Vol. XIX, p. 179, March 2nd, 1781), but the scheme made no progress. In 1786 Pitt was hoping that the building might be begun in a few weeks (Pitt to Wilberforce, Sept. 23rd, 1786, in *Private Papers of William Wilberforce*, by A. M. Wilberforce, 1897). By 1794 a site had been selected (where Battersea Park now is) ; but difficulties had arisen in its acquisition, to overcome which an Act was passed (34 George III, c. 84). The proposal was then eclipsed by Bentham's project of a " panopticon," out of which, after many vicissitudes, Millbank Prison eventually emerged. See Report of Select Committee on Police and Convict Establishments, 1798 ; 39 George III, c. 52 ; 52 George III, c. 44 ; 56 George III, c. 63 ; 59 George III, c. 136 ; and Jeremy Bentham's *Works*, Vol. IV.

1867 (to the Swan River), something like a hundred and fifty thousand convicts must have been poured into Australia, Tasmania and Norfolk Island, a large proportion of whom never returned to England. But the resumption of transportation did not completely solve the problem for the Government. The crowded state of the hulks, and the very considerable cost at which they were maintained, was a perpetual reminder of the need for a proper place of confinement and punishment prior to transportation. We need not here seek to unravel the complication of Bentham's proposal of the panopticon, or model prison, on which he ventured so much of his capital, and engaged in so prolonged a controversy with the Government. In 1810, Sir Samuel Romilly varied his persistent campaign for a reform of the criminal law by a definite proposal to the House of Commons that the long-deferred building of a national penitentiary should be at once undertaken.[1] This proposal, warmly supported by Wilberforce and Whitbread, was met by the Government with the appointment of a Select Committee to inquire into the whole question of transportation, the hulks and the old contract with Jeremy Bentham for a "panopticon." In 1811, this committee got to work, under the chairmanship of George Peter Holford, who was destined to become, for the next two decades, one of the ablest and most persistent of prison reformers.[2] Before

---

[1] *Hansard*, Vol. XVI, pp. 944-6, May 9th, 1810 ; June 5th, 1811.

[2] No life of George Peter Holford, M.P., has been written, and he is not even noticed by the *Dictionary of National Biography*. Yet no student of this period can help being impressed by his Parliamentary and pamphleteering activity between 1811 and 1830, and his work as one of the three "supervisors" who were appointed to build Millbank Penitentiary (the others being Lord Farnborough and the Rev. J. T. Becher). As the most active member of the board of governors of this prison, he was engaged in all the controversies as to the excessive cost, the diet scale, the hard labour and the unhealthiness for which it was attacked (*Memorials o Millbank*, by Arthur Griffiths, 1875, Chs. I to IV). He was born in 1768, the younger son of Peter Holford, a Master in Chancery, of Weston Birt (Gloucestershire). Called to the Bar in 1791, he was, in 1802, elected M.P. for one of the boroughs in the hands of the administration ; and he sat in Parliament (with a few months interval in 1806-7) for twenty-four years, representing successively Bossiney, Lostwithiel, Dungannon, Hastings and Queenborough—all Government pocket boroughs. In 1804 he was appointed by Pitt, Secretary of the Board of Control for India, an office

this committee Holford called his friends Paul and
Becher, as well as the keepers of Newgate and Horse-
monger Lane gaols, skilfully managing to bring into
sharp relief the horrors of the old-fashioned prisons,
as compared with the new establishments of Gloucestershire and Nottinghamshire. This led the committee to report emphatically in favour of " a system
of imprisonment not confined to the safe custody of
the person, but extending to the reformation and
improvement of the mind, and operating by seclusion,
employment and religious instruction."[1] It was the
report of this committee that finally buried Bentham's scheme, and caused the Government in
1812, to set about building Millbank Prison on sixteen acres of marsh bought from the Marquis of
Salisbury for £12,000. For nine long years the
erection proceeded of what was subsequently
described as a "monument of ugliness," and was,
at any rate, one of the most costly of all the buildings

which he held until 1810. On going out of office, he was pressed by the
Home Secretary to become chairman of the Prison Discipline Committee
appointed in that year ; and thus began his career as a prison reformer.
He died in 1839 (see *Annual Register* for 1839, p. 336). Apart from a
youthful volume of poems (1789) and an early book on West Indian
missions (*Observations on the necessity of introducing . . . clergymen into
. . . the West Indies*, 1808), neither of which is in the British Museum,
together with *Thoughts on the Old and New Principles of Political Obedience*,
1793, and a couple of theological treatises, his principal work is his *Account
of the General Penitentiary at Millbank* (1828), a useful treatise on prison
administration. The best idea of his work can be gathered from the
frequent references in Hansard for 1806, 1812-6, 1819-20, 1823-4, and
1826, and in the *Gentleman's Magazine* from Vol. LVIII onwards.
   The following (probably incomplete) list of pamphlets by Holford affords
some idea of his persistent industry : *Speech of G. Holford, Esq., on the
motion made by him . . . for leave to bring in a Bill for the Better Management of the Prisons belonging to the City of London*, 1814 ; *Speech . . . on
the Bill to amend the laws relative to the Transportation of Offenders*, etc.,
1815 ; *The Convict's Complaint, supposed to be written on board the hulks*,
etc., 1815 ; *Thoughts on the Criminal Prisons of this Country*, etc., 1821 ;
A Short Vindication of the General Penitentiary at Millbank, 1822 ; *Speech
. . . in support of an Amendment to withhold from the Visiting Justices
the power of authorizing the employment without their own consent of prisoners
committed for trial*, 1824 ; *Second Vindication of the General Penitentiary*,
1824 ; *Substance of a Speech . . . in committee . . . for consideration of
the laws relating to prisons*, 1824 ; *The Convict's Complaint*, 1815, *and the
thanks of the Convict in* 1825, etc., 1825 ; *Third Vindication of the General
Penitentiary*, etc., 1825 ; *Statements and Observations concerning the Hulks*,
etc., 1826 ; *Letter to the Editor of the Quarterly Review . . . relative to the
supposed ill-success of the General Penitentiary at Millbank*, 1830.
   [1] First Report from the Committee on the Laws relating to Penitentiary
Houses, H.C. No. 199, May 31st, 1811, p. 4.

that the world had then seen since the Pyramids of
Egypt, the total expense from first to last amounting
to not far short of three-quarters of a million sterling.[1]
It may be doubted whether the Taj at Agra, the
Cloth Hall at Ypres or the Cathedral of Chartres, had
cost anything like this sum. From 1821 onward the
National Government had therefore, in addition to
the hulks, its own " model " prison for convicted
criminals ; and, as we may here note, from 1842
onward another at Pentonville. The controversies
about these institutions, to some of which we shall
recur, served only to complicate the interminable
discussions about prison administration which we
shall presently describe.

[1] *An Account of the General Penitentiary at Millbank*, by George Peter
Holford, 1828 ; *Memorials of Millbank*, by Arthur Griffiths, 1875 ; *The
London Prisons*, by W. Hepworth Dixon, 1850 ; *The Criminal Prisons of
London*, by H. Mayhew and J. Binny, 1862.

Jeremy Bentham's voluminous writings on prison administration,
beginning with his pamphlet entitled *A View of the Hard Labour Bill*,
1778, and his volume *Panopticon, or the Inspection House*, 1791, can be
most conveniently read in Vol. IV of his *Works*, edited by Sir J. Bowring ;
see also *La Formation du Radicalisme Philosophique*, by Elie Halévy,
especially Vol. I, *La Jeunesse de Bentham*, 1901.

CHAPTER VI

PRISON ADMINISTRATION FROM 1774 TO 1816

(a) *The County Justices*

WE may now resume the story of the local prisons. The majority of the country gentlemen who, as high sheriffs and Justices of the Peace, were responsible for the administration of county prisons, had remained unmoved by Howard's exposures. They did not even comply with the two Acts of 1774, though Howard himself went to the expense of having them reprinted "in an intelligible form," and sent them to every keeper of a county gaol in England.[1] Within a few years, however, the Justices were everywhere driven to bestir themselves by an unforeseen pressure from without. The sudden stoppage of transportation to the American Colonies had, as we have seen, forced the Government to establish the hulks and project the national penitentiaries. The Act of 1779 had incidentally provided that, pending the completion of these national prisons, the local gaols and Houses of Correction were to be deemed penitentiaries, to which criminals might be condemned in lieu of transportation. Characteristically enough, no one seems to have made

---

[1] *Life of John Howard*, by J. Field, 1850, p. 117. On his subsequent visits he nearly always has to report non-compliance with the express direction of Parliament that a copy of the Act should be hung up in the prison. In spite of the Act of 1774 the Clerk of Assize and the Clerk of the Peace still went on claiming fees from acquitted or discharged prisoners, and these found it prudent to comply even with illegal requests of this sort; see *Proceedings of Grand Juries . . . of the County of Gloucester*, by Sir G. O. Paul (Gloucester, 1808), p. 43.

any preparations to receive this new contingent of
prisoners. " The judges," wrote Sir G. O. Paul,
" proceeded to sentence convicts as directed, whilst
the Justices on their part have neglected to provide
the ' proper places ' to receive them as also directed ;
and of course the ordinary wards of county gaols
became . . . dangerously overcrowded,"[1] causing,
in 1783, renewed outbreaks of gaol fever, which
spread to houses in the neighbourhood of the prisons,
and infected remote parishes to which discharged
prisoners returned. Hence we find " the high sheriff
and grand jury of the county of Berks " petitioning
Parliament in 1783, showing that they " in common
with the rest of the kingdom have suffered during
the late war by the difficulties which have arisen in
inflicting the due and accustomed punishment on
offenders not sentenced to die . . . their gaol is
inconveniently full of convicts, from whence much
danger arises of escapes and of infectious distempers
that may spread."[2] As the House of Commons
found no remedy for this plethora of convicts, there
ensued, throughout the country, a prolonged series
of building operations. By the year 1789, as Howard
with some complacency enumerates, no fewer than
forty-two new gaols or Houses of Correction began to
be built.[3] In most cases, however, the building
operations were greatly drawn out by the inefficiency
of Quarter Sessions as an administrative body ;
and they were often obstructed by the strenuous
opposition of the county ratepayers, so that it was
not until the beginning of the nineteenth century that
they were all completed.[4]

[1] *Proceedings of the Grand Juries . . . of the County of Gloucester in
Designing and Executing a General Reform in the Construction and Regulation of Prisons* (Gloucester, 1808), p. 47.
[2] *House of Commons Journals*, Nov. 20th, 1783. There is a similar
petition from Shropshire (*ibid.*, March 11th, 1784). The Lancashire
Quarter Sessions, considering the same state of things in November, 1783,
decided " that it is absolutely necessary to build a " new House of Correction at Preston " (*Manchester Mercury*, Nov. 25th, 1783).
[3] *Account of the Principal Lazarettos*, etc., by John Howard (Warrington,
1789).
[4] Thus in Worcestershire the Justices' proposal to erect a new gaol in
1802 was stopped by the opposition of a county meeting ; revived in 1808,

Unfortunately, the majority of county benches were satisfied with bricks and mortar. In hardly any of the new buildings was the separate and cellular system completely adopted even for sleeping purposes, ahd in many of the prisons the herding together of all classes of prisoners by day and by night still continued. In the majority of county gaols the gaoler still had to live mainly by his fees, perquisites and exactions ; whilst in many country bridewells the inmates remained without any systematic provision of food. In about half a dozen counties there is evidence that the Justices in Quarter Sessions appointed a prison committee of Visiting Justices, or formally adopted, by way of prison regulations, a few extracts from the 1779 or 1791 Act. But the Visiting Committee did not visit, and the regulations were not even hung up. In Middlesex, for instance, as Sheridan told the House of Commons in 1800, " the Prison Committee . . . did nothing more than meet in the committee-room and examine—whom ? —the very persons from whom they could least expect any impartial accounts whether or not the prisoners were properly taken care of—the gaoler, the doctor and the parson."[1] The ordinary Justices of the Peace had, in fact, not yet realized that what was demanded of them was a laborious personal inspection. As was commented by one of their own number, " The pursuits of pleasure, the attraction of gain, the negligence of many, and the ill-placed confidence of others, lead astray from those duties, which, being equally the business of everybody, are but too frequently neglected ; and the artful gaoler, with words of submissive cant, finds no great difficulty in persuading a bench of magistracy so circumstanced to waive the trouble of visiting his prison."[2] " It is not so much for want of good laws," said a

it was again violently opposed as extravagant, but the Justices persisted (*Worcester Herald*, Aug. 20th, 1808). In 1812 the new gaol is still reported as building (*State of the Prisons*, by James Neild).

[1] See the report of the debate in the *Portsmouth Telegraph*, July 28th, 1800.

[2] *The State of the Prisons*, by James Neild, 1812, p. lv.

county magnate in 1793, " as from their inexecution, that the state of the prisons is so bad. In two different counties the Justices took into consideration the late Act (1791), and gravely resolved to wait till they saw what effect it had in other places."[1] " Notwithstanding these anxious endeavours of many individuals in the House of Commons to promote what seemed to be a reigning spirit without doors," relates in 1808 the ablest of contemporary Justices, " no sooner was the whole scope and purpose of the Act for this county (Gloucestershire) made applicable to all the other counties of England . . . than the spirit of execution ceased ; so that if . . . the Act of the 31st (George III) had contained an ordinance for committing to the flames the modern statutes for the construction and regulations of prisons, the purposes of these laws could not have made a less general progress, or have been more disregarded. I have reason to think," he adds in despair, " that in no one county of England have the powers of the three Acts, of the 22nd, the 24th, and the 31st George III, been fully carried into effect."[2] The one tangible result of Howard's labours, so far as concerns the majority of county prisons, was to prevent the more malignant outbreaks of gaol fever. This distemper, optimistically remarks Howard in 1789, " by which such numbers, not only of guilty but of innocent persons were destroyed, is now almost eradicated,"[3]—probably by the adoption of the most elementary sanitary precautions—" and our gaols may, for the most part, be visited without danger. But it is observed that at this point the spirit of improvement unhappily seems to stop, scarcely touching upon

---

[1] *Observations on the State of the English Prisons*, etc., by Alex. Wedderburn, successively Lord Loughborough and Earl of Rosslyn, 1793, p. 24.

[2] *Address . . . on the subject of framing Rules, Orders and Byelaws for . . . the prisons*, etc., by Sir G. O. Paul (Gloucester, 1808), p. 26.

[3] Some confirmation is afforded by Howard's statement in a private letter in 1785, that the prisoners enlisted in the army and navy during the late war, had not, as formerly had always been the case, infected their regiments and ships (Howard to Whitbread, 1785, in *Correspondence of John Howard*, by J. Field, 1855, p. 91.)

that still more important object, the reformation of the morals of the prisoners."[1]

To this general apathy as to any reform of prison discipline there were, however, some notable exceptions. In Sussex, the Lord Lieutenant, the Duke of Richmond, bestirred himself, immediately after Howard's first visit, to get built new county prisons at Horsham in 1775 and at Petworth in 1781, in which the novel principles of cellular construction, separate confinement and continuous employment were so vigorously applied that these prisons became a terror to the local criminal population.[2] In Wiltshire by 1784 the Justices had, at their principal county gaol, given the gaoler a definite salary, prohibited him from trafficking with the prisoners, stopped the sale of drink in the gaol and also the bringing of it in from outside, excluded all visitors except by Justice's order, and built a row of solitary cells. At this gaol, at Fisherton Anger, near Salisbury, we learn that there had been erected " twenty-four apartments for the reception and separation of

[1] *Society for Giving Effect to H.M. Proclamation against Vice and Immorality—Account of the Present State of the Prisons*, 1789, p. iii. The passage is quoted from Howard's *Account of the Principal Lazarettos*, etc. (p. 233), then just published. As a later prison reformer, Matthew Davenport Hill, observed : " With the exception of those changes which approve themselves to the common instincts of benevolence, such as cleanliness, ventilation, drainage, etc., the seed sown by Howard fell in stony places. Whatever required the faintest tincture of philosophy for its appreciation was lost, and had to be re-found, and in many cases it has been re-invented." (*The Recorder of Birmingham : a Memoir of M. D. Hill*, by R. and F. Davenport Hill, 1878, p. 152.) The so-called " Proclamation Society," printed in 1789 " eight pamphlets containing extracts from Mr. Howard's Account of the Present State of the Prisons, together with a general introduction," each dealing with an eighth part of England and Wales ; and distributed these among the Justices and other leading inhabitants of these respective districts. (See *An Account of the Present State of the Prisons and Houses of Correction in the Chester, North and South Wales Circuits*, 1789, and the similar ones for other districts.)

[2] Lord Mansfield used to relate how he was inclined to blame the Duke of Richmond for extravagance in building the Sussex County Gaol at Horsham four times as large as was required, and how willingly he retracted his opinion on learning that the new gaol had been constructed to contain only the same number as the old one. If it was three parts empty in 1791 it was because prisoners seldom came there a second time. (Holliday's *Life of Lord Mansfield*, see *Prison Discipline*, by J. Field, 1856, p. 102.) These two prisons were the first in England to be constructed on the cellular plan. The severity of their regimen was rebuked in the House of Commons in 1816 (*Hansard*, May 13th, 1816), and solitary confinement was thereupon given up in favour of labour in association.

prisoners. One of these lately condemned for a
year's imprisonment petitioned to be hanged," so
feared was this solitary confinement.[1] In Norfolk,
the "new bridewell erected at Wymondham . . .
under the direction of the public-spirited magistrate,
Sir Thomas Beevor, Bart.," was by 1785 "governed
on a plan very different (from) and far superior to
other Houses of Correction. One part of the plan
was to keep the prisoners apart in several distinct
rooms or cells, and employ them ten or twelve hours
in a day in some useful labour, by which they might
earn a part, at least, of their maintenance, and be
prevented from corrupting each other."[2]   Similarly,
in the West Riding of Yorkshire, an enlightened
magistrate in 1788 drew up on Howard's lines an
elaborate code of rules for the administration of the
new House of Correction then building at Wakefield ;[3]
and when it was opened in 1791, Quarter Sessions, at
the instigation of Lord Loughborough, sent an
officer to Wymondham to learn the system of discipline and employment there in use, upon which a
printed report was circulated to all the Justices of
the Riding.[4] The Lancashire Justices, largely at
the instigation of T. B. Bayley, an enthusiastic
disciple of Howard, opened at Manchester in 1790,
"a spacious and handsome prison," framed upon
Mr. Howard's plan of solitary confinement, for which
purpose there are upwards of a hundred cells so
distinctly separate that the prisoners cannot have the
smallest intercourse with one another." . . . "On
the admission of a prisoner he will be immediately
washed in a bath for the purpose, and his clothes
scoured to prevent any infectious communication.
There are working shops provided for those who can
be employed ; for the refractory there are dark cells,

---

[1] *Observations, Moral and Political, particularly respecting the necessity
of Good Order and Religious Œconomy in our prisons . . . by J. H. Esq.*
(probably Jonas Hanway), 1784, pp. 13-15.

[2] *Newcastle Chronicle,* Aug. 27th, 1785.

[3] *Leeds Intelligencer,* Sept. 16th, 1788.

[4] *Lincoln, Rutland and Stamford Mercury,* March 4th, 1791.

and for the sick there are hospital rooms."[1]   The Suffolk magistrates completed, in 1792, their new gaol at Ipswich, which was, we learn, " divided into four parts, one for debtors, another for convicts, a third for felons and a fourth for women. They have separate cells, and are provided with a comfortable dress at the expense of the county : each has a bedstead, straw mattress, sheet, blankets and coverlet. From the structure of the building no gaol distemper can possibly arise, and every prisoner on his entrance is obliged to strip and be bathed before he is apparelled with the clothing of the house ; nor are strangers admitted to see them."[2]

The partial reforms carried out by the Justices of Sussex, Wilts, Norfolk, the West Riding, Lancashire, Suffolk and others were thrown into the shade by the great campaign of prison reform, extending over more than thirty years, carried on by the ablest, the most persistent, and on the whole, most successful of Howard's followers, Sir George Onesiphorus Paul,

[1] *Leeds Intelligencer*, March 23rd, 1790 ; see *Biographical Memoirs of the late Thomas Butterworth Bayley*, by Dr. Thomas Percival (Manchester, 1802), p. 4 ; and *The Parish and the County*, by S. and B. Webb. It is reported that the popular name of the gaol, " the New Bailey," was taken from that of its chief promoter.

[2] *Leeds Intelligencer*, July 30th, 1792. It was for the assistance of the Suffolk Justices in 1785, who were then thinking of erecting this new gaol at Ipswich, and a new House of Correction at Bury, that Dr. Jebb wrote his *Thoughts on the Construction and Polity of Prisons, with Hints for their Improvement*, by John Jebb (with Preface by Capel Lofft), 1786. The Dorset County Gaol at Dorchester, reformed by Sir G. O. Paul's friend, Morton Pitt, with an exemplary system of account books ; the Stafford County Gaol and the Oxford County Gaol are also mentioned as prisons managed somewhat on Howard's principles. (*Life of Lord Mansfield*, by Holliday ; *Observations on the State of the English Prisons*, etc., by Alexander Wedderburn, successively Lord Loughborough and Earl of Rosslyn, 1793, pp. 8, 20.)   In the minutes of the Bucks Quarter Sessions we find, in 1785, a code of thirteen rules adopted for the gaol, and another, closely resembling it, for the Houses of Correction, enforcing sanitation and work, and providing a fixed diet table for all prisoners, whilst fees of all kinds were abolished. (MS. Minutes, Quarter Sessions, Buckinghamshire, Midsummer, 1785, and Easter, 1786.) They were amplified and improved in 1795 and 1800. (*Ibid.*, Michaelmas, 1795, and Midsummer and Michaelmas, 1800.) In Norfolk, in 1795, a committee was appointed to consider the state of the gaol ; and on its report fees were prohibited, a salary of £160 was given to the gaoler, paid turnkeys were appointed, the prisoners were classified, convicts were put in separate cells, and so on. (MS. Minutes, Quarter Sessions, Norfolk, Oct. 7th, 1785.) We infer that, of the other counties, those which, by 1804, had paid most attention to prison administration, were Cornwall, Devon, Hants, Hereford and Derby.

Bart., an active magistrate of Gloucestershire.[1] In the critical year of 1783 the state of the Gloucestershire prisons amounted to a grave public scandal. At the County Gaol in Gloucester City, the whole herd of prisoners, " those committed for trial, and those convicted, the young and the old, are indiscriminately driven at night into one dark pen. . . . A ponderous chain crosses this place of rest, and passing the middle link of each man's fetter, it is made fast at each end, and the whole number are threaded together. . . . There are at present forty prisoners so threaded together every night."[2] The half a dozen little Houses of Correction scattered up and down the county were no less insanitary, whilst they added the additional cruelty of providing no food for their inmates, who were in a state of semistarvation. The promiscuity and licence which prevailed made the prisons, said the grand jury, " a seminary of vice and a certain introduction to the most infamous practices."[3] Throughout the county, Paul declared, three prisoners died of distemper for every one executed, and of those who died the vast majority were either persons awaiting trial or debtors. What was worse, both the moral and

---

[1] The only life of Paul is that in the *Dictionary of National Biography*. The excellent *Bibliographer's Manual of Gloucestershire Literature*, by F. A. Hyett and W. Bazeley (Gloucester, 1895), records over a dozen separate publications by Paul, between 1783 and 1813, in a bewildering variety of editions. Most of the matter will be found in the little volume entitled *Proceedings of the Grand Juries . . . of the County of Gloucester on Designing and Executing a General Reform in the Construction and Regulation of the Prisons*, by Sir G. O. Paul, 3rd edn. (Gloucester, 1808). See also his *Address to the Magistrates . . . 1789, on a Motion to consider the Appointment of Officers and of adopting Regulations for the Government of the New Prisons*, 4th edn. (Gloucester, 1808) ; his *Thoughts on the Alarming Progress of Gaol Fever* (Gloucester, 1784) ; his *Address delivered at a General Meeting . . . for . . . receiving a Statement of the Proceedings of the Committee . . . to rebuild the New Gaols and Bridewells* (Gloucester, 1792) ; his *Address . . . on the Administration and Practical Effects of the System of Prison Regulation* (Gloucester, 1809) ; and the various editions of the *Rules, Orders and Byelaws* drawn up by him. There are also three pamphlets by him as to erecting a county lunatic asylum, dated 1796, 1812, and 1813, and one of 1803 as to building a new shire hall. As to his position in county administration, see *The Parish and the County*, by S. and B. Webb, 1907.

[2] Subsequently, fourteen of these were discharged as innocent ! (Sir G. O. Paul's *Proceedings*, p. 44.)

[3] *Considerations on the Defects of Prisons and their present System of Regulation*, etc., by Sir G. O. Paul, Bart., 1784.

the physical infection spread to every village to which an acquitted prisoner returned. Paul determined to make the Gloucestershire prisons a model for all England. From 1783 onward, in the minutes of Quarter Sessions and the local newspapers, we watch this indefatigable reformer setting in motion all the cumbrous machinery of county government, drafting resolutions and " presentments " for the grand jury, making speeches at Quarter Sessions, delivering addresses at county meetings, printing and circulating these in pamphlets to the magistrates of the county, and persuading them step by step to prison reform. Yielding to Paul's indomitable energy, the Gloucestershire Justices obtained, in 1786, a Local Act enabling them not only to rebuild their county gaol and Houses of Correction, at a cost of nearly £50,000, but also to carry out the principles of the Penitentiary Act of 1779. The new prisons were built on the cellular system : each inmate had a separate cell, and was, " as far as the nature of his employment permitted," kept during the day apart from his fellows. " Labour of the hardest and most servile kind, in which drudgery is chiefly required, and where the work is little liable to be spoilt by ignorance, neglect or obstinacy, such as treading in a wheel, drawing in a capstern for turning a mill or other engine," was to be the daily routine of all convicted prisoners.[1] Intercourse with friends was strictly forbidden, but the prisoners were to be visited not only by the warders, but once each day by the governor himself, and once or twice a week, separately, by the chaplain and the surgeon. No alcohol or other luxuries were to be permitted, but sufficient food, clothing and bedding were to be supplied to every inmate. Irons, chains and brutalizing punishments were abolished. All fees, exactions, perquisites and opportunities for traffic with the prisoners were peremptorily swept away. The

---

[1] *General Regulations for the Inspection . . . of . . . prisons, etc.,* County of Gloucester, 1790, p. 67. The phraseology is taken from a clause of the 1779 Act.

keeper or gaoler was replaced by a salaried governor, a staff of male and female warders, a surgeon and a chaplain. All this was the work of Paul, and of Paul alone : he was, as has been truly said, " the head and heart of the committee, the draftsman of the Bill, the financier who raised the funds, the clerk of the works at all the five new buildings, the author of the reformed system of discipline, the general Visiting Justice of the county, and the scapegoat on whose head were laid all the stupid anathemas that the scheme provoked."[1] Whatever may nowadays be thought of the sternness of the regimen, or of his whole-hearted adoption of the panacea of cellular isolation, in the sphere of administration he was evidently an inventor and a reformer. His greatest merit was that, in the elaborate " Rules, Orders, and Regulations for the Conduct and Government of the Prisons,"[2] which he drew up for his county, he greatly improved, not only on Howard's general suggestions, but also on the definite injunctions which Eden and Blackstone had incorporated in the Penitentiary Act of 1779. We are, for instance, inclined to believe that we owe to Paul the first expressly formulated scheme for direct administration by the Justices themselves, as distinguished from the mere vesting of personal authority in the governor or gaoler, whether under a farming contract or otherwise. It was from his admirable rules that other county benches slowly and gradually learned such administrative devices, now become commonplace, as the making of all contracts for supplies by the Justices themselves, instead of by the governor or other officer,[3] the requirements that the governor, the surgeon and the

---

[1] *The Prison Chaplain*, by W. L. Clay, 1861, p. 64.

[2] These formed a volume of 84 pages which went through at least four editions : see *General Regulations for the Inspection and Control of all the Prisons*, together with *Rules, Orders and Byelaws for the Government of Gaol and Penitentiary House for the County of Gloucester* (Gloucester, 1790). A revised code, also by Sir G. O. Paul, was published in 1810, and successive editions in 1812 and 1820.

[3] See the tenders accepted by the Justices in full Quarter Sessions, MS. Minutes, Easter and Michaelmas, 1791. It is interesting to note the relative prices paid for bread, 2½d. per lb., and " legs, necks and shins of beef," 1½d. per lb.

chaplain should each keep an exact diary of the day's work, to be regularly presented to the Justices, the institution of a "visitors' book," in which the Visiting Justices were to write their observations, the express recital in minute detail of the duties to be performed by each officer, the elaborate detailed rules for sanitation, the changing of linen, opening windows, etc., and the formulation of fixed and varied diet-tables, minutely specifying each day's meals.   No student of the minutes of the Gloucestershire Quarter Sessions[1] can doubt that it was due almost entirely to Paul's personal working out of every administrative detail, his perpetual reports to, and discussions with, his fellow Justices, and his own " uninterrupted superintendence " of each prison that the Gloucestershire County Gaol and Houses of Correction attained, by 1812, what the most competent observer described as " the highest pitch of perfection in polity " then known.[2]

Meanwhile in Nottinghamshire another prison reformer, the Rev. J. T. Becher, whom we have known of also as an experimenter in workhouse management and an early advocate of Friendly Societies, was developing a more attractive suggestion of the 1779 Act, the profitable employment of the prisoners.   Incidentally he gives us, in his account of the Southwell House of Correction in 1806, a lurid vision of what an unreformed county prison, thirty years after Howard's visits, could still be like. " When a prisoner arrived at the gate," he tells us, " his commitment was inspected, and he was consigned to the ward appropriated to offenders of his denomination, without undergoing any previous investigation to ascertain his cleanliness or health ; by which negligent omission vermin and the itch

---

[1] See, for instance, MS. Minutes, Quarter Sessions, Gloucestershire, Jan., 1790 ; *ibid.*, Jan., 1792 ; *ibid.*, Easter, 1892 ; and his evidence in the First Report from the House of Commons Committee on the Laws relating to Penitentiary Houses, 1811, and in the Report of the House of Commons Committee on the State of the Gaols, 1819.

[2] *State of the Prisons*, by James Neild, 1812, p. 249.   A good description of the Gloucestershire reforms is given in *The Prison Chaplain*, by W. L. Clay, 1861, pp. 63-8.

were not infrequently communicated to the whole
of his miserable associates. If he were convicted of
felony or aggravated misdemeanour, or even charged
with these offences, he was fettered and confined in
the felons' ward : a drunken turnkey, to whom the
small pittance of £5 was allowed by the county, secured
him in the dungeon at night and released him in the
morning. . . . Without moral instruction, without
laborious industry, pinched with hunger, and generally
more than half naked, he dragged about his chains in
all the squalid wretchedness of abject penury until the
day of trial arrived, or the term of his sentence expired ; when, emaciated by the baneful atmosphere of
the dungeon, and unhabituated to the exercise of any
employment by which a livelihood might be acquired,
he was turned loose upon the public to practise all
his former crimes with the additional artifice and
dexterity derived from the lessons of his abandoned
companions. . . . Those committed for inferior
offences, such as trifling assaults, non-payment of
penalties, misbehaviour in service or apprenticeship,
or acts of vagrancy, avoided the miseries of a dungeon ; but were necessitated to use the same apartment for every purpose . . . nearly 18 ft. 6 in.
square ; of this space the bedsteads occupy more
than a fourth part, yet in this contracted place have
been generally collected from seven to eleven men
and often more ; three, sometimes four, and even
five, in one bedstead, lying on loose straw, without
any bedclothes except such as the precarious hand
of friendship or charity accidentally supplied. Night-
tubs, cooking utensils, plates, basins, meat dressed
and raw, potatoes, coals and various articles of diet
or dress all promiscuously jumbled together, dirty
and clean, in this small room; where even the
wretched prisoners complained that the vermin and
filth were to be accounted amongst the most afflictive
severities attending their sentence. Those who in
this or any other part of the prison could procure
friends, were allowed to receive from them daily, or
occasional relief in provisions, money or ale in moder-

ate quantities ; to persons connected with those in the vicinity of Southwell dinners ready dressed were regularly sent ; to others coming from places more remote, sustenance sufficient for a week was brought ; to those belonging to the associated poachers, money was by the fraternity remitted ; and those who had neither friends nor money, being destitute of employment, were barely prevented from starving by the daily county allowance consisting of one pound of bread and one penny in money."[1]

Becher got the Justices to build a new House of Correction, on the windmill plan, with a central house and three wings affording accommodation for six distinct classes of prisoners."[2] The leading idea of his system of prison administration was the encouragement of industrious habits, by the provision of comfortable conditions of life and remunerative work, in pleasant association—a device which we shall discuss hereafter. To stimulate the good will of the prisoner, by sharing profits and giving intellectual and religious instruction was, in fact, the central idea of this system of " discipline." In their leisure time the inmates were supplied with improving books, and " encouraged to read to each other " round the fire. " It is supposed," remarked the House of Commons Committee of 1811, " that the vigilance of those who have the care of the prisoners will be able to prevent any mischief that might result from the communication of a few individuals with each other ; and that, in the small circle in which the offender is allowed to move, he may be expected, under proper management, to form habits of industry and self-restraint, which he will be likely to practise on his return to society."[3]

---

[1] *A Report concerning the House of Correction at Southwell*, by Rev. J. T. Becher (Newark, 1806), pp. 4-5.

[2] New rules were not adopted by the Nottinghamshire Quarter Sessions until 1808 ; and Becher described the reformed system of separate night cells, regular employment in productive work, under salaried officers, with systematic inspection by visiting Justices, before the Committee on the Laws relating to Penitentiary Houses (First Report, H.C., No. 199, May 31st, 1811).

[3] First Report of House of Commons Committee on the Laws relating to Penitentiary Houses, 1811, p. 20.

(b) *The Municipal Corporations*

The two or three hundred gaols and Houses of Correction which were not under the County Justices were even less affected by Howard's influence than the hundred or so of county prisons. The Municipal Corporations, the lords of manors, and the owners of special franchises[1] seem, for the most part, to have paid no attention whatever, either to Howard's strictures or to the injunctions of Parliament. They neither put their vile dungeons and lock-ups into a sanitary state,[2] nor promulgated the regulations prescribed by statute. Still less did the majority of towns go to the expense of building new gaols on an improved plan. Here and there, in the course of the next half-century, a Municipal Corporation put up a new prison building,[3] but the civic authorities, for the most part, paid no more heed to prison administration than did the private owners of gaols. Between 1800 and 1830, as the House of Commons was

[1] Honourable exception must be made of the Duke of Devonshire, who rebuilt, in 1794, the small gaol that he owned at Knaresborough for the Honour of Forest of Knaresborough. Lord Middleton, too, as lord of the Honour of Peverel, built in 1805 a new gaol of four rooms, " in the backyard of a publichouse." (*State of the Prisons*, by James Neild, 1812.)

[2] At the Canterbury City Gaol, Howard notes, in 1779, " no regard is paid to the clause " (in the Act of 1774) " enjoining that once in the year at least the gaols shall be whitewashed." (Howard's *State of the Prisons*, 2nd edn., 1780, p. 227.) Similar observations occur in many other cases.

[3] The Municipal Corporations of Doncaster (1779), Lynn (1784), Cambridge (1788), Northampton (1792), and Leicester (1793) seem to have built new prisons after Howard's criticisms; and their example was followed later by Winchester (1800), Wolverhampton (1800), Penzance (1803), York (1807), Chester (1807), Portsmouth (1808), Lincoln (1808), Wisbech (1809), Ipswich (1810), and Newcastle-on-Tyne. But the chief example was Liverpool, where the corporation built a new House of Correction as early as 1776, and started on a new gaol to replace the " Old Tower," once the fortified mansion of the Stanleys. Unfortunately, when in 1787 the new gaol was finished, the corporation in an economical fit refused to give up the old one, and presently found a profitable use for the new building by letting it to the Government at a high rent for the accommodation of French prisoners of war. Not until 1811 was it devoted to its original use, and then received high praise from all observers. " The new prison according to the Howardian plan for solitary confinement is on a very extensive scale, and has every possible convenience." (*The Representative History of Great Britain and Ireland*, by T. H. B. Oldfield, 1816, Vol. IV, p. 100 ; *Notes on a Visit to some of the Prisons in Scotland and the North of England*, by J. J. Gurney, Pt. II, 1820 ; Sir J. A. Picton's books, *Memorials of Liverpool*, 1875, Vol. I, pp. 217, 247, 293, and *Municipal Archives and Records*, 1886, pp. 133, 234, 256, 311, 371-2 ; *The Manor and the Borough*, by S. and B. Webb, 1908, p. 484.)

informed, the fifty or sixty county authorities in England and Wales spent over three million pounds in building and equipping new prisons. In that period the couple of hundred Municipal Corporations spent only £600,000 on the same service. The only towns that went to any considerable expense in the matter were the City of London, Bristol, Liverpool, York, Newcastle and Nottingham.[1]

In 1812, when we get the next general survey of prisons, nine-tenths of those outside the county jurisdictions seem to have remained pretty much as they were in Howard's time. The most important of all the prison authorities, the corporation of the City of London, was beyond all comparison, the worst. Even the complete destruction, by the rioters of 1780, of Newgate and the Borough Compter—two of the worst of its five prisons—led to practically no improvement. Notwithstanding the suggestions of Howard, the Corporation rebuilt Newgate on the bad old plan of promiscuous herding together, by day and

[1] An account of the total expenses incurred in building . . . the several gaols . . . since 1800, H. of C., No. 316, of 1831 ; *The Manor and the Borough*, by S. and B. Webb, 1908, p. 726.

[2] For the state of Newgate and other City prisons from 1774 to 1818, see the two pamphlets by Josiah Dornford in 1786 ; *Hints respecting the Prison of Newgate*, by Dr. J. C. Lettsom, 1794 ; *A Memorial respecting the improper conduct of the Jailer of Newgate*, etc., by Thomas Lloyd, 1794 ; the *Letter to the Livery of London on the City Prisons*, by Sir Richard Phillips, 1808 ; the evidence given by the keeper of Newgate himself before the House of Commons Committee on the Laws relating to Penitentiary Houses, Nos. 199 and 217 of 1811 ; *State of the Prisons*, by James Neild, 1812 ; Holford's speech in the House of Commons, June 14th, 1814 (*Hansard*, Vol. XXVIII), when the City Corporation managed to defeat a Bill for reform ; the *Letter to the Common Council and Livery of the City of London on the Abuses of Newgate*, by the Hon. H. Grey Bennet, 1814, reprinted in the *Pamphleteer*, Vol. XXII, 1818 ; the two Reports from the Committee of the House of Commons, Newgate and other City prisons (1814), and on the King's Bench, Marshalsea, the Fleet and the City of London prisons (1815), also reprinted in the *Pamphleteer*, Vol. VI, 1815 ; the Report of two Committees of the Common Council of the City of London on Gaols and Gaol expenses (Minutes of Common Council, July 5th, 1814, and March 13th, 1817), and the proceedings in the Common Council thereon between 1814 and 1818 ; the anonymous pamphlet, *A Twelve Months' Visit to Newgate in the Year 1817*, 1819 ; the truly awful description given by Thomas, afterwards Sir Thomas, Fowell Buxton, Bart., in his *Inquiry whether Crime and Misery are Produced or Prevented by the Present System of Prison Discipline*, 1818 ; and the first and second Reports from the Committee on the Prisons within the City of London and Borough of Southwark, Nos. 275 and 392 of 1818. See also *The Old Bailey and Newgate*, by Charles Gordon, 1902 ; and *Chronicles of Newgate*, by Arthur Griffiths, 2 vols., 1875 ; *The Manor and the Borough*, by S. and B. Webb, 1908, p. 668.

night—the untried with the guilty, the young with the old. The administration under the Court of Aldermen was as defective as the building. There was the same old absence of work, and practical absence of discipline. The wickedest convicted felon who could afford to pay the keeper's fees might live in comparative comfort on " the Master's Side," or even get private apartments on " the State Side "— whilst the common herd of pickpockets and burglars, untried persons awaiting trial, and simple misdemeanants, hardened villains and young children, all pigged together on " the Common Side." Porter could be bought in unlimited quantities by any prisoner who could pay for it, and though spirits were forbidden, so much was smuggled in that the prisoners were frequently seen drunk.[1] The turnkeys, as well as the keeper, expected to receive fees, and knew how to make themselves disagreeable if they were disappointed. Irons, and " double irons " were in common use. The lawless extortion of " garnish " made every newcomer, exactly as happened a hundred years before, either " pay or strip." The four other prisons belonging to the City of London were, in their various ways, as old-fashioned as Newgate. One of them, the Borough Compter, which had been rebuilt in 1780-7, was found by Buxton in 1818, in all respects so vile that, after giving a terrible description of its horrors, he declared it " difficult to determine whether the vice it encourages is, or is not surpassed by the measure of misery it inflicts."[2]

[1] Howard had expressly drawn attention in 1789 to the continuance of the sale of liquor in the London prisons : " Though the gaolers' taps are abolished, yet are not publicans continually waiting to serve the prisoners and their company ? Is not beer now sold by the debtors ? And do not turnkeys keep shops in the gaols? " (*An Account of the Principal Lazarettos,* etc., by John Howard, 1789, p. 233.)

[2] *An Inquiry whether Crime and Misery are Produced or Prevented by our Present System of Prison Discipline,* by T. Fowell Buxton, M.P., 1818, pp. 20-34. More than thirty years before Howard had condemned this in the following words : " A new gaol on a bad plan. The wards of the men and women debtors join, so that the prisoners associate. The whole prison very dirty. Garnish not abolished." (*An Account of the Principal Lazarettos in Europe,* etc., by John Howard, 1789, p. 130 ; *Life of John Howard,* by J. Field, 1850, p. 396.) Buxton's minute description in 1818, compared with that of 1812, shows that things had positively got worse since Neild visited this prison (*State of the Prisons,* by James Neild, 1812, p. 396), in spite of the pointed remarks of the House of Commons Committees of 1814 and 1815.

CHAPTER VII

THE RENEWAL OF PARLIAMENTARY
ACTIVITY, 1811-1823

BEYOND an occasional inquiry into the cost of the
hulks and the practicability of penal colonies, the
House of Commons and the Ministers of the Crown—
occupied, it is fair to say, by the war with France—
seem, between 1791 and 1810, to have taken no more
interest in prison administration than the majority
of local authorities. But though the labours of John
Howard, of Blackstone and Eden, of Paul and other
reforming Justices, had done little to raise the general
level of the local prisons, the impression created by
their writings and their experiments[1] lived on as a
ferment, producing, in the first decade of the nineteenth century, a new crop of investigators and
reformers. Chief among the former was James
Neild (1744-1814), who modelled his career upon
that of Howard. Like his great exemplar, he belonged to the commercial class, rising in the prime of
life to the position of a landed proprietor, a Justice
of the Peace for three counties, and in due course
High Sheriff of Buckinghamshire. He had, from

[1] Besides the pamphlets of Paul and Becher already referred to, we may
mention that *On the Prevention of Crime and on the Advantages of Solitary
Confinement*, by Rev. John Brewster, 1792 ; and that by him *On the
Religious Improvement of Prisons*, 1808 ; the *Observations on the State of
English Prisons and the means of improving them*, by Alexander Wedderburn, successively Lord Loughborough and Earl of Rosslyn, 1793 ; *Hints
respecting the Prisons of Newgate*, by Dr. J. C. Lettsom, 1794 ; *A Dissertation on the Diseases of Prisons and Poorhouses*, by Dr. J. M. Good, 1794 ;
and *Thoughts on the necessity of Moral Discipline in Prisons, etc.*, 1797, by
Rev. Thomas Bowen, the chaplain of the City of London Bridewell, on
the condition of which he published two other pamphlets, referred to
elsewhere.

1762 onward, taken a benevolent interest in the relief
of poor debtors, and after retiring from business he
devoted all his spare time for twelve years to jour-
neying over Great Britain, for the purpose of describing, in minute detail, the structure, condition and
administrative methods of more than 350 prisons.
These detailed descriptions appeared in the *Gentleman's Magazine* between 1804 and 1806, and were
embodied, in 1812, in a magnificent quarto, em-
bellished with plates.[1] This fresh use of the concrete
statistical method, done upon identically the same
lines as Howard's work, was enlivened by admirably
written descriptions and fortified by the current
philosophy of punishment. But the time had passed
when the House of Commons could be moved by any
enumeration of individual instances ; and we doubt
whether Neild's work would have made much
impression if the cause of prison reform had not
attracted the support of such potent intellectual and
emotional movements as Philosophic Radicalism and
Evangelical Christianity. From the standpoint of
local government we are not much concerned with
Bentham's proposals in 1794 that the national
Government should allow him to erect and manage on
the contract system a monster " penitentiary " for the
reception of its convicts. But, however absurd we
may deem some of the details of Bentham's administrative projects, it was the publication in 1811, of his
Théorie des Peines et des Récompenses,[2] which gave
to the merely empirical proposals of the prison

[1] *State of the Prisons in England, Scotland and Wales, extending to various
places therein assigned not for the Debtor only, but for felons also, and other
less criminal offenders, together with some useful documents, observations and
remarks adapted to explain and improve the condition of prisoners in general,*
1812. For Neild's life, see *Dictionary of National Biography*. The extraordinary similarity between Neild and Howard, alike in career, position,
pursuits, opinions and even in family life and misfortunes, has been more
than once remarked. He was the founder and treasurer of the Society for
the Relief and Discharge of Persons imprisoned for Small Debts ; and in
1800 he published *An Account of the Persons Confined for Debt*. He died
in 1814, resembling Howard, too, in not living to witness any appreciable
improvement in the prisons which he had described.
[2] Dumont's French edition of this work, published in 1811, was made
widely known to English reformers by the long summary of it in the
Edinburgh Review for 1813.

reformers an intellectual framework connecting them with the wider movement for the reform of the criminal law, and, indeed, also with that for the general reorganization of society on utilitarian principles. It was, however, not enough to regard the problem of prison administration from a purely intellectual standpoint, and it was therefore fortunate that the efforts of the utilitarians were seconded by the no less influential Evangelicals, who managed to create that stir of semi-religious excitement without which, as it has been said, " no philanthropic project is ever fairly launched in England."[1] Chief among these new supporters of prison reform were the Quakers, in close touch with their brethren in Pennsylvania, where societies for the relief of prisoners had been established in the opening years of the century. In 1808 a similar society was started in London.[2] These new forces produced, from about 1810, a distinct revival of Parliamentary agitation.

The first sign of this awakening was Sir Samuel Romilly's eloquent appeal to the House of Commons, early in 1810, for a reform of the whole criminal law, including the administration of the prisons. For the next couple of years the agitation was kept going by the proceedings of George Peter Holford's Select Committee on transportation, the hulks and Bentham's " panopticon," to which we have already referred, and which incidentally threw much light on the prison experiments of Gloucestershire, Nottinghamshire, Sussex, and other counties where the Justices had built " model " prisons.[3] In 1812 Sir Francis Burdett made the House of Commons listen to a recital of horrors perpetrated at Lancaster Castle, the ancient gaol of the county.[4] But the only legislation affecting local prisons that at once ensued was a series of little Acts springing directly

[1] *Our Convict System*, by W. L. Clay, 1862, p. 11.
[2] *An Account of the Origin and Object of the Society for the diffusion of knowledge upon the punishment of death, and the Improvement of Prison Discipline*, 1812.
[3] Three Reports of the Committee on the Laws relating to Penitentiary Houses, 1811-2.
[4] *Hansard*, July 3rd, 1812, Vol. XXIII, p. 895.

from Neild's concern for the poor debtors. The Commissioners of Customs and Excise were authorized to contribute towards the maintenance of the numerous persons committed as debtors for fines and penalties under the revenue laws.[1] The old law requiring every county to contribute towards the poor prisoners in the King's Bench and Marshalsea prisons was made more effective, and extended also to the Fleet prison.[2] Any magistrate was empowered to order parish relief for any poor debtor in a municipal or franchise gaol.[3] A more important Parliamentary campaign, led by the Hon. Henry Grey Bennet, George Holford, and Sir William Eden, with the support of Sir Francis Burdett, Sir Samuel Romilly, and Lord Holland, took place in 1814 and 1815. The Grand Jury of Middlesex formally presented Newgate Gaol as a public nuisance ; and Eden, Holford, and Bennet managed to get a committee on the City of London prisons, which revealed a continuance of all the old horrors.[4] Holford brought in a Bill to compel the Corporation to appoint a special prisons committee, which should get rid of the old contracting system, and directly administer these important gaols. The Corporation fought this measure tooth and nail, the Aldermen declaring such a statutory committee to be derogatory to their

[1] 53 George III, c. 21.

[2] 53 George III, c. 113 (1813), amending 43 Elizabeth, c. 2, 11 George II, c. 20, and 12 George II, c. 29. This Bill excited the animadversions of the provincial counties. Thus, at the Gloucestershire Quarter Sessions, we read: " A Bill (as amended by the Committee of the House of Commons) for the better relief of the poor prisoners confined in the King's Bench, Fleet and Marshalsea prisons, having been submitted to the perusal of this Court, together with a letter directed to the Clerk of the Peace, for the information of this Court, from Henry Thornton, Esq. : this Court having perused the same, are of opinion that the attention of the Members for this County ought to be requested to the progress of the said Bill through the House of Commons, as the least sum, namely £45, thereby proposed to be paid out of the public stock or rates of this County for the relief of poor prisoners confined in the King's Bench, Fleet and Marshalsea prisons, far exceeds the whole expenditure of this County in allowances made to debtors incapable of supporting themselves when confined in the gaols of this county." (MS. Minutes, Quarter Sessions, Gloucestershire, April 27th, 1813.)

[3] 52 George III, c. 160.

[4] Report of the Select Committee of the House of Commons on Newgate and other City Prisons, 1814.

dignity, and the reforms proposed to be unnecessarily extravagant. In the end the Bill was defeated in a thin house by a few votes.[1] Meanwhile a little Bill was got through, giving the Justices in Quarter Sessions more complete authority to appoint salaried chaplains to their gaols and Houses of Correction.[2] Another Act required annual returns to be made to the Home Office, and laid before Parliament, giving exact particulars as to the persons committed to prison in each county or other local jurisdiction.[3] A useful little measure, also arising directly from Neild's criticisms, enabled the Home Secretary to order the removal of any lunatic person from a prison to an asylum.[4] Presently, the prison reformers, headed by Bennet, successfully carried through a more notable reform. In 1814 Bennet had vainly striven to pass, against the resistance of the City of London, a Bill to abolish gaolers' fees.[5] In 1815 he was successful in passing into law, apparently by general approbation, a drastic measure sweeping away all prison fees, and making it expressly a penal

[1] *Hansard*, Vol. XXVIII, June 14th, July 4th and 11th, 1814.
[2] 55 George III, c. 48 (1815), amending 13 George III, c. 58 and 22 George III, c. 64. This was itself amended by 58 George III, c. 32 (1818).
[3] 55 George III, c. 49 (1815).
[4] 56 George III, c. 117 (1816). This measure was by no means universally enforced. The Gaol Returns for 1833 speak of the presence of one lunatic in Cold Bath Fields prison, one at Northampton County Gaol, one at Nottingham County Gaol, one at West Haverford in Pembrokeshire, four at Ilchester, one at the Surrey County Gaol, one at that of Warwickshire, two in the County Gaol of Westmorland, one at Worcester, one in York Castle, one in the House of Correction at Northallerton, five in Newgate, and one in White Cross Street. The House of Correction at St. Augustine's, Kent, accepted insane prisoners when necessary. At Cold Bath Fields prison the reception of such persons was clearly not unusual, as the rules in force between 1831 and 1835 charged the surgeon to visit lunatic prisoners " confined there at the expense of the county," and to " report their state and condition to the Visiting Magistrates at the next general meeting."
[5] *Hansard*, Vol. XXVIII, June 15th, 1814. The total abolition of prison fees, first suggested by Howard, had seemed in 1773 an impracticable reform. It was in vain that Dr. William Smith pointed out, in 1776, that " No Act of Parliament, rule of court or mandate of magistrates will avail against the avarice, extortion and barbarity of gaolers ; and if their fees are not utterly abolished, regulations of every kind will prove insufficient." (*State of the Gaols in London, Westminster, and Borough of Southwark*, by William Smith, M.D., 1776, p. 16.) What was advocated in 1793 was merely that the gaoler should be paid a salary, and should be required to account for all fees and prisoners' earnings. (*Observations on the State of the English Prisons*, by Alexander Wedderburn, successively Lord Loughborough and Earl of Rosslyn, 1793, p. 19.)

offence for any officer to exact any fee from any
prisoner whatsoever.[1]

At this point in the squalid tragedy of the prison-
house there enters on the scene that stately, fas-
cinating and emotional moral genius, Elizabeth Fry
(1780-1845).[2] A wealthy and highly-connected member of the influential sect of Quakers, calmly confident
of her managing skill, her gift for exhortation, and
above all, of the " power of the spirit," this remarkable woman succeeded where Parliament itself had
failed, in persuading the Aldermen of the City of
London to introduce some imperfect, and it is to be
feared, short-lived reforms in the most notorious of
their gaols. Already in the hard winter of 1812-3
she had visited Newgate, and had realized the debasing tragedy of prison life—the disorderly, dram-
drinking, half-naked women, vagrants and felons,
convicted and unconvicted alike, some with little
children clinging to their skirts, penned up promiscuously in crowded wards and yards, reeking with filth
and infested with vermin. At Christmas, 1816, she
started, with a few friends, a beneficent crusade of
moral suasion within the prison walls, offering to the
female prisoners food, clothing, cheerful employment,
religious services and care of their children, in return
for a voluntary subordination to the rule of sobriety,
cleanliness and decent conversation. Her methods,
it is clear, attained her end, at least temporarily,
and the brutal crowd was reduced at any rate to

[1] 55 George III, c. 50 (1815), amended in detail by 56 George III, c. 116
(1816). These measures were made not to apply to the King's Bench,
Fleet, or Marshalsea prisons (in spite of terrible exposures in the Report of
the Committee on the State of the King's Bench, Fleet and Marshalsea
Prisons, and on the new London prison for debtors, 1815), for the curious
reason that as these were not subject to the justices of any county, there
was no fund from which compensation could be given to the officers in
lieu of their fees. It seems to have been thought out of the question to
charge the compensation to national funds—which leads us to believe that
" the Treasury " had much the same character then as now!

[2] See *Memoirs of the Life of Elizabeth Fry, with extracts from her journal.
and letters*, edited by two of her daughters (Katherine Fry and R. E;
Cresswell), 1847 ; *Memoirs of Elizabeth Fry*, by Thomas Timpson, 1847 .
Elizabeth Fry, by Mrs. E. R. Pitman, 1847 ; *Four Biographies*, by L. B,
Walford, 1888 ; *Chronicles of Newgate*, by Arthur Griffiths, 1875, Vol. II
pp. 132-46 ; *Through Prison Bars*, by W. H. Render, 1894 ; *Elizabeth Fry*
by G. K. Lewis, 1910.

outward order. Made widely known by a letter of
Robert Owen in October, 1817, the fame of her work
spread to chapels, churches, and the drawing-rooms
of the wealthy ; and during the next two decades
we see arising "Ladies' Prison Committees" in
provincial towns, which combined, with the questionable devices of almsgiving and sensational revivalism,
a practical concern for the health, decency and future
welfare of the women prisoners. The particular
scheme of prison administration gradually evolved
by Mrs. Fry and her friends, which we shall presently
discuss, was pressed upon local authorities by the
now active "Society for the Improvement of Prison
Discipline," which published frequent descriptions of
the results of its inspections of the gaols, and constantly held up to odium the local authorities which
effected no reforms.[1] The immediate, and we are
inclined to think, the most useful outcome of this
missionary devotion was the stimulus which it gave
to legislative reform. Inspired by the example of
their relative and co-religionist, the powerful families
of the Gurneys, Buxtons, Hoares and Barclays, threw
their energies into prison improvement ; and matter-
of-fact administrators like Paul and Becher, Holford
and Bennet, found themselves reinforced, both in the
House of Commons and in the pamphleteering press,
by these fervent magnates of the financial world.[2]

---

[1] This was the society started in 1808 by William Allen, Basil Montagu,
Sir Richard Phillips and other rather sentimental reformers for the diffusion
of knowledge upon capital punishment, including incidentally prison
reform. In 1816, after a period of suspended activities, this society seems
to have developed into a wider organization, commonly known as " The
Society for the Improvement of Prison Discipline," in which the Gurneys,
Hoares, Frys, Barclays, and their allies took the leading parts. This
society, which lasted right down to the passing of the General Prisons Act
of 1835, set going frequent inspections of the gaols and bridewells, published
valuable descriptions of their condition and other usual reports, and
exercised no little Parliamentary influence. As a guide for these inspections,
the society printed a set of 175 searching questions, covering the whole of
prison administration, from the position and construction of the gaol down
to the arrangements for the discharge of prisoners. (*Inquiries relative to
Prison Discipline*, 2nd edn., 1820.)

[2] The most impressive of the pamphlets of these years was the *Inquiry
whether Crime and Misery are Produced or Prevented by our Present System
of Prison Discipline*, by T., afterwards Sir Thomas Fowell Buxton, Bart.,
1818. This was a graphic description of the horrible condition of about a
dozen prisons in London and other towns, which went through six

Successive Committees of Parliament revealed the unmistakable connection between the rapid increase of crime, the overcrowding of the gaols and the upgrowth of a whole population of juvenile and professional criminals. The statistical returns now laid annually before Parliament under the Act of 1815, supplied irresistible arguments to the reformers.[1] In 1822 Peel succeeded Lord Sidmouth as Home Secretary, and, urged on all sides to consolidate the criminal law, decided to begin with the least controversial department, that of the Gaol Acts, and to embody in his consolidating measure the commonly accepted principles of prison reform, for the application of which an influential Select Committee had just strongly pressed.[2] His Bill, considered by a Select Committee in 1822, and passed into law in 1823, was the first measure of general prison reform to be framed and enacted on the responsibility of the national executive.[3]

editions within the year. See also his *Severity of Punishment*, etc., 1822, and the *Memoirs of Sir Thomas Fowell Buxton, Bart.*, by Charles Buxton, 1872. In 1819, J. J. Gurney, a Norwich banker, and his sister, Elizabeth Fry, made a round of visits to provincial prisons, and published *Notes of a Visit to Prisons in Scotland and the North of England with Elizabeth Fry*, by Joseph John Gurney (1819, reprinted in *The Pamphleteer*, Vol. XX, 1820) ; see also his *Letter to the Magistrates for the Three Ridings of the County of York in reply to the Report of the Visiting Magistrates of York Castle relative to that prison* (York, 1819) ; his *Thoughts on Habit and Discipline*, of which a second edition was published in 1844, and *Memoirs of J. J. Gurney, with selections from his journal and correspondence*, by J. B. Braithwaite, 1854.

[1] " It appears by Parliamentary returns," says the Fifth Report of the Prison Discipline Society, " that in the year 1818, out of 518 prisons in the United Kingdom (to which upwards of 107,000 persons were committed in the course of that year) "—such a total must include every tiny place of confinement in the three kingdoms—" in 23 of such prisons only the inmates were separated or divided according to law ; in 59 of the number there was no division whatever—not even separation of males from females ; in 136 there was only one division of the inmates into separate classes, though the 24 George III, c. 54, had enjoined that 11 such divisions should be made ; in 68 there were but 2 divisions, and so on ; whilst in only 23 were the prisoners separated according to the statute. Again, in 445 out of the 518 prisons, no work of any description had been introduced ; and in the remaining 73 the employment carried on was of the slightest possible description. Further, in 100 jails, which had been built to contain only 8,545 prisoners, there were at one time as many as 13,057 persons confined." (Quoted in *The Criminal Prisons of London*, by Henry Mayhew and John Binney, 1862, p. 97.)

[2] Report of House of Commons Committee on the State of the Gaols, 1820.

[3] 4 George IV, c. 64 (1823).

The "Act for consolidating and amending the laws relating to the building and regulating of certain gaols and houses of correction in England and Wales" represented a great advance in prison administration. Besides consolidating the whole of the statute law on the subject, it for the first time made it peremptorily the duty of the Justices to organize their prisons on a prescribed plan, and to furnish quarterly reports to the Home Secretary upon every department of their prison administration. They were expressly required to adopt, as the basis, Howard's four principles of the provision of sufficient, secure and sanitary accommodation for all prisoners, the transformation of the gaoler or master from an independent profit-maker into the salaried servant of the local authority, the subjection of all criminals to a reformatory regimen, and the systematic inspection of every part of the prison by visiting justices. The Act, moreover, prescribed, in clauses of elaborate detail, most of the administrative devices introduced by Paul, such as the exclusion of the gaoler and other officers, not only from all private trading with the prisoners, but also from any housekeeping or "farming" contracts with the local authority, the supervision of female prisoners exclusively by matrons and female warders,[1] and the requirement that the gaoler, the chaplain and the surgeon should personally visit every cell at stated intervals and keep detailed journals of their daily work, for regular presentation to Quarter Sessions. The prisoners

---

[1] " One of its provisions, which placed female prisoners under officers of their own sex, was due to Mrs. Fry." (*The Recorder of Birmingham : a Memoir of M. D. Hill*, by R. and F. Davenport-Hill, 1878, p. 180.) Even prison matrons had only just begun to be appointed, and female warders were unknown. In 1816, on the formation of the establishment of Millbank Penitentiary, the Dorset prison reformer, Morton Pitt, informed the committee that " the situation (of matron) is a new one. I never knew but two instances of a matron in a prison, and those were the wives of turnkeys or porters." (*Memorials of Millbank*, by Arthur Griffiths, p. 40, of 1884 edn.) No matron was appointed even at the well-administered House of Correction at Preston until 1825. (Annual Report of the Chaplain to Quarter Sessions, 1825.) It may be remarked that, in no fewer than eight of the prisons that he visited (namely, Worcester, Chelmsford, Horsham, Monmouth, Gloucester, Exeter, Bodmin and Brecon), Howard had found women in charge of prisons mainly occupied by men.

were protected against irons and chains and tyrannical punishments by compulsory notification to the Visiting Justices of every instance of their use. More debatable proved the idea of the " classification " of prisoners into five different groups for their association in productive labour, by which it was intended that they should earn their maintenance. With this idea came elaborate provisions for the instruction of the prisoners in reading and writing, for the copious supply to them of pious literature, for their participation in frequent religious services, and even for their taking the Sacrament. These new features were the result of the pressure of Mrs. Fry and her friends embodied in the extensive propagandist work of the Society for the Improvement of Prison Discipline. But though Parliament had brought itself at last to dictate to the Justices the exact system on which they were to administer their prisons, it would not contemplate (nor did Peel even suggest) the appointment of Government inspectors to insist on the law being obeyed,[1] nor did the Act provide any machinery for compelling negligent or recalcitrant local authorities to comply with its requirements. Moreover, it applied only to 130 prisons, being all those of the county Justices, those of the Cities of London and Westminster, and those of only seventeen provincial towns ; and it did nothing to reform either the three great debtors' prisons in London[2] or the one hundred and fifty or so gaols and bridewells in the franchises and the minor municipalities, which were at this date the " filthiest and most abominable in the Kingdom."[3]

[1] In 1821, as later, the very idea of a Government inspector was denounced by the " enlightened Liberal." " We object," said Sydney Smith, " to the office of prison inspector, for reasons so very obvious that it is scarcely necessary to enumerate them. The prison inspector would have a good salary ; that, in England, is never omitted. It is equally matter of course that he would be taken from among Treasury retainers, and that he would never look at a prison."

[2] In spite of a further Report of Commissioners on the State and Management of the Fleet and Marshalsea prisons, and the prisoners confined therein, 1818.

[3] *The Prison Chaplain*, by W. L. Clay, 1861, p. 98. The Municipal Corporations, to which the Act applied, outside London and Westminster,

CHAPTER VIII

RIVAL POLICIES IN PRISON ADMINISTRA-
TION, 1816-1835

THE twelve years 1823-1835, witnessed a steady, but
uneven, application of Peel's great measure to the
130 prisons which came within its scope. The direct
administration of these gaols and Houses of Correction by the Justices themselves now became general ;
and this direct administration, as was inevitable,
brought the country gentlemen face to face with all
the difficulties of the problem. We see arising a
whole group of controversies about the rival advantages of particular devices—separate confinement or
" classified association," profitable employment or
the tread-wheel ; the compulsory setting to work of
persons awaiting trial or their free maintenance—
over which, for the next half-century, active chairmen of Quarter Sessions and zealous Visiting Justices,
prison chaplains and humanitarian critics bombarded
each other and their Members of Parliament with
argumentative reports and pamphlets for, or against,
their several panaceas. We shall attempt here a
brief examination of the various devices tried by
local authorities down to 1835. To estimate their
value the student must keep in mind what the con-
troversialists themselves seldom clearly realized,
namely, the complex character of the object aimed

were Bristol, Canterbury, Chester, Coventry, Exeter, Gloucester, Hull,
Leicester, Lichfield, Lincoln, Liverpool, Newcastle, Norwich, Nottingham,
Portsmouth, Worcester and York. We do not know why these towns,
including both small and large, were specially selected, or why the relatively
large municipal prisons of Leeds, Bath, Dover, Ipswich, Oxford and
Cambridge were exempted.

76

at in the treatment of prisoners. To the original end of safe custody had, by this time, been added as essential the maintenance of the prisoners in health according to the scanty knowledge and low standard of the time. Imprisonment as a punishment had, it was assumed, to be made deterrent, alike to the prisoner himself, and to other persons. It had, at the same time, to be, at any rate, not demoralizing to any part of the population, and—as far as possible —reformatory of the delinquent's bad habits of mind and body. A less openly avowed, but at this stage of local government, a more potent motive of prison administration, was the desire to reduce to the utmost its cost to the community. These five distinct and often mutually conflicting aims were accepted, then as now, with more or less confusion of thought, by all prison administrators and critics. What gave acrimony to the interminable controversy which now set in, was not so much the conflict of evidence as to the efficacy of the particular devices, as the unavowed differences in opinion upon the relative importance to be attached, not merely to the maintenance of the prisoners in physical and mental health, but also to success in deterring, success in reforming, and success in economizing public expenditure.

(a) *The Treatment of Untried Prisoners*

One of the first phases of the controversy concerned the treatment of persons awaiting trial. It was an old commonplace of the criminal law that such prisoners, until conviction, were deemed to be innocent ; and, as a matter of fact, something like one-third of them were eventually acquitted or discharged.[1] Yet, as we have seen, during the eighteenth century, these unconvicted persons were subjected to the same intolerable conditions as the

---

[1] See the Statistics from 1810 to 1831 summarized in the *Report from the Select Committee on Secondary Punishments . . . with Notes and Appendix,* 1832, p. 2.

felon. Even when the worst of the positive abuses
had been remedied—when gaol fever had been got
rid of, fees abolished, bounds set to the tyranny of
the gaoler, extreme promiscuity mitigated—there
was, at the beginning of the nineteenth century, no
reasonable provision made for treating as innocent
the suspected felon awaiting trial, or the person
committed merely in default of finding sureties.
Here is a description of the treatment of untried
prisoners, which that entirely veracious Quaker,
Thomas Fowell Buxton, saw with his own eyes in
1818, in the prisons administered by the Middlesex
Quarter Sessions and the Corporation of the City of
London. " The prisoner, after his commitment is
made out, is handcuffed to a file of perhaps a dozen
wretched persons in a similar situation, and marched
through the streets, sometimes a considerable distance, followed by a crowd of impudent and insulting
boys ; the moment he enters prison irons are ham-
mered on to him ; then he is cast into the midst of a
compound of all that is disgusting and depraved.
At night he is locked up in a narrow cell with perhaps
half-a-dozen of the worst thieves in London, or as
many vagrants, whose rags are alive and in actual
motion with vermin ; he may find himself in bed,
and in bodily contact, between a robber and a
murderer ; or between a man with a foul disease on
one side, and one with an infectious disorder on the
other. He may spend his days deprived of free air
and wholesome exercise. . . . He may be half-
starved for want of food and clothing and fuel. . . .
His trial may be long protracted ; he may be
imprisoned on suspicion and pine in gaol while his
family is starving out of it, without any opportunity
of removing that suspicion, and this for a whole year.
If acquitted he may be dismissed from gaol without
a shilling in his pocket, and without the means of
returning home."[1] Nor were untried prisoners treated

---

[1] *An Inquiry whether Crime and Misery are Produced or Prevented by our
Present System of Prison Discipline*, by Sir Thomas Fowell Buxton, 1818,
p. 15, etc. We read, in 1823, of a scene in Westminster, where " A party

any more considerately in the provinces. In 1822 it was the practice in the West Riding " for the prisoners . . . to be marched from Wakefield to the place where the court is to sit, chained two together by their necks, besides the usual handcuffs on their wrists ; in this way they are marched sometimes to Skipton, nearly thirty-five miles ; to Knaresborough twenty-five miles, and other places of shorter distance, to take their trial. The exposure of fifty or sixty prisoners on the high roads in these populous districts is certainly a great evil as regards the prisoner himself, who is not yet proved guilty."[1] Not until 1823 did any local authorities convey untried prisoners in the decent seclusion of a covered van ; and when in that year the Surrey Justices introduced this reform,[2] their example was not followed even by the Middlesex Justices for four years. It was not until 1827, too, that the West Riding Justices gave up marching their prisoners on foot from town to town, and provided a covered van for their conveyance.[3]

Once lodged in gaol, there seems to have been no question, so long as the prison was regarded merely as a place of detention, of distinguishing in treatment between untried and convicted prisoners, except that, in some cases, the " county bread " was confined to convicted felons ; whilst persons awaiting trial, like the debtors and " fines," lived or starved as they might. By 1815, at any rate, this minimum of food seems to have been in some form or another supplied to all the inmates of a prison. With the gradual reform of prison regimen, the situation of the untried prisoner, so far as health and decency were concerned,

amounting to the unusually large number of 102 prisoners were not long since handcuffed in pairs, chained together, and conducted from this prison (Tothill Fields Bridewell) through the crowded streets of a populous district, about a mile distant, in order to be formally set at liberty by proclamation. The same treatment is observed towards females." (Fifth Report of the Society for the Improvement of Prison Discipline, 1823, p. 60.)

[1] Fourth Report of the Committee of the Society for the Improvement of Prison Discipline, 1822, Appendix, p. 70.

[2] Fifth ditto, 1823, p. 57.

[3] Seventh ditto, 1827, pp. 24, 41, 105, 402.

improved with that of the convicted felon. But the
same identity of treatment continued. Where, as
at Southwell, work was exacted, the same task was
set to all alike.[1] So long as this work was of a profitable nature, conducted on profit-sharing principles,
its provision was not regarded as a hardship, but even
as an indulgence. Presently, however, the simplicity
of the tread-wheel, which we shall subsequently
describe, led to its being substituted in many gaols
for every other kind of employment. The exaction
of this hard and monotonous, and to some persons,
painful toil, with none but derogatory associations,
at once altered the circumstances ; and a heated
controversy arose as to the legitimacy of applying
it to untried prisoners. An unconvicted inmate of
the Northallerton Gaol who had been given the
alternative of a bread and water diet or the tread-
wheel, got the eminent advocate Scarlett to apply on
his behalf for a mandamus to compel the Justices
to afford him better treatment. The Court of King's
Bench decided, however, that though the Justices
were bound to find the prisoners work by which they
could maintain themselves, they had full discretion as
to the kind of work, and that even untried prisoners
could not insist on being maintained in idleness.
"A man who was committed to prison," said Chief Justice Best, "was not to be placed in a better situation
than one who was at liberty . . . as a man at liberty
would not be sustained in idleness, so a man in prison
could not ask more."[2] The use of the tread-wheel for
convicted and unconvicted prisoners alike was accordingly continued in Northallerton and some other

[1] The Nottinghamshire Justices ordered, in their reformed House of
Correction at Southwell, that the governors shall employ on some work
or labour, which is not severe, *all such prisoners as are kept and maintained
at the County expense*, though by the warrant of commitment such persons
are not ordered to be kept to hard labour—the only distinction being that
unconvicted persons, like those sentenced to mere imprisonment, were
allowed to receive one-half of their earnings, whilst prisoners sentenced to
hard labour received only one-fourth. (Second Report of the House of
Commons Committee on the Laws relating to Penitentiary Houses, June
10th, 1811, pp. 109-18.)
[2] 2 Barnewall and Cresswell, 286 ; *Quarterly Review*, Jan., 1824, Vol.
XXX, p. 404 ; see also *Prison Discipline and Secondary Punishments*, by
P. Laurie, 1837, p. 10.

gaols, and was strenuously defended by the chairman of Quarter Sessions for the North Riding.[1] It was, on the other hand, furiously denounced as inhuman and barbarous by Sydney Smith in the *Edinburgh Review*, and enlightened public opinion swayed to and fro between discipline and humanitarianism. In the first draft of Peel's great measure, laid before the House of Commons in 1822, he proposed to authorize the Justices to find employment for the untried prisoner, " in any work of which he shall be capable, at regular wages " from the county fund. This was objected to by Holford, on the ground of expense, it being argued " that such persons ought to provide for their own support."[2] In the Act of 1823, as eventually passed, the dispute as to the legitimacy of the tread-wheel was slurred over, and it was simply made lawful to employ untried prisoners with their own consent.[3] This, however, left unaffected the practice of those Justices who, like those of the North Riding, duly asked their untried prisoners whether or not they would consent to work, but limited the alternatives to bread and water on the one hand, and the tread-wheel on the other. It was an aggravation that the human force which worked the tread-wheel in the Northallerton Gaol was leased out like so much water-power or steam, to a local miller, who exacted much or little labour according to the requirements of his trade.[4] It took another Act to make it clear to reluctant Justices that, in the case of unconvicted persons, the consent to work " shall be freely given and shall not be extorted or obtained by deprivation or threat of deprivation of any prison or other allowance," and it was expressly declared that no prisoner before conviction " shall under any pre-

---

[1] *Letter to the Right Hon. Robert Peel . . . on Prison Labour*, 1823 ; *Second Letter to the Right Hon. Robert Peel, on Prison Labour*, 1824, both by John Headlam ; *Edinburgh Review*, 1821 ; *Quarterly Review*, Vol. XXX, p. 430.

[2] *Substance of the Speech of George Holford, Esq., in the House of Commons, June 21st, 1822, in a Committee of the whole House for considering the laws relating to Prisons*, 1824.

[3] 4 George IV, c. 64, sec. 37 (1823).

[4] *Hansard*, March 5th, 1824.

tence be employed on the tread-wheel either with or without his consent."[1] Here ended this particular controversy, and, with it, all discussion as to the treatment of untried prisoners. So far as we are able to ascertain, local authorities, between 1824 and 1835, refrained from exacting labour on the tread-wheel from unconvicted prisoners, but continued to subject them to the same regimen as actual convicts, except that, in a few exceptional prisons, they were permitted to supply themselves with extra food if they had the necessary means, and to enjoy occasional intercourse with outside friends or legal advisers. To the reader unaware that a not altogether dissimilar condition of things exists to-day, it will seem incredible that neither Parliament nor the Government could bring itself to the point of realizing that the only justification for the imprisonment of unconvicted persons is the necessity of ensuring that they should not escape trial ; and that there is no warrant for subjecting them to any other discipline, discomfort, or involuntary labour than is actually necessitated by their temporary seclusion and by the privacy requisite to prevent both mutual annoyance and mutual contamination, of which it seems plain that the nation should, at least in the first instance, bear the expense.

(b) *The Profitable Employment of Prisoners*

Passing from untried prisoners to the convicts, in no department of prison administration did the rival ends of sparing expense, reforming the prisoners and deterring from future crime, come more sharply into conflict than in that of prison employment. The exaction of a given amount of physical effort had been, from the time of Howard, an essential part of any deliberate system of prison discipline. But the reforming Justice of the Peace, at the opening of the nineteenth century, saw no difference, in deterrent and reformatory qualities, between one kind of

---

[1] 5 George IV, c. 85, sec. 16 (1824).

manual labour and another. What he wanted was to keep the prisoner out of mischief and make him earn as much as possible towards his maintenance. The prison workshop became, in fact, like the eighteenth century " House of Industry," meiely a device for profitably employing one class of paupers, and thus reducing the burden cast upon the rates. In this spirit was couched an order of the Norwich Bridewell Committee for December 10th, 1805, that eighty yards of hempen cloth should be provided, together with hose-yarn for twenty-four pairs of stockings to be knitted by the female prisoners ; and a later order, issued on February 3rd, 1807, for twine for making fishing nets.[1] Thus, all sorts of handicrafts were carried on in the reformed gaols, some of these becoming regular factories, dominated by the hum and clatter of their scores of looms in constant work, and earning a profit which defrayed a large proportion of the cost of the prisoners' maintenance. This transformation of the prisons into "busy scenes of cheerful industry," the men in the weaving shed or tailor's workshop, the women in the sewing room or laundry, delighted the somewhat emotional philanthropists of the Society for the Improvement of Prison Discipline ; and secured, right down to her death, the warm approval of Mrs. Fry.[2] The new House of Correction, for instance, which the Lancashire Justices built at Preston in 1790, was highly commended by Neild in 1806-12 and by J. J. Gurney in 1819,[3] as a model of what a prison should be. It was, from the first, run mainly as a cotton weaving factory, employing constantly a hundred and fifty men on the hand looms of the period, and keeping the rest at tailoring, shoemaking, cotton picking, etc.[4]

[1] MS. Minutes, Bridewell Committee Book, Norwich Justices, Dec. 10th, 1805, and Feb. 3rd, 1807.
[2] The approval of the society lasted until 1821 ; see the enthusiastic *Third Report of the Committee of the Society for . . . the Improvement of Prison Discipline*, 1821.
[3] *Gentleman's Magazine*, June, 1806 ; *State of the Prisons*, by James Neild, 1812 ; *Notes on a Visit to some of the Prisons in Scotland and the North of England*, etc., by J. J. Gurney, 1819.
[4] *The Prison Chaplain*, by W. L. Clay, 1861, p. 105.

The expediency of this prison employment became the subject of prolonged controversy. From the standpoint of those who were above all things anxious to use the prison as a reformatory institution there was much to be said for these experiments. " We treat mankind," said Becher, " as constituted of habits, and our principle is to eradicate those which are bad, and to implant others that are better ;"[1] and he proceeded to cite individual cases in which " a man filthy, diseased, drunken, idle and profane," became, during his imprisonment, "clean, sober, healthy, diligent, and to all appearance a good moral man, by which I mean to imply that he does not swear, nor behave inattentively during the hours of devotion, nor invade the little property of his fellow prisoner, or quarrel with him, or do any act unbecoming a man of sound principles." The manufacturing enterprises of Preston and Southwell undoubtedly provided both a rough and ready technical education, and a potent stimulus to regular industry. The well-conducted prisoner, at the end of his term, found himself in possession, not only of a small sum of money, earned by his own exertion, to tide him over temporary unemployment, but also of a new handicraft, or with increased capacity for working regularly at his old one—not to mention the advantage of a written " character " for skill, good conduct and industry.

Unfortunately, even the ablest of the reforming Justices were not single-minded in their desire to reform the habits of the criminals in their charge. They never shook themselves free from the notion that all prisoners should maintain themselves. As formerly in the Poor Law Houses of Industry, the desire to earn a profit led to the adoption in the prison of administrative devices which went far to neutralize the good effects of stimulating industry. There grew up a system of profit-sharing, under which the comfort of each prisoner, and the sum which he drew

---

[1] First Report from House of Commons Committee on the Laws relating to Penitentiary Houses, 1811, Appendix, p. 38.

at his discharge, depended solely on the productivity of his labour.[1] Hardened criminals, with no intention of mending their evil ways, were able, by superior strength and skill, or their knowledge of a profitable handicraft, to earn comparatively large sums, whilst the weak, unskilled or incompetent inmate, however good his conduct, and however sincere his desire to reform his ways, found himself gaining no more than the minimum subsistence. To attain the maximum of reformatory effect, the reward of the prisoner ought to have been quite unconnected with difference of productivity, and to have taken the form of a payment by time, dependent not on skill, but on regularity and devotion to industry. Even more disastrous than the profit sharing was the association in large workrooms brought about by the desire to make the prisoners' labour profitable. To confine each prisoner to the labour which he could perform in his own cell might have been reformatory, but could not be made remunerative. " Work which is to produce profit," explained an experienced administrator in 1821, " will run counter to discipline and moral improvement. It will often be found convenient to the taskmaster to bring together for purposes of manufacture prisoners who ought not on other accounts to be permitted to associate with each other."[2] These ill-effects were intensi-

---

[1] Thus, at Preston, the county took 40 per cent. of the earnings, the taskmaster 10 per cent., and the prisoners 50 per cent., part being paid at once, and the rest on discharge. (See, for instance, MS. Minutes, Quarter Sessions, Lancashire, April 13th, 1820.) " Prisoners (1815-1824) . . . were discharged with more money in their possession than they could have saved in the same time by free labour " (Chaplain's Report on Preston House of Correction, 1843). Even in the hulks the practice prevailed, in 1812, of " stimulating convicted prisoners to be industrious by allowing them to spend a small portion of their earnings " in extra food. (*Statements and Observations concerning the Hulks*, etc., by George Holford, 1826, p. 25.) Under Becher's new rules, the prisoners in the Nottinghamshire House of Correction at Southwell got, if sentenced to hard labour one-third, if unconvicted or merely sentenced to imprisonment, one-half their earnings. When the prisoners found, we are enthusiastically told, that, already lodged, clothed, fed, warmed and lighted and provided with constant cheerful employment, " by diligence they might be enabled to spend the last day of the week in working solely for their own emolument, unusual contentment and incalculable activity were instantaneously diffused through every ward of the house."

[2] *Thoughts on the Criminal Prisons of this Country*, by G. Holford, M.P.,

fied when the Justices "farmed out" the prisoners'
labour. The Justices found the choice of trades, the
purchase of plant and material, and the selling of the
product involved them in much trouble, and the speculation frequently led to actual loss.[1] We soon find
Paul urging the Gloucestershire Justices to adopt an
easier plan. " I cannot help impressing on the mind
of the magistrates," he said in 1792, " that if the
work is to be made productive the method must be
changed. The buying a variety of new materials,
the vending goods manufactured, requires an attention and control of the magistrates over the officers
that will be scarcely exercised. The labour of the
prisoners should be farmed."[2] " Farming " became,
accordingly, as in the workhouses, the common
expedient for the organization of labour.[3] Sometimes the gaoler or master took the whole proceeds
of the prisoners' work as part of his remuneration.
In other cases an outside employer would pay the
Justices a lump sum for the privilege of sending in
materials for the prisoners to work up. The " farmer " having no interest in rescuing the prisoners
from idleness, or reforming them by regularity, only
provided work as and when it was profitable to himself. The gaoler, who was also a speculator in labour,
combined men, women and children in associated
employment, irrespective of their mutual contamination. Clever artisans who could earn the most
money, or were useful in instructing others in profitable trades, naturally became his favourites for

1821, p. 62 ; *Quarterly Review*, Jan., 1824. At the newly established
Millbank Penitentiary (opened in 1816) all sorts of trades, glass bead blowing, the manufacture of tin ware, rug making, were tried ; but, in 1822, after
a convincing report by Holford, they were all abandoned as failures except
tailoring, shoemaking, weaving and needlework. (*Memorials of Millbank*,
by Arthur Griffiths, p. 45, of 1884 edn.)

[1] It seems always to have paid well at the Preston House of Correction,
a textile factory in a textile-working district, where the net cost of each
prisoner to the county rate was reduced to less than 3d. per day.

[2] MS. Minutes, Quarter Sessions, Gloucestershire, Easter, 1892.

[3] " It was the prevailing opinion at that time (1812) that those who
superintended convicts should be paid out of their earnings." (*Statements
and Observations concerning the Hulks*, etc., by George Holford, 1826, p. 13.)
The National Government leased out to a contractor the labour of the
prisoners in the hulks, and this system was continued for forty years.

prison indulgencies, irrespective of the crimes for which they had been committed ; whilst it was the incorrigibly idle and destructive who were recommended for remission of sentences, or employed merely as wardsmen or cooks.[1] " Trading gaolers," said one of them in 1822, " are the bane of improvement ; if the prison be crowded, it is to their interest to recommend the idle and ignorant to the consideration of the magistrates, and it is not likely they will desire to part with the industrious, orderly mechanic."[2]

There was, however, another objection made to the conception of prison discipline, so much admired by Becher, Elizabeth Fry and the philanthropic school generally. It was urged that it tended to ignore what must always be one main object of the treatment of criminals, that of deterring from future crime, by supplying every person with a strong motive for resisting the temptation to transgress the laws of the land. It was presently complained that, under the system of profitable employment, the prison became, for many a poor labourer or mechanic, rather a comfortable place. The healthy surroundings, ample but simple food, and regular employment in association compared favourably with his lot when out of gaol. It began to be alleged that the great increase in the numbers committed to prison was due to their positive attractiveness. " Our gaols and Houses of Correction," it was said by Baron Western in 1821, " are generally considered by offenders of every class rather as a sure and comfortable asylum whenever their better fortunes forsake them, a sort of refuge for the unfortunate of their profession."[3] " If prisons," he remarked, " are to be made into places in which persons of both sexes and all ages may be well fed, clothed, lodged, educated and taught a trade ; where they may find pleasant society and are required not

---

[1] *Ibid.*

[2] *Thoughts on the Defective State of Prisons*, by Thomas Le Breton, Keeper of the County Gaol of Kent, 1822, p. 36.

[3] *Remarks upon Prison Discipline, etc., a letter addressed to the Lord Lieutenant of the County of Essex*, by C. C. (afterwards Baron) Western, 1821, p. 54.

to take heed of the morrow, the present inhabitants should be turned out, and the most deserving and industrious . . . should be invited."[1] It was this aspect of the case that aroused the indignation of the " common sense " school. " I would banish," wrote Sydney Smith in the widely read *Edinburgh Review* of 1822, " all the looms of Preston Gaol, and substitute nothing but the tread-wheel or the capstern, or some species of labor where the laborer could not see the results of his toil—where it is as monotonous, irksome and dull as possible—pulling and pushing, instead of reading and writing—no share in the profits—not a single shilling. There should be no tea and sugar, no assemblage of female felons round the washing-tub—nothing but beating hemp and pulling oakum and pounding bricks—no work but what was tedious, unusual and unfeminine."[2] A general revolt set in against the once-favourite panacea of profitable employment. The capitalist employers outside began to object.[3] To the " com-

---

[1] *Ibid.*, p. 16. The underlying assumption of such critics was expressed, in 1835, by Whitworth Russell (then about to be appointed an inspector of prisons) ; that it was not desirable, under " any circumstances to give to a prisoner that which would place him in a better situation than he would have been had he never entered prison." (First Report of House of Lords Committee on Gaols and Houses of Correction, 1835, p. 116.) But this was to fall into the same verbal fallacy as the champions of the New Poor Law. What was required was to make the conditions of prison as of workhouse life, less pleasurable, *taken as a whole*, than private employment, not necessarily less really advantageous to the inmate, or even less pleasurable in particular respects. " There are, I fear," rejoined Holford, " numbers of persons in this country who wear clothes which are insufficient to protect them from the inclemency of the weather, or who are lodged in close and ill-ventilated apartments, or who inhabit damp and unwholesome situations, or are employed at noxious trades, or work at unseasonable hours, or are subject to other hardships or privations of the like nature ; but I have never heard it contended that these evils, from which it is not in our power to relieve other classes of the community, are on that account to be imposed upon prisoners . . . The dietary of a prison becomes therefore a medical question." (*Thoughts on the Criminal Prisons of this Country*, by George Holford, 1821, p. 57.)

[2] *Edinburgh Review*, Feb., 1822. Under the stress of this attack, the Society for the Improvement of Prison Discipline, which had enthusiastically supported the regime of profitable employment in its Third Report of 1821, devoted much of its next report to a repudiation of a policy of undue indulgence, and strenuously asserted that " severe punishment must be the basis of prison discipline." (Fourth Report, 1822.)

[3] A citizen of Birmingham writes to Lord Sidmouth that " a manufacturer of pins in this place employs the prisoners in the gaols of Warwick, Stafford and Northampton in the making of pins by which means the

mon sense " school of prison reformers, it must have seemed a fortunate circumstance that the industrial revolution was rendering it every day increasingly difficult to make any actual profit out of the demoralized and indiscriminately collected gaol inmates. " The late improvements in machinery," Sir G. O. Paul told a House of Commons Committee in 1819, " have so . . . annihilated the objects of work by hand that the power of supporting a system of hand labor in prison, to be productive of emolument, is entirely out of the question."[1]

(c) *Isolation versus Classified Association*

Another controversy as to prison discipline, destined after 1835 to become the most virulent and most notorious of them all, was already latent in the divergent practice of the various county benches. This concerned the amount and kind of human intercourse to be permitted to the prisoner. The gross promiscuity of the old prisons had led Howard constantly to insist on the importance of " separation " and " classification," by which he seems to have meant solitary sleeping cells, which he had seen at Ghent in 1775 and in Swiss prisons in 1776, with common dayrooms and workrooms, each to be used in common by the prisoners belonging

---

distress of the poor of this place is greatly augmented, and poor rates considerably increased to the injury of numerous families and in direct contradiction to an Act of Parliament made for that purpose. . . ." The Home Office is asked to interfere, but replies that application must be made to the local magistracy. (Home Office Papers, Nov. 8th, 1821.)

[1] Report of House of Commons Committee, P.P. VII, 1819, p. 403. " It has long since been discovered in most of the gaols and Houses of Correction in this country, that manufactures can seldom be carried on in a prison, whatever means may be used to encourage or stimulate the work of the prisoners, with any reasonable prospect of gain, and very rarely without much risk of loss. There may be a few prisons situated in parts of the country where manufactures are flourishing, to which persons may be willing to send material from the neighbourhood, paying for the workmanship of them when they receive the manufactured article ; but such employment must be precarious, and liable to cease at any moment, and it can never be prudent in those who manage Houses of Correction to manufacture articles for sale on behalf of the county to any considerable amount, owing, among other reasons, to the uncertainty of finding a market for them." (*An Account of the General Penitentiary at Millbank*, by George Holford, 1828, p. 198.)

to a distinct class.   The General Penitentiary
Act of 1779 had carried the plan a step further,
by providing, as the severest discipline, for separate
cellular confinement during both day and night,
accompanied by religious instruction and " well
regulated labor."[1]   Howard's disciples first put these
ideas into practice at the new Sussex county prisons
at Horsham and Petworth, where the isolation seems
to have been strict and the discipline at first severe.
Sir G. O. Paul, acting on the advice of his chaplain,
" discarded the system of classes " according to term
of sentence, prescribed by the Penitentiary Act,
and adopted " a more temperate system for the whole
term " of imprisonment for all convicted persons.
The Gloucestershire regimen was a carefully thought-
out plan of separate sleeping and separate employment in isolated cells, varied with daily chapel,
twenty-minutes' tread-wheel and twenty minutes'
walk—all in silent association—and professedly tem-
pered, every day or every few days, by regular visits
from and conversation with the master and the chaplain, the surgeon and the Visiting Justice.   Other

[1] 19 George III, c. 79, sec. 8, 38, etc. We shall recur, in a subsequent
chapter, to the controversy as to " solitary confinement " and the so-called
" Separate System." The earliest English proposal for " separate apartments for condemned prisoners "—meaning only prisoners condemned to
death—appears to have been made by the Christian Knowledge Society
in 1710. Merely for the sake of safe-keeping without fetters, Mandeville,
in 1725, had strongly urged its adoption in Newgate for tried and untried
prisoners alike : " I would have," he said, " everyone of the malefactors
locked up, by himself, and they should never be suffered to converse
together. . . . Build a hundred small rooms, perhaps of 12 ft. square. . . .
They should all have such conveniences that those who were shut up in
them should, during their stay, have no occasion to stir out of them on
any account. . . . Thus we might secure prisoners without galling them
with irons before we are sure that they deserve to be punished at all."
(*An Enquiry into the Causes of the Frequent Executions at Tyburn, etc.*, by
B. Mandeville, 1725, pp. 37-8.) The reformatory effects of solitary confinement were strongly urged in an able pamphlet of 1771, entitled *A Letter
to Sir Robert Ladbroke, Knight, Senior Alderman . . . of the City of
London ; with an attempt to show the good effects which may reasonably be
expected from the confinement of criminals in separate apartments*, by Rev.
Samuel Denne, Vicar of Wilmington, 1771. After Howard's visits, it was
fervently advocated by Jonas Hanway ; see especially his *Solitude in
Imprisonment with profitable labor and a spare diet, the most humane and
effectual means of bringing malefactors who have forfeited their lives and are
subject to transportation to a right sense of their condition, etc.*, 1777 ; and
the idea was patronized by Archdeacon Paley in his *Moral and Political
Philosophy* of 1785.

reformed prisons adopted similar combinations of cellular isolation during the night, and non-intercourse during the day. What specific results in reforming and deterring these experiments may have had are insufficiently recorded. Already in the speeches and writings of prison reformers between 1810 and 1823, we note some reaction against the strict enforcement of non-intercourse. This change of opinion was due partly to rumours of insanity being caused by the rigorous solitude of Petworth and other highly-reformed prisons, and partly to the use of this punishment for seditious offenders.[1] But the experiment of cellular confinement prior to 1835 can, in most counties, scarcely be said to have been tried, as before it could be thoroughly tested, the new prisons were found quite inadequate for the great increase of persons committed. The population of the principal counties was increasing by leaps and bounds, and this was accompanied from 1811 onwards, and especially from about 1816, by a great increase in crime.[2] Rather than incur the expense of additional new buildings, even the reforming Justices fell back on the easier expedient of " classification." This meant associating the whole of each class—such as felons, misdemeanants, debtors, " fines," untried prisoners, women and boys—in a common dayroom or workroom, and even installing two, three or four of a class in a single sleeping cell.[3] It was, to many Justices, a recommendation that the reversion to associated labour in a common workroom, by permitting the use of machinery and division of

[1] Thus Sir Samuel Romilly complained, in 1810, of " the levity with which [sentences of solitary confinement] have of late years been inflicted. . . . Persons . . . for the offence of uttering seditious words have, at Courts of Quarter Sessions, been sentenced to two years of solitary imprisonment." (*Hansard*, June 5th, 1810, p. 350.)

[2] A good statistical sample of this increase is afforded by the return of commitments to the Suffolk County Gaol at Bury St. Edmunds for the years 1805-34, given in the Report of the House of Lords Committee on Gaols and Houses of Correction, 1835, p. 231.

[3] When, in 1816, the newly-appointed governor of Millbank Penitentiary was sent on a tour of inspection, he reported that " the system of individual separation was not carried into effect except at the Gloucester Penitentiary." (*Memorials of Millbank*, by Arthur Griffiths, p. 39 of 1884 edn.)

labour, made less difficult the profitable employment of the prisoners. At Ilchester in 1822 the Commissioners found that the eagerness with which prison labour was pursued had brought about a condition of utter promiscuity. Seven shops had been constructed on the ground floor for the manufacture of woollen and linen cloth and the trade of shoemaking. In the upper story spinning-machines had been installed and a carpenter's shop built. To meet the demands of what tended to become a highly organized industrial community, the principle of classification was necessarily disregarded, prisoners being selected to associate with one another according to their varying degrees of proficiency, so that a young offender, if inexperienced, might be placed under the tuition of a hardened criminal who possessed strength or a highly developed knowledge. In regard to the women, this cult of industry took the obnoxious form of compelling untried prisoners to work in the wash-house in the company of convicts. The particular class of prison reformers who now came to the front very much preferred the associated dayrooms, trusting for reformatory influences to the contagious outbursts of religious emotion generated by prayer meetings. The sterner administrators, whilst not resisting this daytime association, found in a continuous application of the tread-wheel throughout the day the deterring influence which Paul had sought in the strict isolation of each prisoner from any intercourse from the others. The Act of 1823, as it emerged from the House of Commons, abandoned the idea of individually separate confinement which had inspired the legislation of 1779-1791, adopting, instead, the now favoured principle of classification. Up and down the country the Justices promptly followed the lead given by Parliament, the more readily because the counties were thus spared what seemed the colossal expense of completely cellular construction. In Gloucestershire itself, immediately the Act was passed, Quarter Sessions appointed a Committee to revise the prison rules according to the new statute, providing especially for the classification of prisoners, so that in particular "juvenile offenders may be kept separate from old, hardened and great offenders."[1] The Buckinghamshire Justices prudently allocated their five prisons to four distinct classes, each with male and female divisions, so that the " Old Gaol " and the "Old Datchet" prisons were wholly given up to persons awaiting trial for felony, the " New Datchet " prison to persons awaiting trial for misdemeanours, the " New Gaol " to convicted felons, and the " Bridewell " to convicted misdemeanants.[2] So completely had Parliament gone back on separate cellular confinement that the 1824 Act expressly provided that " where in any prison there shall be only one prisoner belonging to any class, such prisoner may be assigned, with his or her consent, to any other class of prisoners of the same sex."[3]

The result of this reaction was quickly noted by the more observant gaol chaplains, prison masters and Visiting Justices. To allow unchecked intercourse among prisoners in a common working room, or even on a common tread-wheel—still more, to lock up three or four together in a sleeping cell—was to bring back all the opportunities for mutual contamination which had excited the sternest reprobation of the more prudent followers of Howard. It was really no diminution of this evil to specialize the contamination. " If each [gaol] class," it was afterwards noted, " respectively be composed of burglars, or assault and battery men, or sturdy beggars, they will acquire under it increased proficiency only in picking locks, fighting, or imposing on the tender mercies

---

[1] MS. Minutes, Quarter Sessions, Gloucestershire, Oct. 14th, 1823, Jan. and Easter, 1825.

[2] MS. Minutes, Quarter Sessions, Buckinghamshire, Jan., 1824. So in Nottinghamshire it was ordered that " the House of Correction situate at Southwell . . . shall be applicable to the following classes of prisoners : First, prisoners convicted of felony ; Second, prisoners convicted of misdemeanours ; Third, prisoners committed on charge or suspicion of felony ; Fourth, prisoners committed on charge or suspicion of misdemeanour, or for want of sureties ; Fifth, vagrants." (MS. Minutes, Quarter Sessions, Nottinghamshire, Oct. 13th, 1823.)

[3] 5 George IV, c. 85, sec. 13.

of mankind."[1] But the very basis of the classification—the kind of offence for which the prisoners were being punished[2]—in no way corresponded with their habitual characters. No distinction was made between a theft committed by a professional criminal, nearing the end of a long career of crime, and a theft into which a starving youth had been tempted as a first offence. Moreover, occasionally " the burglar was sent to prison for trying his hand at begging, a professed sheepstealer for doing a little business as a thimblerig man, and a London thief for showing fight at a country fair."[3]

Thus, whilst the Act of 1823, with its classification ideal, may have levelled up many of the worst gaols among the hundred and thirty to which it applied, it positively lowered the standard in the best of the reformed prisons. Prison administration had by this time become a matter of systematic and continuous observation, and the evil effects of even classified association were quickly noted by the ablest critics. Presently English public opinion began to be influenced by the news of the remarkable results achieved by certain American experiments in completely solitary " separate " and " silent associative " imprisonment, with and without labour. We do not need to explore the heated controversy which went on between the prison reformers of New York and Boston, Pennsylvania and Virginia, as to the merits of their respective systems.[4] What reached

---

[1] *Modern Prisons*, by Col. (afterwards Sir Joshua) Jebb, 1844.

[2] This was the basis adopted in the sixty-eight county and corporation gaols in which the Municipal Corporation Commissioners Reports, and the Parliamentary Gaol Reports for 1833, show classification to have been enforced in its entirety ; and also in the twenty which had recourse to a partial system. The same is true of the model House of Correction established at Southwell, as is clear from the system of rules adopted in 1823. The futility of the classification system is forcibly described in *Prison Discipline*, by Rev. J. Field, 1858, pp. 30-62 ; see also *Chapters on Prisons and Prisoners*, by Rev. Joseph Kingsmill, 1852, and *Modern Prisons, their Construction and Ventilation*, by Sir Joshua Jebb, 1844.

[3] *Modern Prisons*, by Col. (afterwards Sir Joshua) Jebb, 1844, p. 8.

[4] We shall recur to the American experiments, which led to heated controversy. It must suffice to point out here that (whilst earlier reported in France by the Duc de la Rochefoucauld-Liancourt and in England by the book, *A Visit to the Philadelphia Prison*, by Captain R. F. Turnbull, 1796),

England, and that not until about 1830, was the consensus of experience and opinion upon the importance of preventing all intercourse between one prisoner and another. Meanwhile the most heroic of prison chaplains, John Clay, was beginning at the Preston House of Correction his thirty years' detailed study of prison life. Disheartened at the effects of "profitable employment," and disgusted at the mutual contamination of the prison yard, he began to insist, in his annual reports to the Lancashire Quarter Sessions, on the necessity of "non-intercourse discipline . . . of some system of non-intercourse"—if the "Separate" was too costly, at any rate, the "Silent."[1] Not until 1834, however—when the West Riding and Cumberland Justices had already put an end to association in their prisons—could Clay induce the Lancashire Quarter Sessions to take up "the system of silence and non-intercourse by and amongst prisoners which hath lately been adopted with great success in the gaols at Wakefield and Carlisle."[2] In Middlesex, where the prisons were densely crowded, and very badly administered, eight or ten of the Justices—among them, Samuel Hoare, Mr. Sergeant (afterwards Sir Albert) Pell, Samuel Mills, and George Byng, M.P., formed a sort of league for reform.[3] They thought themselves fortunate, in 1829, in getting appointed as the governor of the House of Correction at Coldbath Fields, a certain George Laval Chesterton, who perceiving "that the paucity of cells . . . presented an irremediable obstacle to the adoption of the Separate

they appear to have become effectively known in this country in 1828-34 by the *Travels in North America* of Captain Basil Hall, 1829 ; *Three Years in North America*, by James Stuart, of which a second edition was published in 1833, and Edward Livingston's Report on a Code of Discipline for the Louisiana prisons, based on solitary confinement, which (*A System of Penal Law*) was published in London in 1828 ; and above all by the elaborate report entitled *Penitentiaries of the United States*, by W. Crawford, 1834.
[1] *The Prison Chaplain : a Memoir of John Clay*, by W. L. Clay, 1861, p. 120.
[2] MS. Minutes, Quarter Sessions, Lancashire, Sept. 11th, 1834. The new rules were not actually adopted till a year later. (*Ibid.*, Sept. 10th, 1835.)
[3] *Revelations of Prison Life*, by G. L. Chesterton, 1856, Vol. I, pp. 16, 32, 35, 37 ; *Peace, War, and Adventure*, by the same, 1853, pp. 241-5.

System," introduced in 1834 the " Silent System "—
a population of 914 prisoners being suddenly " ap-
prised that all intercommunication by word, ges-
ture or sign was prohibited."[1] This return to non-
intercourse discipline, which presently spread to
other counties, where " a fictitious, artificial and
superficial " isolation[2] was substituted for the " real
isolation " of cellular confinement, coincided with a
new epoch in English prison history, and started a
more specialized controversy lasting for a whole
generation, which will be dealt with in a following
chapter.

(d) *The Tread-wheel*

In the revulsion of feeling against the profitable
employment of prisoners, we find prison administrators turning between 1818 and 1826 eagerly to the
tread-wheel (less correctly designated tread-mill). " I
should . . . use no other secondary punishment than
the tread-mill," wrote Sydney Smith, as a magistrate
for Yorkshire, to the Home Secretary, " varying in all
degrees from a day to a life. . . . This punishment
would be economical, certain, well-administered,
little liable to abuse, capable of infinite division, a
perpetual example before the eyes of those who want
it, affecting the imagination only with horror and
disgust, and affording great ease to the Government."[3]
This form of penal labour had been suggested in so
many words by the Penitentiary Act of 1779, which
directed the Governors to keep the prisoners " to
labour of the hardest and most servile kind, in which
drudgery is chiefly required, and where the work is
little liable to be spoiled by ignorance, neglect or
obstinacy, and where the materials or tools are not
easily stolen or embezzled, *such as treading in a wheel,*

---

[1] *The Criminal Prisons of London,* by Henry Mayhew and J. Binny,
1862, pp. 287-8.
[2] *Modern Systems of Criminality,* by C. Bernaldo de Quiros, 1911, pp.
180-3.
[3] Sydney Smith to Robert Peel, March 27th, 1826. (*Sir Robert Peel,*
edited by C. S. Parker, 1899, p. 402.) This, it will be noted, was after
the publication of the Parliamentary Return Papers on the Effect of the
Tread-wheel in the prisons where it has been established, 1825.

or drawing in a capstern, for turning a mill or other machine or engine."[1] The suggestion of a " walking-wheel " was revived by Bentham in 1796,[2] and a tread-wheel was in use at the Gloucester County Gaol in 1811, with the express object, as the rules declared, of enforcing " the hardest and most servile kind " of labour contemplated by the 1779 Act.[3] A simple form of tread-wheel, easily applicable to all prisons, was devised about 1818, by William (afterwards Sir William) Cubitt (1785-1861), then an engineer at Lowestoft, for use in the Suffolk County Gaol at Bury ; and it was from this example that the practice spread.[4] The cheapness and simplicity of the " stepping-mill," or " everlasting staircase," as it was called, the severity of the physical labour which it exacted, and the manner in which this " wheel-stepping " was hated by the prisoners, all commended the new device to Quarter Sessions, and " tread-wheels "—grinding corn, or grinding nothing but air, raising water, or supplying power to hemp-beating, cork-cutting, or other machines—were fitted up in every reformed prison. " It was heresy . . . to question its reforming efficacy on convicts ; the only point on which there existed any difference of opinion was as to the number of diurnal revolutions which yielded a maximum of reforming power. Some magistrates kept their prisoners treading from morning to night,

[1] 19 George III., c. 74, sec. 33. At Mont St. Michel (France) the prisoners were made to hoist up all the supplies by a huge tread-wheel ; and the same mechanical device has been frequently used in all ages.
[2] *Letters on the Management of the Poor*, by Jeremy Bentham (Dublin, 1796).
[3] The very words of sec. 33 of the 1779 Act are copied in the *General Regulations for the Inspection and Control of all the Prisons . . . for the County of Gloucester*, 1790, p. 67. Sir G. O. Paul, in 1811, described how all able-bodied male prisoners were " taken, two by two, from their cells to tread in a wheel the power of which raises the water to the top of the building," each pair of prisoners doing a spell of about twenty minutes in the day, and then resuming their other employment in the working cells. (First Report from House of Commons Committee on Laws relating to Penitentiary Houses, May 31st, 1811, p. 24.)
[4] See Cubitt's life in *Dictionary of National Biography* ; *Description of the Tread-mill invented by Mr. W. Cubitt* (Society for the Improvement of Prison Discipline), 1822 ; *Description of the Patent Improved Tread-mill* by William Hase (Norwich, 1824) ; *Revelations of Prison Life*, by G. L. Chesterton, 1856, Vol. I, pp. 224-5 ; Papers on the Effect of the Tread-wheel where it has been established, 1825 (Parliamentary paper).

13

till they half-killed them ; others were content with
requiring a modicum of wholesome exercise on the
wheel for three or four hours a day.''[1] In a short
time a great storm of controversy arose. It was
alleged on the one hand, and vehemently denied on
the other, that labour on the tread-wheel was so
exhausting as to break down the prisoners' health ;
that it led to rupture and other bodily injuries ; and
that it amounted in some cases to positive torture.
Independent observers denounced it as certain to
counteract any efforts making for the reform of the
prisoner's character. The controversy continued
long after 1835, and we need not here pursue its
various ramifications. It is, however, clear that the
Justices' enthusiasm for their device, and their ignorance of its effects on the human body, led them, in
many cases, to impose excessive tasks. Its use for
women had, after a generation of cruel experiment,
to be entirely given up. All the early tread-wheels,
moreover, constructed so that six, twelve, or eighteen
prisoners stepped side by side, allowed them full
opportunity of conversing together, and so brought
back much of the evil promiscuous association. Yet,
in spite of all criticism, it spread from gaol to gaol,
vehemently attacked by humanitarians, not only as
cruel, but also as ineffective in working any reform of
the convict ; and no less obstinately defended by
Justices in search of a punishment at once cheap
and easy of application, and potent as a deterrent.
We infer, from the mass of conflicting partisan
statements, that the tread-wheel was a success, in
so far as it afforded a cheap and easy method of
forcing prisoners to work. When exacted in suffi-

---

[1] *The Prison Chaplain*, by W. L. Clay, 1861, p. 98. " There is so little
uniformity as regards the number of hours devoted to labour, the height
of the steps of the wheel, and the rapidity of its rotation, that in some
prisons the punishment is nearly three times as severe as in others. . . .
In Bedford Gaol the labour performed is equal to an ascent of 5,000 feet
. . . while in Knutsford House of Correction it is 14,000 feet." (*Report
from the Select Committee on Secondary Punishments . . . with notes and
appendix*, 1832, p. 6). The Warwickshire Justices were proposing, in
1824, to require the equivalent of 17,000 feet. (*Quarterly Review*, January,
1824, Vol. 30, p. 409 ; Sixth Report of the Society for the Improvement
of Prison Discipline, 1824, p. 305).

cient quantity this form of penal discipline certainly deterred persons from using the gaol as a convenient place of refuge in seasons of adversity. On the other hand, the weight of evidence indicates that labour on the tread-wheel was habitually injurious to the bodily health of women, and occasionally to that of men, whilst it was always physically depressing, personally degrading, and unproductive either of mental initiative, or emotional regeneration.[1]

This battle between the respective adherents of reformatory and deterrent labour continued to rage throughout the next generation, and may be said, indeed, to be still one of the unsettled questions of prison administration. It seems, in fact, to be impossible to find a regimen simultaneously combining deterrent painfulness and reformatory invigoration. This was pointed out in the celebrated article on prisons which James Mill contributed to the *Encyclopædia Britannica* in 1823, in which he advocated strenuously the plan of " reform by industry," as against Elizabeth Fry's panacea of " reform by religious emotion," and also against the " common. sense school " of Sydney Smith and others, which sought only penal deterrence. In this article, amid much which has lost interest for the present generation, his elaborate dissertation included one suggestion

[1] See the Parliamentary Paper, entitled " Communications made to or received by the Secretary of State for the Home Department respecting the use of Tread-wheels in Gaols." (H. of C., 1823); *Correspondence Relative to Prison Labour*, by Sir John Coxe Hippisley, 1823 ; *A Letter on the Nature and Effects of the Tread-wheel*, by John Watt Briscoe, 1824 ; the fifth and sixth Reports of the Society for the Improvement of Prison Discipline, 1823 and 1824, which give elaborate details of the variety of tasks ; *Report from the Select Committee on Secondary Punishments . . . with notes and appendix*, 1833 ; *Prison Discipline*, by J. Field, 1848, Vol. I, pp. 28-31 ; *Revelations of Prison Life*, by G. L. Chesterton, 1856 ; *The Criminal Prisons of London*, by Henry Mayhew and J. Binny, 1862, pp. 174, 288, 303-7 (where the modern tread-wheel is described in detail, with a picture) ; and Report of the Home Office Committee on Prisons, 1895, which led to its final abandonment.

The tread-wheel was introduced into the Berkshire County Gaol at Reading soon after 1822 (*Prison Discipline*, by J. Field, 1848, p. 28) ; into the Middlesex House of Correction at Coldbath Fields, and the Surrey House of Correction at Brixton, in the year 1822 (MS. Minutes, Quarter Sessions, Middlesex, 1822, and *Gentleman's Magazine*, July, 1822) ; into the Lancashire House of Correction at Preston in 1825 (*The Prison Chaplain*, by W. L. Clay, 1861, p. 111).

which has, so far as we know, never been put in operation. James Mill urged that whatever might be indispensable as deterrent punishment and the far more important reformatory treatment might, with advantage, be sharply separated, and made to follow one on the other. It was for the judge to determine by his sentence the nature and amount of the punishment, properly so called, to be inflicted on the criminal, in order to deter him and others from similar transgressions. After the punishment had been inflicted, the criminal might be detained in confinement and subjected to an appropriate regimen, designed exclusively with a view to reforming his character, and fitting him to become a productive citizen. Have we here the germ of the system now called Preventive Detention and the Indeterminate Sentence? James Mill laid stress on the distinction between the judicial function of deterring and the administrative function of curing. We should prefer to regard both the deterrent punishment, if there is anything to be said for its infliction, even in the form of loss of liberty and initiative, and the reformatory treatment, which ought to be the main factor, as parts of a cure, designed, on the one hand, to supply for the future an adequate inhibitory motive, and on the other, to develop in the patient good habits and mental initiative.

(e) *Administrative Chaos*

These leading controversies only imperfectly represent the divergencies of prison discipline and regimen adopted by local authorities between 1823 and 1835. From the standpoint of the prisoner himself, the nature and frequency of the punishments to which he was subjected for breaches of the now elaborate prison rules, were as important as the amount and kind of the labour regularly exacted from him. Heated were the discussions among justices and philanthropists as to the expediency of flogging, or as to the relative advantages of the dark cell, starvation diet and extra turns on the tread-wheel.[1] On the other hand, there were cliques and coteries of prison reformers who attached more importance to the kind and amount of religious exhortation and instruction given in the gaol, varying, as this did, from a perfunctory service on Sundays for those who cared to attend, up to daily revivalist prayer meetings by enthusiastic evangelists of both sexes.[2] Already in 1810 Windham had declared himself " very jealous as to the manner in which religious instruction was inculcated." It might, he said, " be so done as to generate a sort of mischievous fanaticism, superinducing hypocrisy upon their original depravity."[3] Religious administrations were certainly intended to exercise a very direct influence upon prison discipline, as may be seen from the elaborate instructions to the chaplain at the Norwich Bridewell, so highly praised by James Nield. A curious incident at Monmouth Gaol in 1825 suggests the prison authorities to have been anxious to enforce the Anglican supremacy in gaols, as the chaplain refused to admit a Nonconformist minister, conversant with Welsh, to attend a condemned prisoner who could speak no English. At York Castle, on the other hand, a priest was admitted to those of the political offenders who were Catholics, and, from the keepers' statements, it appears to have been customary to have recourse to him on all such occasions.[4] In the all-important matter of diet, the Justices adopted haphazardly anything from a stinted allowance of bread and water, up to three meals a day, full, nutritious and appetizing, and

[1] See, for instance, the discussion in the House of Commons when the indefatigable H. Grey Bennet, M.P., vainly objected to the clause in the Prisons Bill authorizing the private whipping of prisoners on the sole authority of the prison governor. He stated that 6,959 floggings had taken place in the English prisons during the preceding year (*Hansard*, July 7th, 1823). Also the anonymous pamphlet, *Observations on the Offensive and Injurious Effect of Corporal Punishment*, 1827 ; and that entitled, *Additional Observations on Penal Jurisprudence and the Reformation of Criminals*, by William Roscoe, 1823.

[2] See the previous references to Elizabeth Fry ; and her *Observations on the Visiting, Superintendence and Government of Female Prisoners*, 1827.

[3] *Hansard*, Vol. XVI, p. 949, May 9th, 1810.

[4] Home Office Papers, H.O. 20 (66, 84), 1820.

agreeably varied according to a weekly menu. Some prisons, moreover, permitted even convicted men to supplement the regular dietary by purchasing more luxurious food, tea, coffee, beer and tobacco. It is needless to say that the various dietetic policies, which were hotly discussed in connection with the leading case of Millbank Penitentiary, were pursued with the very minimum of reference to physiology or psychology. The close connection now believed to exist, not only between diet and physical health, but also between the properties of specific quantities and qualities of foodstuffs, on the one hand and the development of cruelty, sensuality, will-power and intellectual alertness on the other, was entirely beyond the ken of that generation. Thus, the extremes of semi-starvation or over-feeding were dictated more by parsimony or sentimental kindness than by any theory or observation as to deteriorating or reformatory results thereby produced.[1]   Moreover, the keener observers were beginning to point out that, not only the material conditions to which prisoners were subjected, but also the personalities with whom they came into contact, could not fail

---

[1] The cost of food varied from threepence up to sixpence per day. " The same inequality exists in the diet of the prisoners; the weekly cost of feeding a prisoner in the Gaol at Hereford being 3s. 7¾d., and in the House of Correction at Preston, 1s. 11½d." (*Report from the Select Committee on Secondary Punishments . . . with notes and appendix*, 1832, p. 6).   An elaborate table of different prison dietaries for hard labour is given in the Fifth Report of the Society for the Improvement of Prison Discipline, 1823, Appendix, pp. 129-172.

To give one instance of the contrasts in prison diet, we may adduce the Somerset House of Correction at Shepton Mallet, where, in 1833, each prisoner had, daily, one pound of bread, one pound of potatoes, six ounces of beef without bone, and one-and-a-half pints of oatmeal gruel; and, when working on the tread-mill, also a pint-and-a-half of soup, or gruel when leaving work. (This, by the way, was exactly the diet adopted at the General Penitentiary, Millbank, in 1823, see the Report of the Select Committee of that year on the Penitentiary.)   On the other hand, at the Cornwall County Gaol, at Bodmin, the daily ration was, for the first month, only a pound-and-a-half of bread, with the addition, after that period, of a portion of gruel. (First Report of Poor Law Inquiry Commissioners, Appendix A, Chapman's Report, p. 460.)   In Suffolk, at the same date, an Assistant Commissioner comments on the " absolute uselessness of punishing mothers " (of illegitimate children) " by sending them to gaol where they are well fed and moderately wrought. . . . When the period of their confinement expires, they come in a condition which renders them exceedingly liable to repeat the act for which they were sent to prison." (*Ibid*, Stuart's Report, p. 339.)

to influence their mental state. A leading tendency in the new regimen was the emphasis laid upon the punitive aspect of prison life in limiting intercourse between the governor or warder and the prisoners to the mere issue of instructions or the hearing of complaints. Provision for this was made in the regulations for Chester Castle issued in 1802, and in those existing for Winchester and Fisherton Anger Gaols in 1822.[1] The objectionable results of the employment of criminals as assistant turnkeys, warders, yardmen, monitors and even as schoolmasters, already being urged towards the end of the eighteenth century,[2] were presently insisted upon. On the other hand, to engage for every large prison a regularly salaried staff of minor officials, adequate to the rapidly increasing number of prisoners, seemed to the majority of the Justices a wanton extravagance.[3]

[1] " Nor shall unnecessary conversation be held (on the part of the prisoners) with them (the gaolers) at any time " (Regulations for Chester Castle, 1802). The Governor " must not, at any time, and more particularly in the presence of Visitants to the Prison, hold unnecessary conversation with the prisoners, but must give his commands and receive their wants in as few words as possible." On the other hand, it was provided that " the Governor must guard himself against every impulse of anger or personal resentment ; he must command with temper, enforce his just authority with firmness, and punish resistance without favour or partiality. With the legal powers entrusted to him it cannot be necessary to strike his prisoners, unless in cases of self-defence ; much less can it tend to any good purpose to give his orders in a violent or insulting tone, or attended with oaths. . . . The same humanity and temper which is required of the Governor in the execution of his duties must be insisted on by him in the conduct of every inferior officer of the prison, none of whom shall ever strike any prisoner, except in self-defence, or in the defence of any other person from any assault or menacing action, tending to assault, from the prisoner . . ."

[2] Desultory Reflections on Police, with an Essay on the Means of Preventing Crime and Amending Criminals, by Sir William Blizard, 1785.

[3] The magistrates, we are told, said to the reformers, " Remember the pressure of the times ; you must suggest nothing that is expensive." (First Report of House of Lords Committee on the State of the Gaols, 1835, p. 237.) Dogs were frequently used instead of warders. Even in Gloucestershire we incidentally learn, " the practice of using mastiffs instead of officers continued . . . till 1820. . . . From 1810 to 1820 there were, in the county prison, ten officers and two dogs." (Remarks by the County Chairman upon the Tables published by David Ricardo, Esq., February, 1850, in his pamphlet upon the Appointment of a Government Auditor, Gloucester, 1850.) So extensive was the use made of prisoners as minor gaol officials that when, in 1835, " the Duke of Richmond's Act interdicted the employment of convicts, and the monitorial system was abolished, the magistrates of Middlesex " found themselves

All these controversies concerned, however, only those local authorities which, under the influence of the 1823 Act, had more or less assumed direct responsibility for the state of the prisons under their jurisdiction. Up and down the country about 150 little gaols and Houses of Correction belonging, in about 120 different towns, to the smaller municipal corporations, the lords of manors and owners of special franchises had, for the most part, remained totally unaffected by any notions of reform. Peel, in omitting these prisons from the scope of the Acts of 1823 and 1824, had expressed the hope that those responsible for their maintenance would themselves remedy the evils.[1] The private owners of franchises did nothing at all.[2] Only in about a score of cases was the power to contract for the maintenance of borough prisons in the county gaols made use of by the smaller municipal corporations.[3] Here and there

compelled to add in the Coldbath Fields House of Correction alone no fewer than " eighty-two new officers under the designation of sub-warders." (*Revelations of Prison Life*, by G. L. Chesterton, 1856, Vol. II, p. 3.)

[1] " Upon mature deliberation," he said, in 1824, " I have resolved to abstain from legislating for the prisons of local jurisdictions, except so far as to enable them to contract with the counties. It is not that I am insensible of the lamentable and disgraceful situation in which many of them are, but I indulge the hope that many of them will contract with the counties, that many of them will build new gaols, and that when, in a year or two, we come to examine their situation, we shall find but few which have not, in one or other of these ways, removed the grievance of which such just complaint is made. When that time arrives, if I find that there are local gaols in which classification and employment are neglected, I shall not hesitate to ask Parliament for powers to compel them to make the necessary alterations." (See quotation in Sixth Report of the Society for the Improvement of Prison Discipline, 1824, p. 14.) This Parliamentary promise was not fulfilled. The evidence given in 1835 showed that the Home Office paid no heed whatsoever to the subject. (First Report of House of Lords Committee on the State of the Prisons, 1835, pp. iii., 275-7.)

[2] At Birmingham, in 1828, Joseph Parkes declared that " the dungeon is a reproach to a Christian country, and the native land of Howard. From twenty to fifty people are, I understand, generally in confinement, and if they cannot pay for better accommodation, chaffed straw is their bedding. Broken windows, through which cold and wet enter in streams, have been deemed a convenience, and justified lest fever and malaria should be engendered in the damp and pestiferous air of the dungeon." (*The State of the Court of Requests and the Public Office of Birmingham*, by Joseph Parkes, 1828, p. 5)

[3] *Report from the Select Committee on Secondary Punishments . . . with notes and appendix* (1833, p. 50). Out of the two hundred towns (having, we infer, about 130 gaols and houses of correction in actual use in 1832, some having been closed), we find the tiny borough of Bucking-

the corporation of a borough exempted from the 1823 Act might bring itself to build a new prison, but then only on the old lines, without undertaking what seemed the unnecessary expenditure involved in cellular construction.[1] Right down to 1835 it could be assumed that " a corporation prison " was " the worst prison in the world."[2] Some even of the counties and large towns which had been brought within the scope of the 1823 Act did little or nothing to reform their prisons in compliance with its requirements. Few prison authorities made the statistical returns required ; in few cases did the prison chaplain make the annual report called for by the Act ; in very few prisons had matrons been appointed for

ham contracting with the Bucks Justices (MS. Minutes, Quarter Sessions, Buckinghamshire, Easter, 1832) ; the borough of Abingdon "purchased the privilege of committing to the county bridewell by a grant of the land on which that bridewell is erected." (First Report of Municipal Corporation Inquiry Commissioners, 1835, Appendix, Vol. I, p. 5.) Salisbury Devizes and Calne, sent their prisoners to the Wilts County Gaol, and contributed to the county rate (pp. 1,343, 1,233, 1,267) ; Maidstone, finding its gaol quite insecure, closed it about 1826, and contracted with Kent for its prisoners (p. 765) ; Newport (I. of W.), joined with the rest of the Isle of Wight in erecting a prison for the whole island, paid for by a special rate (p. 784) ; the City of Worcester sent its convicts sentenced to hard labour to the County Gaol (p. 157). In 1826, a Parliamentary Return showed that only fourteen small boroughs had contracted with their respective counties, whilst nine more were in negotiation (H. of C., April 10th, 1826: Seventh Report of the Committee of the Society for the Improvement of Prison Discipline, 1827, p. 398). Between thirty and forty small towns had closed their prisons, or allowed them silently to lapse. (See Fifth Report.)

[1] The following boroughs exempted from the 1823 Act, seem to have built new prisons sometime between 1811 and 1834 ; Barnstaple (First Report of Municipal Corporation Commission, 1835, p. 431) ; Basingstoke (p. 1,102) ; Bideford (p. 439) ; Bradninch (p. 458) ; Carmarthen (p. 214) ; Dover (p. 951) ; Falmouth (p. 502) ; Feversham (p. 973) ; Plymouth (p. 584) ; Rochester (p. 860) ; Sandwich (pp. 1,045-52) ; South Molton (p. 614) ; Tewkesbury (p. 126) ; Tiverton (p. 627) ; Winchester (p. 168). The central government was as neglectful as the local authorities. By 5 Geo. IV, c. 85, sect. 7, the various local authorities having prisons outside the scope of the 1823 Act were required to make annual returns to the Home Office as to the state of their prisons. This provision was disregarded, and the Home Office, which has never cared for regular reports of the local administration for which it was nominally responsible, made no attempt, right down to 1835, to obtain the returns. (House of Lords Committee on the State of the Gaols, 1835, p. 275.)

[2] First Report of House of Lords Committee on the State of the Gaols 1835, p. 183 ; as to the condition of these smaller prisons, see Second ditto, pp. 334-7, and Appendix, pp. 175-95. It is fair to say that these prisons exempted from the 1823 Act were, for the most part, very small, having each only half-a-dozen prisoners. Only in about a dozen towns (chief among them Bath, Leeds, Dover, Oxford, Cambridge, Ipswich and Ely) were there as many as twenty inmates in a prison.

the female wards.[1] The two most important of
prison authorities, the County of Middlesex and the
City of London, remained, to the last, pre-eminent
in maladministration. The Justices of Middlesex, for
instance, could still be properly upbraided in the
House of Commons, as late as 1828, for maintaining
prisons actually increasing in iniquity, vilely overcrowded, grossly disorderly, and in a state of incredible filth.[2] The corporation of the City of London
continued frankly impenitent as to the condition of
Newgate, which, a leading alderman declared, " I
do not think you could improve."[3] On this, the
House of Lords Committee reported emphatically,
in 1835, that " imprisonment in Newgate, Giltspur
Street and the Borough Compter . . . must have the
effect of corrupting the morals of their inmates and
manifestly tend to the extension rather than to the
suppression of crime."[4]

(f) *The Beginning of Central Supervision*

To the political student of the twentieth century,
or to the busy House of Commons politician of to-day,
it will seem incomprehensible that nothing should
have been done by the Home Office to bring about the
redress of the worst of the scandals of the London and
provincial prisons. We fail nowadays adequately

[1] First Report of the House of Lords Committee on the State of the
Gaols, 1835, p. 275; Second ditto, p. 333. " Of 136 prisons which are
included in the Act (4 Geo. IV, c. 64) 36 only had a sufficient number
of cells to admit of each offender being placed apart at night. The total
number of persons confined in these prisons at one time in the last year
(1834) was 18,197, but the number of sleeping rooms and cells therein
was only 11,704. . . . There are, altogether . . . about 1,300 day rooms."
(House of Lords Committee on the State of the Gaols, etc., 1835, Appendix,
p. 146.) Thus, seventy years after Howard began his visits, there were,
in all England, even with 136 professedly reformed prisons, only 36—
the detailed returns indicate only 24—in which it was possible to maintain
the primary condition of " non-intercourse at night " (*Ibid*, pp. 147-50.)
[2] Dr. Lushington, M.P., in *Hansard*, February 28th, 1828. The Middlesex County Gaol at Clerkenwell had, in 1834, only 32 sleeping apartments
for 414 prisoners, and the House of Correction at Coldbath Fields only
417 cells in which to put 1,245 prisoners. (House of Lords Committee
on the State of the Gaols, 1835, Appendix, p. 148.)
[3] Sir Peter Laurie. (See Fourth and Fifth Reports of the House of Lords
Committee on the State of the Gaols, 1835, p. 457.)
[4] First Report of House of Lords Committee on the State of the Gaols,
etc., 1835, p. iii.

to realize both the absence of administrative machinery between the central and local governing authorities, and the almost complete lack of responsibility of the Cabinet for what was being perpetrated in the prisons of the King. Right down to the end of Lord Sidmouth's term of office as Home Secretary in 1822, we find the very scantiest attention paid in Whitehall to what was going on in the local gaols and bridewells. We owe, apparently, to the advent of Peel almost the beginning of departmental supervision of prison administration. We learn from a letter of the Earl of Egremont of April 19th, 1822, that he had, in his capacity of Lord Lieutenant for Sussex, distributed, to the Chairman of the Quarter Sessions and the Visiting Magistrates, copies of a communication from the Home Office relating to the condition of the County Gaol. Somewhat earlier the surgeon of Lancaster Castle transmitted a report on the sanitary condition and health of the prison; while on the death of a prisoner in Coventry Corporation Gaol, the Home Office procured a report of the results of the inquest and of statements made by the gaoler, the surgeon and a fellow-prisoner of the deceased, and a summary description of the whole episode.

It must be remembered that Peel had at his disposal no official staff by which he could continuously inform himself of what was going on in the prisons. There were no Home Office inspectors or Government doctors. Some of the reformers of the eighteenth century had realized the necessity for some social tissue connecting the local prison with the National Government, as well as between the keeper of the local prison and the owners thereof. The only suggestion that seems to have been made was that this link should be supplied by the County Justices. Such a project was in harmony with an already existing practice, for in 1703 the Corporation of Norwich recorded its desire that the "Justices of peace doe proceed forthwith in repairing and enlarging the Gaol of this City according to the late Act of Parliament." What, therefore, had been achieved a century later was the awakening, at least in some of the Justices, of a more lively sense of their responsibilities. The magistrates certainly regarded themselves as the source of authority for dealing with any emergency arising out of prison administration, subject to the final ruling of the Quarter Sessions or the Judges on Circuit. In the course of correspondence with the Home Office in 1822 on the subject of prisoners' letters, the Dorset magistrates drew attention to the following definition of their powers, contained in the Prison Regulation adopted in 1802 : " That if any of these rules should appear inconvenient in practice, such may, at any time, be suspended by the Visiting Magistrates, and that the reason of such suspension be reported by them to the next General Quarter Sessions of the Peace—to be held for the said county, in order that any regulations that may be thought necessary may then be adopted." At Dorchester Gaol, the difficulties arising out of the unusual duties imposed by the presence of such a political offender as Richard Carlile drove the keeper to pay almost daily visits to the local Justice of the Peace, Archdeacon England, who issued instructions to meet each special case, and reported his decisions to the Home Office. At Ilchester, Henry Hunt's treatment was regulated from a similar source, and during the first six months of his confinement the *Magistrates' Journal* bore witness to the practical significance of their regime. An instructive letter may be quoted in which the Visiting Magistrates apply to the Home Office for instructions. The Prison Discipline Act of 1824 contributed more strength to the arm of the Justices by the seventeenth section, which empowered any Justice, without being appointed a Visitor, to visit any prison and to report any abuses he might discover at the next General or Quarter Sessions of the Peace.

It must not, however, be overlooked that a different theory of the Justices' authority existed which rendered them immediately subordinate to the sheriff. A movement in this direction appears during a discussion of the action of the magistrates in debating some regulations of their own authority for a new gaol built at Fisherton Anger in Wiltshire in 1822. A debtor imprisoned there alleged in a petition to the Home Office that they curtailed the privileges of the debtors, and questioned their validity. During the inquiry which ensued, Peel corresponded, not with the magistrates, but exclusively with the High Sheriff of the county. It was left to him to transmit the opinions and suggestions of the National Government to the Justices, and to convey in answer their vindication of their conduct.

At Dorchester Gaol the superior powers of the sheriff seem to have been recognized by the magistrates, for Carlile having uttered threats of his power to escape during November, 1823, the Chairman of Quarter Sessions invited the sheriff to meet the visiting magistrates and himself to examine the prisoner in the presence of the gaoler and his assistants. When reporting this to the Home Office, the Chairman defined his view of the relations subsisting between sheriff and Justices in terms which admitted of no misapprehension, and he was not corrected by the Home Secretary.

With such inadequate powers, and under such uncertainty as to their authority, the Justices of the Peace, it is plain, could effect but little as supervisors of the local prisons. Their haphazard and spasmodic intervention, kindly intentioned as it usually was, must have rendered the administration even more uncertain and chaotic than it would otherwise have been. Yet for a dozen years after Peel's assumption of office in 1822, the Home Office struggled on without any better machinery for supervision and control of the gaols and bridewells, and without any other means of securing the enforcement of the Statutes of 1823 and 1824 than was afforded by the perfunctorily rendered annual gaol statistics and the occasional, and almost accidental, correspondence over particular cases that happened to be reported to Whitehall.

Such was the state of the prisons when, in 1832, the Whig Government and the Reformed Parliament took over the administration of the nation's affairs. The wholesale demoralization of the Old Poor Law and the political partizanship of the close municipal corporations were the first to be investigated of the evils of English local government. Incidentally, these two commissions of inquiry, with their scores of peripatetic assistant commissioners, confirmed the allegations of the little knot of prison reformers, and brought to notice the intimate connection that existed between pauperism and prison discipline, corrupt municipal corporations and overcrowded and insanitary gaols. The Whig Ministry, in all its projects of reform, was dominated by two leading assumptions, both of them derived at second-hand from Bentham, and untiringly pressed on them by Nassau Senior and Chadwick, namely, the value of uniformity of administration throughout the country and the impossibility of attaining this uniformity without a large increase in the activity of the central government. The prison was a sphere in which these principles were specially applicable. From the standpoint of criminal jurisprudence it seemed intolerable that persons convicted of similar crimes and sentenced to identical punishments should be in one place subjected to physical privation and torturing labour ; in another, contaminated by dirt, disease, idleness and licentious intercourse ; whilst in others they were supplied with plentiful food, profitable employment, comfortable lodging and technical and religious instruction. The divergent results of these opposite policies were registered, sometimes in appalling statistics, in the calendar of convictions and reconvictions of the different county and borough assizes and sessions. Some more uniform treatment of convicted prisoners seemed imperative, alike for equity and for social reform. The need for expert centralized inspection and control was equally manifest. Half a century of experience had proved beyond doubt that it was futile to pass elaborate Acts of Parliament, if there was no official machinery for ensuring that these Acts should be obeyed by the multitude of local prison authorities. It was hopeless to expect that the country gentlemen, busy commercial men, or little shopkeepers, acting as Visiting Justices or borough aldermen, would observe, record and enforce the complicated, difficult and costly requirements of " enlightened " prison discipline. The terrifying increase in the number of commitments to prison made the problem of prison administration at once gravely urgent and peculiarly difficult.[1]   These points were brought out with emphasis by a House of Commons Committee of 1832, when the hands of Ministers were too full to permit of new legislation.[2]   This could not, however, long be delayed. It was plainly only in order to register a foregone conclusion that a committee was appointed by the House of Lords in 1835, under that veteran prison reformer, the Duke of Richmond, to inquire into the state of all the prisons in England and Wales. The recommendations of this Committee, which were supported by the most comprehensive and the most searching survey of English and Welsh prisons yet produced,[3] were immediately embodied in an Act " for effecting greater uniformity of practice in the government of the several prisons in England and Wales, and for appointing inspectors of prisons in Great Britain.[4]

[1] " The real truth is," said Peel in despair, " the number of convicts is too overwhelming for the means of proper and effectual punishment." (Peel to Sydney Smith, March 14th, 1826, *Sir Robert Peel*, edited by C. S. Parker, 1899, p. 402.) " The number of persons charged with criminal offences and committed to the different gaols of England and Wales for trial . . . was, in (the) seven years ending December 31st, 1817, 56,308 ; ditto, 1824, 92,848 ; ditto, 1831, 121,518." . . . These numbers do not comprise offenders of every description who passed through the prisons, being exclusive of summary convictions before magistrates, vagrants, prisoners for re-examination and debtors. (*Report from the Select Committee on Secondary Punishments* . . . *with notes and appendix*, 1832, p. 3.)

[2] See the separate publication, *Report from the Select Committee on Secondary Punishments* . . . *with notes and appendix*, 1833. In the current phraseology of the day, " secondary " punishments included every kind of sentence short of the " capital " punishment of hanging.

[3] See the voluminous five successive reports of the House of Lords Committee on the State of the Gaols and Houses of Correction, 1835, with their elaborate statistical returns and lengthy descriptions.

[4] 3 and 6 William IV, c. 38 (1835).

By this revolutionary statute the immemorial autonomy of the two hundred local authorities in England
and Wales which still maintained prisons, was, at
one blow, destroyed. For the next forty years county
and borough justices go on administering their gaols,
and paying for them out of local funds, but subject
always to ever increasing regulations made by the
Home Office on every detail of prison life ; inces-
santly watched and criticized by a staff of salaried
inspectors reporting to the Secretary of State and to
the public ; and obliged, from time to time, to introduce whatever changes in regimen were dictated by
prison reformers in Parliament. Thus, just as the
" private venture " gaol keeping of the eighteenth
century had been succeeded by the anarchic local
autonomy of the first third of the nineteenth century,
so this itself was, from 1835 onward, superseded by
the Whig regime of centrally controlled local administration under professional officers. It is with this
epoch of prison administration, passing, in 1878, into
a completely nationalized service, that we have now
to deal.

CHAPTER IX

CENTRAL INSPECTION AND CONTROL:
FIRST PERIOD, 1835-1864

DURING the forty years that followed the Act of
1835, we watch the successive administrators at
Whitehall struggling with the actual administrators
of the prisons to bring about prison reform. Unfortunately there was no agreement as to what was
desirable. The period was one of almost incessant
controversy. The philanthropic movements of the
preceding half-century remained powerful factors.
But the prison reformers were divided among themselves as to the means by which the regimen of the
gaols and bridewells was to be regenerated. What
they quarrelled about ; and what Justices and Home
Office officials perpetually experimented with, were
particular devices by which prisoners might be sufficiently punished to deter others from crime ; prevented from escape, disorder or rioting ; kept in
what was then deemed reasonable health, and possibly even reformed in character. The last thing
that was thought about was the relation in which the
administration of prisons should stand towards the
government of the country. It says much for the
condition of Political Science in the England of
1835-1877 that what we now see to be one of the most
fundamental issues—whether the keeping of the
King's prisons should be a function of local or of
national government—was scarcely even raised until
the very end of the period, to be then summarily

decided by Parliament upon grounds having little relevance to prison administration.[1]

(a) *Cellular Isolation*

Foremost among these problems of prison regimen was the controversy that raged over the enforcement of cellular isolation. We have already referred to the proposals of prison reformers of the eighteenth century that, as the obvious way of preventing the scandalous evils of unrestrained association among prisoners, these should all be provided with separate sleeping apartments. What Howard apparently desired was that each prisoner should sleep alone, but that all should work during the day in supervised association with each other. This was presently improved upon by making the cellular isolation complete, by day as well as by night. We come therefore to the endless controversy as to the advantages and drawbacks of solitary confinement, with the various mitigations that the experience of a century has suggested. In the form of the " Separate System," combined with silence among prisoners in association, it became in England the official panacea for all the defects of prison administration ; as, indeed, it has very largely remained down to the present day. The determined adoption by the Home Office officials, from 1835 onwards, successively ratified by Lord John Russell and Sir James Graham, of this combination of physical and mental isolation of each prisoner is, perhaps, the most momentous official decision in English prison history.

In order to appreciate the controversy that arose over this policy of cellular isolation and the absolute prohibition of speech among the prisoners—a con-

---

[1] By far the most important sources of information for the period 1835-64 are the various official documents, notably the twenty annual reports of the Inspectors of Prisons, 1836-59 ; the eleven reports of the Surveyor-General of Prisons (Colonel Jebb), 1844-62 ; the reports of the Directors of Convict Prisons, 1851-79 ; the Report of the Committee on Prison Discipline in Gaols and Houses of Correction in England and Wales, 1850 ; the Reports of the Commissioners on the Birmingham and Leicester prisons, 1854 ; and the Report of the House of Lords Committee on the present state of discipline in Gaols and Houses of Correction, 1863.

troversy which continues to this day—we must here interpose some account of its origin.[1] The well-meaning but unimaginative philanthropists among the Evangelicals and Quakers of Pennsylvania, who had succeeded in abolishing capital punishment in 1786, were shocked at the moral contamination involved in the association among the prisoners in their gaols, and repelled by the sight of the gangs of prisoners with shaven heads, working on the roads in fetters and iron collars. Zealous reformers accordingly devised the system of cellular isolation, not merely (as Howard had advocated) during the time for sleep, but throughout all the twenty-four hours of the day and night, and for the whole period of the sentence. The old Walnut Street prison at Philadelphia, about 1790, was provided with thirty solitary cells, in which prisoners slept, ate and worked without ever emerging from their narrow isolation. In 1818 even this was improved on, for the new prison then erected was wholly arranged in solitary cells, in which not even the provision of work broke the terrible monotony. This " benevolent " imposition of absolutely solitary confinement for long terms aroused the greatest enthusiasm among large numbers of wholly philanthropic people, and led to official inquiries from the most enlightened European countries.[2]

[1] For exact particulars as to the Pennsylvania proceedings (which do not appear to have originated with the Society of Friends as a body, though some leading Quakers were among the religious philanthropists concerned), see " The Silence System in British Prisons," by Stephen Hobhouse, in *The Friends' Quarterly Examiner*, July, 1918 ; reprinted as a pamphlet.

[2] *Penitentiaries of the United States*, by W. Crawford, 1834. Crawford had been the delegate sent by the British Government to investigate the American prison systems. Official investigators were sent at about the same time by the governments of France, Belgium, and Prussia. They saw each other in the United States, and their several reports, whilst differing considerably in character and weight, all concurred generally in recommendation of cellular isolation. The commissioners from France were Alexis De Tocqueville and G. de Beaumont (*Le Système Penitentiaire aux États Unis*, 2 vols., 1837). E. Ducpetiaux went from Belgium (*La Réforme Penitentiaire*, 3 vols., 1837-8) ; whilst Prussia sent the celebrated experts, C. J. A. von Mittermaier (*Die Gefangnissverbesserung insbesondere die Bedeutung und Durchfuhrung der Einzelhaft*, 1858), and Dr. N. H. Julius, who promptly translated Tocqueville and De Beaumont's book into German, and also published *Nordamerika's Sittliche Zustande*, 1839, and

Now, it is important to recognize that, in this introduction of solitary confinement, what was primarily aimed at was the religious and moral regeneration of the prisoner, which, it was supposed, would be promoted by uninterrupted introspection. Solitary confinement was, in all seriousness, humanely imposed as a reformatory device. It arose, indeed, in the monasteries. It had been introduced into prison discipline by Pope Clement IX in the erection in 1703 of the cellular prison of San Michele at Rome. For the same reason it was advocated by Bishop Butler in a sermon of 1740, and patronized by Archdeacon Paley in his *Moral and Political Philosophy* of 1785. By the time that a dreadful experience had proved beyond all possibility of denial that uninterrupted introspection and self-communion in solitary confinement did not, in fact, lead to penitence and moral regeneration, but that it did result in loss of health, mental depression, a permanent lowering of mental and physical capacity, the most agonizing suffering, much insanity, repeated attempts at suicide and an appalling death rate, it was found to be, very naturally, of all punishments, the one most dreaded by criminals. Moreover, of all prison systems it afforded the smallest chance of escape and gave least trouble to the officials. It needed the least staff and (once the capital cost of the building had been provided) it was the most economical. Finally, it seemed to possess, so far as the prison regimen was concerned, the great quality of uniformity. The cells could be made identical in size, shape and bareness ; the utensils (and also the food) could be absolutely standardized ; the necessary visits to each cell could be rigidly regularized. Because of its attractiveness in these respects, we shall find the system of an absolute mental and physical isolation of each prisoner, for which the name of solitary confinement will be as far as possible repudiated,

England's Mustergefängniss in Pentonville, 1846. The effect of their official reports to their respective governments was to set going in Western Europe the building of cellular prisons.

exercising for a hundred years a constant attractive
" pull " on prison regimen.

The results of the genuine solitary confinement, as
practised in Pennsylvania and elsewhere, were too
appalling to permit of its introduction to this country,
in all its rigour, by the Home Office of 1835. What
the most enlightened prison administrators aimed at
enforcing in Millbank Prison, and at prescribing for
the prisons under Local Government, was officially
designated the " Separate System," which was
regarded as quite a humane arrangement. " In the
Act (2 and 3 Victoria c. 56)," says Colonel (afterwards
Sir Joshua) Jebb, " which rendered separate confinement legal, it was specially enjoined that no cell
should be used for that purpose which is not of such
a size, and lighted, warmed, ventilated, and fitted
up in such manner as may be required by a due regard for health and furnished with the means of
enabling the prisoner to communicate at any time
with an officer of the prison." It was, moreover,
required by the same Act, that each prisoner should
have the means of taking exercise when required ;
that he should be supplied with the means of moral
and religious instruction, with books, and also with
labour and employment. It does not seem, so far,
as if there were any lessening of the solitude. Indeed, the Separate System is elsewhere defined, by
the Surveyor General of Prisons, as that mode of
penal discipline " in which each individual prisoner is
confined in a cell, which becomes his workshop by
day and his bedroom by night, so as to be effectually
prevented from holding intercourse with or even
being seen sufficiently to be recognized by a fellow-
prisoner." Another exponent of the advantages of
the Separate System gives us its real difference
from solitary confinement. Under solitary confinement, the chaplain of Pentonville Prison tells us,
" the prisoner is wholly deprived of intercourse with
other human beings." Under separate confinement
" he is only kept rigidly apart from other criminals,
but is allowed as much intercourse with instructors

and officers as is compatible with judicious economy."[1] We must give full weight to this distinction between the system of solitary confinement and the official view of the English " Separate System." But we imagine that, to the prisoner himself, the most serious point was that, under both systems, he was locked up alone in his own cell for twenty-two (or even more) hours out of the twenty-four. His cellular isolation was an invariable fact. The extent to which his solitude was, in practice, mitigated by " social intercourse " with the governor, the chaplain, the doctor and the warders, on the occasion of their visits to his cell, was, we fear, to say the least, uncertain.

An alternative to complete cellular isolation had been found at the prison at Auburn, in New York State, in the prisoners working by day in association, but in absolute silence.[2] This so-called " Auburnian," or " Silent System " was strongly advocated by those who were unable to contemplate the building of new cellular prisons sufficient to accommodate separately for working purposes all the prisoners of the country. Moreover, by permitting work in silent association, it made possible the introduction of a much greater variety of employment, by which it was hoped to make the prisoners pay for their own keep, and from which it was reasonably expected that better results could be obtained than from the tread-wheel or the crank. The obvious drawback was that prisoners could never be prevented from trying to communicate with each other ; so that the system of silent association was found not only to require a very extensive supervisory staff, but also to lead, in practice, to a terrifying number of punish-

---

[1] *Results of Separate Confinement at Pentonville*, by Rev. J. T. Burt, 1852, p. 92 ; compare *Prisons and Prisoners*, by Joseph Adshead, 1845, and *Gaol Revelations*, by a Governor, 1852.

[2] " This form of discipline is said to have been originated in the Belgian prison of Ghent, visited by John Howard in 1775 ; and it is, in essential features, the system which we know in our British prisons to-day—only at Auburn the silence was enforced most cruelly with the constant use of the whip." (*The Silence System in British Prisons*, by Stephen Hobhouse, 1918, p. 9.)

ments for breach of the rule of silence. Here, for the moment, we leave the problem, in order to trace the course of events from 1835.

What becomes at once apparent from the records is that the inspectors whom the Home Office appointed,[1] and whose reports, after 1835, became the principal sources of information about the English prisons, were strongly prepossessed in favour of the physical and mental isolation of every prisoner. The Home Office appears, from the outset, to have committed itself in favour of the system of cellular isolation. The Government seems almost to have charged the inspectors to collect evidence favouring the new panacea, and to have judged all prisons according to the degree in which it was adopted. This, of course, is easily accounted for by the horrible evils of the unrestrained association that still continued in nearly all prisons under Local Government.

Already in 1836, as the inspectors entered upon their service, the condition of Newgate, the first prison they visited, supplied them with illustrations for a thesis in defence of isolation. They drew a lurid picture of the Chapel Yard.[2] "Here," they declared, "were associated together the convicted, and the untried, the felon and the misdemeanant, the sane and the insane, the old and young offender. . . . In Ward No. 12 were six prisoners, four convicted and two untried. . . . Here we found a man aged 38, under sentence of twelve months' imprisonment for an assault on a lad, with an intent

---

[1] After the Act of 1835, four prison inspectors were appointed for England and Wales (besides one for Scotland). To W. Crawford, who had been sent to report on the American penitentiaries, and Rev. Whitworth Russell, late chaplain at Millbank Prison, were assigned the Home and Midland Counties ; and it was their eleven reports, 1836-1847, passionately devoted to the separate system, that were noticeable. The two other inspectors who dealt respectively with the Northern and the South-Western Districts, made less impression. Of the whole inspectorate it was said that three were for the Separate System, and two opposed to it (*The Prison Chaplain*, by W. L. Clay, 1861). For Crawford (1788-1847), who had been secretary to the London Prison Discipline Society, and had devoted himself to philanthropy, see *Dictionary of National Biography*. He died suddenly in 1847 whilst actually attending a meeting of the Commissioners of Pentonville Prison, in the prison itself.

[2] Parliamentary Papers, 1836, xxxv, 4, 7, 8, 17.

to commit an unnatural offence ; two lads of 17 and 18 years of age, one under a fourteen days' sentence ; the other untried, being charged with a slight offence for which he was afterwards sentenced to a month's imprisonment ; a man, aged 35, under sentence of transportation for life, for forgery ; another aged 34, under seven years' sentence of trans-portation ; and the sixth, aged 34, for the non-payment of several small sums of money. . . . In No. 20, the receiving ward, all offenders are kept on their first committal, without any reference whatever to the varieties of case or character, until the surgeon has seen them, which is generally in the forenoon of the morning after they are committed. . . . Such of the prisoners as the surgeon has declared to be in a fit state to be removed into the wards, have then their places assigned to them, a duty which belongs to the principal turnkey of the second station; but, as he is frequently absent on various occupations, it is constantly performed by the inner gateman of the second station, a convicted prisoner. One of the principal turnkeys informed us that on an average this gateman, a prisoner, assigns to the prisoners their wards at least three days in the week. Thus the important duty of classifying the prisoners, so far as the accommodation of the gaol will permit, is entrusted to a convict, himself a wardsman, and who, of course, takes care to select for his own ward those whom he thinks best able to pay his ward dues ; and so great is the authority exercised by him, and so numerous are his opportunities of showing favouritism, that all the prisoners may be said to be in his power. If a man is poor and ragged, however inexperienced he may be in crime, or however trifling may be the offence for which he has been committed, his place is assigned among the most depraved, the most experienced, and the most incorrigible offenders, in the Middle Yard. . . .

" Early in the morning, each day during the session week, all the male prisoners against whom bills of indictment have been found, are mustered in the

Master's Side Yard, and, before the sitting of the
court, are taken down to the Bail Dock, sometimes
as many as sixty or seventy together. Here they are
often kept day after day, expecting their trials, sometimes from 8 or 9 o'clock in the morning until
eleven at night. Some of the prisoners have spoken
of this as the time of their greatest suffering : one in
particular said, ' There we are mixed up with horrid
characters, and are like wild beasts in a den. The
conversation is gross and horrible ; some behave
more as if they were going to a fair than to a trial.
They annoy all those who are not of their set, and
who seem alive to a sense of their situation.' Here, as
everywhere else in Newgate, we find the evils of
prison association."

The attempt to combat the evils of association in
prison life by subjecting the inmates to a system of
classification, founded upon the offences committed
or upon psychological examination, the inspectors
dismissed in terms of emphatic disapproval. " It is
maintained," they said, " that, by a proper classification, we may get rid of the apprehension and mischief of gaol contamination. We deliberately deny
this. This opinion is based upon a foundation which
both reason and experience abundantly prove to be
delusive. Classification is professedly regulated by
one or other of these two standards—gradation in
crime or diversity of character. Now we submit that
an attempt to classify according to the degree of
imputed guilt is entirely futile ; the standard itself
is purely technical, inasmuch as the law places in the
same category crimes which, in moral atrocity, are
separated by the widest assignable interval. But
even granting that the legal denomination embraces
crimes of the same degree of moral turpitude, the
imputed guilt of the prisoner will not necessarily
consign him to the society of his equals in moral
depravity ; because a most atrocious character may
happen to be committed on a charge involving only
trivial criminality. Is this accident, then, to associate him with trivial offenders ? By the system of

classification by crime, it must be so ; but the advocates of this system seek to avoid the lamentable consequences of this branch of the arrangement by taking refuge in the other. They offer to determine the class in which the prisoner shall be placed by the actual moral habits and character of the offender. They profess to determine the case by a reference to a test of which they cannot have any cognizance ; by an inquiry into circumstances which are impenetrably veiled from all human scrutiny—the internal habits and disposition of the mind and heart! "

With the advocacy of cellular isolation, the condemnation of its only serious rival, work in association under the sway of rigidly enforced silence, was clearly involved. In the following extract from their second report, the inspectors pass judgment with a fullness of detail which depicts the whole system as exemplified under peculiarly favourable circumstances, with the wide modifications that these would require in the structure of prison administration. The importance of this passage is enhanced by the fact that it condemns in advance almost exactly the system which has been the basis of the English prison system for the last twenty years. " We say, in the first place," they declare,[1] " that so far as the prevention of intercourse is concerned, the Silent System is not efficacious. If it be granted that communication may be carried on by signs, or in a subdued tone of voice, then it is in evidence that this system does not and cannot prevent such intercourse. The difficulty of enforcing the prohibition of intercommunication under this system is felt and acknowledged by some of its warmest advocates. . . . Upon [the prisoners] the persuasion of the obvious fact, that communication cannot be prevented, will operate most prejudicially ; it will act at once as a constant spur and a premium to their ingenuity, which will have abundant scope to exercise itself amidst the

---

[1] Parliamentary Papers, 1837, xxxii, 2, 3, 4. This adverse account of Coldbath Fields Prison should be compared with that of the governor, in *Revelations of Prison Life*, by G. L. Chesterton, 1856.

multiplied and perplexing engagements of the monitors. . . . The truth of this is demonstrated by the following among other remarkable facts, that in the prison of Coldbath Fields, in which the Silent System is believed to be brought to the greatest degree of perfection, under the management of a highly intelligent and able governor, who has at his command every possible advantage for working the system, there were in the year 1836 no less than 5,138 punishments " for talking and swearing. . . . The warmest advocates of the silent system admit that they cannot carry it into operation without that constant employment of means which are obviously adverse to the spirit of the constitution, and to the first principles of justice. They confess that they must be permitted to inflict punishments for every detected violation of the rules. . . . Nor is the nature of those punishments less objectionable than their frequency. They consist in reduction of food, or in confinement in dark and ill-ventilated cells ; both of which have such a tendency to impair the prisoners' health, that the governor has thought it necessary to reduce the punishment to a degree that impairs its efficacy. Nevertheless, the prisoners persevere in counterfeiting ill-health, and, for the purposes of carrying on the deception, they frequently resort to practices of an abominable and revolting nature. Here then, My Lord, is one punishment, or to speak more correctly, here are many punishments superimposed upon that to which the prisoner was originally sentenced, who is thus oppressed by sufferings and privations beyond the awards of law. . . . But there is another evil inherent in this system, which will tend more effectually to secure its condemnation. We allude to the employment of prisoners as wardsmen and monitors to aid in carrying it into operation. This practice (an unavoidable one under the system in question) is directly opposed to every principle of justice. Is a culprit, probably the greatest delinquent in the prison walls, probably the most ingenious villain, the most finished hypocrite, certainly one of the most guilty in the eye of the law (for it is only from those whose term of imprisonment is long that such agents are selected)—is this man to be released from the condition of a criminal suffering for his offences, and placed in a situation which invests him with authority, which is every moment felt over his fellow-prisoners, every one of whom is perhaps less stained with moral turpitude than himself? In confirmation of this reasoning we find it stated by the governor of the Westminster Bridewell 'that the oldest thief makes the best monitor.' Some notion may be formed of the extent to which this unjust principle must prevail under the Silent System from the fact that, in Coldbath Fields Prison, containing on an average nine hundred prisoners, no less than 218 of them are removed from the operation of the law and the endurance of their punishment, by being appointed to offices of trust or authority : besides these 218 prisoners, there are 54 regular officers ; so that here we have 272 persons appointed to superintend 682 prisoners (i.e., 900 minus 218 who have appointments), being in the ratio of one officer to two and a half prisoners—an exorbitant proportion. This intelligent governor also says that he is much discouraged at times by circumstances of the following nature : after he has taken pains in instructing an individual for the purpose of qualifying him to be an officer of the prison, he finds all his labour lost, by the person so instructed feeling alarmed at the arduous nature of the duties, and declining to undertake them. The governor further states, in reference to his selection of fit and proper persons to serve as monitors, etc., that in order to make that selection he must rely in a great measure upon the knowledge and recommendation of the turnkeys, a circumstance which affords scope for patronage and has a tendency to produce serious evils ; that in order to keep the monitors up to the performance of their duties, it is necessary to receive reports against them from prisoners. . . . At one prison a man, who had filled the office of monitor under the Silent System in another prison, was so persecuted by his fellow prisoners, that the governor, unable otherwise to protect him, was obliged to remove him to a separate cell, as the only means by which he could shield him from the vengeance to which his conduct as monitor exposed him from those over whom, in the discharge of his duties, he had previously, and in another prison, exercised authority. . . . But the amount and severity of the punishment involved in the Silent System is not felt chiefly by the convicted prisoner ; it falls with even greater weight upon the untried. From the novel character of the system, from the multiplicity as well as trifling nature of its regulations, some time must necessarily elapse before the recently committed prisoner can be made acquainted with them ; the consequence of this is, that the earlier portion of the prisoner's confinement, that too which precedes his trial, is the most irksome and vexatious. His thoughts and attention must be occupied in acquiring a knowledge of the rules and a readiness in practising them ; or else in undergoing the various punishments to which his ignorance, his inadvertence, or his stubbornness exposes him. . . . That the untried prisoner is subjected to a greater proportion of suffering than the convicted, we find instanced in one prison where ninety untried prisoners were visited with 224 punishments ; whilst 236 convicted prisoners were visited with 574 punishments. They assemble together social beings, interdict communication between them, and then punish them for yielding to that most powerful of human impulses—the desire of interchanging thought with those with whom they are compelled to associate. Here is a difficulty contrived with perverse ingenuity, as if merely for the purpose of overcoming it, and when it fails, as it must perpetually, the system revenges itself upon the prisoner for the remissness of the officer.''

The system of physical isolation continued to receive tributes from the inspectors couched in varying degrees of warmth, one devoting some pages to a graphic description of the torments which befell the unconvicted prisoner on his apprehension, when it was usually his fate to be conducted to a police station, "where the means of separation are so defective, that he may be confined with drunkards, burglars and pickpockets. With these companions he may pass the night and also the Sunday, if apprehended on the preceding evening. When brought up to the Police Office, he is taken through the public streets, and at the office he finds a collection, from the various stations, of some of the worst characters in London, to whom he thus becomes personally known. A case lately occurred of a prisoner being robbed by his fellow-prisoners in a lock-up room of one of the Police Offices, where he was detained upwards of five hours, and where nine men and four women were placed together in the same apartment. If remanded for re-examination or committed for trial, the prisoner is sent to the gaol in a van employed for the conveyance of prisoners. There are three of these vans constantly engaged for this purpose. They are 8 ft. 4 in. long, 4 ft. 5 in. wide, and 5 ft. 5½ in. high, and will each conveniently accommodate about twenty prisoners ; but upwards of thirty are occasionally conveyed. No officer, either male or female, is inside the van. It can excite no surprise that, under such circumstances, scenes of gross indecency constantly occur. We have ourselves been frequently present when the van has reached the prison and seen profligate characters, of both sexes, after being thus mingled together, descend from that carriage with clothing not sufficient to cover their nakedness. That robberies should occasionally take place in these carriages must, we conceive, be regarded as a matter of course. Prisoners in a state of the most beastly drunkenness, infected with the itch, covered with vermin and most obnoxious from their filth and effluvia, the desperate burglar, the notorious pickpocket, the abandoned prostitute, and even the unnatural offender, are here crowded together in the smallest possible space ; and among them are not

infrequently prisoners of decent habits accused of
trifling offences, servant girls, refractory apprentices,
and others creditably brought up and reputably
connected."[1]

The inspectors' Third Report of 1838 was preceded
by a hundred pages of introduction devoted to the
defence of cellular isolation in which all the arguments
in its favour are marshalled ; and in conclusion the
erection of a model penitentiary is urged, where the
system might be put into force as a pattern for all
the county and borough gaols. This extremely able,
but as we should now say, strongly biased report
may not unfairly be described as, " after Howard's
book, the most important volume in the history of
prison discipline."[2] Like the Poor Law Report of
1834 and the Municipal Corporations Report of 1835,
which are open to a similar condemnation for bias,
it carried conviction to those who read it, and resulted
in immediate legislation. We can to-day see its
faults and its shortcomings, but, at the moment it
was irresistible. It was, for all its ability, a piece
of " unfair special pleading. All the strongest
evidence against their theory was suppressed, and
the arguments of their opponents [were] feebly
stated "[3] by these zealous inspectors. It was answered in more than one quarter ;[4] but it prevailed.
The new Prisons Act of 1839 (2 and 3 Vic. c. 56)
repealed the classification clauses of 4 Geo. IV, and
gave explicit approval of separate confinement by
defining the conditions of its enforcement, and by
providing for the issue of certificates to those prison
authorities which complied with the Home Office
demands.

The immediate result of this Act was probably not
so much to stimulate local authorities to extend
physical isolation as to arouse criticism upon the

[1] Parliamentary Papers, 1837, xxxii, 18, 19.
[2] *The Prison Chaplain*, by W. L. Clay, 1861, p. 183.
[3] *Ibid.*, p. 185.
[4] See, for instance, the article in *The Monthly Law Review* for October
and November, 1837 ; *Revelations of Prison Life*, by G. L. Chesterton,
1856, Vol. I, pp. 314-37.

existing methods of its administration. The Westminster Bridewell was unfavourably reported on by
an inspector, and the Superintending Committee of
Millbank Prison decided to mitigate the severity of
its regimen on account of a " distressing increase in
the number of persons who had become insane."
But in the main the tide was greatly in favour of
cellular isolation, and the opening of Pentonville
in 1842, and the completion in 1845 of the " Prison
Palace " at Reading,[1] seemed to establish it as an
accepted article of faith.

It must not be supposed that the triumph of cellular isolation was wholly the work of the Home Office.
An active minority of prison reformers took the same
side. Lord Brougham's Committee, appointed in
1847 to consider the administration of criminal justice with special attention to juvenile offenders,
reported in favour of cellular isolation as opposed to
the Silent System with classified association, but
added an injunction that the greatest caution should
be used in its application when accompanied by hard
labour. The evidence given was largely but by no
means unanimously in its favour. Clay, the able
chaplain of Preston Gaol, pronounced it to be the only
possible basis for a system of reformation ; and the
governor of Tothill Fields Prison supported him with
the allegation that of all forms of punishment it
aroused the most active apprehension in the prisoner's mind. Mr. Sergeant Adams, on the other hand,
while refusing credence to the reports that solitary
confinement produced insanity, considered that it
left the prisoner in a state of " harmless docility."
Captain Maconochie, then governor of Birmingham
Borough Gaol, carried his opposition much further.
On his first appearance before the Committee, he
declared that a two years' sentence of separate confinement was more damaging than fourteen years'
transportation, and that at Pentonville the prisoners
were in a state of complete physical and mental
prostration. On a later occasion he modified his

[1] *Prison Discipline*, by J. Field, 1848.

attitude so far as to deny that mental alienation could be directly traced to this system, but he maintained that its reformatory influence was counterbalanced by a condition of extreme mental irritation prevailing during the early stages, and by the reaction which followed when men became gradually acclimatized, and settled down and "made themselves comfortable." Other witnesses, if not hostile, were distinctly critical. The chaplain of Bath Gaol considered it dangerous to maintain the system with all its rigour right up to the moment of a prisoner's discharge. He therefore advocated a relaxation during the latter half of the sentence.

Outside the ring of prison specialists, too, considerable hostility must have existed towards solitary confinement, as a whole generation later, when opposing the Prisons Bill of 1877, Newdegate stated in the House of Commons that more than thirty years previously he had visited the United States, and had been so much impressed with the evils of the system, that in conjunction with some Warwickshire and Middlesex magistrates he had opposed its introduction throughout England, and had delayed it until sweeping reforms could be effected. The prevailing looseness of opinion on the whole subject was advertised by the fact that, in its Report, Lord Brougham's Committee made much of the illusory distinction between " solitary " and " separate " confinement. The same diversity of opinion appeared in the evidence given before Sir Geo. Grey's Committee on Prison Discipline in 1850. The Committee itself summed up strongly in favour of separation. It condemned the want of uniformity in applying the system and resolved that every prison should contain enough cells to secure separate confinement for every prisoner. All untried prisoners should be kept in separation ; and short-sentence men should serve their whole time in cellular isolation, whilst the early portion of a long sentence should be served under the same conditions.

Of the witnesses, the prison inspector, J. G. Perry,

advocated separation for a reason hitherto rarely noted. He considered that it stimulated charitable feelings towards a prisoner on his discharge, as employers of labour considered that he had passed through a process of reformation, whereas prison life spent in promiscuity they treated as a sure means of impairing a man's character ; and they therefore refused applications for employment from those who had emerged from a period of imprisonment of that kind. Other advocates of separation, including the governor of Reading Gaol, spoke of it as eminently deterrent to the vagrants ; but in this they were contradicted by the governor of Wakefield Prison. The surgeon of Pentonville Prison stated that such cases of insanity as he had observed had occurred only in the early stages of confinement. A suggestion recalling the previous committee was made by the Duke of Richmond, who emphasized the need experienced in Pentonville Gaol for a period of work in association before the prisoners were brought together on the transports.

Charles Pearson, to whose insistence the Committee was largely due, presented a separate report, attacking the cellular system of confinement in its head-quarters at Reading Gaol. He alleged that it involved a violation of the law in neglecting to enforce hard labour,[1] and encouraging, as it did, long hours of drowsy idleness, that it fostered all the evils incidental to solitude. He considered that its inefficacy was proved by the number of punishments inflicted at Reading, and declared that murders committed upon wardsmen were generally the work of prisoners placed in separate confinement, whose minds were so exasperated by the system that they mistook perfectly indifferent conduct for tyranny or ill-treatment.

However, notwithstanding much adverse criticism

[1] In the Reading Gaol, the insistence of the chaplain (Rev. J. Field) had led to the prisoners being pressed to spend almost their whole waking life in committing to memory the Old and New Testaments, merely varying their perpetual reading by such light work as they chose. Hence the nickname of the " Read, read, reading gaol."

from men who were devoting all their energies to the problem of prison reform, as well as from prison officials themselves, cellular isolation constantly extended its range of adherents. In 1857 the inspectors reported that, in the Southern and Western district, " so universal . . . is the testimony in favour of the Separate System in the English prisons . . . that there remain only two county prisons in which it has not been adopted, either wholly or in part ; and in those exceptional instances new buildings are now in progress which promise soon to assimilate them to the more perfect establishments of the kind."[1] This diversity of opinion was reflected in the administration of the prisons. The Surrey and Middlesex gaols were very backward ; the City of London House of Correction at Holloway alone maintaining a complete form of separation. Others, again, seemed anxious simultaneously to reap the benefits of the two rival systems, and the Preston House of Correction provided in 1857 for both the " separate " and the " silent " treatment within its walls. As usual, the inspector spoke with the utmost confidence of the enormous superiority of the methods which made for a stronger measure of " perfection." The next Committee appointed to report on gaol discipline, sitting under Lord Carnarvon in 1863, to which we shall subsequently have occasion to refer, considered that " the system generally known as the Separate System must now be accepted as the foundation of prison discipline, and that its rigid maintenance is a vital principle to the efficiency of county and borough gaols."[2] The Committee recommended legislation which should render its adoption obligatory upon all gaols, a behest which they conceived might be most strictly enforced by making the Treasury grant in aid of the cost of the prison conditional upon its fulfilment. They urged emphatically that the principle should pervade the whole system of discipline, for in their opinion neither in the school, nor at

[1] Parliamentary Papers, 1857, vii. 406
[2] Ibid., 1863, ix, 5.

chapel, nor during exercises was there any adequate reason for its relaxation. No important voice was now raised against complete cellular isolation.

We may regard this House of Lords Committee of 1863 as the last occasion on which even an opportunity was allowed for cellular isolation to be seriously treated as an open issue. In the same year the inspectors presented the following enthusiastic account of the extension of isolation since 1843.[1] " In laying before you this report, it is very satisfactory to refer to the great and manifold improvements that have taken place in the construction and discipline of prisons in England and Wales since the enactment of Statute 2 and 3 Victoria, Chapter 56, by which the separate confinement of prisoners, as contra-distinguished from solitary confinement, was first sanctioned by law.   In the year 1843, when I had the honour to be appointed to my present office, there were two prisons only in the part of the country now comprised in the southern district, in which advantage had been taken of the provision of the Act, the County Gaol of Shrewsbury and the City Gaol of Bath, the former having undergone alterations in 1840 to fit the cells for separate confinement, and the latter having been rebuilt with cells upon the plan of Pentonville Prison two years afterwards.   These prisons, at the time to which I refer, contained less than an aggregate number of 200 certified cells, whereas at the present time there are more than 8,000 in the southern district which have received the legal sanction to be used in the same form of discipline. . . . Nor has the expectation of the public on the large outlay of money in the building and improvement of prisons been disappointed ; immediately on the change of discipline followed so great a reduction in the number of commitments that in many instances the prisons, although suited in size to the supposed exigencies of the several jurisdictions, were, in a few years found to be unnecessarily spacious ; and in many instances cells forming part of the

[1] Parliamentary Papers, 1863, xxiii, 5.

excess were left to the Government for the confinement of transports and penal servitude prisoners during their probationary period."

In the next year the Bill which was to become the Prisons Act of 1865 put an end to doctrinal controversy by definitely requiring that every prison should contain cells for separate confinement, equal in number to the highest average of prisoners housed in it. It was doubtless a good thing that Howard's demand for a separate sleeping apartment for each prisoner should at last become the law of the land. Unfortunately, as we think, this plainly necessary reform was, in the minds of prison administrators, bound up with the far more doubtful device of cellular isolation during the greater part of the prisoner's waking life.

(b) *The Enforcement of Penal Diet*

The attempt to institute uniform dietaries throughout all the prisons was also a distinguishing feature of the era of control—an attempt taking the form of superseding by positive injunction the previous prohibition of luxuries.

On this point the reformers had to reckon with a public opinion which suspected a tendency to pamper the prisoners, and feared that an ample diet would render a gaol agreeable as a place of residence. In the middle of the century the Recorder of Birmingham, Matthew Davenport Hill, was asked by a Committee sitting on Criminal and Destitute Juveniles, whether he considered the gaol dietary too liberal. His answer may be quoted as an expression of a very common attitude :[1] " From all the information I can obtain it is so beyond all doubt, and the mischiefs that flow from that, which I conceive an error, are very fatal indeed. I remember some twenty years ago this was the state of things. There were three classes of persons : there was the soldier who kept guard over the convict ; there was the convict, and

---

[1] Parliamentary Papers, 1852, vii, 61.

there was the pauper. Now, one would say, according to a natural justice, the soldier who was in execution of his duty, and a member of an honourable profession, should have the best diet ; the pauper, who is to be considered, by law at least, as the victim of misfortune, should have the second best ; and the convict, who is in prison in consequence of his own crime, should have the worst diet. That order was exactly reversed. The convict had the best diet, the pauper the second best, and the soldier had the worst. A convict has been heard to say, when some little diminution in his rations was made, ' We shall be treated as bad as soldiers by and by.' "

It is due to the Home Office to admit that, in its efforts to deal with this very difficult question, it did not allow itself to be unduly influenced by popular clamour. In 1842, Sir James Graham, perhaps the ablest of all the successors of Peel at the Home Office, instructed the inspectors to report to him upon the whole system of prison administration, with special reference to the question of diet. Their report was adopted as the basis of a code of prison administration, which the Home Secretary immediately communicated to the Chairmen of Quarter Sessions in a circular dated January 27th, 1843. The inspectors laid down the principles which directed official action in this matter until 1863. " The principle," they said, " which we are of opinion ought to be acted on in framing a scale of prison diet, and that which we have endeavoured to carry into effect as far as possible in the annexed scale, is, that that quantity of food should be given in all cases which is sufficient and not more than sufficient, to maintain health and strength, at the least possible cost ; and that, whilst due care should be exercised to prevent extravagance or luxury in a prison, the diet ought not to be made an instrument of punishment. . . . We are of opinion that there always ought to be three meals each day in prison, and that at least two of the three should be hot ; that there should be variety in the kinds of food forming the diet, with occasional changes, and that a considerable portion of the food should be solid ; that in the selection in the kinds of food, it is essential for the maintenance of health to include substances which are necessary for the support of the various parts of the body."

The dietaries actually adopted appear in the accompanying tables.

THE GRAHAM DIETARIES OF 1843.

I. WITHOUT HARD LABOUR.

	Class 1.	Class 2.	Class 3.	Class 4.
	Less than 7 days.	7 days to 2 r.	21 days to 4 months.	More than 4 months.
	ozs.	ozs.	ozs.	ozs.
Bread	112	168	140	168
Potatoes	—	—	64	32
Meat	—	—	6	12
Total solid food	112	168	210	212
	pints.	pints.	pints.	pints.
Soup	—	—	2	3
Gruel	14	14	14	14
Cocoa	—	—	—	—
Total liquid food	14	14	16	17

II. WITH HARD LABOUR.

	Class 2.	Class 3.	Class 4.	Class 5.
	7 to 21 days.	21 days to 6 weeks.	6 weeks to 4 months.	More than 4 months.
	ozs.	ozs.	ozs.	ozs.
Bread	168	140	168	154
Potatoes	—	64	32	112
Meat	—	6	12	16
Total solid food	168	210	212	282
	pints.	pints.	pints.	pints.
Soup	1	2	3	3
Gruel	14	14	14	11
Cocoa	—	—	—	3
Total liquid food	15	16	17	17

The immediate results of the measure may be seen in the report issued at the beginning of the year 1844 for the preceding year.[1] " I have," says the inspector, " particular pleasure in reporting that, in the

[1] Parliamentary Papers, 1843, xxv, xxvi, 253.

very great proportion of the prisons comprised within this extensive district, the means taken for ensuring prisoners a certain quantity of plain and wholesome food have been attended with great success by the very general adoption of the official dietaries or their equivalents. . . . Among other evils foretold as the certain result of this interference with the food for prisoners, there is one more warmly insisted upon than others, and which I advert to, rather from the strenuousness of its advocates, than from its real importance. I allude to the anticipation that by the adoption of those dietaries, or their equivalents, the situation of the convict as to food, would be so superior to that of a considerable proportion of the humbler classes, that it would induce a preference for a prison, and thereby directly encourage crime. . . . But I am prepared to show, that even if the morals of the people were as vitiated as apprehended, the quantity of food prescribed for prisoners by authority is no encouragement to crime, but directly the reverse, and prisoners are less likely to be satisfied with the new diets than the old. I have already found this to be the case, in one instance at Chester, where the prisoners declared that they liked the quality of the new, but preferred the quantity of the old. The reason is obvious. The food prescribed in the official dietaries consists of various articles, all alimentary of the human body, and generally solid in form. The ordinary diet for prisoners, previous to the recent interference of authority, was most disproportionately given in a liquid form, consisting, independently of the bread, of thin gruel, and in some cases with the addition of thin soup, well satisfying the immediate cravings of hunger by its bulk, but affording no sufficient supply to the constantly consuming elements of the human body. Hence the numerous trifling cases of dyspepsia and other ailments connected with the digestive functions which, under long imprisonment, crept into serious maladies, breaking down the constitution or ending in death. That the new dietaries are of a sufficiently

nutritious character, though less repletive than the
former, I have no doubt ; and I have just received
the voluntary evidence of a keeper of a House of
Correction in an agricultural district, which had been
previously remarked for its sharp discipline and spare
food, where the Justices had, of their own accord,
adopted the official tables upon the recommendation
of the circular from the Home Office."

It is by no means easy to estimate the significance
of these dietaries in English prison history, as their
adoption was very far from being universal, or even
widespread. We may draw some inferences from
the treatment accorded to certain modifications
proposed by the Home Office four years later. In
1850 the Chairman of the Berkshire Visiting Justices,
in the course of evidence given before the Committee of the House of Commons, made the sin-
gular and instructive statement that the Berkshire Quarter Sessions had approved the Home
Office dietary, but added "that he had had no
authority to introduce it." Further information on
this point is obtained in a resolution of the Committee of 1863, which noted that Sir James Graham's
dietary had been so modified, wherever it had been
accepted in any shape, that its fundamental principle,
the avoidance of any penal character, had been directly
ignored. Absence of uniformity in this, as in every
other form of administration, characterized the
county and borough prisons. One of the witnesses,
Doctor Edward Smith, who had been summoned on
account of his careful researches into the question,
said that Sir James Graham's dietaries had been
adopted in only half the gaols, extraordinary discre-
pancies existing in the others. He compared Cardiff,
where no meat at all was allowed, with the Middlesex
gaols which provided 6 ozs. of cooked meat on four
days in the week ; and he added : " There is no
uniform dietary enforced by the Government, and I
think that that is a fundamental defect. A dietary
is recommended by the Home Office, and any scheme
of dietary must be sanctioned by the Home Secre-

tary ; but there is none enforced, and the result is
that the Visiting Justices of the different prisons
adopt such a plan as seems to them to be good within
the limits which are allowed by the Home Secretary.
Therefore it seems to me that the want of an authorized and enforced system of dietary by the Home
Office is that which leads to all the diversity now
existing in that respect."[1]

Thus, during the twenty years, 1843-1863, a standard dietary existed, approved and recommended by
the Home Office ; but in the absence of all means of
enforcing its adoption, the diets in actual use varied
from the lavish feeding of the Middlesex gaols, and
some of the large borough gaols, to the county prisons
where the Justices generally aimed at placing the
food on a standard below that of the workhouses.

We may believe that, in the minds of the Home
Office administrators it was, very largely, with the
object of remedying this state of things that the
House of Lords Committee of 1863 was appointed.
This Committee, to which we shall hereafter allude,
was able to secure the renewed attendance of Edward
Smith, as the medical practitioner who had devoted
most attention to working class and convict diet.
Poor as his science must now seem, it was the best
available at the time. For some years the results
of his researches had been published in pamphlet
form, or among the transactions of learned societies ;
and at the instance of the British Association he had
recently reported elaborately upon the dietaries in
use at the Coldbath Fields Prison, and at the West
Riding Gaol at Wakefield, investigating the strain
produced by various forms of labour by experiments
performed upon himself. It had been his endeavour
to determine the lowest adequate measure which
supplied the human system with the elements of
nutrition in their due proportions. This he fixed at
1,400 grains of carbon and 70 grains of nitrogen. He
considered it a necessary condition for the adoption
of a scientific dietary that the prisoner's mode of life

---

[1] Parliamentary Papers, 1863, ix, 76.

should be assimilated as far as possible to that of the ordinary labourer, noting that close confinement admitted of less vital action and less conversion of food tissue. Under such circumstances the nitrogenous element, which was supplied mainly by meat and milk, required intensification by a heavier meat diet. But labour in the open air might, he alleged, be treated as a positive substitute for meat, and must therefore be a necessary and constitutional part of every prison system. In no case must the need for an increased diet consequent upon intensified labour be measured directly by the increased waste of the body, as, whilst the latter might, in the case of treadwheel labour, be multiplied five or six times, the consumption of nitrogen did not increase in any proportionate degree. He thought that the needs thus arising might generally be met by an increase in the farinaceous foods ; and he prescribed, as the basic elements of his dietaries, bread, rice, oatmeal, potatoes, milk and meat liquor. He advised that food should be served hot, as in that state it was a vital stimulant.

Having reached these conclusions, Dr. Smith naturally looked unfavourably upon the existing dietaries, which he pronounced injurious to the prisoner and a loss to society. He expressed approval of the cardinal principle underlying Sir James Graham's dietary, that the prisoners' food should not be used as an instrument of punishment, but considered that the dietary itself was conceived without the smallest regard to the value of foodstuffs as scientifically determined. He declared the lowest classes, appointed for prisoners serving short sentences, to be utterly inadequate. The nutritive elements of Class I resolved themselves into 350 grains of carbon and $17\frac{1}{2}$ of nitrogen, as against 1,400 and 70 grains which he had fixed as the minimum. Frequent repetition of short sentences on such a basis would produce a most prejudicial effect. The higher classes of dietary he pronounced over-abundant, in view of their excessive allowance of meat. He pointed to the establishment of a uniform scale of dietary for all prisons as the ideal to be striven for, and recommended the appointment of a special committee to undertake a series of experiments, on the prescribed basis of the dietary of the agricultural population, accompanied by light labour and open-air exercise. So soon as the uniform system of hard labour should be introduced it would become possible to secure uniformity of diet throughout the whole scale of prison life.

In the meantime the Government had not been inactive. In November, 1863, a Commission consisting of the medical officers from Millbank, Dartmoor and Gosport prisons, who had been appointed some time earlier to inquire into the dietary of convict establishments, was asked by Sir George Grey to include county and borough gaols within its sphere of research. In a letter, dated December 18th, it was explained that the Home Secretary did not repudiate the fundamental principle of Sir James Graham's dietary, but interpreted it to mean that whilst health must be maintained, all approaches to luxurious living had to be avoided. The familiar principle was once more solemnly rehearsed that prison fare was not to compare favourably with that of free labourers or workhouse inmates. And, finally the Commission was instructed to inquire into the advisability of placing long sentence prisoners, at the very beginning of their terms of imprisonment, upon the dietary of the class to which they had been allotted.

The conclusion of the Commission, whose report was submitted on April 28th, 1864, formed, in some sense, an answer to the charges and suggestions of the Committee of the House of Lords. Dr. Edward Smith was treated with scanty respect. It was pointed out that his presumed discoveries had been made under constantly changing circumstances. In the first instance the experiments had been performed upon himself and other private individuals ; the conclusion had then been compared with the circumstances of Lancashire operatives, persons of middle age ; and, finally, their results had been applied to the inmates of prisons, a much younger class of men, serving five different periods of imprisonment, varying from less than one week to more than four months. It further transpired that tables of weighing drawn up at three different gaols set forth results which corresponded in no way with those recently proclaimed by Dr. Smith as subsisting between the alleged needs of the human system and the increase or decrease of weight occasioned by the several dietaries of 1843. The positive results of the Commission's labours lost in independence of character by the admission, at the outset, that scientific experiments could possess only a limited value. The Commission had therefore felt compelled to accept in general terms the guidance of the inspectors; and it pronounced in favour of the Home Office dietary as adequate to provide a rough practical scale, but standing in need of modification at almost every stage.   In passing a general criticism on this dietary they considered it quite impossible to " study this table without coming to the conclusion that Sir James Graham did unconsciously introduce a strong penal element into classes one and two, and a slight element of luxury into class five ; for, on the one hand, we have no knowledge of any class of persons who voluntarily limit themselves to bread and water gruel for a week, still less for three weeks at a time, and, on the other hand, we think that the cocoa in class five is both pleasant and costly enough to be considered a luxury."[1]

In framing its own scale of diet, the Commission explained that it had been governed by the principle of causing all prisoners sentenced to the longer term to pass through every scale in the dietary.   In this decision it had been influenced by reports submitted upon an experiment undertaken at the West Riding Prison at Wakefield. On September 1st, 1862, the Visiting Justices had sanctioned the adoption of an experimental diet, in which a more generous allow-

[1] Parliamentary Papers, 1864, xlix, 569.

ance of food was to be the reward of industry and good conduct. They defended this enterprise on the ground " that their experience and observation had led them to entertain for some time strong objections to the existing arrangement by which prisoners, sentenced for the longer terms of imprisonment, were placed on the higher diet assigned to such terms as soon as they entered the prisons. They believed that the best arrangement of a prison dietary would be one by which the prisoner having assigned to him, at first, the lowest possible diet consistent with the maintenance of health, should be enabled to earn by industrious exertion, a diet gradually improved through progressive stages. Common sense seemed to them to indicate that the amount of food given should have some relation to the labour undergone, and that the natural stimulus offered by having an object to work for would act beneficially on the prisoner in a sanitary as well as in an industrial point of view."[1] The experimental diet, except for the Class 1 prisoners serving ten days or under, exceeded the ordinary diet in extent, and except for Class 1, the loss of weight occasioned by it was less. Unfortunately for the Commission, the medical officer of the prison reported unfavourably upon the experiment, alleging that it resulted in increased mortality, loss of weight, and failure in health and strength. On May 1st, 1863, the experiment was abandoned at the instance of the Secretary of State.

The Commissioners, however, were of opinion that the Visiting Justices had been successful in their attempt to show that the experimental dietary was not answerable for this depreciation in the prisoners' health, urging that these cases of mortality were exceptional. They, therefore, advocated a resumption of the experiment, and the introduction of its principles into every county and borough gaol.

To the injunction of the Home Secretary that the prisoners' fare should not contrast favourably with the meals within the reach of the free labourer, the

[1] Parliamentary Papers, 1864, xlix, 608.

Commissioners returned an answer which deserves to be quoted.[1] "It is," they said, "extremely difficult to ascertain what the ordinary food of free labourers is. Even if the inquiry was limited to that class of free labourers which is known to be the worst fed, namely, agricultural labourers, the true facts of the case would not be readily obtained. And even if it were to appear that, as a class, their food was badly chosen, badly cooked, and insufficient in quantity . . . it would not be incumbent upon us in framing dietaries for prisoners, to imitate their bad example, or to conform ourselves to their exceptional circumstances. The duty which the authorities have to discharge in respect of the diet of prisoners, seems to us to be strictly analogous to that which they already perform in regard to other matters which involve their health and strength ; and just as it would not be right to subject our prisoners to the dirt, overcrowding, and defective ventilation to which the majority of them had been exposed when they were free, so ought it to be with their food. The quality and amount of it ought to be determined, not by the standard of any class of labourers, but by the actual necessities arising out of the prisoners' altered circumstances. . . . Of the able-bodied in-mates of the workhouse, we will only observe that, while they differ materially from the prisoner in the consciousness which they have of freedom to quit their temporary asylum, they can only be brought into comparison with prisoners under short sentences, for whom even Sir James Graham provided a scanty and unattractive dietary."

The difficulty occasioned by the diverse kinds of "hard labour," the Commissioners attempted to meet by suggesting that "no labour which does not visibly quicken the breath and open the pores should be described as hard "; and they held it to be more economical to "apportion the punishment to the diet than to raise the diet to the level of the punishment."

[1] Parliamentary Papers, 1864, xlix, 556-620.

Guided by these considerations, the Commissioners adopted a scheme which they calculated would save the nation £16,000 a year. It is set forth in the accompanying table.

This dietary represents the last attempt to arrive at uniformity during the rule of the local authorities. The result is made clear by Sir George Grey's words in the House of Commons during the debates in the Prisons Bill of 1865. "I sent," he said,[1] "the dietary tables, suggested by the Committee to whom this subject was referred, to the authorities of every prison in the kingdom. In some prisons they have been adopted, and in other reasons have been given for not adopting them. . . . They have brought me to the conclusion that you cannot lay down absolutely a fixed dietary scale, and that if you have a maximum and a minimum the difference would be so wide that it would be of little use. The recommendations of the Committee, however, have led to improvement in the existing dietary tables, and to a greater approximation to uniformity than has prevailed at any former period." The result of forty years of " chipping and changing " in prison diet was to leave the question practically as unsettled as ever. The results of particular dietaries were, in fact, scarcely more definitely ascertained than the objects and purposes to be aimed at were agreed upon.

(c) *The Enforcement of Penal Labour*

The subject of prison labour has already demanded some attention as presenting difficulties in the administration of cellular confinement, and as a question to be solved before any satisfactory scheme of diet could be adopted. In some respects it raised more issues than any other topic of prison discipline. It was not only the field upon which the protagonists of an exclusively penal and deterrent regimen met the advocates of reformatory treatment, but it was beset with difficulties of a technical nature in connection

[1] *Hansard*, Vol. 177, 1865, Feb. 13, p. 217.

DIETARY PROPOSED BY SELECT COMMITTEE.

Parl. Papers, 1864, xlix, 618.

			Class I.	Class II.	Class III.	Class IV.	Class V.	
Breakfast	Every day	Bread	ozs. 6	ozs. 6	ozs. 8	ozs. 8	ozs. 8	Food of female prisoners apportioned on the principle of deducting 1-6th from weight of man to, and deducting ¼ from, articles of food served in solid form. Hard labour men to receive extra cheese, gruel, and meat.
		Gruel	—	1 pt.	1 pt.	1 pt.	1 pt.	
Supper	„	Bread	6	6	6	8	8	
		Gruel	—	—	1 pt.	1 pt.	1 pt.	
„	Sundays	Bread	8	8	10	10	12	
		Cheese	—	1	2	3	3	
Dinner	Mondays Wednesdays & Fridays	Bread	6	6	4	4	4	
		Potatoes	—	—	12	16	16	
		Suet Pudding	—	—	8	12	12	
		Indian Meal Pudding	6	8	—	—	—	
„	Tuesdays Thursdays Saturdays	Bread	6	6	8	8	8	
		Potatoes	8	12	8	8	16	
		Soup	—	—	¾ pt.	1 pt.	1 pt.	

with the interpretation of the term "hard labour," as used in the Acts of 1824 and 1835. Finally, it brought the life of the prison into immediate touch with the outer world, through the competition of prison industry with capitalist enterprise and free labour.

We have seen that the previous era of prison reform had called into being a special instrument, the tread-wheel, for providing the prisoners with penal and irksome work. The cellular system now called for a new invention which was supplied in the crank, devised about 1846 by one Gibbs, of Pentonville.[1] In the early years of the period under review the crank was widely adopted, being installed either wholly in the prisoner's cell, or with its regulative machinery outside the cell. The whole field of prison industry ranged between institutions such as Coldbath Fields Prison, where a sternly punitive un-productive system of labour was enforced, and those such as that of Wakefield, which aimed avowedly at fitting their inmates for the pursuits of an indus-

---

[1] Report of Surveyor-General of Prisons, 1847, p. 17. As seen, about 1860, at Coldbath Fields Prison the crank is thus described : " Crank labour consists in making 10,000 revolutions of a machine resembling in appearance a Kent's Patent Knife Cleaner, for it is a narrow iron drum placed on legs, with a long handle on one side, which, when turned, causes a series of cups or scoops in the interior to revolve.   At the lower part of the interior of the machine is a thick layer of sand, which the cups, as they come round, scoop up, and carry to the top of the wheel, where they throw it out and empty themselves, after the principle of a dredging machine.   A dial-plate, fixed in front of the iron drum, shows how many revolutions the machine has made.   It is usual to shut up in a cell the man sent to crank labour, so that the exercise is rendered doubly disagreeable by the solitude. . . . As may easily be conceived, this labour is very distressing and severe. . . . A man can make, if he work with ordinary speed, about twenty revolutions a minute, and this, at 1,200 the hour, would make his task of 10,000 turns last eight hours and twenty minutes." (The Criminal Prisons of London, by Henry Mayhew and John Binny, 1862, p. 308.)

In its modern form (see the description in Appendix 15 to Annual Report of the Prison Commissioners for 1879) the crank handle turned a cylindrical drum, to which clip-brakes of various construction were applied so as to retard its motion by friction.   These clip-brakes had admittedly failed in the past to supply a resistance which could be relied on as " definite, uniform and constant, under all circumstances " ; but it was contended, in 1879, that these mechanical imperfections had been overcome, and that it was then possible to instal machines in each cell " by which the amount of force exerted by any prisoner could be measured as easily as his ration of food could be weighed."   We do not find that the prisoners were convinced of this undeviating constancy.

trious existence. Between these two extremes lay almost every kind of occupation. There was the type which frankly stood to make the prison self-supporting, as in the County Gaol at Dorchester, where in 1838 the inspectors found the inmates engaged in almost every form of simple industry, of which the annual profits occasionally approached a hundred pounds. On the other hand, there were instances of most futile attempts to conform to Home Office instructions. In 1852, at the County House of Correction at Wisbech, the inspector saw the occupants engaged in the useful and instructive task of separating white and black oats, " three pints being considered the day's work."

There seems undoubtedly to have been a powerful opposition to unproductive penal labour from the very outset on the part of persons who represented the various elements collected around prison life. In 1837, the governor of the House of Correction at Coldbath Fields, George Laval Chesterton, who readily admitted a reputation for unflinching severity, described at length the risks to health attendant upon the infliction of tread-wheel punishment. " The prisoners,"[1] he said, " coming off the wheels warm, for relief, and sitting in that state, on the stages, must be bad. I think tread-wheel labour injurious to the health of some of the prisoners—to corpulent, or infirm, and aged, or tall persons ; but not to boys, lads, or men of light weight, if in good health. . . . I find that the men in general are greatly distressed, after three months' continuous labour, but tall and heavy men in a less time ; they fall away in flesh, get into bad condition, and become generally depressed ; the effect upon those who had been addicted to hard drinking, and who are sentenced to very long terms of imprisonment, is, in most cases, seriously injurious to the system. . . . With regard to women, I believe tread-wheel labour, if judiciously used, is highly beneficial to health, particularly in

[1] Parliamentary Papers, 1837, xxii, 94 ; see also his *Revelations of Prison Life*, 1856, Vol. I, pp. 224-5.

cases of disorderly women, prostitutes, etc., committed for periods not exceeding three months, and who generally come into prison in a deplorable condition from drink and intemperance, and quit it in good health. . . . I do not think that the state of the mind produced by tread-wheel labour is favourable to moral reformation. It is more severely felt by some prisoners than others. It decidedly gives rise to every deception and falsehood. The prisoners occasionally attempt to avoid taking their turn ; they watch opportunities for this purpose ; they deceive the doctor ; they feign sickness of various kinds (seldom on meat days, however, unless after dinner). . . . There is scarcely a man who comes here sentenced to hard labour, who, by his own account, has not had some most afflicting illness, or met with some serious accident disabling him from hard work. This state of mind cannot be favourable to reformation. . . ." The inspectors in the general survey of 1843 expressed an even more outspoken disapproval of this mode of punishment, and urged its confinement within the narrowest limits. " We are of opinion," they said,[1] " that tread-wheel labour is often very unequal in its operation, and that, under certain circumstances, it is prejudicial to health, particularly where there is predisposition to disease ; that in default of proper precaution it exposes the prisoners to serious accidents; and that it is liable to abuse. For three reasons, therefore, and in order to check the excessive use of the tread-wheel labour, we are of opinion :

1. That tread-wheel labour is improper for females.
2. That tread-wheel labour is improper for boys under fourteen years of age.
3. That no prisoner who is not sentenced to hard labour should under any circumstances be placed on the tread-wheel.
4. That no prisoner should be placed upon the

---

[1] Parliamentary Papers, 1843, xxv, xxvi, 6.

tread-wheel, or put to other hard labour, without the previous permission of the Medical Officer.

. . . We are of opinion that it is very desirable that useful employment, with the necessary materials and instructions, should be provided for all prisoners, in order that all convicted prisoners sentenced to hard labour, but not placed on the tread-wheel, and all prisoners sentenced to simple imprisonment (except those of the first division) may be put to work ; and that prisoners before trial, debtors, and misdemeanants of the first division, may have the option of employment."

In 1850 the surgeon to the House of Correction at Kirton-in-Lindsay spoke in the following terms of the tread-wheel as a factor in the greater frequency of illness and in the impaired moral of the inmates of that gaol. " Before the tread-wheel was introduced," he said,[1] " there was much less illness than there has been since. . . . The majority of prisoners, except the skulkers, lose in weight. It is impossible by any vigilance to prevent this skulking to escape the tread-wheel. Some of the prisoners are sure to baffle you. They frequently swallow soap, which has the effect of purging them and bringing on a low fever, during the continuance of which it is impossible to put a man on the wheel. They formerly ate large quantities of salt, in order to bring on fever, and to prevent this they were deprived of their salt bags. . . . I think it very desirable as a matter of health, as well as in a moral point of view, that some other employment should be substituted for the tread-wheel labour ; and as an immediate measure, I would recommend that, during the last quarter of an hour before breakfast, and the last half-hour before dinner and supper, the prisoners should leave the wheel and walk about to cool themselves gradually, instead of going straight into the cold passages to get their meals."

Governing opinion, however, seems to have looked

[1] Parliamentary Papers, 1850, xxviii, 442.

upon strictly penal labour with a consistently favourable eye. Such, at least, is the inference which it would seem proper to draw from the resolutions of the two Committees. In regard to the first, the Committee of 1850, we may treat the predominant motive as a desire to fulfil the injunctions of the two Prison Acts. For, apart from an approving reference to the universal infliction of crank labour at Leicester County Gaol, the subject is directly approached only in the twenty-fifth Resolution of the Report, where the opinion is expressed that " provision ought to be made in every prison for enforcing sentences of imprisonment with hard labour."

In the evidence given before that Committee almost every aspect of the subject was touched upon. Labour of a predominantly agricultural character found a warm advocate in Charles Pearson, to whose efforts the appointment of the committee was largely due. He defended it as readily learned, susceptible of considerable variation and beneficial to the health of prisoners. He laid stress upon its economic merits, drawn from the cheapness of the appliances required, and the remunerative character of its output. Captain Maconochie, governor of Birmingham Borough Gaol, opened another line of inquiry by stating that a gentleman of Birmingham had protested against the adoption of productive labour as involving the menace of unfair competition with free labourers. This particular anxiety was no doubt powerful in hindering many gaols from having recourse to industrial occupations, one of the Leicestershire Visiting Justices telling the Committee that the County Prison had refrained from introducing the local industry of stocking frames, as the authorities anticipated that, while the real influence of such a step upon the markets must be very slight, a fierce outcry would be raised, exaggerating it beyond measure.

The subject of prisoners' earnings was variously regarded. The chaplain of Durham Gaol thought it desirable that prisoners should be allowed to earn a certain sum, which they might receive on their discharge as a means of giving them a fresh start. In opposition to this, the Earl of Chichester, a Commissioner of Pentonville, said that at Millbank each prisoner had received at one time the full amount of his earnings, but this practice had been found to neutralize the penal aspect of imprisonment, and had been abandoned. Crank-labour was attacked and defended with equal warmth. The prison inspector, J. G. Perry, considered it extremely injurious as the prisoner felt himself degraded by the unproductive character of the work, which gave rise to increased animosity against the law and its officers. They, in their turn, found in their power to vary the intensity of labour an opportunity of gratifying their spite against any individual prisoner.

The chaplain of Bath Prison repeated these charges adding that the crank offered no real index of the labour expended. He considered that the appointment of a task which left the prisoner entirely dependent upon the warders' goodwill justified him in describing crank-work as a species of " torture." Moreover, its futility as a deterrent was demonstrated by the fact that, notwithstanding these elements of intense severity, committals became no less frequent.

The advocates of the crank quite frankly grounded their case upon its harshness and irksome severity. One of the directors of the Government Convict Prisons, Captain O'Brien, considered that it possessed the advantage of being readily adaptable to the physical capacity and condition of the health of every prisoner. Amongst its warmest defenders were the governor and the chaplain of Leicester County Prison. In the year 1848 crank labour was in this gaol extended to all convicted prisoners sentenced to hard labour. The work was of a very severe character, a maximum of 14,000 revolutions being daily demanded of each adult male prisoner. In consequence there were numerous cases of failure to accomplish the appointed task, and punishments rained thick and fast. During a single month (January, 1849) the punishment of confinement in the solitary cells was ordered on as many as eighty-five occasions, and floggings were proportionately numerous. Despair and insubordination became rife, and the inspectors took note of " that dogged spirit of resistance that is eminently characteristic of the inmates of this prison." Still unshaken in their conviction of the excellence of task-work on the crank, and desirous of avoiding an increase in the number of floggings, the Visiting Justices, acting entirely upon their own authority, modified the character of the labour so as to make punishment the immediate and unavoidable consequence of a failure to carry out the appointed task. They adopted the simple expedient of making the prisoners' meals dependent upon the performance of a certain amount of labour. Thus, 1,800 revolutions were required to earn breakfast, 4,500 more for dinner, 5,400 for supper, leaving still 2,700 to be performed afterwards. This system continued in force until May, 1852, by which time the very numerous cases in which privation of meals was inflicted had given rise to a dropsical disease termed " crank oedema," which at last caught the inspectors' attention. On crank work, in general, the following judgment was passed in the report of the Royal Commission.[1] " We think . . . that it ought to be applied only to persons confined for short terms of imprisonment, whom it may be difficult, perhaps impracticable, to train to industrial labour. In the next place, we think it ought to be applied, not in separate cells but in association, in a large apartment, or a detached building. . . . When the prisoner is working at the crank machine alone within his cell, the means of increasing the intensity of the labour, with or without his knowledge, being in the hands of the prison officer . . . the prisoner will be almost sure . . . to conceive the belief that the intensity of the labour has been arbitrarily and for mere purposes of severity, increased by the prison

---

[1] Parliamentary Papers, 1854, xxxiv, p. xiii.

officer, and thus a feeling of irritation against the prison authorities is daily engendered."

The special use to which the crank had been put at Leicester was condemned as constituting an infringement of the Act of 1824. "We entertain," they said, "also strong objection to task-labour which is not of a productive or industrial description ; nor do we think that such labour, as it is tasked at the crank-machines, is strictly in conformity with the provisions of the 10th Section of the Gaol Act, 4 Geo. IV. Cap. 64, which enacts that every prisoner shall be employed so many hours in every day, not exceeding ten . . . and clearly indicates that continuous hard labour during the day, not dependent upon the completion of a set task, was contemplated by the legislature."

After pointing out that the crank was introduced to provide a deterring influence which seemed to be demanded by the well aired and decently furnished cell under the Separate System, the Commissioners continued :[1] "We are of opinion that it would be desirable altogether to discontinue the present system of tasked labour at the crank machine, and to substitute for it continuous labour during the day, with intervals of rest, as it has been practised at the treadwheel ; the cranks, when so used, being set at the same fixed weight for all prisoners. . . ."

It is thus clear that there was a considerable body of opinion hostile to purely penal labour, and in some instances in favour of the substitution of industrial and productive tasks. The House of Lords Committee of 1863 provided another opportunity of stating the position. Both inspectors condemned the crank in much the same terms as they had employed thirteen years before, and the Chairman of the Berkshire Justices roundly stated that it had proved a failure, adding :[2] "You may tell a man that he shall work so many turns and have no breakfast, as was the case at Birmingham, so many turns or no dinner, or so many turns and no supper, but it was found that,

[1] Parliamentary Papers, 1854, xxxiv, p. xiv.
[2] Ibid., 1863, ix, 240.

first of all, there is something in the Saxon blood which every now and then rebels, and you cannot make a man work ; then what are you to do ? At Birmingham the food was withdrawn, and the men at last became so ill that some of them died. There was a great inquiry into the matter in a court of law; and the result was, that the governor was sentenced to three months' imprisonment." The governor of Taunton Gaol said that vagrant and workhouse offenders were quite undeterred by the prospect of crank labour. The most genuinely idle men, to meet whose cases it was specially designed, regarded it without dismay. In his prison it was reserved as a punishment for acts of insubordination.

It is interesting to note that on this occasion, in addition to the usual arguments advanced in favour of industrial labour, it was contended that a distinctly penal element might be imported into it. One prison inspector, J. G. Perry, urged that such occupations might be regulated to suit each man's strength, since anyone acquainted with the trade could easily judge whether a prisoner was working up to his full capacity. He stated that it had been found particularly beneficial for criminals convicted as receivers, vagrants, trained and habitual thieves, and men committed for murderous assaults. His brother inspector suggested the introduction of task work into industrial occupations as a means of executing sentences of hard labour. The Governor of Taunton Gaol considered that the same end might have been attained by lengthening the hours of labour ; making a statutory day's work consist of eleven hours.

The desire for uniformity, together with the powerful voice of Colonel (afterwards Sir Joshua) Jebb, easily carried the day. The House of Lords Committee summed up with an almost vindictive emphasis in favour of tread-wheel and crank. Pointing out that an undesirably wide variety of methods of enforcing hard labour existed, the Committee considered it urgently necessary to secure an authoritative definition of the term by Act of Parliament. It was most undesirable that the wish to foster industrious habits or to make prison labour remunerative should in any way hamper the enforcement of hard labour as a penal measure. Moreover it was doubtful whether industrial labour in prisons could ever be continuously remunerative. The Committee declared itself unable to accept the statement that the crank or tread-wheel produced an irritating or deteriorating effect on the prisoner ; and it registered a special protest against the terms advanced by Inspector Perry. Nothing but the tread-wheel, the crank and shot drill, could, in the opinion of their lordships, be fitly described as hard labour. The Committee further proposed that, in default of a complete uniformity which the varying lengths of sentence rendered impossible, a daily working period of eight hours should be awarded to hard labour prisoners during the first three months of their first year's imprisonment, and of six hours for the second three months. This recommendation, it was pointed out, fell far short of giving practical effect to the powers of punishment sanctioned by the Act of 1824.

The findings of the Committee were intended to influence the Secretary of State in drafting his Bill. He, however, asked the inspectors for their views upon the verdict of the Committee. The inspectors once more denied that the tread-wheel, crank or shot drill constituted the only employment which could justly be designated hard labour, which was rather the fitting term to be bestowed upon any occupation whatever when imposed by task. They repeated their former statements as to the inequalities involved in labour at the two first-named machines and the failure of such tasks to exert a deterring influence ; and they added that shot drill had already been abandoned at Coldbath Fields Prison. They strongly advocated oakum picking as easily adjustable to each prisoner's powers and as permitting of work in solitude in his own cell. The uncertainty produced in the Home Secretary's mind by these irreconcilable divergences was reflected in his introduction of the Bill. "It is very easy," he observed,[1] "to say that certain employments shall be considered hard labour, but it is impossible without subjecting the authorities of prisons to great inconvenience, and depriving them of their fair discretion, to say, as recommended by the House of Lords Committee, that hard labour shall consist of nothing else but the tread-wheel, crank and shot drill. . . . I propose, therefore, to enumerate certain kinds of hard labour, with a view to indicate generally the views of Parliament in the subject. After that I should propose to give to the Visiting Justices, with the concurrence of the Secretary of State, a discretion as to what kind of hard labour shall be adopted where the enumerated kinds are not or cannot be enforced. A maximum of hours . . . now exists by law. I propose that that shall be also a minimum to be undergone by persons during the earlier part of a prisoner's sentence. I have adopted this view after communication with persons of experience, who think it extremely desirable, in order to stimulate the industry and good conduct of prisoners, that power should be given to the magistrates to diminish even the minimum amount of hard labour after a certain period of the sentence has expired."

In the 1865 Act, in its final form, the subject of labour received but scanty notice. It was laid down that hard labour should be divided into two classes, the first comprising work upon the tread-wheel, crank, shot drill, stone-breaking and kindred occupations ; while the second should admit of any hard bodily exertion that the Justices might provide. Not a word was said of industrial labour, unless, indeed, by way of implied condemnation in the specific injunction that every prison in which prisoners under sentence of hard labour were confined must provide the necessary appliances for executing the sentence. The Home Office was plainly hostile to any development of industrial or remunerative labour in gaols, but the Minister thought it more discreet not expressly to prohibit it.

(d) *Two Prison Reformers and a Scandal*

These three questions, the merits of the separate system, the principles of prison diet, and the character of prison labour, were, so far as concerned prisons, the main problems of legislators and administrators during this period. Great diligence and not a little ingenuity was shown by the Home Office in complying with the demands of the Acts of Parliament whilst nevertheless leaving some margin for local conditions or the exigencies of special cases. But it is impossible to avoid the conviction that the failure of prison administration of these years lay less in unwise decisions upon points of administrative detail, than in the refusal to conceive of the prison regimen as a whole. What was important was the net result on the prisoner's body and mind of his sojourn in gaol—a topic that needed fresh study by courageous minds prepared to ignore the phraseology of Acts of Parliament. To this deficiency must be ascribed the very scanty attention paid by prison inspectors and Parliamentary Committees alike to the subject of the prisoners' education. In the majority of gaols a perfunctory compliance with the tenth regulation of the Gaol Act was the utmost limit of mental training. Even in prisons like Norwich Castle, where the magistrates were sufficiently enthusiastic to enforce a love of learning under the penalty of close confinement in his cell for the defaulter, the instruction must have been derisory in view of the statement of the chaplain that " in no case has he suffered them (the prisoners) to learn to write except as a stimulant to further improvements ; he promises that they shall learn to write, as soon as they have got to a certain point in reading." This curious prejudice was shared by the chaplain of Swaffham House of Correction, who told the inspectors that it would be " very disadvantageous and productive of evil, if the prisoners were taught to write." With regard to teaching writing and arithmetic at Reading, "the chaplain feels that much discretion ought to be used in communicating this extent of secular knowledge to criminals. Such instruction might prove injurious both to the culprit himself and to society. . . . It is only, therefore, when the feelings and conduct of an offender give the hope of his reformation, that instruction, beyond that of teaching to read, is imparted."[1] Where a library existed, the books were not of a character to awaken a taste for literature in those who, in the most favourable instances, had only a rudimentary facility in reading and writing. At Maidstone Gaol the books had been assembled under the chaplain's direction and comprised " 13 Volumes of Tracts, 2 Volumes of Cheap Repository Tracts, 2 Volumes of Bishop Wilson's Sermons, *Bishop Home on the Psalms*, Law's *Serious Call*, Josephus on the Jewish Wars, Burnet on the Psalms, Bishop Watson's *Apology*, Bishop Porteous' *Evidences*, Jones on the Trinity, Bishop Hall's *Comfort to the Afflicted* " ; and we read also of Leslie's *Short Method with the Deists* ; and the same author's *Short and Ready Method with the Jews.*[2]

Such an absurd collection was by no means peculiar to Maidstone. In fact, education in gaol meant, to the chaplains of the time, little more than the reduction of the prisoners to a state of abject submission supposed to be produced by compelling them to contemplate pictures of the eternal sufferings to which they were destined.

In contrast with the obtuseness of prison administrators of this period appears the work of two reformers, of whom one devoted himself to direct legislative action, whilst the other tried experiments in prison regimen within the limits that the law imposed.

The first, Charles Pearson,[3] belongs to the generation educated by Sir Samuel Romilly and Sir T. Fowell

---

[1] *Prison Discipline*, by J. Field, second edition, 1848, Vol. I, p. 158.
[2] Parliamentary Papers, 1837, xxxii, 387.
[3] As to Charles Pearson, who is not included in the *Dictionary of National Biography*, see *The Prison Chaplain*, by W. L. Clay, 1861, pp. 256-60.

Buxton. He was, he tells us,[1] "Under-Sheriff of London and Middlesex for the years 1832, 1833, and 1834. During that time I may say that I almost resided in the prisons of the City. I . . . made a close investigation of the circumstances and motives of action of the prisoners confined there. I have for the last third of a century, visited almost every prison in every town that I have been in, both at home and abroad ; and I have read every work which has been published within my reach upon the subject. I have filled the stituation of Chairman of a Committee of the Corporation for the administration of justice, whose duty it was to inquire into these subjects ; and I now hold the office of City Solicitor, which is in the nature of a public prosecutor in the City, and my duties and habits have led me to a close and constant examination of all matters connected with prisons and prison discipline."

In 1847 he secured election to the House of Commons (for Lambeth) solely for the purpose of securing a decisive hearing to his views on prison reform. In January, 1849, he held a sort of convention of prison reformers in the City of London, at which he expounded his plans during six days' sessions. On May 15th of the same year he moved for the appointment of a committee to report on the practicability of establishing a uniform system of prison discipline. The Home Secretary promised to grant a committee early in the following session, and it was appointed in February, 1850. Pearson was naturally included in its membership ; but he also gave evidence before it, developing his opinions at length and embodying them in a separate report. His scheme was a medley of shrewd administrative reforms and wildly impracticable schemes of making prison labour economically profitable ; and it is chiefly interesting as foreshadowing some of the changes actually adopted in 1877.

Pearson aimed at a prison regimen that should be genuinely reformatory ; but what he contemplated was less the mental improvement of the prisoners

---

[1] Parliamentary Papers, 1850, xvii, p. 469.

themselves than the deterrence of the whole class from which they were drawn. A true intellectualist, he thought that if prison life was widely known to be irksome and hard, the potential criminal would weigh its discomfort against the difficulties of free labour ; and that he would reach in his own mind, the conclusion that " Liberty was the best policy." His powerful criticism of the existing system struck at the whole method of dealing with crime, from the sentence of the judge to the minutest detail in the administration of the gaol. He quoted statistics to show that committals had increased within three-quarters of a century more than tenfold ; from 1,174 in a year in Howard's time to 13,422 in a year shortly before 1850. After making allowance for the growth of population and the increased vigilance of the police, Pearson saw the main cause of the increase of criminals in the comfort of modern prison life. This he contrasted with the ordinary workmen's existence in the following terms : " I am," he said,[1] " stating a fact, and an opinion founded on my experience, that inasmuch as prisoners are now better lodged, better fed, better taught, better attended medically, and that the education and moral and religious instruction, and all the material and comforts of life are greater for prisoners than they are for people in free life, the conviction produced upon my mind is, that to this state of things is to be attributed a large amount of the increase of petty offences, by which persons find a refuge in a gaol ; and that the old system, wicked and bad as it was, did deter prisoners from the commission of crime. . . ." For an ideal prison administration, he proposed[2] " as one branch of punishment, enforced silence, perfect and absolute silence. . . . I contemplate . . . a restriction to seven hours sleep. There is nothing that a criminal so much covets as that dreamy, drowsy, lazy, idle, yawning, imaginative state, between sleeping and

---

[1] Parliamentary Papers, 1850, xvii, 472.
[2] Ibid., 1850, xvii, 509.

waking, when he is living, as it were, in an imaginative world. There is nothing which is calculated so to rivet upon a man his evil passions and feelings, as the habit which is fostered in our gaols of permitting, if not compelling, a man to be in a warm bed for 10 hours, such as we have heard of, between the sheets in a warm hammock, in a warm room at Reading. To tame the fiercest animals we resort to the privation of sleep, and there is no criminal who would not feel the utmost repugnance to that monotony of life which stinted him to a small measure of sleep, and required him to observe strictly the hours prescribed. I propose . . . that instead of a soft hammock he shall be on a hard bed. . . . The life of a prisoner should be punishment. . . . I propose that he shall be fed with the zero diet of the gaol, water and coarse bread. . . . I propose that he shall wear a coarse parti-coloured prison dress, I have no sympathy for the humanity that spares the nice feelings of a criminal by rejecting a prison dress ; it is necessary for security ; it is necessary for distinction ; and, in my judgment, it is one of the exigencies of a sound system of prison discipline that convicted prisoners should be all clothed in a prison dress."

With this discipline Pearson sought to combine pecuniary reparation for the offence committed against society thereby actually fostering habits of industry ; and to this end he proposed a drastic alteration of the sentences of imprisonment. " I contemplate," he urged before the committee,[1] " that the Secretary of State shall be entitled to commute the sentence of years or months, which shall have been passed by the Court, into a number of hours' labour, reckoning each day as ten hours, so that in case of a sentence of a year's imprisonment, it would be a sentence for 3,000 hours of labour ; taking 300 days in the year as the probable days of health and labour, and taking ten hours as being the mean quantity required. I propose that the prisoner

[1] Parliamentary Papers, 1850, xvii, 511.

shall be allowed to work out his liberation by his industry at that rate ; and that an hour's work shall entitle him to a halfpenny worth of food. . . ."

To effect these reforms, the whole administration had to be changed. The Secretary of State was to be entrusted with the duty of translating the sentences of the Court into terms applicable to the conditions of life. Pearson proposed that " all prisoners sentenced to reformatory punishment for any period between three months and four years, ought to suffer their sentence in district prisons, to be erected and maintained out of the Consolidated Fund, under the inspection of a Prison Board, responsible to Parliament, and acting under the authority of the Secretary of State."

" Such district prisons should be placed in suitable situations adjoining, or near to, the great trunk railways, and should be constructed in the most economical form consistent with the health and safe keeping of the criminals, with a sufficient quantity of enclosed land for their labour and maintenance.

" One uniform system of penitentiary punishment should be adopted in such district prisons, with a view to the punishment and reformation of criminals, under the supervision of the proposed Prison Board . . . a considerable portion of time (say 28 hours per week) should be devoted to public and private worship and mental and moral instruction, with seasons of solitude for reflection and self-examination ; . . . each prisoner should rest in a separate cell and should be allowed only a stinted number of hours (say 52 per week) for sleep on an iron or guardroom bedstead, with a mat, and as much bedding as is requisite for needful warmth and health ; . . . as well for punishment as to prevent mutual contamination, silence and non-intercourse between the prisoners ought to be constantly enforced ; that they should be required to perform continuous and hard work, to defray the charges of the establishment, and that the quantity and quality of their diet, and the duration of their imprisonment, should be made dependent upon their good conduct and amount of labour, reckoning a given number of hours' work (say ten) as cancelling one day of the sentence of the court.

" To teach prisoners to obtain dominion over their own actions, and to acquire fixed habits of industry and self-control, Mr. Pearson's plan . . . proposes further to stimulate the exercise of these indispensable requisites to a permanent reformation, by awarding to the most industrious and best conducted prisoners small gratuities, to be accumulated for them on their discharge, or, at their own option, to be applied in keeping alive domestic and social sympathies, by supplying some relief, however small, to their families, ofttimes suffering the extremities of destitution and disgrace from the misconduct of those to whom, by all the laws of God and man they had a right to look for protection and support."[1]

A characteristic detail remains to be stated. Pearson mistrusted the Government as manufacturer, and advised that the prisoners' labour should be left to contractors,[2] on the principle that, taking as an example agriculture, the contractor should pay a fixed rate for land, labour, and manure to the Government, and supply the needs of the prison at a fixed tariff, deriving his profit from the surplus. Assuming the prison to house 1,000 prisoners, 500 would be employed upon the land, the remainder working at other trades to meet the needs of prison life, in accordance with their former occupations. These also would be employed by contract, the contractors sending in their own officers to supervise the work, subject merely to the approval of the Government. This project was supported by the evidence of an experienced agriculturist, who undertook to contract for a period of years, paying 10d. a day for the daily labour of 500 prisoners. He professed himself ready to pay, at the expiration of two years, an additional sum of £500 a year for the land and manure,

---

[1] Parliamentary Papers, 1850, xvii, p. xxiv.
[2] Ibid., 1850, xvii, 483.

upon a contract to supply officers and prisoners at ordinary prices with all the food they might require. Two architects estimated the cost of a penitentiary on Pearson's lines, with all accessories, at less than £80,000.

Pearson's scheme of prison reform, the outcome of much study and practical experience, which had the approval of some competent prison administrators,[1] ended with the Committee of 1850. The Committee referred to it in terms of vague appreciation, but said that circumstances forbade its immediate realization.[2]

What was destined to be the last generation of the local administration of prisons was marked by many small experiments, but these were only in the details of gaol administration, and contemplated nothing beyond minor improvements. The figure of Captain Alexander Maconochie, is therefore, unique as one who was permitted to make actual trial of a system which avowedly demanded, as an essential condition of its fulfilment, a sweeping revision not only of prison methods but of society's whole outlook upon crime.[3] The system of punishment which he

---

[1] *Revelations of Prison Life,* by G. L. Chesterton, 1856, Vol. II, pp. 6-10, 48-52. On the other side, see *Substance of a Speech in reply to the Objections against Separate Confinement by C. Pearson,* Rev. S. Field, 1849 ; and *A Common-sense View of the Treatment of Criminals, with remarks on C. Pearson's plan,* by Rev. J. Kingsmill, 1850.

[2] Seven years later, at the very end of his life, Pearson tried to set on foot a public agitation. He wrote to the Lord Mayor of London, speaking in bitter terms of the Committee's neglect of his work, and calling upon the City to lead the way in a new campaign of prison reform. But he was not heeded. (*What is to be Done with Criminals ?* by Charles Pearson, 1857.)

[3] Alexander Maconochie (1787-1860), after service in the Royal Navy, in which he attained the rank of captain, became secretary to the Governor of Van Diemen's Land, and afterwards held appointments in the penal establishments, where he published his *Thoughts on Convict Management, and other subjects connected with the Australian Penal Colonies,* 1839. In 1846 he published *Crime and Punishment,* in many ways a remarkable book, which gained him no little notoriety in the little world of prison reformers. Appointed to be governor of the Birmingham Prison in 1849, he sought to put in operation his " mark " system, but the experiment was brought to an end in 1851 by his enforced retirement, as the Justices disapproved of his leniency. His assistant, Lieutenant Austin, appointed to succeed him, became infamous by the cruelties practised on the prisoners. Maconochie published various pamphlets, including *The Mark System and Prison Discipline,* 1845, 1846, and 1855 ; *On National Education as bearing on Crime,* 1855 ; and *Prison Discipline,* 1856, making more than

had designed was much more deeply rooted in psychology than at first sight appears. Scientific penology was then practically unknown in England ; and Maconochie, an officer in the Royal Navy, did not express his reasoning upon human nature in scientific terms, or, indeed, in language that did justice to his real, though necessarily imperfect, penetration. But a single paragraph, the conclusion to his book, entitled *Crime and Punishment,* published in 1846, strikes a new note in dealing with the criminal as something other than an object for pity and reprobation, or as a " scare-crow for the community."

" When men are smitten with adversity in ordinary life, and thus punished for previous follies or misconduct, they are not condemned to this adversity for a certain time, but until they can retrieve their position. They suffer under this task, they sorrow over it (but without resentment), they struggle with it, their characters improve under the various efforts and emotions called out by it . . . frequently they rise even higher than before. . . . And so it might be without punishments, if we would model them on the same type. They are now for the most part barbarous in every sense, in their want of skill and adaptation to high purpose, and in the crime and misery they thus gratuitously produce. We might make them beneficent in every sense, merely by copying the wisdom that is around us : and when this is fully understood, it is not to be imagined but that every

a score in all between 1838 and 1851. Maconochie's pioneer work in prison administration has been extravagantly praised in some quarters. To W. L. Clay he was " the noble-hearted old man " who " passed from maleficent neglect to beneficent death " (*The Prison Chaplain,* by W. L. Clay, 1861, p. 254). Matthew Davenport Hill, the Recorder of Birmingham, presided at a great celebration on his enforced retirement from the Birmingham Gaol in October, 1851, and praised him highly in *Meliora* (No. 13). He even included him in a volume of British worthies entitled *Our Exemplars,* 1860 (and new edition, 1880), declaring that " to Captain Maconochie is owing more than to any other one individual living, the rational and humane system of prison discipline which, though very slowly, yet surely, is extending itself through our land. His theoretic views and his practical application of them . . . have operated as a leaven upon public opinion, while they have been a polestar to individual effort." On the other hand, since his death in 1860, his efforts have been forgotten, and he is not even included in the *Dictionary of National Biography.*

lover of his kind will take even an eager interest in bringing about the change. The real difficulty is to influence the inquiry."[1]

Maconochie's judgment upon the existing prison discipline and his project of the " Mark System," rested on this view.

" In the management of our gaols," he writes,[2] " and other places of punishment, we at present attach too much importance to mere submission and obedience. We make the discipline in them military, overlooking a distinction, specifically drawn in the Mark System, and to which too much importance cannot be attached, between the objects of military and improved penal discipline. The ultimate purpose of military discipline is, to train men to act together ; but that of penal discipline is, to prepare them advantageously to separate. The objects being thus opposite, the processes should equally differ : but we make them the same, and reap accordingly. A good prisoner, it has been observed, is usually a bad man, and in the circumstances this result is sufficiently intelligible. Men kept for weeks, months, years, under a severe external pressure, and praised and encouraged in proportion as they submit to it, are in a direct course of preparation to yield to other forms of pressure as soon as they present themselves. They go in weak, or they would not probably be prisoners, and they come out still more enfeebled."

" The whole organization of the Mark System, then, is directed to cure this defect in our present penal arrangements. It offers wages (marks) to stimulate to voluntary as opposed to compulsory exertion ; it imposes fines in the same currency to deter from, rather than otherwise prevent misconduct ; it charges in them for supplies issued, in order to create an interest in voluntary moderation, and it promises the recovery of liberty only to a definite accumulation of them, over and above all that may be thus expended, thereby affording the strongest

---

[1] *Crime and Punishment,* p. 47.   [2] *Ibid,* pp. 28, 29.

stimulus to systematic exertion, prudence and self-command, the virtues best suited to sustain men against external temptation after discharge. The qualities of immediate obedience and submission are thus not sacrificed, for the absence of them may entail corresponding fines : but they are obtained by means of the exercise of the higher virtues, not by their being placed in abeyance. They will become proofs of strength, not weakness—and will cultivate what they thus exhibit."

Before the Committee of 1850, when he appeared to give evidence as governor of Birmingham Gaol, Maconochie explained his system in greater detail : " I think," he said,[1] " that . . . time sentences are the root of very nearly all the demoralization which exists in prisons. A man under a time sentence thinks only how he is to cheat that time, and while it away ; he evades labour, because he has no interest in it whatever, and he has no desire to please the officers under whom he is placed, because they cannot serve him essentially ; they cannot in any way promote his liberation. Besides this, in the desire to while away his time, he conjures up in his mind, and indulges, when he has the opportunity, in every sort of prurient and stimulative thought, and word, and even, where he can, act. . . . Now the whole of these evils would be remedied by introducing the system of task sentences. . . . A man under a task sentence would strip his coat to work, he would set a proper value upon time, which under a time sentence is hated, and he would exert himself in such a way that he could not but improve, *he must improve.* The difficulty in imposing task-sentences is the finding a general expression for labour. *I have proposed marks to represent labour.* . . . If the Secretary of State were to say that ten marks a day, as a matter of course, should be the expression for good fair average labour in a gaol, and were to give directions to governors and Visiting Justices to accommodate their calculations of piece-work to that scale, I experience

---

[1] Parliamentary Papers, 1850, xvii, pp. 447-8.

myself no difficulty whatever in so gaining a universal expression, and I think that no difficulty whatever would be found. The next thing which I think extremely injurious at present is a fixed diet irrespective altogether of exertion to earn it. Therefore when I gave a man ten marks a day I would require that he should keep himself, according to arrangement which could easily be made in the gaol, with the distinct understanding that only those marks that he could save out of his ten marks a day should count towards his liberation. . . . There would be a constant stimulus to effort, on the one hand, to gain marks, and to self-denial, on the other, to retain them With all that, there still would be no great gain unless an opportunity was afforded the prisoner of working in his cell in his overtime above the ten hours a day which he owes to the Government.

"I derive in Birmingham extreme benefit from that . . . the good effect of it is infinite ; it cannot be expressed ; it would make every prisoner stand, as it were, upon his own feet . . . adversity in ordinary society is not imposed for a certain time, but is imposed until a man can work out of it . . . and gaining the will to the requisite exertion in order to get out of it is, I think, the whole secret between that which is injuriously penal and beneficially penal. . . ." Sentence would, accordingly, be passed by creating against the prisoner a fictitious debt of 3,000 marks for example, and until he could earn them "he would show himself unfit to return to society, by wanting that diligence and industry, and exertion and prudence which are the only means by which a poor man can keep out of gaol."

The final point to be noted in Maconochie's plan is the provision intended to stimulate the social instinct in a prisoner, by means of the formation of groups of six or eight prisoners, after the lapse of a certain period passed in separate confinement, and "pooling" the marks of all the members in a common stock, so that the responsibility of the well-being of such a group rested upon each of its members.

Maconochie's system had the good fortune to be given a certain amount of trial, only to be overwhelmed in the greatest scandal of English prison history of the nineteenth century. In 1849 the Visiting Justices of Birmingham chose him as the first governor of their newly constructed gaol, expressly in order that he might give his theories a trial, so far as the statutes permitted. Unfortunately, as we infer, Maconochie spent too much time in promulgating his theories, and demonstrating them to committees and other inquirers, and too little to the detailed administration of the prison committed to his charge. Noticing some relaxation of discipline, the Justices promptly placed a large part of the current administration in the hands of a deputy governor, Lieutenant Austin, with whom Maconochie failed to agree. Austin introduced a regime of great severity, from which Maconochie dissented, but which he failed to prevent. He did, indeed, complain to the Justices in 1851 of Austin's severity, whereupon Austin tendered his resignation. This the Justices refused to accept, suggesting rather that Maconochie, with whose humanitarian views they failed altogether to sympathize, should himself relinquish his post. This enforced retirement in October, 1851, brought Maconochie's short-lived experiment to an end.

The whole episode was destined to be darkened by a terrible scandal. Early in 1853, eighteen months after Maconochie had left the prison, rumours became prevalent in Birmingham of terrible cruelties perpetrated in the Borough Gaol. At the inquest held upon a prisoner who had hanged himself, the chaplain casually mentioned the use of illegal methods of punishment, an allusion which attracted the attention of the Home Office inspector (Perry). He thereupon investigated the facts for himself, and reported to Lord Palmerston, the Home Secretary, that illegal punishments had been inflicted on an extensive scale. A committee of the Visiting Justices had in the meantime examined the question and reported on it to the Home Secretary. The character of this examination was unsatisfactory, as the Justices had refused to receive the evidence of certain persons, discharged officers and others, who wished to give evidence. The magistrates made a " whitewashing " report, contradicting both the prison inspector and a memorial presented by some of the inhabitants. A Royal Commission was appointed to probe the matter thoroughly.

The Report of this Commission, in conjunction with that of another Commission on cruelties in the Leicester prison, made a deep and lasting impression on public opinion ; and contributed not a little, though at an interval of a quarter of a century, to popular acquiescence in the measure of 1877.[1] The report revealed the existence in the Birmingham prison of a system of wanton and unmitigated tyranny, inflicted by way of punishment for failure to perform impossibly heavy tasks upon the crank. The crank in use had been copied from the type installed at Leicester, and, in the opinion of the Commissioners, called for much greater efforts than the weights attached to them appeared to imply. The daily task amounted to the performance of 10,000 revolutions by 6 o'clock. When this was not carried out, the prisoner was kept in the crank cell until late at night, and if the work was still not done, he was deprived of his supper, receiving no food till eight o'clock next morning, when he was given only bread and water. To meet the numerous cases of failure to comply with these demands, followed by outbursts of hysterical violence, a special punishment jacket—also a Leicester invention—was introduced. In the hands of Captain Maconochie its use had been strictly confined to prisoners who became dangerous.

[1] The report was published in 1854, and will be found in Vol. XXXI of the Parliamentary Papers of that year. The *Times* of September 15th, 1854, and the other newspapers of that month may also be consulted. The revelations formed the basis of the well-known novel and play by Charles Reade, *It's Never too Late to Mend* (1856).

But under Lieutenant Austin's rule, it was frequently used as a punishment for all kinds of offences, becoming in the Commissioners' words an "engine of positive torture." The case of suicide already alluded to arose immediately out of the infliction of prolonged periods of solitary confinement during which the punishment jacket was repeatedly applied. The Commissioners decided that the suicide was a "deliberate act of self-destruction, committed by the prisoner to relieve himself from bodily and mental suffering. . . ." They added the grave condemnation, "We are of opinion, that by the order and with the knowledge of the governor, he was punished illegally and cruelly, and was driven thereby to the commission of suicide."

The worst instances of cruelty were associated with this instrument of restraint. But there were other punishments involving illegality, not only on the part of the governor, but also on the part of the magistrates who sanctioned their use. A sentence of whipping, imposed upon two boys who had been guilty of repeated acts of disobedience, was carried out continuously day by day, twelve lashes being dealt on one day, and six more the next, *and so on until the boy became obedient.* The Commissioners recorded their "strong dissent from and disapprobation of such a scheme of punishment. The notion of persevering in the infliction of bodily pain day after day until by its repetition the 'obstinacy' of a prisoner is subdued, and he is coerced into a declaration of submission, appears to us to be opposed to every principle upon which punishment ought to be administered." Another abuse was the disregard of the distinction between separate and solitary confinement, so that the majority of prisoners were left utterly idle in isolated cells. Of the surgeon the Commissioners state :[1]

"We found that scarcely one of the more important regulations laid down for the guidance of this officer had been observed by him. Until a recent

[1] Parliamentary Papers, 1854, xxxi, p. 29.

period, he had not kept any record of the health of prisoners, on their admission into the prison, and on their discharge from it ; and his examination of prisoners on their admission, one object of which ought certainly to have been the ascertaining whether they were in a fit state to undergo the ordinary discipline, and to perform the ordinary labour, seems to have been made in a most careless and superficial manner, and without any reference to that question. In regard to all these instances of the non-performance of prescribed duties, however, it is to be observed, that perhaps the prisoners really suffered but little in consequence of them, since it was too evident, from the admission of Mr. Blount himself as well as from the statements of other witnesses, that his inspections of prisoners, when performed, were of such a character as to be generally quite useless as means of detecting illness, and that although instances of great suffering and injury to health from excessive labour and want of food, must constantly have come under his notice, he rarely interfered to relieve the prisoners from the operations of a discipline and modes of punishment which few could have been capable of supporting. . . . The treatment of those really sick, or at least complaining of illness, was characterized by the same contravention of rules, and the same absence of all apparent sympathy with the persons so afflicted. It is very doubtful whether such as daily complained of illness, and desired medical aid, were regularly visited by Mr. Blount. It is certain that he frequently refused them means of relief when he did visit them. . . . It is lamentable enough that several prisoners have thus died in their cells, some to the last lying in their hammocks, although there was a part of the building purposely fitted up as an infirmary for the reception of the sick ; but that which especially marks the small amount of care exercised by the governor and the surgeon, who must here both be held in different degrees responsible with regard to unfortunate fellowmen at the point of death, whose sole guardians they were, is the fact that on three occasions prisoners have died in their cells with no fellow creatures present ; being found dead by the warder entering some time afterwards."

The Commissioners summarized their judgment of the administration of the gaol in terms of the utmost severity.[2]

"With respect to Captain Maconochie, we are fully satisfied that he is a gentleman of humanity and benevolence whose sole object in undertaking the government of the prison, was to promote the reformation of the prisoners, and the well-being of society, by means of the system of moral discipline which he hoped to establish there. Nevertheless, as we have seen, he was led in the pursuance of these objects to sanction the infliction of punishments which were not warranted by the law and the employment of which was the more to be regretted, inasmuch as such a course is apt to lead to the use, in the hands of persons not restrained by the same benevolent feelings, of practices equally illegal, and more objectionable from their greater frequency and their greater severity.

"Again, we have no reason to doubt that Lieut. Austin assumed the government of the prison with the *bona fide* intention and desire of doing his duty. . . . Unhappily, however, he appears almost from the first to have adopted the notion, that the principle of strict separation, combined with hard labour, was to be effectually maintained by no other means than by the instant infliction of punishment for every infraction of the discipline or failure in the labour ; and we have already seen that, not content with the administration of punishments authorized by the law, nor with the application of those of an unlawful kind which had existed in the time of Captain Maconochie, he introduced of his own authority another, not only utterly illegal, but most objectionable from its painful, cruel, and exasperating character, which he practised with a frequency distressing to hear of, for offences often too trivial to call for any severity of punishment at all, and upon offenders quite unfit to be subjected to it, combining with it also other inflictions and privations, and directing and witnessing their application with a lamentable indifference to human suffering, until the penal system of the gaol became almost a uniform system of the application of pain and terror. . . . For the punishment of the strait jacket, Lieut. Austin never obtained or asked the sanction of the magistrates ; he never made it known to the inspector of prisons ; and he discouraged as much as he could all remonstrance against or interference with it on the part of the officers of the prison. Many of the severities actually practised were probably unknown to him, but he must be held to a great extent morally responsible for them all. And, upon the whole, we are constrained to declare our conviction that his conduct in his office, as disclosed in evidence before us, was deserving of the most severe censure."

Of the Visiting Magistrates as a body, the Commissioners[1] were " compelled to say that they seem from their absolute confidence in Lieut. Austin's administrative capacity, to have suffered the performance of their duty almost to degenerate into a mere routine form. In truth, no real supervision was exercised by them. They met once a week at their board room in the gaol ; they had read to them the formal reports of the events and the statistics of the prison, but they never examined either the journals of the officers, or the books in which the discipline and its effects were or ought to have been recorded, and from which, imperfect as they were, they would have learned, or at least must have suspected the existence of much illegal punishment and much deplorable suffering. . . . The governor and the surgeon habitually neglected the rules of the prison without their interference, and to a great extent without their knowledge. The attempts at suicide, which occurred so often in the gaol and which must have been reported

---

[1] Parliamentary Papers, 1854, xxxi, p. 37.

to them, appear hardly to have excited their serious attention."

A blaze of public indignation followed the work of the Commissioners. On the enforced resignation of the governor and the surgeon the citizens held a meeting to protest against the Visiting Magistrates taking it upon themselves to select the successors, and after a declaration to the effect that the Justices had forfeited all claim to the confidence of the people of Birmingham, to demand the appointment of a stipendiary magistrate. Austin, the governor, and Blount, the surgeon, were criminally proceeded against, and found guilty, the first named being sentenced to three months imprisonment, which—we fear, characteristically enough—he was allowed to serve as a first-class misdemeanant. Blount, the surgeon, was never even called up to receive sentence, and was allowed to go unpunished.[1]

The report of the Commission on the Leicester prison revealed cruelties similar in character to those at Birmingham—the imposition of excessive tasks at the crank, the frequent infliction of cruel punishments for failure to perform these tasks, including repeated floggings and reduction of food. It was this last that led to exposure, through the emaciated condition of one of the victims attracting the attention of the inspector. The revelations, however, were less serious than in the Birmingham case, the Commissioners expressing the opinion that "no grave personal imputation rests upon any of the persons concerned in the government of Leicester County Gaol." The governor and surgeon were both acquitted of any charge of cruelty, and the blame fell mainly upon the Visiting Magistrates. A lengthy correspondence took place between the Home Office and the Justices, in the course of which the latter showed themselves to be unaware of the illegality of their action in failing to acquaint the inspector or the

---

[1] For the trial of Austin and Blount in August, 1855, see *Annual Register* for 1855, pp. 120-4, and *Suggestions for the Repression of Crime*, by Matthew Davenport Hill (who was Recorder of Birmingham at the time), 1857, pp. 232-8.

Secretary of State with their intention of adopting an entirely new punishment, the stoppage of meals. This expedient they referred to somewhat disingenuously as a " postponement " of meals ; and they proceeded to justify its enforcement by pointing out that it was the only punishment left to them in a prison in which " separate confinement " was inflicted upon all prisoners as a general regimen and not reserved as a punishment for acts of insubordination. They ignored, that is to say, the distinction to which the Home Office clung, between separate and solitary confinement.

With the scandalous revelations of Birmingham and Leicester we close the first period of the era of Central Supervision and Control. In particular details, the cruelties in those prisons were, we may hope, exceptional. Yet enough is known—enough has perhaps been described in the foregoing pages— of what was happening in the other prisons of the time to arouse the most disquieting suspicions. The most uncomfortable reflection is that the worst-administered prisons were not those in which the evils were greatest. The misery of the prisoners, and as we must now acknowledge, even the cruelty with which they were unwittingly treated, may have been at their worst where the prison regimen had been most deliberately devised, and the system most exactly applied. It should for ever make for humility in prison administrators to reflect that it is doubtful whether the sum of human suffering was not in this period, during long stretches of years, greater at Millbank and Pentonville penitentiaries, than at the worst of the prisons under Local Government. And, as we shall see in the ensuing chapter, it was not for many years that the lesson was learnt—if, indeed, it has yet been learnt.

The very idea of cellular isolation by day as well as by night, which dominates this period, came, in the twentieth century, to be condemned by Enrico Ferri as " one of the great aberrations of the nineteenth century."[1] We may recall the burning indignation of Charles Dickens over what he saw of its application in the United States, "In its intention," he said, "I am well convinced that it is kind, humane, and meant for reformation ; but I am persuaded that those who devised this system of prison discipline, and those benevolent gentlemen who carry it into execution, do not know what it is they are doing. I believe that very few men are capable of estimating the immense amount of torture and agony which this dreadful punishment, prolonged for years, inflicts upon the sufferers. . . . I hesitated once, debating with myself whether if I had the power of saying 'yes,' or 'no,' I would allow it to be tried in certain cases, where the terms of imprisonment were short ; but now I solemnly declare that with no rewards or honours could I walk a happy man beneath the open sky by day or lay me down upon my bed at night with the consciousness that one human creature for any length of time, no matter what, lay suffering this unknown punishment in his silent cell, and I the cause or I consenting to it in the least degree."[2]

The Home Office officials, as we have seen, and their allies among prison reformers, always denied that the Separate System which they advocated was equivalent to solitary confinement. But, as has been well said, " they were infatuated about isolation. They would have the system, the whole system and nothing but the system. They made the separation so thorough that its depressing influence took all the starch out of the prisoners' characters, and rendered both their wits and their wills limp and flabby."[3]

What it is hard to forgive is the deluded self-complacency which led them to ignore the way the system actually worked. How could Colonel Jebb,[4]

<hr/>

[1] *Modern Systems of Criminality*, by C. Bernaldo de Quiros, 1911.
[2] *American Notes*, Chapter VII, " Philadelphia and its Solitary Prison," pp. 119-120, by Charles Dickens, 1842.
[3] *Our Convict Systems*, by W. L. Clay, 1862, p. 19.
[4] Colonel (afterwards Sir) Joshua Jebb (1793-1863), see *Dictionary of National Biography*, was the distinguished officer of the Royal Engineers whom the Home Office secured, from 1837 onwards, as technical adviser in the construction of cellular prisons. In 1844, he was formally appointed

for instance, who knew how the prisons were administered, bring himself to assert " that *scarcely an hour* in the day will pass without [the convict] seeing one or other of the prison officers," or that will not be taken up with "constant employment or labour "?[1]

It was a strange perversion of the facts for the chaplain of Pentonville Prison to declare that, whilst the convict " is kept rigidly apart from other criminals, *he is allowed as much intercourse with instructors and officers* as is compatible with judicious economy."[2]

Right down to 1896 the Secretary of the Howard Association, completely satisfied with the system as enforced by the Prison Commissioners, could assure the public that the convicts "have *numerous visits* in their cells from the officers, chaplain, schoolmaster, and from suitable persons from outside, together with industrial occupation, books, instruction and daily exercise."[3]   On the other hand, the advocates of " the Silent System," and work in association—where " real isolation is replaced by a fictitious, artificial and superficial one "[4]—were equally disingenuous. They ignored the evil effect of the incitement to deceit and evasion, the incessant breaches of the rule and the frequent punishments, and they even denied that the enforcement of silence was injurious. " The legitimate opportunities," said the governor of Coldbath Fields Prison, "nay, the demands, for the use of speech are

to be Inspector-General of Military Prisons, and also to the new post of Surveyor-General of Prisons, which he combined, in 1850, with the chairmanship of the then established Board of Directors of Convict Prisons. He was made K.C.B. in 1859.   Right down to his death, in 1863, he exercised a dominative influence in prison administration.   His book, *Modern Prisons, their Construction and Ventilation*, 1844, governed the structure of subsequently erected places of imprisonment all over the world.   A posthumous volume containing many of his official reports and memoranda, entitled *Reports and Observations on the Discipline and Management of Convict Prisons*, was edited by his friend, the Earl of Chichester.

   [1] *Modern Prisons : Their Construction and Ventilation*, by Colonel (afterwards Sir Joshua) Jebb, 1844, p. 10.
   [2] *Results of Separate Confinement at Pentonville*, by Rev. J. T. Burt, 1852. See also *Prisons and Prisoners*, by Joseph Adshead, 1845.
   [3] *Penological and Preventive Principles*, by W. Tallack, edition of 1896, p. 120.
   [4] *Modern Systems of Criminality*, by C. Bernaldo de Quiros, 1911, pp. 180-3.

numerous. The daily responses in chapel, communications with the governor, the chaplain, the schoolmaster and various officers, all tend healthfully to employ the tongue."[1]

It is to be feared that a potent influence in the general adoption of the system of cellular isolation was the fact, as stated in 1850, that " the officials like it ; it gives them very little trouble, so, without pretending to understand its complicated effects, moral or mental, they almost all swear by it."[2]

[1] *Revelations of Prison Life*, by G. L. Chesterton, 1856, Vol. II, p. 27. On the other hand, we do not know that there is any evidence of silence in gaol producing actual dumbness, as described in the novel, *La Fille Elisa*, by Edmond de Goncourt.

[2] *London Prisons*, by W. Hepworth Dixon, 1850, p. 154. See, on the whole subject, *A System of Penal Discipline, with a Report on the Treatment of Prisoners in Great Britain and Van Diemen's Land*, by Henry P. Fry, 1850 ; and *Prisons and Reformatories, being the Transactions of the International Penitentiary Congress*, by Edwin Pears, 1872.

CHAPTER X

PENAL SERVITUDE

ONCE more we have to interpose a reference to the establishment of prisons under the National Government. Just as transportation to North America became impracticable after 1776, so transportation to New South Wales had to be given up in 1840.[1] Just as the establishment of the hulks and the erection of Millbank Prison followed from the first interruption of transportation, so the construction of Pentonville Prison in 1842, as a model on the cellular plan for the purpose of working out in practice a new system of prison discipline, followed on the second interruption. After a decade of experiment the new system was definitely established by the Penal Servitude Acts of 1853 and 1857.

The system of prison administration introduced by these Acts, and subsequently amended by statutes of 1864, 1871 and 1891, was a combination of all that was then deemed most enlightened.[2] Contrary to the

[1] The Parliamentary inquiry of 1837 condemned the system absolutely, "as being unequal, without terror to the criminal class, corrupting to both convicts and colonists, and extravagant from the point of expense." (*The English Prison System*, by Sir Evelyn Ruggles-Brise, 1921, p. 24). Transportation to New South Wales was abolished by Order in Council in 1840. For Van Diemen's Land there was an attempt at a system of "progressive stages," under which the convicts could gradually earn their freedom and pardon; but this proved a demoralizing failure, and further transportation was stopped in 1846. Under a new system of "Ticket of Leave" men continued to be sent thither until 1852, when the colony (renamed Tasmania) refused to receive any more. Transportation to the Swan River Settlement (now Western Australia) continued until 1867, the last convicts remaining until 1872. For reference to authorities as to the transportation system, see footnote on p. 44.

[2] For the system of Penal Servitude, see the successive Reports of the Commissioners appointed in 1842, and those of the subsequent Parliamentary Inquiries, notably the Royal Commissions of 1863 and 1878-9,

common impression, its essential feature was not,
and has never been, any specially rigorous enforcement of penal labour. It would, indeed, have been
difficult to have devised any harder or more continuous labour than that exacted in many of the prisons
under Local Government,[1] notably as revealed to a
horrified public opinion by the reports of the Royal
Commissions on the Birmingham and Leicester gaols.
The essential features of Penal Servitude in English
prison history (quite unlike that of *travaux forcés*
in France, for which it has often been mistaken)
have been the combination of (*a*) the enforcement, for
a fixed period (originally eighteen months) of rigorous cellular isolation and complete non-intercourse,
day and night, accompanied by the plank bed,
a restricted diet, a prescribed task of isolated
labour, and deprivation of all humanizing privileges ;
with (*b*) a subsequent period of associated labour

and the Departmental Committee of 1895 ; *The Punishment and Prevention of Crime,* by Sir Edmund Du Cane, 1885, Ch. VI, " Penal Servitude" ;
*An account of the manner in which sentences of Penal Servitude are carried
out,* by the same, 1882 ; *The Criminal Prisons of London,* by H. Mayhew
and J. Binny, 1862 ; *Scenes from a Silent World,* by F. Scougall, 1888 ;
The Story of Dartmoor Prison, by Sir Basil Thomson, 1907 ; *Secrets of
the Prison House,* 2 vols, 1894, and *Fifty Years of Public Service,* by A.
Griffiths, 1904 ; *The Treatment of Prisoners,* 1904 ; *Wards of the State :
an Official View of Prison and the Prisoner,* by T. Hopkins, 1913 ; *In an
Unknown Prison Land,* by George Griffith ; *Our Prison System,* by A.
Cook, 1914, and *Las Prisones de Londres y las nuestras,* by F. Cabrerizo,
1911. On another plane, but affording some valuable suggestions and
criticisms are such books (some of them dealing only with local prisons)
as *Six Years in the Prisons of England,* by a merchant (Frank Henderson),
1868 ; *A Month in Her Majesty's Prison, Leicester,* by T. P. Barrow,
1882 ; *Twelve Months in an English Prison,* by S. W. Fletcher, 1884 ;
Eighteen Months' Imprisonment, by D. S., 1884 ; *Leaves from a Prison
Diary,* by Michael Davitt, 2 vols, 1885 ; *Five Years' Penal Servitude*
(Anon.), 1882 ; *Life in English Prisons* (Anon.), 1896 ; *Pentonville Prison
from Within* (Anon.), 1904 ; *The Mark of the Broad Arrow,* by a Convict,
1903 ; *Penal Servitude,* by Lord William Nevill, 1903 ; *Twenty-five Years
in Seventeen Prisons,* by No. 7, 1903, second edition, 1906 ; *Mrs. Maybrick's
Own Story : My Fifteen Lost Years,* 1905 ; *My Prison Life,* by Jabez
S. Balfour, 1907 ; *A Burglar in Baulk,* 1910, and *A Holiday in Gaol,*
1911, both by Frederic Martyn ; *My Life in Prison,* by D. Lowrie, 1912 ;
and *Prisons and Prisoners,* by Lady Constance Lytton, 1914.

[1] The phrase, "imprisonment with hard labour " was first used in
the Statute, 16 George III, c. 43, as an alternative for transportation.
Presently, as prison discipline stiffened, all those sentenced to imprisonment were put to penal labour, usually of the same kind. Any difference
between " imprisonment " and " imprisonment with hard labour " came
to lie in other aspects of prison regimen than in the kind or amount of
labour expected.

under the Silent System, originally upon public works. in the open air ; at first (until 1864) with increased diet, and, later, with opportunities for " progressive stages " of improvement in conditions, and for earning a partial remission of the original sentence ; and (c) conditional discharge on a " Ticket of Leave," originally to an overseas colony, and subsequently at home under police supervision for a prescribed period.[1]

In order that the new system might be worked under the best conditions money was not spared for the erection of new cellular prisons on the latest model, first at Pentonville at a cost of £85,000 in 1842 ; then at the Isle of Portland in 1848 ; then at Dartmoor, where the old place of confinement of the French prisoners of war was practically rebuilt at great expense in 1850 ; in 1853 Brixton Prison was taken over from the Surrey Justices and expensively adapted for the reception of all the women convicts ; and in 1856 a large prison for men was opened at Chatham. Presently more than five thousand men or women were under this " most enlightened treatment," the number increasing by 1880 to more than 10,000 in thirteen different prisons.

As we are not writing the history of national prison administration, we cannot here examine the results of the system of Penal Servitude, upon which, in the course of the latter half of the nineteenth cen-

[1] The most novel feature in the system was that subsequently known as the " Progressive Stages " ; essentially the principle of inducing docility and diligence in the prisoners by the stimulus of rewards in the shape of more comfortable conditions, and partial remission of sentence. This, we are now told, was due chiefly to " the tireless efforts made at that time by Sir Joshua Jebb and his colleagues " at the Home Office (*The English Prison System*, by Sir Evelyn Ruggles-Brise, 1921, p. 29). It was applied experimentally in Ireland by Sir Joshua Jebb, and merely continued by Captain (afterwards Sir Walter) Crofton, Chairman of Irish Prisons Board, whose evidence on Progressive Stages and Police Supervision before the House of Commons Committee of 1855 has led to the system being ascribed to him. The " mark system," as we have mentioned, had already been invented by Captain Maconochie. *Reports and Observations on the Discipline and Management of Convict Prisons*, by Sir Joshua Jebb, edited by the Earl of Chichester, is largely made up of detailed criticisms of the differences between the English and Irish systems. See also *Reformatory Prison Discipline as Developed by Sir Walter Crofton*, by Mary Carpenter, 1872.

tury, there was perpetual controversy. What is important is that the prison regimen that it prescribed inevitably became, as "the most enlightened" of the time, the type towards which the regimen of the prisons under Local Government was steadily made to approximate. What is significant is that this regimen, even where applied under the most advantageous conditions, had to be successively modified, in one feature after another, on the Home Office itself becoming convinced of the very serious injury that it was inflicting on the unfortunate prisoners.

We can give only a few examples. At Pentonville Prison,[1] for instance, where what was euphemistically called the separate system was applied in full vigour, the convicts admitted were, from 1843 to 1849, most carefully selected for their physical fitness to stand the strain of hard labour under discipline. The effect on them of " eighteen months solitary " was, to the bewilderment of the Commissioners of Convict Prisons, " a great number of cases of death and of insanity "—to wit in each year as many as 120 cases per 10,000 of mental disease, says the prison doctor, being a ratio twenty times as great as in, not the general population, but all the other English prisons of the time. Accordingly the period of confinement in Pentonville Prison was reduced, first to twelve months and subsequently to nine months. Still " there occurred an unusually large number of cases of mental affection among the prisoners, and it was therefore deemed necessary to increase the amount of exercise in the open air, and to introduce the plan of brisk walking, as pursued at Wakefield "[2] For half a century we may trace in the official reports this effect of the " Separate System " on the mental

[1] For the administration and regimen at Pentonville see, in particular, apart from the official reports, *The Criminal Prisons of London*, by H. Mayhew and J. Binny, 1862 ; *London Prisons*, by W. Hepworth Dixon, 1850 ; *Results of Separate Confinement at Pentonville*, by Rev. J. T. Burt, 1852 ; *Pentonville Prison from Within* (Anon.), 1904 ; and the enthusiastic German description, *England's Mustergefangniss in Pentonville*, by Dr. N. H. Julius, 1846.

[2] Reports of Commissioners of Convict Prisons, 1853 ; *The Criminal Prisons of London*, by H. Mayhew and J. Binny, 1862, p. 115.

health of the prisoners, notably in the continual attempts of the Home Office to discover ways of mitigation compatible with the retention of the system itself. Unfortunately, the statistics of health, insanity and suicide among prisoners, which appear portentous, have been so manipulated and discredited from one side or another, as to be inconclusive. What is clear is that far more prisoners have contracted tuberculosis, gone out of their minds or committed suicide than the prison authorities have liked.[1]

What is, we think, significant is the elaboration of the precautions taken. For any consideration of the effect of the regimen on those who were subjected to it, whether as to the degree of their suffering or as to the upsetting of their sanity, the number of suicides in prison is not so eloquent as the extraordinary physical precautions that the Prison Commissioners have been successively driven to take in order to prevent attempts at suicide.[2] The percentage of cases of prisoners being driven actually mad, and transferred to lunatic asylums, is nowadays not so significant as the relaxations which had to be introduced in order to stave off insanity. What we do not find is any adequate study of the effect of the whole regimen (including so near an approach to solitary confinement) on the physical and mental state of those prisoners whose sanity just survived their ordeal. "In a medical point of view," deposed, very early in the controversy, a doctor of great ex-

[1] Whatever there may be to be said against the regimen at Coldbath Fields Prison, it is to its credit that it could be said that, whereas the wide freedom of movement allowed made suicide possible, " twenty years elapsed . . . without our having had to deplore a single suicide. For many years, the daily average number of convicts exceeded one thousand " (*Revelations of Prison Life*, by G. L. Chesterton, 1856, Vol. II, p. 80).

[2] Thus various alterations were successively made in the internal fittings of the cells so as to make suicide by hanging extremely difficult ; and when it was found that prisoners got into such a state of mind that numbers of them could not be restrained from jumping from the upper corridors, and so being dashed to pieces, the action taken by the prison authorities was, not to alter the regimen which produced that state of mind, but, without change in the regimen, merely to cover in all upper corridors by strong wire netting, so that jumping to destruction became physically impossible. (See Annual Report of the Prison Commissioners, 1890, Appendix 18.) This is typical of many similar precautions.

perience, " I think there can be no question but that separate or solitary confinement acts injuriously, *from first to last*, on the health and constitution of anyone subjected to it."[1] "As to convicts on discharge," testified an experienced Salvation Army officer in 1895, " I should like to say that we find a greater number of them incapable of pursuing any ordinary occupation. They are mentally weak and wasted, requiring careful treatment for months."[2] Generation after generation, the English prison system, under the most enlightened administration of the time, seems to have continued to return its victims to the world of competitive industry in a state of mind and body in which most of them must necessarily have had the greatest difficulty in earning a livelihood by honest work. We cannot find that the Home Office of this period had any scientific investigation made of the results of penal servitude on the industrial capacity of the discharged convict, or even on his comparative efficiency on admission and discharge respectively.

But this is not the place in which to estimate the success or failure of the system of Penal Servitude in the prisons under Home Office administration. We must return to our account of prisons under Local Government, bearing in mind the strong and persistent " pull " on prison regimen which the system of Penal Servitude henceforth exerted on Justices of the Peace and Home Secretaries alike.

[1] Dr. Attfield, long resident surgeon at Millbank Prison, and afterwards Medical Superintendent of the West Australian Convict Establishment, quoted in *Criminal Correction*, by C. P. Measor, 1864, p. 54.

[2] Colonel Baker, of the Salvation Army, Evidence before the Departmental Committee of 1895, p. 279.

CHAPTER XI

CENTRAL SUPERVISION AND CONTROL :
SECOND PERIOD, 1865-1877

WE come now to the assumption by the Home Office
of increased powers of control. After the revelations
of the Royal Commissions on the Birmingham and
Leicester prisons in 1854, we see the inspection of
the Home Office becoming steadily more minute,
vigilant and continuous ; and the criticism and instructions addressed to those responsible for the
administration of the prisons under Local Government taking a more mandatory tone. Public opinion
was uneasy, but favoured no particular reform. The
Royal Commission of 1847 had definitely concluded
that the absolute separation of prisoners from each
other was the only sound basis upon which a reformatory discipline could be established with any reasonable hope of success. The Select Committee of the
House of Commons under Sir George Grey, initiated,
as we have described, by Charles Pearson, had
endorsed that opinion in 1850. Moreover a whole
generation of experience had convinced the Home
Office officials that a rigorous application of the
Separate System, whatever might be its effect on the
prisoners, was the only practicable alternative to the
obvious evils of promiscuous association which still
characterized the majority of the county, borough
and franchise prisons. Hence we see, after the
Crimean War, a steady approximation to this system
all over the country.

A further step had now to be taken. The Home

Office, it must be remembered, could not, at that date, peremptorily order the County Justices or the Municipal Corporations to rebuild or alter their prisons, or even amend their prison rules. The Act of 1835 had required all rules framed by local prison authorities to be submitted for the approval of the Secretary of State, but did not enable him to require new rules to be made. An Act of 1844 had empowered him to appoint a Surveyor-General of Prisons, who could exercise influence on plans for new buildings, but could not require new prisons to be built. No action was taken on the proposal for a Central Prison Authority, which was made in 1850 by the Select Committee, which Charles Pearson had got appointed ; but its recommendations that the Separate System, as carried out in Pentonville Prison, should be generally applied to all prisons (though for not more than twelve months for each prisoner) gradually became increasingly influential. Every reforming Justice of the Peace, who, in these years, got effected any improvement in the county gaol, worked in the direction of cellular isolation ; but there was still no power to make this or any other system universal, and a couple of hundred separate prison authorities could not possibly arrive at uniformity.

The opportunity for a step forward came in the opening of the 'sixties. A sudden increase in the number of robberies with violence in the streets of London led to a renewed outburst of the popular demand for greater severity in the treatment of convicted prisoners. The rapid passing, in the session of 1862, of the so-called "Garotters' Act," inflicting flogging on convicted garotters, did not satiate the popular craving for vengeance. In 1863 a Select Committee of the House of Lords on prisons and prison discipline, over which the Earl of Carnarvon presided, led to a drastic tightening up of the administration, under which not the "professional criminal" only, but all the unfortunate inmates of the gaols, suffered for a whole generation. The

Committee showed little trace of the humane consideration for the well-being of the prisoners, which had inspired Howard and Neild, Buxton and Maconochie. It had lost all patience with indolent or obstructive Justices of the Peace. It specifically condemned the lack of uniformity that prevailed in the 193 local prisons which were, in 1863, still maintained in England and Wales alone, and which differed widely, alike in the severity of the punishment and in the treatment of the prisoners. The Committee once more insisted on a general application of the Separate System, in all its rigour, not because it was reformatory, but expressly because it was terrible to criminals. The full period of nine months rigid cellular confinement, day and night, was to be henceforth insisted on for all convicts, expressly because of the deterrent effect that it was believed to have. "We think, too," said the Committee, "that this wholesome effect on their minds might be increased" by even greater severity! In Ireland, they found, the prisoners were put on a specially low diet for the first four months. Even more ingenious seemed to their lordships the Irish plan of giving to the convicts, thus rigidly confined to their cells, only the simplest and most routine drudgery by way of work, expressly because this enabled the governor to dispense with the visits to the cells of the instructors, which were thought to "mitigate the irksomeness of separate confinement." The Lords Committee greatly favoured these ingenious devices, which they hoped would "give a more deterrent character to separate imprisonment in the English prisons," on every inmate of which, young and old, male and female, first offender and hardened recidivist, the Lords declared that "hard labour, hard fare, and a hard bed," should be inflicted.

No protest was made against Lord Carnarvon's report,[1] and steps were at once taken to act upon its

[1] There seems to have been a falling off in the output of books on prisons in the eighteen-sixties. We may mention three volumes by F. W. Robinson, *Female Life in Prison,* 1862 ; *Memoirs of Jane Cameron, female convict,*

terrible recommendations. The fixed wooden bed
was installed in every cell and the hammock removed.
The cell doors, which had been opened in the daytime after the first two months of each man's sentence, were henceforth kept closed and bolted
during the whole nine months. The assemblage of
selected convicts in educational classes was discontinued. "Everything was done to render the
separation real and complete; exercise was taken
in separate yards, and masks were worn to prevent
recognition."[1] On the tread-wheel, and even in
attendance at divine service in the chapel, the most
elaborate structural arrangements were made to
prevent the prisoners from seeing each other. The
Directors of Convict Prisons avowed in their report
that their object was to make the universal term of
strict cellular isolation as deterrent as possible. The
Home Office lost no time in getting new legislation,
which should enable the same regimen to be enforced
in all the local prisons. The Prisons Act of 1865
effected what the County Justices and Municipal
Corporations regarded as a revolution, by depriving
them, so far as their maintenance of prisons was concerned, of their immemorial autonomy.[2] Every prison

1864; and *Prison Characters*, 1866, all three " by a Prison Matron "; the
two volumes by Mary Carpenter, entitled *Our Convicts*, 1864; also three books
by an ex-official, C. P. Measor, entitled *The Convict Service*, 1861, *Criminal
Correction*, 1864; and *The Utilization of the Criminal*, 1869. More suggestive is Archbishop W. B. Ullathorne's essay *On the Management of Criminals*,
1866, in which he explains why solitary confinement of criminals is unfavourable to repentance. We may mention also the two pamphlets by Sir
Walter Crofton, *Convict Systems and Transportation*, 1863; and *The
Immunity of " Habitual" Criminals*, 1861. We have already cited *The
Criminal Prisons of London*, by Henry Mayhew and John Binny, not published until 1862, but compiled years previously; and *Six Years in the
Prisons of England*, by a Merchant (Frank Henderson), 1868.

[1] *The English Prison System*, by Sir E. Ruggles-Brise, 1921, p. 65. The
mask, which was discontinued in English prisons at the end of the nineteenth century, was continued in Continental prisons. It was only discontinued in Belgium in 1920, when M. Emile Vandervelde was Minister of
Justice.

[2] We may note, so far as concerned the town prisons, that although, in
municipalities, the Town Council remained the " prison authority," the
Borough Justices were given the power of appointing the prison officers,
with the result that they became, even in those towns where this had
previously not been the case, the actual administrators of the prison.
But Local Acts were unaffected; and in Bath, for instance, the Town
Council made the appointments.

authority was positively required by the Act to provide separate cells for all the prisoners, duly certified by the Inspector of Prisons as being structurally and in all other respects in accordance with the statutory requirements. The old distinction between the gaol and the House of Correction was abolished. The prisoners had all to be subjected to penal labour in prescribed forms, either (first-class) on the tread-wheel, the crank or the capstan, or at shot drill or stone breaking, or (second-class) such other labour that the Secretary of State might approve. All prisoners over sixteen were required to be kept to these prescribed forms of first-class labour for at least three months, before they could even qualify for second-class labour. The local authorities were specifically required to frame new dietaries, which had to be such as the Secretary of State might approve. The Secretary of State was given effective means of enforcing compliance with all these statutory requirements by being expressly authorized to withhold, at his sole discretion, the Grant in Aid of the prison expenditure. The governor of the prison was authorized, without any safeguarding conditions, of his own volition to punish any prisoner by close confinement for three days and nights on bread and water. In addition, the Visiting Justices could order one whole month in a punishment cell, or (for a prisoner sentenced to hard labour) a flogging. The use of irons or other forms of mechanical restraint (notwithstanding the terrible revelations of what went on in the Birmingham Gaol) was expressly authorized, though under restrictions. The code of rules for all prisons was, by what must now seem an extraordinary blunder in Political Science, enacted in minute detail in a schedule to the statute ; and was thus made unalterable, even in the smallest respect—however much local circumstances might be found to differ, whatever might be the conditions of particular gaols or particular prisoners, and what-ever unforeseen discoveries might be made—except by another Act of Parliament. It speaks volumes as to the composition of the Parliament of 1865 that this draconic law should—after all the revelations of prison horrors in 1854 and otherwise—have been passed with little protest or objection.[1]

It was afterwards alleged, with some justification, that it was the Act of 1865, not that of 1877, which constituted the turning point of English prison administration in the second half of the nineteenth century. It was the 1865 statute which definitely decided upon the prison régime that lasted until the very close of the century, whilst the statute of 1877 which we shall presently describe, only changed the administrative machinery. In the Prisons Act of 1865 the prison administrators at the Home Office had, at last, got what they wanted. A uniform prison policy, exactly on the lines which they had been laying down for a whole generation, had now been specifically prescribed by the authority of Parliament. What seemed full powers were given to the Home Secretary to ensure that the Act should be carried into effect. There was no lack of willingness at Whitehall to put the new powers in force. There was, immediately, a general stirring up of the local prison authorities, a great issuing of circulars and instructions, an increased vigour in the inspections and in the inspectors' criticisms and complaints.

Under the Act of 1865 a great deal was accomplished. In the first place, rather than face the expense of putting their prisons in a proper state, many of the smaller prison authorities in the boroughs and fran-

---

[1] The statute contained some useful features. For the first time, the local prison authority was empowered to make, from public funds, some grant in aid of prisoners on their discharge. Every prison had to have not only a gaoler or governor, but also a doctor and an Anglican chaplain ; and every prison for women had to have a matron. A coroner's inquest had to be held on every prisoner who died in gaol, and no one connected with the prison was allowed to serve on the jury. Moreover, it was for the first time enacted that no prisoner should be employed in the discipline of the prison or in the service of any officer or in the service or instruction of any other prisoner. It had thus taken nearly a hundred years since Howard wrote to get the abuse stopped of prisoners acting as wardsmen, or being placed in positions in which they were inevitably tempted to favour or tyrannize over other prisoners.

chises, were prevailed upon to give up their prisons altogether, and leave the task to the County Justices. In the course of fifteen years from 1862, no fewer than eighty[1] out of the 193 prisons of that date—all, of course, the smaller ones which had sometimes no prisoners at all, sometimes only a few dozen—were entirely discontinued ; and with them disappeared the most extreme and the most picturesque of the instances of " lack of uniformity," with which the inspectors' reports had been filled. Moreover, everywhere the discipline was tightened up, the penal labour increased in severity, the separation of prisoners from each other more strictly enforced. Some slight approach towards uniformity was, on the lines described in Chapter IX, made in prison dietaries, though the dietetic problem had been found too difficult for the Justices to solve.

In 1869, by the Act abolishing imprisonment for debt, one of the chronic factors in prison disorder was got rid of. Even if the local administrators had all been as zealous and as competent as the best among them, no place of confinement could, as we now see, possibly have been maintained in a decent state so long as the law required the admission of a whole class of inmates to whom the common prison discipline could not be applied. The mere presence, in nearly all the local prisons, of persons detained only for non-payment of debts, rendered nugatory all attempts at a uniformity of regimen. " To their introduction of improper articles," it was said, " there is hardly any restriction ; to their intercourse with strangers there is scarcely any restraint. . . . Their sympathy is always excited in behalf of the criminals, and manifested by their supplying them, clandestinely, with food, tobacco and other articles ; and in occasionally affording them the means of communication. The Debtors' Ward, in a well-ordered prison, is sure to be the exception to general cleanliness, and the debtors themselves the disturbers of general

---

[1] Fourteen of these (thirteen in boroughs and one in a franchise) had been expressly closed by the Act of 1865 itself.

quiet."¹ But the debtors were mainly responsible, also, for the continuance of the discreditable little prisons of the " liberties " and " franchises " up and down the country. In 1837, for instance, the " Debtors' Gaol " for the " Hundred and Forest Courts " of Macclesfield seems to have made practically no advance since the visits of John Howard. " The keeper," we read,² " receives no salary, and it is a matter of some difficulty to find anybody willing to undertake the charge. The person now in that situation is collector of the Corporation market tolls, for which he receives £1 16s. a week, and is inspector of weights and measures at a yearly salary of £10 besides fees. No allowance is made to the prisoners in case of extreme distress, and they have been occasionally relieved by the other prisoners, or the keeper. No attempt to preserve order or discipline among them ; they do as they please. Drunkenness is frequent, and upon the admission of a fresh prisoner the gaol is described as being a scene of uproarious hilarity. . . . Two debtors at present confined here state that the . . . garnish of ten shillings is lowered to five, which they paid, and it was expended in liquor. The keeper makes each prisoner pay 3s. 6d. a week to him for bedding and coals, the bedding not being his property. . . ." It was in vain that the inspector urged the abolition of this and similar debtors' prisons at Rothwell, Halifax, Knaresborough and Richmond.

From the outset the inspectors had denounced the whole class of debtors' prisons.³ " The discreditable condition of the gaols for debtors, attached to peculiar jurisdictions, and the condition of their inmates, have long been the subject of animadversion in these reports. . . . In the hope that it may be useful, I proceed summarily to describe the imperfections of these gaols under peculiar jurisdictions,

¹ Parliamentary Papers, 1836, xxxv, 164.
² Ibid., 1837, xxxii, 536. What the debtors' prisons were like may be seen in Scenes and Stories by a Clergyman in Debt (written in a debtors' prison), 1835 ; also Prison Reminiscences, by H., 1859.
³ Ibid., 1844, xxix, 233.

with the evils consequent upon imprisonment in them, and showing how desirable is their suppression.

"1. The absence of any legal provision for the maintenance of prisoners in execution when not in county gaols, and their consequent distress, being often in want of food, the Poor Law Commissioners having notified that the Poor Rate cannot be applied for the relief of such prisoners while in gaol.

"2. The accommodation in many of these prisons is limited to the bare walls. No respect being paid to religion by the performance of Divine service ; no medical assistance in cases of sickness, no provision of food, bedding, light nor fire. No authority exercised by which the brutal or hardened are restrained from practising on the weak or better disposed. Idleness and corrupting influence prevails in all, unchecked and unreproved. It is worthy of remark that imprisonment in the gaols of the Courts of Request at Sheffield was found to make so little impression, that it was deemed necessary to heighten its severity, by ordering that prisoners should not be allowed to employ themselves in any kind or description of work. I may add that I never went into these prisons without finding a party engaged at cards, or some other idle game. . . .

"4. In the cases of collusive arrests these peculiar jurisdictions are often selected by the fraudulent, that they may be subjected to as little restraint as possible whilst waiting in prison for the session of the Insolvent Court ; and also that in case of a remand, they may be free from the restrictions imposed on debtors in a county gaol. . . .

"5. In another jurisdiction for the recovery of small debts, in an agricultural district, it was observed that but few executions were ever taken out, but just before the harvest months, when these prisons became thronged, executions being put in force for the purpose of compelling the debtor to an arrangement or of depriving him of the advantage of his labour, by keeping him in prison during the period. Under such circumstances the labourer had no possible

means of extrication from debt, after a first involv-
ment, except by wearing out the amount by lying in
prison ; for by giving up to the creditor the wages
accruing from harvest labour, he must have again
got into debt during the winter months, when work
was short. . . ."[1]

After 1869, though unfortunate debtors still continued to be committed to prison, as they do to this
day, they were imprisoned as offenders,to be punished
for contempt of court. They could therefore, it was
with some callousness contended, be subjected to the
prison regimen applied to other offenders ; and their
presence ceased to afford an excuse for a lack of the
uniformity after which the Home Office strove.

Notwithstanding the statutory transformation of
mere debtors into offenders punishable for contempt
of court—notwithstanding all the improvements set
in motion under the Act of 1865—it was presently
realized that the desired results had not been obtained.   It was all very well for Parliament to ordain
that every prisoner should be placed in cellular isolation, and for the Home Secretary to insist that this
should be done.   But in all but a few of the seven or
eight score prisons under Local Government—and in
all but a part of the structure even of these few—
the provision of separate cells for all the prisoners
involved an enormous building programme, which
neither County Justices nor Municipal Corporations
were willing to undertake at the ratepayers' expense.

[1] How the admission of debtors undermined the administration of even
the county prisons is shown by the account given of Lancaster Castle in
1856.   The inspector reports (Parliamentary Papers, 1856, xxxiii, 410):
" In the governor's journal I observe four cases in which the friends of
debtors had been detected endeavouring to bring spirits into the prison.
A severe example was made in one case, the daughter of a debtor being
convicted in a penalty of £10, or in default to be imprisoned for two months,
for an attempt to carry rum into the Debtors' Gaol ; and it is to be hoped
this may deter others from similar attempts."
I also observe the following entries in the same journal :
" *October 27th.*—'About half-past midnight the gate-warder on duty found
P.C., a bailiff to the Liverpool County Court, lying helplessly drunk outside
the castle gates, and with him a man who requested the warder to take
charge of the said P.C.   About 7 o'clock the next morning the same parties
presented themselves at the castle gates, when the companion of P.C.
turned out to be a debtor in his (P.C.'s) custody.   I have reported C.'s
shameful conduct to the High Bailiff of the Court! ' "

It was all very well for Parliament to enact, in minute detail, a uniform code of rules for all prisons, and to prescribe specified forms of penal labour. But the application of prison rules, and the adoption of particular forms of labour necessarily depended on considerations of structure and equipment in the several prisons, which could not be changed merely by the stroke of a pen, and could not be made even to approximate to uniformity without great expense. Moreover, the couple of thousand Justices of the Peace and members of Municipal Corporations, who were still the legal owners of the hundred or more separate prisons, felt that they were themselves responsible for the prison administration, whatever rules Parliament might enact, and whatever the Home Office inspector might say. At least they thought that it must be within their discretion how the rules should be applied, how the required dietaries should be framed, and how the specified penal labour should be exacted ; and on all these points the freely exercised discretion of a hundred or more separate authorities seriously departed from the uniformity that the Home Office had never ceased to desire.[1]

One of the most striking differences among the hundred or so local prisons[2] at this period was in respect of their policy in the matter of the labour imposed on the prisoners. The Home Office administrators had become convinced, as the controversies of the past half-century had demonstrated, that all efforts to make profit out of the prisoners' labour, by manufacturing goods for sale in the open market, inevitably led to gross inequalities in the treatment of prisoners, to practically unrestrained association among them, and—what was becoming a matter of troublesome political agitation—to complaints from employers and Trade Unions of the unfair competition of " Prison Labour." In the convict prisons

[1] The average number of prisoners in confinement, which had gone down in the years of good trade and continuous employment, 1871-2, to some 17,000, had again risen by 1877 to over 20,000.
[2] By 1877 the total number of local prisons in England and Wales had been reduced to 113.

these difficulties had been largely overcome by the
employment of all the prisoners physically fitted for
such labour on tasks of excavation and constructional
work for the Government itself, on which the
convicts at Chatham, Portsmouth, Portland, Dartmoor and other prisons were engaged.   Those
not physically fit for such work were employed
mainly in the domestic services and rough tailoring
required for the prisons themselves.   In the local
prisons, however, the utmost diversity prevailed.
Some of the County Justices and Municipal Corporations clung desperately to the idea of making the
prisons self-supporting;   and though the Act of
1865 had made obligatory the penal labour of the
tread-wheel or the crank for the first period of long
sentences, the Home Secretary had not been able to
exclude all other employment, and the prisoners
might still be put to other tasks that might be approved.   The Home Office was not able, in fact, to
bring to an end, in some important gaols and Houses
of Correction, the most extraordinary developments
of profit-making enterprise.   In the West Riding
gaol at Wakefield, for instance, right down to 1878,
the manufacture of mats of all kinds produced a
gross revenue of £40,000 a year.   Elsewhere clothes
were made up for contractors : all sorts of brushes
were manufactured for home and foreign markets ;
there were extensive boot and shoe manufactures ;
and large sales were made of various other articles.
Steam-power was often employed, and extensive
machinery provided.   " Trade managers," as well as
instructors (who acted as foremen) were engaged at
substantial salaries, with additional bonuses dependent on the profits of the undertaking.   Governors
and warders were also encouraged to promote the
enterprise, to the inevitable detriment of prison discipline, by being themselves allowed to share in the
profits.   In some cases commercial travellers were
employed to effect sales, and even agents in foreign
countries.   The prisoners were naturally encouraged
to work by special bonuses and gratuities, and

sometimes actually paid at piece-work prices. The
trade managers, as well as the governors, were entrusted with these awards ; and diligent prisoners
were also given additional food, even to the extent,
occasionally, of meals of hot mutton chops ! [1]

It will easily be realized how much the Home
Office administrators chafed, between 1865 and 1877,
under their practical inability to enforce, upon the
County Justices and Municipal Corporations, the
uniformity in prison regimen to which so much
importance was attached. It was, however, long
thought impossible to make any further inroads on
the autonomy of the local prison authorities.
Presently a new factor came into play. The General
Election of 1874 had brought into power a government pledged not to increase, but actually to relieve
the burden of rates upon the rural districts, and
especially those which it fell to the County Justices
to levy upon their tenants and neighbours. The
Home Office officials found their hands stayed,
not only when they strove to put down profit-making
in prisons, but also when they sought to enforce the
Act of 1865 by compelling the County Justices to
incur the expense of building new gaols on the
cellular plan. It began to be realized that the maintenance of more than a hundred separate local prisons,
some of them containing only a few dozen or a few
score inmates, was, in itself, a great waste of public
money ; and that to insist upon every such prison
authority equipping itself, not only with a complete

[1] Among the prisons with the greatest manufacturing and trading developments were Wakefield (*Annals of the Wakefield House of Correction*,
by J. H. Turner, 1904), Preston (*The Prison Chaplain*, by W. L. Clay, 1861),
Manchester, Bedford, Chelmsford, Maidstone, Bodmin, Lewes, Warwick,
and Coldbath Fields (*Revelations of Prison Life*, by G. L. Chesterton, 1856),
and Holloway (London). See, as to this prison labour, Report of House of
Lords Committee on Prison Discipline, 1863 ; Report of Home Office
Committee on Prisons, 1895 ; Report on Prison Labour in Foreign Coun-
tries, 1895 ; Report of Home Office Committee on the Importation of
Goods made in Foreign Prisons, 1895 ; Correspondence between the
Board of Trade and the Government of India on Prison-made Goods, 1897 ;
Statement by the Prison Commissioners on the Action which has been
taken to carry out the Recommendations of the 1895 Report,. 1898 ; *The
English Prison System at the end of the Nineteenth Century*, by Sir Evelyn
Ruggles-Brise, 1921, " Labour in English Prisons," pp. 131-141.

staff, but also with a completely cellular building—as Parliament had, in effect, enacted, at the instance of the Cabinet itself—would be an inexcusable extravagance. To compel the building of new county gaols at the ratepayers' expense had become, in fact, after 1874, politically almost impossible. The new Cabinet was pledged actually to reduce the County Rate.

At this point, it was inevitable that the recommendation of Charles Pearson before the Select Committee of 1850 should be revived. If the burden on the County Rate had to be reduced, what would be more effective than altogether to relieve the county of the expense of maintaining the prisons? In this way, it was urged, the rural ratepayer would save nearly half a million pounds a year, besides cutting himself loose, at a blow, from all the portentous new liabilities now discovered to have been imposed, with a steadily rising tide of prisoners to be maintained, by the Act of 1865. Faced with the prospect of these liabilities, and tempted by the reduction of the rates within their grasp, the Justices of the Peace, it was suggested, would no longer very strenuously resist the transfer of the whole function of prison maintenance from local to central government. Such a transfer, it was argued, would not only enable the Home Office to get over the dilemma in which it was placed by the breakdown of the 1865 Act, and enable, at last, an ideal prison administration to be everywhere carried out, without the difficulties inevitably connected with local control, but would also effect a net economy of expense. To get rid of the unnecessary multiplicity of local prisons would create such a saving as would suffice to cover the entire cost of the requisite new buildings, for which the Government could not, in the political circumstances of the moment, easily find the money in any other way. We do not know how the motives were mixed, in the Home Office officials who advised, or in the Cabinet which adopted the proposal for the transfer of the prisons from local to central government. But it is clear that the consideration of how otherwise to avoid an actual increase in the County Rate, and how else to get the money for the new cellular prisons to which Parliament and the Government had been by the Act of 1865 committed, played a substantial part. The Bill which Mr. R. A. (afterwards Viscount) Cross introduced in 1876 and passed into law in 1877—which involved, as was expressly claimed, no important departure from the prison regimen that was supposed to be everywhere enforced—was, in fact, made politically possible, not so much by the state of the prisons, as by the successful campaign for a reduction of the local burdens on the rural landowner, farmer and ratepayer, which had formed so large a part of the General Election of 1874.[1]

---

[1] The Prisons Act of 1877 (40 and 41 Victoria, c. 21), thorgh encountering even less opposition than had been expected, was not passed without a struggle. In 1876 the Second Reading was carried by over 200 majority, but lack of time prevented the Bill becoming law. When it was reintroduced in the subsequent session, with some verbal changes conciliatory to the Justices, it was denounced as " a gigantic and almost unparalleled centralization," as " a distinct slur on local government and management," and as " sapping the foundations of the constitutional system " of " independent local administration." But the Radicals who joined with a few discontented Conservatives in opposing the measure on the Second Reading found (as stated by Mr. Peter Rylands) that " the bribe held out of the relief to local burdens," coupled with the argument of increased administrative efficiency, was irresistible to the county members whom the 1874 election had returned to Parliament. In the long-drawn-out Committee stage, they even obtained a further financial concession. The Bill proposed that local prison authorities which had failed to provide sufficient prison accommodation should be required to contribute to the Exchequer at the rate of £120 per cell of their deficiency. It was thereupon demanded, and eventually conceded, that other local authorities, which had provided cellular accommodation in excess of what was found to be the maximum number of their own prisoners, should be reimbursed by the Exchequer for their excess accommodation, whether or not this was likely to be required for the kingdom as a whole, in any prisons that the Home Office did not discontinue within two years. Under this clause no less than £127,478 was paid to the counties for 1,376 cells, which proved, eventually, to be of very little use (Punishment and Prevention of Crime, by Sir Edmund Du Cane, 1885, p. 69). The subsequent stages of the Bill were fiercely fought by the Irish members, who struggled, with some slight success, to get amendments adopted which would prevent (in the Local Prisons) some of the worst inhumanities with which the Irish condemned to penal servitude for treason-felony had become acquainted in the convict prisons (see Hansard for 1877). The harsh treatment of the Irish prisoners, who ought, it was said, to have been treated as political prisoners (see Political Prisoners at Home and Abroad, by G. Sigerson, 1890) had been described in John Mitchel's Jail Journal, editions of 1868, 1876 and 1913; in Irish Rebels in English Prisons, by J. O'Donovan Rossa, 1882 ; and, with great restraint and a noble freedom from bitterness, in Leaves from a Prison Diary, by Michael Davitt, 1885.

CHAPTER XII

THE ACT OF 1877 AND THE "DU CANE RÉGIME"

THE Prisons Act of 1877 (40 and 41, Victoria, c. 21) effected a revolution almost unique in the history of English Local Government. A great administrative service, extending throughout the whole country, which had been for centuries within the sphere of Local Government, was transferred *en bloc* to a department of the National Government. In no other branch of public administration has such a change been made in England. Whenever such a transfer has been proposed—as it has been at different dates for police, for elementary schooling, for lunacy, for main roads, and indeed, for other services—the characteristic English preference for local over central administration has hitherto always proved too strong to be overcome. In prison administration alone has centralization prevailed. It does not fall within the plan of this book to attempt any judgment upon all the results of the administrative revolution for which the then Home Secretary and the Conservative Cabinet of 1874-80 were responsible. But we may conclude our account of English prisons under Local Government by a final chapter describing the application of the Act of 1877, and the inauguration in the prisons, in substitution for the rule of the County Justices and Municipal Corporations, of what afterwards became known as the "Du Cane régime."

By the Act of 1877 the ownership of all the local prisons was vested in the Secretary of State, and their general superintendence was committed—as that of

the national convict prisons had been by the Act of
1850—to a body of Commissioners, not exceeding
five in number, to be appointed by the Home Secretary, to assist him in the work ; to act under his
instructions and to be responsible to him for the whole
administration.[1] Of these Commissioners the first
chairman was Colonel (afterwards Sir Edmund)
Du Cane, a distinguished officer of the Royal Engineers who had succeeded Sir Joshua Jebb as Surveyor-
General of Prisons under the Act of 1844, and had
been mainly responsible for the structural and other
arrangements of the modern convict prisons. He
was at that time, and continued to be, also Chairman
of the Board of Directors of Convict Prisons, so that,
although technically still divided into two parts, the
whole of the English prisons came, in fact, under a
single administration.[2]

On April 1st, 1878, the entire population of the
local prisons of England and Wales—the number of
prisoners being then absolutely at its maximum in
the whole history of the nation, namely 21,030[3]—
was transferred from the care of the County and
Borough Justices and the Municipal Corporations to
that of the Secretary of State and his Prison Commissioners. The Home Office went promptly and vigorously to work. Out of the 113 local prisons transferred
to them, no fewer than thirty-eight were instantly
closed on the day of transfer ; and in the course of
the ensuing decade nineteen more were got rid of,

[1] Thus there was not, and there has never since been, any lessening of the
power and authority of the Secretary of State, and no derogation of the full
ministerial responsibility of the Home Secretary for everything that happens
in the prisons. This was made quite clear by the wording of the Act and
was definitely stated by the chairman of the Prison Commissioners (*The
English Prison System at the end of the Nineteenth Century*, by Sir Evelyn
Ruggles-Brise, a paper read at the 1900 International Prisons Congress
at Brussels). The Prison Commissioners are just as much the agents of the
Home Secretary as are the clerks in the Home Office.

[2] The other Commissioners were W. W. Hornby (1877-91), J. W. Perry
Watlington (1877-80), and W. J. Stopford (1877-98). In succession to J.
W. Perry Watlington, R. S. Mitford was appointed in 1882 ; in succession
to W. W. Hornby, E. (afterwards Sir Evelyn) Ruggles-Brise was appointed
in 1892. But Sir Edmund Du Cane, who served until 1894, was, throughout his whole chairmanship, the dominant influence.

[3] In addition to some 10,000 in the convict prisons.

the total number of " local " (as distinguished from
" convict ") prisons being reduced by 1894 to no
more than fifty-six. The business of taking over the
institutions, situated all over the country, on a single
day, and consolidating them into two-thirds, and
eventually into no more than half of their number ;
" organizing the staff, every member of which had
statutory rights reserved to him ; rearranging the
buildings, and establishing uniformity " was, as Sir
Godfrey Lushington rightly claimed in 1895, a task of
" prodigious magnitude on which an immense amount
of thought, contrivance and skill " was expended.[1]

The first object of the Commissioners seems to have
been administrative efficiency and economy, and of
this the first condition, as they conceived it, was uniformity. The accounts, for instance, of the various
prisons were found in what seemed to the administrators at Whitehall to be a terrible muddle, no two
institutions keeping their books on the same plan,
or classifying their innumerable items of receipts
and expenditures in the same way. A model system
of book-keeping, with a perfect classification of
items of account was at once devised, and set going
in every prison. But more important steps were
promptly taken towards uniformity of prison regimen. Committees of officials were appointed to
devise what seemed to them the most suitable
dietary, the most scientific schemes of penal labour,
the most efficient administrative devices, and so
on, the result of these deliberations, which were
carried on without publicity, upon exclusively
official information, and with the minimum of
outside criticism, being in each case prescribed
for uniform adoption from one end of the kingdom
to the other. A new and elaborate code of
prison rules was presently promulgated, made up
of the best of the rules embodied in the 1865
Act, with such modifications as experience had
dictated. The staff of every prison was organized
upon a strictly uniform scale, with exactly pre-

[1] Report of Home Office Committee on Prisons, C.7702, 1895, p. 3.

scribed arrangements for the services of the governors, the chaplains, the medical officers, the schoolmasters, the warders, and what not.[1] It was expressly in order to bring the treatment of the sick up to the necessary uniformity of standard that a Medical Inspector of Prisons was appointed.

The extent to which this fetish of uniformity was pushed seems to-day extraordinary. For not only was the uniformity to extend to all parts of the kingdom, to all features of the regimen, and to all departments of each prison, but it was even carried so far as to ignore, almost entirely, all the differences among the prisoners themselves. The very smallest distinction was made between prisoners of different ages, or of different sexes, or of different social antecedents, or of different bodily physique, or of different mental attainments. To Sir Edmund Du Cane a prisoner was a prisoner, and practically nothing else. We can now see how calamitously such a blind uniformity in the application of a regimen which was, to say the least, dangerous in its possible effects, reacted on three great classes of prisoners, for whom very different arrangements needed to be made. Thus, prior to 1895, practically no attention was paid to the special and peculiar problem of the female prisoners, who were being committed to prison to the number of nearly a thousand every week of the year, two-thirds of them for drunkenness or prostitution, three-quarters of the whole having been previously convicted, most of them repeatedly. In and out of prison passed this mournful procession of unfortunate victims, most of them committed for short sentences which left no room for the beneficial influences of the much-vaunted " System of Progressive Stages." Under the "Du Cane régime," their treatment was as nearly as possible that meted out to the men who made a lifelong profession of preying

---

[1] In all the staffs of the 113 prisons taken over on April 1st, 1878, there were found to be only fifty schoolmasters! But even to-day the prison " schoolmasters " are, for the most part, men of only slight technical qualifications for teaching.

on the public in the way of fraud, cheating or robbery with violence. Right down to 1895, too, practically no heed was paid to the " feeblemindedness," which characterizes a large proportion, variously estimated at from 3 to 20 per cent., of all the inmates of our prisons. Unless a prisoner could be certified definitely as insane—in which case he was supposed to be removed to an asylum—all, whether sharp-witted and cunning, or stupid to the extent of actual mental deficiency, had to undergo the uniform treatment. Lastly, and in some ways most tragic of all, there was a total neglect to consider how best to treat the youthful criminal, boy or girl, whether convicted for the first time or recidivist. For the children between twelve and sixteen who were then being committed to prison for every kind of petty offence, as for what we have since learned to call the juvenile adult, between sixteen and twenty-one—the age at which, as we now know, the great majority of our life-long criminals are formed—the Prison Commissioners of 1878-94 had nothing but their uniform regimen applicable alike to the ingenious forger, the professional burglar, the hungry pilferer, the drunkard and the prostitute.

Second only to the desire of the Commissioners for an exact uniformity of administrative efficiency in all the prisons, was their insistence on a rigorous uniformity of severity. The Act of 1877 had not, it is true, expressly prohibited the employment of the, prisoners on productive work ; and the susceptibilities of Parliament had even been appealed to by a preamble to the section relating to labour which was certainly understood to imply that productive labour of a skilled character would be retained.[1] But Sir Edmund Du Cane and his colleagues evidently thought that productive employment, coupled with " instruc-

[1] Section 11 of 40 and 41 Victoria, c. 21, begins by declaring that " Whereas it is expedient that the expense of maintaining in prison prisoners who have been convicted of crime should in part be defrayed by their labour during the period of their imprisonment, and that with a view to defraying such expenses, and also of teaching prisoners modes of gaining honest livelihoods, means should be taken for promoting in prison the exercise of and instruction in useful trades and manufactures, so far as may be con-

tion in useful trades," was not consistent with the uniformity of deterrence at which they aimed. In nearly all cases it involved labour in association, which was incompatible with the rigorous cellular isolation that the policy of deterrence was held to require. The phrase of the House of Lords Committee of 1863—that the prisoners should all endure " hard labour, hard fare and a hard bed "—seems to have been taken seriously as the Government policy, and applied with a ruthless uniformity which the noble lords had possibly not contemplated. Along with the uniform dietary and the universal plank bed came—in spite of all the evidence existing against it—uniform " first class hard labour by means of the tread-wheel, the task of which was regulated by the most minute instructions as *the* task for hard labour in prisons."[1] And along with the universal infliction of a uniform task upon the tread-wheel or the crank (for the latter remained extensively in use) came the insistence upon cellular confinement and absolute non-intercourse among the prisoners for the whole length of each man's sentence, which, in the worst cases, extended to two years. " The governor," laconically said the rule, " shall enforce the observance of silence throughout the prison." Opportunity was taken to bring to an end the various profit-making enterprises of the local prisons. The bonuses and allowances to officers and prisoners were abolished, and the foreign agents, the commercial travellers and most of the salaried trade instruc-

sistent with a due regard on the one hand to the maintenance of the penal character of prison discipline, and on the other, to the avoidance of undue pressure on, or competition with, any particular trade or industry."

[1] *The English Prison System*, by Sir Evelyn Ruggles-Brise, 1921, p. 72. An amendment by Mr. Serjeant Simon, forbidding the use of the tread-wheel, had been rejected in the House of Commons by 229 votes to 72. The official committee on penal labour, and notably Dr. Gover, the Medical Inspector of Prisons who reported specially on the subject (Annual Report of the Prison Commissioners, 1891, Appendix 15), deprecated the previous practice of some prisons in allowing forms of labour which were not " penal and deterrent in character," and insisted that every prisoner should, " for at least a portion of his sentence, be employed upon this repugnant description of work." Shot-drill was, however, abolished, and the use of the capstan abandoned, whilst stone-breaking was steadily diminished. There remained only the tread-wheel, which the official reports now rehabilitated, and the crank.

tors were dispensed with. Mat-making was, in fact, almost entirely abandoned, in deference to the agitation of the capitalist mat manufacturers, who (in conjunction with the operatives whose agitation they incited and subsidized) were able to demonstrate that the extraordinary development of the prison industry at Wakefield and elsewhere, in which no fewer than 3,000 prisoners were continuously engaged, had seriously encroached upon their profits. Such other industries as were continued had more and more to be confined to work that could be done by each prisoner in his separate cell. One of the most extensive of these occupations was oakum picking, in which between 3,000 and 4,000 men were employed ; and this was kept on even when (by the substitution of iron ships for wooden ones) the demand for oakum fell away, and the industry ceased to yield any profit at all. The disagreeable and monotonous task of picking old rope to pieces, which needed no instruction, which might be imposed upon prisoners of any physical strength or mental capacity, which could be performed in silence in absolute cellular isolation, and which was rendered all the more "penal" in character because of its very unprofitableness, became, under the Du Cane régime, after the hated tread-wheel and crank, the favourite form of prison labour.[1]

We should do the Prison Commissioners of 1878-94 an injustice if we inferred that in prescribing a uniform application of cellular isolation, absolute non-intercourse among the prisoners, the rule of silence, oakum-picking, and the tread-wheel, they ignored the effects of this rigorous treatment upon the mental and physical condition of the vast population committed to their charge. They were familiar with the controversies of the past half-century. They were aware of the proved results of solitary confinement in Millbank Prison, of the tread-wheel

---

[1] See, for all this, the Annual Reports of the Prison Commissioners, 1879-85 ; and *The Punishment and Prevention of Crime*, by Sir Edmund Du Cane, 1885, especially Chap. IV.

in Pentonville Prison, of the incessant stimulus to
deceit and the frightful frequency of punishments
which the strict enforcement of silence had everywhere produced. "Cellular labour," wrote Sir
Edmund Du Cane himself, at the very time that he
was making it the basis of his prison regimen, " is
decidedly brutalizing in its effects. To men of any
intelligence it is irritating, depressing and debasing
to the mental faculties ; to those already of a low
type of intelligence it is too conformable to the state
of mind out of which it is most desirable that they
should be raised."[1] It is hard to understand how
the Prison Commissioners of that date justified their
action. But they believed that in no other way
could they achieve the object of uniformity in
the application of a deterrent system which they
understood the Home Secretary, in compliance with
the recommendations of the House of Lords Committee of 1863 (though without the express concurrence of the Parliament of 1877) to have definitely
decided upon. What the Prison Commissioners
seem to have believed was that it was possible, by
a uniform efficiency of administration upon " enlightened " principles, in which governors, medical officers,
chaplains, schoolmasters and warders were given
precisely detailed rules with which they were required to conform, to prevent the evil consequences
that had admittedly happened in the diversely
administered prisons of 1821-77. No small part of
the thought and work of the Commissioners during
these years was devoted to the administrative improvements by which they aimed at preventing their
uniform regimen of deterrence from actually injuring
the health of the prisoners. Some slight improvement
was made in the bathing arrangements. All overcrowding was stopped. The most elaborate precautions were gradually taken to make the prison buildings absolutely sanitary, and to exclude all infectious
disease. The medical care of the sick was greatly

---

[1] *The Punishment and Prevention of Crime*, by Sir Edmund Du Cane,
1885, p. 175.

improved, minute regulations were issued, and professional inspection was introduced.   The hospital accommodation, nursing and medical treatment were raised to a standard which, whilst it could bear no comparison with that of voluntary hospitals, had never before been known in prison.   Prison statistics are rightly regarded with some suspicion, and the prison death-rate is much affected by the practice of releasing prisoners who are expected to die, but it is probable that the officially recorded reduction of the death-rate among prisoners, from 10.8 per 1,000 in 1877 to 5.6 per 1,000 in 1898, fairly represents a vast improvement in the average physical health of those in confinement.   What was ignored, and hardly ever publicly discussed, was the significant fact that the great majority of prisoners lost weight, and those committed for short terms often to a serious extent.   Nor can it have been realized how exceptionally high was the death-rate from tuberculosis in comparison with that of the population at large, nor how much this susceptibility to tubercular disease might depend upon specific dietary insufficiencies, the exclusion of direct sunlight, the inevitable accumulation of dust, and the perpetual desire to prevent draughts, which characterized even the best ventilated prisons.

With regard to the mental condition of the prisoners the evidence is, perhaps, least satisfactory. The prison schoolmaster was directed to give instruction in reading and writing to those who were found to be illiterate ; but we do not gather that there was any ·real improvement, between 1878 and 1894, in the education imparted to the prison population as a whole.   The prison libraries began, at any rate, to contain some books apart from the theological homilies which used to characterize them.   Those prisoners who were Roman Catholics were no longer deprived of access to a priest, or left without religious services.[1]   The visits of the Anglican chaplains to

[1] There had been a strange agitation—one of the most foolish of the waves of rabid " Protestantism " that marked the Victorian era—against the

each prisoner's cell may have become somewhat more frequent than the one or two a year which had in some large prisons been the average. We may well believe that the improved training of governors and warders, the elaborate rules directing in minute particulars their treatment of the prisoners, and the greatly increased supervision and inspection must have done much to prevent the worst of the arbitrary tyranny which had, in the past, often driven prisoners to despair. The wearing of masks, for instance, was abolished. The Commissioners may fairly claim in their favour the reduction of suicides among prisoners from 17·6 per 1,000 in 1877 to 7 per 1,000 in 1896. But it is not clear how far this reduction of achieved suicides corresponded with a genuine diminution in the percentage of prisoners driven into insanity or despair, and how far it was merely the result of the extraordinary precautions introduced into the prisons with the object of making it almost impossible to commit suicide, to which we have already referred.[1]

To prevent the actual cruelties which had from time to time occurred in the prisons, Parliament had definitely limited the power of the governor to inflict punishment. He was not allowed to place any prisoner in the punishment cell and on punishment diet for more than three days, though the Visiting Justices might inflict as long a term as fourteen days. His use of irons was strictly limited to the restraint of prisoners actually guilty of physical violence in gaol. The Home Office followed this up by stringent and precise rules intended to ensure that any excess of punish-

appointment of Roman Catholic chaplains to prisons. This agitation, of which Mr. Whalley, M.P., and Mr. Newdegate, M.P., made themselves the spokesmen in the House of Commons, had prevented some County Justices from providing religious ministrations for their Roman Catholic prisoners.

[1] We cannot forget that the percentage of suicides may go down, coincidentally with an actual increase in the percentage of insanity (*History of Penal Methods*, by George Ives, 1914, p. 231). The statistics officially given as to the percentage of suicides appear to vary in unexplained ways ; and it does not seem that much reliance can be placed upon this item of prison statistics. Sometimes we read of the percentage of deaths by suicide to the total deaths in prison, and sometimes the percentage to the average daily population.

ment or other cruelty should become automatically known to the inspectors and to the Prison Commissioners. We may hope that the greatly increased stringency of inspection, the elaborate keeping of records, and the steady improvement in the prison staffs effected some substantial improvement in this respect, although the matter is not one on which definite evidence is available.[1]

What the Prison Commissioners of 1878-1894 most prided themselves upon, and what they very largely relied on to mitigate their deterrent regimen, was the system of " Progressive Stages," to which allusion has already been made. The lot of the prisoner at the beginning of his sentence was, admittedly and intentionally, extremely hard—so hard, as possibly to be quite unendurable over a lengthy period. But it was made possible for every prisoner, after a certain time, to procure for himself, by absolute obedience and perfect docility, progressive stages of alleviation, to which, minute as they may appear, he could look forward, and from which it was supposed that he might derive so much encouragement as to counteract all that was injurious in his cellular isolation and silent toil on the crank or tread-wheel. The difficulty was to find alleviations compatible with the uniformity of which such a fetish had been made. Improvement in diet had been abandoned, not only as unnecessarily adding to expense, but also as illogical, because anything beyond a sufficiency of food amounted to luxury unjustifiable for prisoners.[2] Reductions in the task of work were equally illogical, because the task was, from the outset, fixed at the precise point between what would allow opportunity for

---

[1] Unfortunately, as has been remarked, prison inspection, under the Du Cane régime, was directed almost exclusively to structure, sanitation, the physical health of the prisoners and their exact obedience to orders and docility under discipline. It does not seem to have taken any account of their mental condition or degree of suffering.

[2] On the other hand, it was not found illogical to reduce the diet by way of punishment. This reduction to bread and water, or to other low diets, was inflicted in the years 1873-8 in no fewer than 40,000 cases annually—a number reduced in the course of the next six years to an annual average of about half as much (*Punishment and Prevention of Crime*, by Sir Edmund Du Cane, 1885, p. 105).

indolence and what would cause excessive fatigue. The Prison Commissioners of 1878-94 were accordingly driven, as their successor admits, actually " to add to the penalty prescribed by the Court by imposing, in the name of the Progressive Stages System, certain penalties and incapacities as a peculiar feature of the early stages."[1] It was not merely that the cells were purposely made as bare and repellent as could possibly be contrived, with opaque glass to the hermetically closed windows so as to prevent even a glimpse of the sky. Nothing was allowed in the way of personal possessions—not a picture or even a photograph of the prisoner's wife or child—to break the monotony of the cell wall, or to keep alive any feeling of family affection. The rule of silence was enforced merely for the sake of enforcing a discipline which had been found to be disagreeable. They were kept in absolute ignorance of public affairs. These were the conditions of all prisoners at all stages. But during the First Stage they were not only kept strictly to " hard labour of the first class " for ten hours every day, six hours of which was to be on the tread-wheel or crank, but were allowed no mattress to sleep on during the whole period, no school instruction, no books of any sort, and no chance of earning, by good marks, any gratuity or remission of sentence. Those promoted to the Second Stage were put, after one month, on hard labour of the second class, which might mean industrial employment ; they were allowed to sleep on a mattress five days a week ; they might, under certain circumstances, receive a small amount of school instruction, and have school-books in the cell ; they were allowed Sunday exercise ; and they had the opportunity of earning a gratuity not exceeding one shilling. In the Third Stage, the hard labour was the same, and also the chances of school instruction and the use of school books ; but the mattress might be enjoyed for six nights in every week, and as much

---

[1] *The English Prison System*, by Sir Evelyn Ruggles-Brise, 1921, p. 73.

as eighteenpence might be earned as gratuity. For those who attained to the Fourth Stage, the hard labour might possibly be superseded by selection for an office of trust about the prison ; the mattress might be enjoyed every night in the week ; library books as well as school books might be read ; the gratuity to be earned rose to the giddy height of two shillings, and the prisoner was allowed to write and receive letters, and to receive visits, at certain intervals, and under stringent restrictions. It will be seen how small were the improvements to be gained even by the best conduct. At a later date the privilege was added of being allowed to earn, by good marks, a slight diminution in the length of the sentence.[1]

Whatever may be said in criticism of the exceptional rigour of the preliminary period, the system of progressive amelioration of the prisoner's condition, dependent on his conduct in gaol—at the elaboration of which Maconochie and Crofton and Jebb had all worked in their several ways—seems to have had some success, in the narrow sense of producing the " good prisoner," in the convict prisons, where the inmates were all serving long sentences. The Prison Commissioners prided themselves on its " remarkable and undeniable success " as " an aid to discipline, industry and good order.[2] " The risk or fear of losing remission marks operates," it could be said, " as a powerful deterrent against idleness or misconduct, and it has been found, generally, that

---

[1] It is hard to recognize in the above exact description of the " Progressive Stages," Sir Edmund Du Cane's optimistic account of the system in 1885. " The principle on which this system is founded is that of setting before prisoners the advantages of good conduct and industry by enabling them to gain certain privileges or modifications of the penal character of the sentence by the exertion of these qualities. Commencing with severe penal labour, hard fare and hard bed, he can gradually advance to more interesting employment, somewhat more material comfort, full use of library books, privilege of communication by letter and word with his friends, finally the advantage of a moderate sum of money to start again on his discharge, so that he may not have the temptations or the excuse that want of means might afford for falling again into crime (*The Punishment and Prevention of Crime*, by Sir Edmund Du Cane, 1885, p. 77). Details of the system will be found in the Annual Report of the Prison Commissioners, 1879, Appendix 12.

[2] Annual Report of the Prison Commissioners, 1885, par. 49.

under the influence of this salutary provision there
has been a marked improvement in the tone and
demeanour of the prisoners, while, at the same time,
an aid has been furnished for maintaining order and
discipline."[1]
Unfortunately, the Prison Commissioners of 1878-
94 failed to remember that the twenty thousand
prisoners committed to their charge in the local
prisons were, unlike the inmates of the convict
prisons, not serving long sentences.[2] The vast
majority of them were committed only for a few
weeks, and only 2 per cent. for six months or more,
whilst no sentence exceeded two years. Hence the
proportion who could derive much benefit from the
system of Progressive Stages was minute.[2] The
extra rigour imposed in order to be subsequently
removed, fell, however, upon all.[3] A similar criticism may be made upon the educational arrangements made by Sir Edmund Du Cane. It was not
worth while seeking to teach for the half an hour or
the one or two hours, per week, which could be set
aside from the demands of labour, men committed to
prison for only a few weeks ; or, indeed, as the Commissioners seem to have thought, for any period less
than four months. Hence the great mass of prisoners
got no benefit from the much vaunted system of
prison education, and the enlarged staff of prison

[1] *The English Prison System*, by Sir E. Ruggles-Brise, p. 81 (with regard
to the subsequent application of a similar principle to the local prisons).
[2] In 1903, 61 per cent. of the men and 66 per cent. of the women were
committed for fourteen days or less. If we take three months as the short-
est time in which any appreciable advantage could be got, either out of
any " System of Progressive Stages " or out of the ministrations of the
chaplain or schoolmaster as they were, in fact, made, we find that, in 1903
only 6 per cent. of the men and only 2 per cent. of the women were sentenced
for longer than that term. (Prison Commissioners' Report for 1903.)
[3] " The only precedent for dealing with short sentences "—that is to say,
the only one that the Prison Commissioners of 1877-98 chose to regard—
" was that afforded by military prisons. It is well known that the Committee on Military Prisons of 1844, which was in favour of hard penal treatment, shot-drill, cranks, etc. (in use in military prisons as a punishment for
recalcitrant soldiers) exercised a considerable influence with local authorities in administering civil prisons ; and the reproach, so often directed to
the Local Prison system "—under Sir Edmund Du Cane—" that it was
too military in its character, was probably due to this source." (*The
English Prison System*, by Sir Evelyn Ruggles-Brise, 1921, p. 73.)

schoolmasters. When a prison chaplain had in his charge, as was sometimes the case in the large new gaols that were being erected, as many as 800 or 1,000 prisoners (which, if he spread his time evenly over all, meant an average of less than ten minutes per month for each inmate), he found it as much as he could do to get round the cells of those serving sentences of substantial length, and he could not possibly visit all those committed only for a few days or weeks. Nevertheless the system of cellular isolation for everyone was maintained with inflexible rigour, and the Prison Commissioners remained to the end, absolutely complacent about it. " The Separate System," wrote Sir Edmund Du Cane in 1886, "never was more uniformly and universally carried out than now, and never stood in higher repute. All our (local) prisons are on the Separate System . . . a sign of the efficiency of the system."[1]

One of the unforeseen results of the transfer of the local prisons to the administration of a Government Department was to put a stop to even the small amount of publicity that had since 1835 prevailed. The Home Office inspectors of the prisons under the administration of the County Justices and Municipal Corporations between 1835 and 1878 had, as we have seen, never scrupled to report in the most outspoken way as to the abuses that they discovered. Successive Home Secretaries had allowed the inspectors' reports to be presented to Parliament and placed on sale, without suppression or omission. The publication of a blue book is not the most effective way of arousing public attention, but this, at least, made it possible, from time to time, to give the world some impression of what passed behind the prison bars. The reports of the inspectors upon the administration

---

[1] Sir Edmund Du Cane to W. Tallack, 1886 ; printed in *Penological and Preventive Principles*, by W. Tallack, 1896, p. 168. The first edition of this work, by the secretary of the Howard Association, appeared in 1889. For his lifelong advocacy of the cellular system, see his *Cellular System*, 1872 ; and his *Defects in the Criminal Administration and Humanitarianism, with special reference to the prison systems*, etc., 1872.

of what had become their own Department were quickly found to be different from those made upon the administration of other authorities. Moreover, when the inspectors expressed themselves freely upon particular abuses, it was deemed inconvenient to make their strictures known to the public. Any reports of this character became confidential documents ; and the Prison Commissioners presented to Parliament their own general reports, in which they described their own administration. We need not ascribe to Sir Edmund Du Cane any conscious or deliberate intention of concealing from Parliament and the public what was happening in the prisons. But the inevitable bias of any official administration is to avoid the trouble that is caused by scandals, and even by the questions put in the House of Commons by members who had got hold of the particular abuses from which no administration can ever be entirely free. Nothing was therefore published that was likely to give rise to Parliamentary complaint, or afford a handle to newspaper criticism. The visits of non-official persons to the prisoners were severely discouraged.

It is true that the local prisons were, under the Act of 1877, each provided with a Visiting Committee of Justices of the Peace appointed by Quarter Sessions, the members of which were statutorily empowered, under section 14 of the Prison Act of 1877, to visit every part of the prison, and to see, privately if desired, every person in confinement. We have seen that, even when the prisons were nominally administered by the Justices themselves, their inspection had been in the last degree perfunctory ; and that it had served sometimes as a screen— even in such bad cases as those of Birmingham and Leicester—to negligent or tyrannous prison officials. When the gaols and Houses of Correction came to form part of a centralized administration, outwardly clean and sanitary, and regulated by a minute code of rules which seemed, to the unpractised country gentleman, to leave no room for abuses, the perfunctory inspection by the Visiting Committee of the work of officials whom they had not appointed, and over whom they could exercise no authority, became, in nearly all cases, absolutely valueless. If any criticisms were inserted in the volume provided for that purpose, no publicity was given to them. Whether or not they were ever communicated to the Prison Commissioners, the zealous Justices of the Peace usually heard no more of the matter. The result was, it is reported, that it became extremely rare for any useful criticism to be made. A great darkness shrouded the whole prison system.[1]

The " Du Cane régime " appeared, accordingly, at first sight, to have achieved a great success. The annual reports of the Prison Commissioners maintained a tone of complete self-complacency.[2] There were no public scandals. No tales of prison horrors comparable with those of a previous generation were told, or at any rate, not in such a way as to be heard by the newspapers or the governing class of the period. The average number of criminals who were at any one time maintained at the public expense—a number which had, down to 1877, continued to increase—now steadily fell.

[1] It is, we think, characteristic that so long as Sir Edmund Du Cane was in command, the Home Office and the Prison Commissioners refused to take part in the International Prison Conference, which had been definitely established after a conference in London in 1872, and in which the prison administrators of nearly every civilized country conferred with scientific investigators and philanthropists for the improvement of systems of punishment. Great Britain did not join this International Prison Conference until 1895. British government delegates attended congresses of 1895, 1900, 1905 and 1910 with (as they declared) some intellectual profit ; and the Conference was invited to hold its quinquennial congress of 1915 in London, this being prevented only by the war.

[2] Sir Edmund Du Cane and his colleagues could claim for their system the support of a majority of those who, on the Continent of Europe, took an intellectual interest in prison administration. In an interesting article by M. Ernest Bertrand, governor of the Central Prison at Louvain (an unrepentant advocate of cellular isolation), we are told (" Les reformes penitentiares " in Revue de Droit Penal et de Criminologie, March and April, 1921) that " The International Prison Congress of 1900 at Brussels may be said to have set the crown upon the head of the Cellular System : a unanimous satisfecit was pronounced upon this system as it was carried out in Belgium. France, Prussia, Spain, Italy, and many other nations, had successively adopted, more or less completely, the same principle, which the United States had revived from Bentham and Pope Clement XI. The credit of this principle had never ceased to grow, at least on this side of the water, right down to the declaration of war (1914)."

Nevertheless public opinion became gradually once more uneasy about the state of the prisons. It could not be concealed that " recidivism "—the repeated convictions for renewed crimes of those who had passed through the prisons apparently unameliorated and undeterred—did not diminish, and seemed, in fact, in certain categories of criminals, even to increase. Those who, like the Salvation Army officers and other philanthropists, had to do with discharged prisoners, reported unfavourably upon their mental condition. It began to be said that the boasted improvement of the prisons was, after all, merely in externals ; that the buildings only had been made sanitary, and that although the prisoners might be kept in what was called bodily health, they left the prison physically weakened, and were often so mentally broken down by their confinement as to be incapable of earning an honest livelihood. " If we look," it was said, a little later, " for the really essential changes during a hundred years, we find just these :

" 1. A surface cleanliness of apparent perfection ;
" 2. Conversation, prison visits and arrangements tending towards a decent sociability between prisoners and prisoners, and between prisoners and the public, reduced and rendered difficult by multitudinous byelaws."

" On the one hand a cleanliness obtainable only by irritating industry disproportionate to its proper value : on the other hand a reduction of such facilities as are most likely to prevent a prisoner from degenerating to a social alien, an automatic machine or a lunatic."[1] What began to be said, in fact, in less restrained language, was that the prisons were " whited sepulchres," less scandalously cruel in particular cases, but possibly more insidiously injurious to the great mass of their unfortunate inmates than

[1] Introduction by A. F. Murison, p. viii, to *The Criminal and the Community*, by James Devon, 1910.

the unreformed gaols that they had replaced.[1]
We are warranted in some such judgment upon
" the Du Cane régime " that followed the Act of
1877 by the careful and restrained conclusions of the
experienced administrator who, in 1895, succeeded
Sir Edmund Du Cane as Chairman of the Prison
Commission. " At a relatively small cost the prison
buildings soon after the Act were brought up
to a high standard, both in construction and in
sanitation. It may be that in some respects his
desire for economy led him too far in the direction
of retrenchment, both in buildings and in service.
. . . There had been, moreover, a decrease in the
yearly death rate, in the number of suicides "—*it will
be noted that no claim is made for any decrease in insanity*—" and in corporal punishments, and in the yearly
average of dietary punishments." In shor⁺, Sir
Edmund Du Cane " had completely succeeded . . .
in promoting uniformity, economy and a generally
improved administration."[2] Nothing is said, it will
be noted, as to the effect on the prisoners themselves,
and on the after-life of the hundred thousand or so
men and women who were annually subjected to the
régime. We must supply the omission by the grave
reflection, authoritatively made in 1895, that " the
moral condition in which a large number of prisoners
leave the prison, and the serious number of recom-
mittals, have led us to think that there is ample cause
for a searching inquiry into the main features of
prison life."[3]
It was a long time before the gradually accumu-
lating public criticism took effect. At last, after the
General Election of 1892,when Mr. Asquith was Home
Secretary, the Government was, in 1894, prevailed
upon[4] to allow an inquiry into the whole prison sys-

[1] Kropotkin could even declare that " our model and modern penitentiaries were a hundred times more corrupting than the dungeons of the
Middle Ages " (*Paroles d'un révolté*, 1885, p. 243).
[2] *The English Prison System*, by Sir Evelyn Ruggles-Brise, 1921, pp. 1-37.
[3] Report of Home Office Committee on Prisons, 1895.
[4] It should be recorded to the honour of the Rev. W. D. Morrison, who
had had a long term of service as prison chaplain, that it is said to have
been largely owing to his representations that the Committee was appointed.

tem, not, indeed, by any independent authority, but by a Departmental Committee of carefully selected members, presided over by the Under-Secretary of State (Mr. Herbert, afterwards Lord Gladstone), who was himself sharing with Mr. Asquith in the responsibility for the prison administration. It is not too much to say that this Committee, less by its specific recommendations than by its very serious reflections on the failure of the Du Cane régime and by the new spirit which it put into the Home Office administration, started, after unexplained delay, what we may hope to have been the beginning of a beneficent revolution.[1]

The Committee of 1894-5 made a keen, and somewhat minute inquiry into the principles and practice of the Prison Commissioners, although it was found impossible for the members to visit many of the prisons, or to gain much from the experience of the subordinate prison officers—let alone consult many ex-prisoners, or the prisoners themselves! The Committee paid a due meed of testimony to the complete success which Sir Edmund Du Cane had achieved in the direction of uniformity, discipline and economy ; and to the attention given to organization, finance, order, sanitation and statistics. But as Sir Edmund Du Cane was fortunately on the point of retiring from office on reaching the age of superannuation, the Committee felt free, so far as the condition of the prisoners was concerned, to pass, in carefully restrained language, what was nothing short of a condemnation of the Du Cane régime itself. The

An impressive article by him, entitled " Are our prisons a failure ? " appeared in the *Fortnightly Review* in May, 1894. His books, *Crime and its Causes*, 1891, and *Juvenile Offenders*, 1896, were influential and suggestive. Other books of this period were *Jottings from Jail*, 1887, and *Prisons and Prisoners*, both by the Rev. J. W. Horsley ; *Experience of a Medical Officer in the English Convict Service*, by J. Campbell, 1884 ; *Scenes from a Silent World*, by F. Scougal, 1889 ; *In Base Durance* : *Reminiscences of a Prison Chaplain*, by Rev. F. Meredyth, 1891 ; *Secrets of the Prison House*, by Arthur Griffiths, 1894 ; *Kirkdale Gaol* : *Twelve Months' Imprisonment of a Manchester Merchant*, 1880 ; *Twelve Months in an English Prison*, by S. W. Fletcher, 1884 ; *Eighteen Months' Imprisonment*, by D. S., 1884 ; and *I was in Prison*, by F. Brocklehurst, 1898.

[1] Report of Home Office Committee on Prisons, 1895.

effect on the hundred thousand or so men and women
on whom it was annually imposed had not been kept
in mind. "The great, and as we consider the
proved danger of this highly centralized system has
been and is that while much attention has been
given to organization, finance, order, health of the
prisoners and prison statistics, the prisoners have
been treated too much as a hopeless or worthless
element of the community, and the moral as well as
the legal responsibilities of the Prison Authorities
has been held to cease when they pass outside the
prison gates." That the system completely failed
to effect any reformation of character was admitted by the highest authority in the Home Office
itself. The Permanent Under-Secretary of State
described the nature of the influence upon the prison
population in terms with which the Committee were
constrained to agree. "I regard as unfavourable to
reformation," said Sir Godfrey Lushington, "the
status of a prisoner throughout his whole career ;
the crushing of self-respect; the starving of all moral
instinct he may possess ; the absence of all opportunity to do or receive a kindness ; the continual
association with none but criminals, and that only as
a separate item among other items also separate ;
the forced labour and the denial of all liberty. I
believe the true mode of reforming a man, or restoring
him to society, is exactly in the opposite direction
of all these." And this experienced official added,
in terms indicating how little the Home Office even
thought of any alteration, "But of course this is a
mere idea. It is quite impracticable in a prison. In
fact, the unfavourable features I have mentioned are
inseparable from prison life." The Committee took
a different view. "We do not agree," they unanimously declared," that all these unfavourable features
are irremovable. . . . We think that the system
should be made more elastic, more capable of being
adapted to the special cases of individual prisoners ;
that prison discipline and treatment should be more
effectually designed to maintain, stimulate or awaken

the higher susceptibilities of prisoners, to develop their moral instincts, to train them in orderly and industrial habits, and whenever possible to turn them out of prison better men and women physically and mentally than when they came in."

It became plain, moreover, that the " Du Cane régime " had achieved no greater success in deterrence than in reformation. The average population in prison had fallen off, but the Committee found no warrant for the self-complacency of the Prison Commissioners in imagining that their rigorous regimen of deterrence was diminishing either the amount of crime or the number of criminals. The diminution in the average prison population which had been so triumphantly adduced as a proof of the success of the "Du Cane régime " was shown to be almost entirely accounted for by a reduction in the average length of sentence awarded by the judges and magistrates. The recidivism was as great as ever. " The broad deduction may be made," it was later remarked, " that so long as the classical conception of punishment remained, i.e., the mechanical application of the letter of the law to an abstract type of offender, no great impression was being made either in the number or character of offences. Statistics varied from year to year under the influence of special circumstances ; but the great stage army of offenders in all the categories continued its unbroken array, with a monotonous regularity ; and it seemed almost a mockery to talk of social progress, when, in the background was the silent, ceaseless tramp of this multitude of men, women and children, finding no rest but behind prison walls, and only issuing thence to re-enter again."[1]

The Committee, accordingly, did something to get the " Du Cane régime " upset, so far as its aim was to deter by severity. It recommended the abolition of the tread-wheel, the crank and, "as much as possible," of all similarly " penal " forms of labour. It insisted on the adoption of productive labour, not, as formerly,

[1] *The English Prison System*, by Sir E. Ruggles-Brise, 1921, p. xix.

for the sake of the profit to be made by the State, but
because of its good effect on the minds of the prisoners.
The Committee evidently regarded with the gravest
suspicion the very foundation of prison discipline,
the system of cellular isolation itself, even with all
the mitigations on which the advocates of the " Separate System " laid such stress. So carefully chosen
a Committee could not bring itself to recommend the
total abandonment of what had, for more than half
a century, been an official panacea. The Committee
declared it to be, as enforced in penal servitude, " a
terrible ordeal," and recommended that the period
should be reconsidered—some of the members privately conveying their opinion, it is said, to the
Home Secretary, in favour either of total abolition
or of the period being reduced to no more than a few
weeks.[1] It was made quite clear, as was indeed
officially recognized, that " the public inquiry of
1894 into prison administration was a practical
condemnation of the separate or cellular system
except for short periods. It swept aside the old-
fashioned idea that separate confinement was desirable on the ground that it enables the prisoner to
meditate on his misdeeds. It held that association
for industrial labour under proper conditions could
be productive of no harm."[2]

So long as any remnant of the system of cellular
isolation was maintained by day, the confinement
was, at any rate, to be mitigated in certain directions.
There was to be a larger discretion allowed to Visiting
Justices to permit visits to and communications
with prisoners. " The present practice of imposing silence except for the purposes of labour and
during the visits of officials and authorized persons, for
a period it may be of fifteen or twenty years, seems to

[1] Not until 1910-1, however, was this recommendation acted upon. In
March, 1911, it is said, after the Home Secretary, Mr. Winston Churchill,
had witnessed the moving performance of Mr. Galsworthy's tragedy of
Justice—the period of what was popularly known as solitary confinement
was reduced to one month for all but recidivists, for whom it was made
three months.

[2] *The English Prison System*, by Sir Evelyn Ruggles-Brise, 1921,
p. 137.

us unnatural." At least, the privilege of talking (withdrawn in 1877) should be restored to prisoners under long sentences. Sunday exercise (which had been suppressed in order, as it was alleged, to avoid an increase in the prison staff sufficient to allow to the warders one day's rest in seven) should be reinstituted, and gymnastics should be organized. There should be a larger and more varied supply of books. The exhortations of the prison chaplain should be varied by the invitation of selected outside preachers. The prison medical officers should keep a continuous watch for any signs of impairment of mind ; and for this purpose they should be chosen from among candidates showing some proficiency in the study of mental disease and lunacy. And, what to social students will seem most revolutionary of all, the large proportion of prisoners deemed to be weak-minded should not be subjected to the ordinary prison regimen, but should be concentrated in a special prison, where they could be detained under special medical supervision. It should, indeed, be considered, the Committee recommended, whether such persons should be treated as criminals at all.

The Report of the Committee of 1894-5 was wholeheartedly adopted by the Government ; and the Home Secretary (Mr. Asquith), in appointing Mr. (afterwards Sir) Evelyn Ruggles-Brise to be Chairman of the Prison Commissioners, expressly directed that the recommendations of the Committee should be put in operation throughout the whole prison system.[1] We may, indeed, recognize, from that date, a certain change of tone in the central prison administration. Unfortunately, as the Prison Commissioners seem to have thought, it was only very slowly, and very incompletely that reforms could be effected.[2] It took three years before a new Act could be obtained (the Prisons Act, 1898), which, by making every

---

[1] *The English Prison System*, by Sir Evelyn Ruggles-Brise, 1921, p. 77.
[2] Statement by the Prison Commissioners on the action which has been taken to carry out the recommendations of the Departmental Committee of 1895 (1898).

Prison Commissioner ex-officio a Director of Convict Prisons, practically (though not formally) merged into one the two separate Boards of Commissioners for convict and local prisons respectively, and enabled the Home Secretary at any time to make new rules and alterations applicable to all the prisons and fortified by the sanction of Parliament. This Act, carried through by Sir Matthew White Ridley, set up, for the first time, an independent and unofficial Board of Visitors for each convict prison, analogous to the Visiting Committees of the local prisons. The Act also took it out of the power, even of a Director of Convict Prisons, to order a flogging ; corporal punishment was henceforth to be ordered only by the Board of Visitors or Visiting Committee, and then only subject to confirmation by the Home Secretary and in cases of gross personal violence to a prison official and acts of mutiny. New rules made under this Act, which came into force on May 1st, 1899, embodied some of the spirit and some of the specific recommendations of the Committee of 1894-5. The tread-wheel·and the crank were finally banished from the prisons. The privilege of gaining a remission of part of the sentence by good marks was, after some delay, extended to all inmates sentenced to more than one month's imprisonment. Work in association, after the initial month of cellular isolation (which the Prison Commissioners could not bring themselves to abolish), was extended to all the inmates of the local prisons. At the same time, upon the report of a special departmental committee, the dietaries were made more varied and somewhat more generous.[1] But it was not until 1901—six years after the Committee had reported—that the feeble-minded inmates of the local prisons even began to be segregated, and placed under special treatment.[2] In the opening years of

---

[1] Report of Committee on Prison Dietaries, 1899. The contrast, alike in tone and in substance, between this report and that of 1878 on Prison Dietaries, is most marked.

[2] A beginning was made, with the inmates of convict prisons only, in 1897, when convicts deemed to be distinctly feeble-minded began to be

the twentieth century the dietaries were at last
reformed in such a way as somewhat to diminish the
prisoners' usual loss in weight, with the incidental
result, in conjunction with other new regulations, of
presently reducing the death rate from tuberculosis
by nearly one half![1] The economic problem of
prison labour was eased by the frank acceptance
(after the prescribed initial period of cellular isolation) of work in association under continuous and
rigorous supervision, either in the service of the
prison itself (including domestic work and the culti-
vation of land), or in production for all the various
government departments (including tailoring, shoemaking, carpentry, printing, bookbinding and tin-
work, and the manufacture of mailbags and baskets
for the Post Office). However inadequate the trade
instruction may have been, however imperfect the
work, and however little use the occupation to the
prisoners themselves, it may at least be said that,
gradually, the prison productions disposed of by sale
to the public sank to a very small amount ; and practically the whole prison population became engaged in
the direct provision of what was required by the
Government itself.[2] Another recommendation of the

segregated at Parkhurst Prison (Isle of Wight). Such a segregation had
been recommended as long before as 1879, by the Penal Servitude Committee of that year ; but under the Du Cane régime no opportunity had
been found to carry it out.

[1] We may cite, among the books of this period, as to the condition of the
English prisons and the direction of reform—besides the works of Rev.
W. D. Morrison and Rev. J. W. Horsley, and the books by prisoners them-
selves, already mentioned : *Prisons, Police and Punishment,* by Edward
Carpenter, 1905 ; *Selected Papers,* 1866-1901, of the Howard Association,
1901 ; *Annals of Wakefield House of Correction,* by J. H. Turner, 1904 ;
Young Gaol Birds, by C. E. B. Russell, 1910, and *Young Delinquents,* by
M. G. Barnett, 1913 (taking up the advocacy begun by Mary Carpenter's
Juvenile Delinquents, 1853) ; *Our Prison System,* by A. Cook, 1914 ; *Wards
of the State : an official view of prison and the prisoner,* by T. Hopkins,
1913 ; *Our Prisons,* by A. Paterson, 1911 ; *Crime and Criminals,* 1910, and
The Modern Prison Curriculum, 1912, both by R. F. Quinton ; *The
Criminal and the Community,* by Dr. James Devon, 1912 ; *History of
Penal Methods,* by George Ives, 1914 ; *An English Prison from Within,*
by Stephen Hobhouse, 1919; *A Prison Chaplain on Dartmoor,* by Rev.
Clifford Rickards, 1920; and *The English Convict,* by Charles Goring,
1913 ; together with publications of the Humanitarian League, the Penal
Reform League, the Howard Association and the Discharged Prisoners'
Aid Societies.

[2] Already in 1898 the Prison Commissioners could say that " practically
speaking, all prison labour is for government departments " (Statement on

Committee of 1895 was very tardily carried out by the systematization and slightly more liberal endowment of the voluntary agencies providing for the employment and kindly care of discharged prisoners, to the advantages of which the men and women discharged from the convict prisons were, for various technical reasons, not admitted until 1911.[1] An even more hopeful though much retarded outcome of the Committee of 1894-5 was the legislative action taken between 1907 and 1914 with the intention, as yet very imperfectly carried out, of clearing the prisons alto-

the action taken with reference to the recommendations of the Committee of 1895). In our *Industrial Democracy*, 1897, pp. 787-8, we pointed out that the economically injurious effect of " prison labour " was not that it " deprived workmen of employment " or employers of profitable business, but that sales of prison-made goods were apt to lead to a progressive lowering of prices and wages. The evil lay, not in prison production, but in the actual placing upon the market of the prison-made products. If these are sold at competitive prices, " they must inevitably undercut the wares made by self-supporting operatives, who will therefore find their employment rendered less continuous than it would otherwise be, and *who will accordingly be unable to resist the reductions forced upon them by their employers.* This is not, as is often argued, because the institution labourers displace other operatives, but because they lower the price of the product. The psychological effect on the market is even more serious than the direct displacement of custom. Every private manufacturer fears that he may be the one destined to lose his customers to the institution which need not consider cost of production at all ; and this fear supplies the buyers with an irresistible lever for forcing down price. The harm lies in this lowering of the Standard of Life of other classes, not in any mere diversion from them of possible additional custom. Hence there is no economic harm, and nothing but gain, in the inmates of institutions producing for consumption or use inside the institution. This has no tendency to lower prices or wages outside, any more than the fact that sailors at sea or in harbour wash their own clothes lowers the wages of laundresses on land." (*Industrial Democracy*, edition of 1920, p. 788.) Thus, the policy now adopted by the Prison Commissioners of confining prison production practically to the supply of the various government departments, without offering anything for sale, is not open to economic objection, and excites no Trade Union protest.

[1] For the beneficent work of the Discharged Prisoners' Aid Societies, for which Acts of 1823, 1862 and 1865 authorized the grant of subventions by the Local Prison Authorities out of the rates, and the Act of 1877 a grant from the Exchequer, see the admirable summary in Chapter xiv of Sir Evelyn Ruggles-Brise's *English Prison System*, 1921 ; and the various reports of the separate societies, notably those of London, Birmingham, Worcester, Gloucester and Wakefield. It was one of the suggestions of the Committee of 1894-5, that these societies should be made the subject of official inquiry with a view to their being systematized, made absolutely co-extensive with the discharges and brought into a single organization, The Prison Commissioners made their inquiry in 1896, and issued new rules in 1897. In 1909 it was decided to form a central association under official supervision to deal on discharge with all convicts whom the local societies had not previously dealt with. Not until 1918, however, was the Central Discharged Prisoners' Aid Society formed to co-ordinate the whole work.

gether of a large class of offenders for whom the prison regimen was plainly unsuited. Thus, in 1907, the Probation Act, making more effective a provision in the Probation of First Offenders Act, 1887, which had remained largely inoperative, enabled a Court, instead of pronouncing sentence, to release the prisoner on probation, under the supervision of a Probation Officer, if it was thought that the prisoner's age, health, mental condition, antecedents or character, or the triviality of the offence, or any extenuating circumstances, made such a course desirable.[1] With the Prevention of Crime Act of 1908 came the institution of an entirely new system of reformatory treatment for some of the more serious offenders among the " juvenile adult " criminals, of whom the common gaol ought to be altogether relieved ; and the comparative success of this " Borstal " regimen seems to open up a vista of further reforms.[2] The Prevention of Crime Act of 1908 introduced, too, a new variety into English prison administration. The judge was empowered, in addition to any sentence of penal servitude of not less than three years, to impose a further term, not exceeding ten years, of Preventive Detention. This gave effect to a suggestion which had been discussed ever since the Committee of 1894-5, for exceptional measures against hardened " professional " criminals, whose whole lives were spent in preying upon the public. They had been shown to be deterred neither by prolonged imprisonment nor by penal servitude. What was desired was some system by which they could be indefinitely segregated, without conditions of excessive severity, to be released only if and when

[1] For the very hopeful " Probation System "—even now by no means fully in operation—see *Memorandum on the Probation System in America*, Cd. 3401, 1907 ; the numerous American reports ; *Origin and Progress of the Probation System*, by Thomas R. Bridgwater, 1909 ; *Probation and Probation Officers*, by Miss N. Adler, 1908 ; *The Probation System*, by Cecil Leeson, 1914 ; and Chapter ix, of Sir Evelyn Ruggles-Brise's *The English Prison System*, 1921.

[2] For the achievements and prospects of " the Borstal System," see the successive reports of the Borstal Association, and the admirable summary in *The English Prison System*, by Sir Evelyn Ruggles-Brise, 1921, Chapter viii, pp. 85-100.

they were believed to be willing to abandon their predatory careers. Parliament "shied" at the idea of an "Indeterminate Sentence," and a Bill of 1903 failed to become law. Five years later, however, the principle of a comparatively mild Preventive Detention, after completion of (but not, as some advocated, in substitution for) a term of penal servitude, was embodied in the Act of 1908. A special prison at Camp Hill, in the Isle of Wight, has now been set apart, in which this supplementary detention takes place under pleasant surroundings, and with the minimum of penal discipline. It is too soon to form any confident opinion as to the results of this experiment, which is, however, proving hopeful. Unfortunately, owing to certain defects in the law, and the indisposition of the Judges to follow the lead of the Legislature, the advantages of the Camp Hill Prison are but little utilized. In another direction the Mental Deficiency Act, 1913, will, it is hoped, gradually relieve the prisons of "many persons of both sexes who hitherto have spent their lives in and out of prison—the despair of the Courts, a source of perpetual trouble to the police, and of nuisance to their neighbours, would, on inquiry and mental observation, be found to be irresponsibles, and proper subjects for medical care rather than the grim severity of ceaseless and useless imprisonment. The long and mournful roll of incurable recidivists would cease to haunt our prisons and public places, and under institutional care would at least be removed from evil-doing, if they did not regain, under medical care, their opportunity for reinstatement in normal industrious life."[2] Finally, the Criminal Justice Administration Act, 1914, by its insistence on time being allowed for the payment of

---

[1] The Prison Commissioners have themselves virtually admitted that mentally defective criminals have continued to be improperly confined in prison, owing to the lack of accommodation for them elsewhere. "The absence of institutional provision for defectives, and particularly State accommodation for males, exercises a paralysing influence on operations under the [Mental Deficiency] Act as regards the disposal of criminal defectives." (Report of the Commissioners of Prisons and the Directors of Convict Prisons for 1915-6, Cd. 8342.)

[2] The English Prison System, by Sir Evelyn Ruggles-Brise, 1921, p. 16.

fines, and its permission to the Court to place offenders between sixteen and twenty-one under supervision until the sum is paid, is already enormously reducing the number of persons committed to prison in default of payment of a fine. Unfortunately, what with the slowness of Justices and their clerks to get out of their habit of instant commission to prison of every kind of convicted offender,[1] and what with the manifold interruptions caused by the Great War, none of these statutes has yet been put into operation either fully or ubiquitously. It seems unfortunate that it does not lie within the habits of the Home Office or of the Lord Chancellor's Department to maintain a constant watch upon the practice of all Courts of Justice (and, of course, particularly those of Summary Jurisdiction), in order that any habitual neglect to take advantage of these statutes, and even every marked statistical deviation from the average in the extent to which they are applied, should be made the subject of inquiry, and, where necessary, of private expostulation. Such a continuous supervision of the practice of the Courts, with a view to a more prompt and more complete compliance with

---

[1] " Custom, routine and the fatal ease, and saving of trouble to all concerned, has, in the past, induced the tendency to regard the warrant of commitment to prison as the ordinary and only expedient for satisfying the claims of justice." (*Ibid.*, p. 13). Thus, it is perhaps in the direction of the " individualization of punishment "—really considering how best to deal with each person convicted of an offence, according to his age, sex, antecedents, attainments and character—that least progress has so far been made in England. It was here that the " fetish of uniformity " of the " Du Cane régime " probably worked most harm. On the other hand, it must in fairness be said that the English system assumed (down to the institution of " Preventive Detention " by the Act of 1908) that it was not for the prison administrators to " individualize," or " fit the punishment to the crime," but for the sentencing tribunal. Unfortunately, in spite of successive statutes, judges, magistrates and justices' clerks are extremely slow to appreciate that it is their duty to " individualize," even to the extent of acting under the Probation Act (thus, the Chaplain of Wakefield Prison said in 1916, " Unfortunately, there can be no doubt whatever that full advantage is not being taken of the powers conferred by recent statutes. In some Courts the Probation Act is only applied in case of felony " (Report of the Howard Association, 1916, p. 18) ; and Parliament, except in the small degree involved in Preventive Detention, has so far refused to adopt the principle of the Indeterminate Sentence (See *The Individualization of Punishment*, by R. Saleilles, 1911 ; Proceedings of the Washington Congress of International Prison Conference, 1910 ; *The English Prison System*, by Sir E. Ruggles-Brise, 1921, ch. v).

ameliorative statutes, has the support of high official
authority.[1]

With these changes we are brought down to the
prison administration of the present, which is described in the volume entitled *English Prisons To-day,
being the Report of the Prison System Enquiry Committee*, by Stephen Hobhouse and A. Fenner Brockway, 1922. To that authoritative description, which
incidentally reveals the extent to which the reforms
have been actually put in operation, and where they
are found to fall short, the present work should serve
only as an historical introduction.[2]

---

[1] " I would not advise," says the Chairman of the Prison Commissioners,
" the imposition of any official system independently of the Courts, but
only that the political heads of the Judiciary should take steps to satisfy
themselves that Probation, as a system, *is working efficiently at every
criminal court in the country* before whom offenders of all ages liable to the
penalty of imprisonment are brought. (*The English Prison System*, by
Sir E. Ruggles-Brise, 1921, p. 13.)

A like supervision and inquiry might, with advantage, be exercised over
the commitments to prison of debtors deemed to be in contempt of court.
It cannot be satisfactory that the proportion of such commitments should
vary enormously from one County Court district to another, according to
the idiosyncrasies of County Court Judges and Registrars (the latter being
generally remunerated by fees). The Lord Chancellor, speaking in the
House of Lords on February 15th, 1907, is reported as saying that " in
some County Courts—though he did not impugn the good faith of the
Judges—the administration of the Debtors' Act had led to great hardships."

[2] For exhaustive lists of books and reports on criminology and penology,
the student will consult *A Preliminary Bibliography of Modern Criminal
Law and Criminology*, by John H. Wigmore (North Western University,
Chicago, 1909) ; *Lehrbuch der Gefangnisskunde*, by K. Krohne ; and *A
Contribution towards a Bibliography dealing with Crime*, by Sir J. G. Cum-
ming, K.C.S.I., 1914.

EPILOGUE

I

WE make no attempt to pass judgment upon the English prison system at any stage of its development. As regards the past, any deliberate assessment of the character and effects of the prisons of any particular period would not only be, perforce, wanting in accuracy, but would, moreover, now serve no useful purpose. As regards the prisons of to-day, the student must be referred to the minutely detailed and extremely comprehensive survey in the simultaneously published volume entitled *English Prisons To-day, being the Report of the Prison System Enquiry Committee*, by Stephen Hobhouse and A. Fenner Brockway. But we permit ourselves certain observations upon the history that we have sought to relate.

II

Apart altogether from what is called penology, or the general theory and practice of the punishment of offenders against social laws and conventions, the history of English prison administration should be of first-rate interest to the student of Political Science, from the light that it throws upon important general problems of public administration. If we inquire how the public services should be divided, as between central and local government, the administration of English prisons—passing in 1877 from local to central—is a leading case, from which we may derive both instruction and warning. If we seek to formulate the relations that ought to exist between the actual administrators of local institutions and services on the one hand, and the central supervisory department and its inspectors on the

other, the successive experiences of the English
prison service, in 1837-77 and 1878-1921 respectively,
are full of lessons. A third point of fundamental
importance is the effect of permitting the performance of public functions, or the discharge of the
duties of a public office, to be made—apart from the
receipt of a determinate (though not necessarily an
unvarying) stipend—a source of private profit. This
is by no means a past issue. It is true that no instructed person in this country would to-day propose
(as Jeremy Bentham did only a century ago, and
Charles Pearson did as late as the middle of the
nineteenth century) to " farm out " the prisoners to
their gaolers or to labour contractors—a practice
still prevalent in various other countries. But it
has come to be a matter of very serious consideration
to what functions and to what offices the conception
of being of a public nature should be, in this respect,
applied.

III

Although the question of whether the administration of prisons should fall within the sphere of central
government, or within that of local government, as a
problem of Political Science, has scarcely been seriously discussed in England, the case for the with-
drawal of the prisons from the local authorities of
1877 was, in our judgment, irresistible, though not
for the reasons usually adduced in support of that
measure. We are less impressed to-day than the
prison officials of the Home Office of 1876-7 appeared
to be, with the necessity, in the interests of even-
handed justice, of securing an absolute uniformity of
prison regimen and prison discipline for all persons
serving sentences of equal duration, to whatever part
of the country they belonged. A crude identity of
this sort, which has the very smallest relation to
equality, can have but a limited value in Political
Science. Nor were the financial economies to be
effected by national unification of the prison service
so important or so indisputable as to warrant, in

themselves, so great a revolution. The claim for a reduction in the rates levied on the county areas, which we may, without uncharitableness, assume to have been the determining factor in the political decision to centralize the prison administration, might (as experience has since demonstrated) have been more advantageously met, in so far as this was just or expedient, by an extension of the system of Grants in Aid.[1] In any case, it is not by the argument of " high rates " that the transfer of *any particular service* from Local to Central Government can be justified. Apart from all these considerations, it was, as we can now recognize, more than anything else, the unsuitability of the areas administered by the hundred or so local prison authorities, coupled with the diversity of these authorities themselves—not to speak of their own manifold shortcomings—that would have anyhow made necessary their super-session as autonomous prison authorities. Even when the average daily population of the prisons for England and Wales exceeded 30,000, none of the local authorities (except perhaps those of the then undivided counties of Middlesex and Lancashire) acted for areas of sufficient census population to warrant their separate administration of even one gaol or penitentiary of the size that separate sleeping accommodation for each prisoner, and useful work in association practically involves. With a prison population reduced to fewer than 10,000, not sixty or seventy, but more like a dozen or a score of pro-perly constructed prisons should be enough for the whole country. What is even more important, no one building—as we can now see—ought to suffice for any area. If we are to have places of confinement at all, and to make them such as the conscience of the nation can approve, they must (though the Home Office has so far only very imperfectly learned this lesson) be specialized for prisoners of different sexes, ages, sentences and conditions of physical and mental

---

[1] See *Grants in Aid : a Criticism and a Proposal*, by Sidney Webb (second edition, 1920).

health, and possibly also for prisoners of different degrees of mental capacity, different antecedents and different characters. The case is one in which, as Chadwick used to say, we must " aggregate in order to segregate." No practicable readjustment of the areas of counties and boroughs could, even after the Local Government Act of 1888, have created units of local government on a geographical basis suitable for efficient prison administration according to modern ideas. We suggest that the intellectual error made in 1876-7, and one often but less excusably repeated in our own day, was the assumption that, because the administration of prisons by the County and Borough Authorities had become inadmissible, the administration of all the prisons by a Department of the Central Government was necessarily the best, or more correctly, the only alternative. One of the lessons of Political Science is that the " opposite of the wrong " is seldom, if ever, found to be "the right."

IV

It is worth while to consider some of the characteristic features of centralized administration by a Government Department, as exemplified, first by the Directors of Convict Prisons, and then by the Prison Commissioners, as branches of the Home Office of 1844-1921.

We are struck, first, by the loss of publicity which the transfer of the administration from local to central government has involved. Since 1878 the prison has become " a silent world," shrouded, so far as the public is concerned, in almost complete darkness. This is due, in the first place, to the policy, to which every well-ordered administration is prone, of " No admittance except on business." The widespread and repeated visitations and minute investigations of John Howard and James Nield, of J. J. Gurney and Sir Thomas Fowell Buxton, or even the popular descriptions of the London prisons which Henry Mayhew was allowed to compile about 1860, would not be permitted by the Home Office of to-day, on the ground that they would constitute an unnecessary interference with the official administration. Although it would be incorrect to say that special permission to inspect the interior of a prison is invariably refused, such visits from outsiders are, in this generation, so severely discouraged, and are purposely made so unremunerative in the way of discovery of how the machine actually works, that they have been, since 1878, and still are very infrequently made. Moreover, the conditions under which such visits are allowed very effectively discourage any wide promulgation of what is seen ; and they practically never lead to the publication of anything that would enable the public to realize what is actually going on within the prison walls.[1] Along with the practice of exclusion of the outsider, for which a plausible argument may be made, there goes an official policy of deliberate reticence, in order not to give any opportunity for troublesome questions to be raised in Parliament, and so as not to afford material for critical articles in the public press.[2] The information published to the world is reduced to a minimum. From the passing of the Prisons Act of 1898 down to the outbreak of war in 1914 only brief, uninforming and obviously censored reports by governors, chaplains and doctors were published. Since 1914 no reports whatever by the persons actually engaged in the administration of the several prisons have been permitted to appear.[3] No person engaged in

---

[1] We ought to notice the work entitled *Our Prisoners*, by A. Paterson, 1911. The author seems to have been granted very special opportunities for preparing this book, which gives, to say the least, a glowing impression of the perfection of prison administration, with the minimum of criticism or even of suggestion. This exception to the practice indicates, we venture to think, an additional danger incidental to the policy of secretiveness. In 1922 the author was appointed a Prison Commissioner.

[2] We are informed that the " Standing Orders " and special instructions for governors, chaplains, doctors and warders are not published, and are not supplied to any inquirer.

[3] A special exception was made in the case of Dr. Charles Goring's report in 1913, on his investigation into the physical characteristics of the prison population, from which, however, any description of the nature and effects of the prison regimen was purposely omitted.

the administration is allowed to publish any book or article on the subject of his work[1] without the permission and imprimatur of the Commissioners, which, as a rule, they appear to be reluctant to give. The reports of the inspectors to the Prison Commissioners are, since 1878, all treated as confidential documents, and only such extracts as the Commissioners think it expedient to embody in their own report are presented to Parliament. It is true that there is a small number of Visiting Justices for each prison, and a carefully selected body of Lady Visitors for the women's prisons. But any criticisms, suggestions or reports that are from time to time made by these authorized visitors are not published, as they might easily be, if only in an appendix to the annual report which the Prison Commissioners make on their own administration. Even when a special inquiry has to be made into some alleged scandal, the inquiry is nowadays always entrusted, not to some person unconnected with the administration,[2] but to one or more officers of the Prison Service ; it is held in private ; the evidence is not published ; and the report is a confidential document, which the Home Office keeps to itself, sometimes without publishing even the decision of the Prison Commissioners or the Home Secretary on the subject. It is scarcely too much to say that, since 1878—apart from the proceedings of the departmental Committee of 1894-5 and a few official committees on minor matters—the Prison Commissioners' deliberate policy has been to ensure that the only source of authoritative information about

[1] Here, again, significant exceptions have been sparingly made. The chairman of the Prison Commissioners, together with one or two selected members of the staff, have, since 1900, read papers (naturally not of a critical character) to the International Prison Congresses ; and, in 1921, Sir Evelyn Ruggles-Brise, near the end of his long service, allowed his book, *The English Prison System*, which had been printed in Maidstone Prison, to be communicated to various newspapers for review, and it was presently published in regular form.

[2] There was, we believe, no independent Commission or Committee to inquire into any alleged prison scandal in England and Wales between 1880 and 1914 ; there seems, indeed, to have been practically none since the Royal Commissions into the administration of the Birmingham and Leicester prisons of 1854.

what is going on in our prisons should be the series of annual reports by the Commissioners themselves, which naturally tell the public only so much of the facts as the Commissioners think to be, in the public interest, expedient.

We do not adduce this example of official reticence and secretiveness, with the consequent loss of publicity, by way of animadversion on the Home Office. A like policy may be seen in the War Office and Admiralty, the Ministry of Labour and the Office of Works. It is, in fact, characteristic of all bureaucracies dealing with an extensive staff, and directly carrying on administration over a wide area. Nor does it prevail, as we shall presently explain, in all the branches of public administration, for which the Home Secretary is responsible. It is worth while to seek to discover what exactly is the cause and the argument for such a denial of publicity.

It is often said by way of justification for this policy of reticence and secretiveness, that any other course, and notably the publication of criticisms of the administration of particular institutions or particular officers, would be seriously prejudicial to the administration itself and especially to the maintenance of " discipline." It will be noted, however, that no such consideration prevents public criticism and the communication of the inspectors' reports, special inquiries by disinterested outsiders, and full publication of the proceedings in the newspapers, when the administration concerned, as is the case with regard to nine-tenths of the administration of this country, is that of some authority other than that of the government department itself. The maintenance of discipline, and the upholding of the credit of the administration, dependent as it so largely is on public confidence, is vital in all branches of Local Government, in the railways, in the merchant marine, in the mining industry, in the management of lunatic asylums and reformatories, and indeed, in every considerable service. But the various government departments, including the Home Office itself, when the administration concerned is not that of a government department, rightly disregard the natural yearnings of every administration for secrecy with regard to its own weaknesses or failures ; and the reports of inspectors and special investigators with regard to the action or inaction of local governing bodies, the nonfeasance or malfeasance of their officials, the condition of schools and colleges, and the causes of accidents at sea, on the railway or in the mine, are given effective publicity. The Home Office itself relies on publicity in the right quarters for the efficacy of the supervision of the Board of Control over lunatic asylums, and that of its own inspectors over factories and workshops on the one hand, and industrial and reformatory schools on the other. It is, seemingly, only when the administration is its own that a government department finds that inspection and public criticism by disinterested outsiders are incompatible with discipline and the best administration.

Nor can we attach weight to the argument that there is something peculiar in the administration of a prison that makes publicity specially undesirable. We find almost exactly the same policy of reticence and secretiveness in all government departments directly administering other institutions. And when the prisons were administered by local authorities, the Home Office, as we have seen, saw no reason why its inspectors' reports should be treated as confidential documents and withheld from publication. However scathingly the inspectors criticized the prison governor, or the prison administration generally, the Home Office of 1835-77 did not find that it was destructive of discipline or inimical to good administration to issue these reports to the world, any more than does the Home Office of 1921 with regard to its inspectors' reports on reformatory schools. We are inevitably led to the conclusion that it is not the character of the service or any peculiarity of the Home Office, but the very nature of direct administration by a central government department that leads to this systematic denial of publicity.

A second feature of direct administration by a government department—exemplified in the Home Office administration of prisons, but peculiar neither to that office nor to that service, is the reluctance and the difficulty with which such a directly administering national department associates voluntary agencies closely with its own administration. This, indeed, is not a criticism that arises out of the transfer of the prisons from local to central government, as the former prison authorities made even less use of voluntary agencies in connection with their work than does the Home Office of to-day. Moreover, some local governing bodies, notably the Poor Law authorities, have nearly always shown themselves, right down to the present time, unable to utilize or even to appreciate the valuable services of voluntary agencies of any kind. But, speaking generally, it may be said that the comparatively modern and rapidly growing local administrations in the wide fields of Health and Education have shown much more appreciation of the value of a close association of voluntary agencies with official work than has any directly administering government department. This close association, moreover, has already effected great improvements in the services concerned,[1] and promises increasingly to supply a necessary corrective of an exclusive bureaucratic administration. It is, accordingly, a drawback to direct administration by a government department that it exhibits a special reluctance to, and finds, in fact, exceptional difficulty in sharing its work with voluntary agencies,

[1] We refer not only to the manifold work of School Managers, Children's Care Committees, Country Holiday Fund Committees, etc., but also to such educational institutions under voluntary administration as industrial and reformatory schools, endowed schools and colleges, training colleges, technical institutes and universities ; not merely to volunteer health visitors and district nurses, infant welfare and maternity centres, hospital visitors and after-care committees, but also all the varied non-governmental medical institutions from " First Aid Centres " and voluntary hospitals to convalescent homes, and institutions for the incurable.

whether in using philanthropic institutions under voluntary management or in organizing systematic co-operation between officials and voluntary workers. We have analysed elsewhere the advantages of voluntary agencies, in comparison with public authorities, local or central.[1] We need only recall here that we enumerated three special advantages offered by voluntary agencies, which public authorities found it impracticable to provide. The voluntary agency (which is seldom to be relied on for continuity, can never cope with the whole need, and has various economic and other drawbacks) can (a) much more freely than any public authority try promising experiments ; (b) lavish an altogether disproportionate amount of time, labour, money and attention on selected individual cases ; and (c) bring to bear religious influences of peculiar potency which are nowadays outside the scope of a public authority.

The centralized administration of the Prison Commissioners has not entirely neglected the help of voluntary agencies, and—to say nothing of the institution of Visiting Justices—it has, during recent years, steadily increased its co-operation with them. Especially in the provision of "after care" by Discharged Prisoners' Aid Societies, in the supervision and assistance of "first offenders" and defendants released on probation, in the development of the "Borstal System," and in the somewhat sparing utilization of the voluntary services of lady visitors of female prisoners and those of outside clergymen and lecturers has the Home Office shown its appreciation of the value of voluntary agencies in co-operation with its own administration.

We hesitate to include in this volume any proposal for prison reform. But merely as examples of the scope for the further utilization of voluntary agencies we venture on some suggestions. Assuming that the idea of imposing solitary confinement as a punishment is abandoned, and with it all notion of

[1] *The Prevention of Destitution*, by S. and B. Webb, edition of 1920.

deliberately adding what we may call intellectual and emotional starvation to the deprivation of liberty, we cannot help thinking that, without increasing public expense, much more use might advantageously be made of carefully chosen volunteers—so as to make their ministrations not occasional and exceptional, at the option of particular governors, but regular daily or weekly incidents of prison life—(*a*) to conduct religious services, so as to free the prison chaplain for more adequate personal intercourse with the prisoners in his charge ; (*b*) to give lectures to the prisoners in their hours of leisure ; (*c*) to hold classes in literary education, and to teach handicrafts ; (*d*) to provide musical services and concerts, and (*e*) to visit individually in their cells, for helpful conversation, such prisoners as are willing to receive them. At Borstal there has already been set a precedent for the co-operation of outsiders in organized games. Unless there still lingers an intention to punish by intellectual and emotional starvation—which appears to us, to-day, as a relic of barbarism—it does not seem right that a prisoner should be locked up in solitary confinement in his cell without any opportunity for personal intercourse, as early as 4.30 p.m. daily, to remain alone and unprovided with occupation until 6.30 a.m. next morning.

A more revolutionary suggestion may be added. As a means of reformation of character, the official prison administration admittedly has achieved only the smallest success, whether for persons committed for short terms for offences connected with drunkenness and prostitution, or at the other end of the scale, for those sentenced to penal servitude for serious crimes. Might there not be found, in this matter, some assistance in a quite exceptional co-operation with voluntary agencies ? Would it be quite out of the question for the Home Office to try the experiment, for a limited term of years, of entrusting the entire administration of one of the prisons to (say) the Salvation Army, the Society of Friends, the

Church of England, or the Roman Catholic Church, if any of these volunteered for so onerous, and yet so important a public service? Naturally, no prisoner would be sent to serve his sentence in the prison under such a voluntary agency except at his own request. The denomination volunteering to undertake the experiment would necessarily be required to retain all the present safeguards against escape, to remain subject to official inspection, and to incur no increased expense. But within prescribed limits there seems no insuperable objection to permitting, as a temporary experiment in a selected prison, any alteration of the prison regimen that might be thought conducive to genuine reformation. After a period of (say) five, seven or ten years the results could be tested in every possible way, in comparison with those of the prisons under official administration. The problem presented by incessant recidivism is, in all its aspects, too serious, and the progress that we are at present making towards its solution is too discouraging, to warrant us in refusing any reasonable experiment that voluntary agencies might, out of public spirit and philanthropy, be willing to undertake.

V

There is a characteristic difference between the administration of English prisons under Local Government prior to 1878 and that of the Directors of Convict Prisons and the Prison Commissioners, in the relation between (a) the actual administrators of the several prisons ; (b) the official inspectors of that local administration ; and (c) the official authorities in whom the decision as to policy has been vested. When the power of and the responsibility for government is in one authority, and the inspectors are officers of another authority, a greater degree of impartiality, more fearless criticism, and a wider freedom of suggestion can be secured than is ever possible, in practice, when all the officers concerned—local

administrators, inspectors and the office staff of
the governing authority—are members of one and
the same service, and to a large extent, parts of a
single official hierarchy. It is one of the incidental
advantages of Local Government that it makes easy
the institution of a system of independent and trustworthy inspection of the administration, directed by
and responsible only to the Central Government. We
see this exemplified in the experience of the inspection of educational institutions by the Ministry of
Education and, within the Home Office itself, in that
of lunatic asylums by the Board of Control. The
experience of the English prison administration in
1835-77 and 1878-1921 respectively indicates how
much was lost in this way, not only as regards publicity but also as regards unrestrained and trustworthy inspection, when the local government of
prisons was merged in a centralized system. The
rights of inspection, criticism and suggestion conferred by the Act of 1877 on the Visiting Justices
were intended, it may be, to make good this loss.
They have, it will be admitted, fallen very far short,
alike in respect of obtaining publicity and in respect
of securing efficient inspection. This failure is due,
we think, not merely to the necessary shortcomings
of amateur and voluntary service, untrained and
spasmodic, as compared with the work of professional
officers continuously covering the whole field, but
also for another reason. Local inspection of central
government administration will always be less
effective than a centrally organized inspection of
local government administration. The dignity, the
authority, the very magnitude necessarily characteristic of a national administration, in comparison with
the powers of any local body, must inevitably make
inspection and criticism of the greater by the lesser
far less influential and effective than when the lesser is
being looked after by the greater. Even if the officers of the national authority have not always a
larger outlook, a wider experience and a greater
knowledge than those of a local body, they will

naturally believe themselves to be in these respects superior, and, what is more important, they will be normally so regarded. Whatever may be the short-comings of the inspection and criticism which the Ministry of Education maintains with regard to the schools, or which the Board of Control exercises with regard to the lunatic asylums, does anyone suppose that the inspection and criticism would gain in effectiveness or influence if the administration of all the schools or asylums were to pass to a central government department, whilst the rights of inspection and criticism of them were transferred, in exchange, to the local authorities ? When administration has to be centralized nationally, the most that can be, in practice, obtained from local bodies or local residents—and this, although no substitute for systematic inspection and professional criticism might be made of great value—is such indication of the public wants or desires, and such expression of popular complaints as is afforded to the Post Office by the Local Advisory Committees of Telephone Users, and to the railway administration by such habitual users of the service as the societies of commercial travellers and the Chambers of Commerce. Local advisory committees of this kind ought, in our judgment, to be instituted and officially recognized in connection with every government department.[1] But they afford no substitute for systematic inspection by professional officers, the possibility of which, accordingly, counts as a point to the credit of Local Government.

VI

To the student of Political Science, it must thus be concluded, the centralization of prison administration under a department of the National Government seems very far from being an unmixed gain. But we cannot, it is clear, go back to the state of

[1] On the whole subject, see *A Constitution for the Socialist Commonwealth of Great Britain.*

things in which every important local authority in England and Wales maintained its own undifferentiated common gaol. In so far as we continue to have to put people in prison, we need a highly differentiated series of institutions, according to the ten or a dozen main classes into which the prisoners should be divided ; and possibly not more, for the whole kingdom, than one or two buildings of each sort. Moreover, the aggregate cost must, in fairness to all districts, continue to be pooled, at any rate, so far as the bulk of the expenditure is concerned ; and this consideration of itself negatives any complete local autonomy. On the other hand there are great advantages to be gained, as has been indicated in the preceding paragraphs, by a more complete separation of day-by-day administration from inspection and final control of policy than is practicable when every officer from the humblest warder up to the chairman of the Prison Commissioners or the Secretary of State himself is a member of one and the same official hierarchy.

It does not, however, seem impossible to devise a constitution for the national prison system under which the final control of policy and the inspection, together with the provision of the cost, might remain in a central government department, whilst the day-by-day administration of each institution could be entrusted to another body. Assuming that (apart from the police station " lock-ups," and the special places of detention for persons under remand or awaiting trial, which it would be a positive advantage to dissociate from the prisons) ten or a dozen prisons, each specialized to meet the needs of a particular class of prisoners, were found to be adequate for the whole of England and Wales, the improvement in the means of locomotion nowadays makes it practicable to commit each person sentenced to detention to the institution adapted to his case.[1] The Prison

---

[1] It should, of course, be part of the provision for the maintenance of the prisoner's family, by whomsoever this is made, that the expenses of visits to the prisoner by near relatives should be found.

Commissioners must remain responsible for the welfare of every prisoner as the Board of Control is for that of every certified lunatic. But we do not see why it should not be practicable for the Prison Commissioners to entrust the actual conduct of each prison, either to a committee of the County or County Borough Council in the area of which it is situated ; or to a joint committee of several such local authorities ; or even, as we have suggested, to any religious or philanthropic body willing to undertake with proper safeguards an onerous, but socially valuable experiment. If the Home Office could, in this way, relieve itself from the detailed administration of a number of institutions all over the country, which can never be managed entirely satisfactorily from Whitehall, the service would gain by the restoration of publicity, by the greater freedom and vigour of the inspection, by the increased ease with which a trial could be given to promising experiments, and by the valuable new assistance that could be afforded by voluntary agencies. Even the substitution of variety for uniformity, in so far as it permitted a certain freedom of local initiative and opportunity for experiment, we should count as, on balance, a gain. The fact that, in 1877, there seemed no other alternative to a disastrous anarchy of autonomous local administration than a completely centralized system should not prevent us—after more than forty years of trial of an unnecessarily simple " nationalization " in the crude form in which it was conceived by Sir Edmund Du Cane—from deliberately seeking to construct a more highly organized administration.

VII

The reflection emerges that, when all is said and done, it is probably quite impossible to make a good job of the deliberate incarceration of a human being in the most enlightened of dungeons. Even the mere sense of confinement, the mere deprivation of liberty, the mere interference with self-initiative—

if in any actual prison the adverse regimen were, in practice, ever limited to these restrictions—could hardly ever, in themselves, have a beneficial result on intellect, emotions or character. We suspect that it passes the wit of man to contrive a prison which shall not be gravely injurious to the minds of the vast majority of the prisoners, if not also to their bodies. So far as can be seen at present, the most practical and the most hopeful of " prison reforms " is to keep people out of prison altogether ! It is in this direction that the present Prison Commissioners, and Parliament and the Home Office, have been, during the last two decades, making most progress. It has been discovered that we can keep people out of prison by the simple expedient of not sending them there. By refusing to commit to prison any child under a certain age, or any prisoner certifiable as of unsound mind ; by freely allowing bail on practicable terms to poor defendants as well as to those with means ; by making the utmost possible use of the Probation of Offenders Act ; by substituting, wherever practicable, sentences of binding over, or fine, for short terms of imprisonment ; and by invariably according time for payment of a fine, instead of instantly committing in default of payment, some magistrates, and even some assize judges, have demonstrated that—notably in the case of "First Offenders"; a large proportion of the former admissions to prison were unnecessary. The total number of persons committed to prison within the year has fallen from 197,941 in 1904-5 to 43,267 in 1920-1. And although this fall is not to be ascribed wholly to the above-mentioned beneficent advances in law and practice, the effect on the statistics of these mere changes in the temper of the judicial authorities is reported to have been most marked, and so far as can be learned the results have been almost entirely good.[1]

[1] Mr. Justice McCardie, at the Glamorganshire Assizes, asked Police-inspector Rees Davies his experience as to the future of persons bound over under the First Offenders Act. Inspector Davies replied that his experience was that they never went back to a life of crime. The Judge said he had

Unfortunately, not all Assizes and Quarter Sessions, and especially not all Petty Sessions, have yet adopted the new attitude of mind ; and they continue—in the case of the unpaid Justices, largely through the routine minds of magistrates' clerks—almost recklessly to commit to prison offenders who would elsewhere be spared this demoralizing and dangerous experience. It seems a pity that there should be no one in the Lord Chancellor's Department or in the Home Office with a pretty taste in statistics, who would set himself to compile, year by year, the percentages, for all the various Petty Sessions and all the various Quarter Sessions and Assizes, of defendants (i) respectively allowed and refused bail ; (ii) discharged as being under age ; (iii) dealt with as persons of unsound mind ; (iv) discharged as " First Offenders " ; (v) released on probation ; (vi) merely bound over ; (vii) sentenced only to pay a fine ; (viii) allowed time for payment ; (ix) sentenced to imprisonment merely in default of payment of fine ; (x) committed for " Borstal " treatment ; (xi) sentenced to imprisonment without the option of a fine or to penal servitude ; and (xii) sentenced to preventive detention after penal servitude. A similar compilation might be made for the various County Courts, of the percentages of debtors committed (largely through the several Registrars) for contempt of Court in failing to discharge their judgment debts, and for the various Petty Sessions, of persons committed for non-payment of rates and taxes. It is reported that such a statistical comparison would reveal the fact that the modern expedient for " keeping people out of prison," beneficent though they have proved to be, are being adopted by different

listened to the inspector's statement with considerable interest, because he had asked himself the question many times, " What was the result of binding over first offenders who previously bore good characters ? " I have come to the conclusion, supported by the view of one of the most experienced inspectors (continued the Judge), that in many cases first offenders have been saved from a future criminal life by the exercise of a wise mercy on the part of the Judge. In my opinion the words of Inspector Rees Davies are of an important character, not only to every Judge but every magistrate who sits in a criminal Court of law.—(*Times*, November 16th, 1921.)

judicial authorities in different parts of the country, to such very different degrees, as to be explicable, even when full allowance is made for differing local circumstances, only by failure to carry out, or even to understand, the new policy. With such comparative statistics before him—especially when they came to extend over several years—a Lord Chancellor or a Home Secretary who took himself seriously as a Minister of Justice would know how, with all proper discretion, to bring home to the minds of those judicial authorities who were making the most extravagant use of the device of imprisonment that they were falling behind the more enlightened of their colleagues. It is suggested that if none of the judges and magistrates sent any higher percentage of recruits to join the sad army of the prison population than the present average for all the Courts, the aggregate total of commitments might possibly be reduced by as much as a quarter.

Another direction in which the number of persons committed to prison needs to be reduced is that indicated by Parliament by passing the Mental Deficiency Act ot 1913. Whether the proportion of prisoners who are mentally defective is only 2 or 3 per cent., as some say, or as high as 20 or 30 per cent. as other persons report, it is now definitely recognized that their committal to, or retention in the ordinary prison is useless to society, injurious to themselves and subtly demoralizing to the other prisoners. Unfortunately, the narrowiy restricted terms of the Act, and even more, the indisposition of the various authorities concerned to make use of it, have, so far, prevented any application of it to more than an infinitesimal proportion of the mentally defective inmates of our prisons. Moreover, an extension of the principle of specialized segregation seems required. The elaborate mental tests applied to all the millions of recruits to the United States army during 1917-8 revealed the fact that an unexpectedly high percentage of adult men seemed to have retained the mentality of a child of ten or twelve. Apart altogether, from the question of congenital mental deficiency, it seems desirable that there should be a systematic scientific investigation (for which that of Dr. Charles Goring affords a precedent) of the mental capacity of the whole prison population, on the lines so successfully planned in the American army. Without attaching all the importance to these mental tests that their inventors believe them to possess, it seems probable that such an investigation would reveal a large proportion of prisoners for whom the regimen of a prison was inept, and who ought (as the Home Office Departmental Committee of 1894-5, suggested) to be in quite another kind of institution. It would probably show also that much of the present prison regimen needs specializing in order to be adapted to the requirements of prisoners of widely differing mental grades.[1]

[1] " Uninvestigated offenders," observes Dr. Hamblin Smith, the medical officer of the Birmingham Local Prison, " are the most expensive luxury that any community can indulge in " (*British Medical Journal*, 17 December, 1921, p. 1036). The interesting and valuable experiments conducted at this prison, under the auspices of the Visiting Justices, with the tacit consent of the Prison Commissioners, are suggestive as to the possible results of more systematic devolution.

INDEX

Abingdon County Bridewell, 105.
Account Keeping, Uniformity in, 203.
Acton, William, 26.
Act for consolidating . . . the laws relating to the building and regulation of gaols . . . in England and Wales, 74-6.
Adams, Mr. Sergeant, 128.
Adler, Miss N., 228.
Admiralty, 238.
Adshead, Joseph, 118, 178.
"Aggregate in order to segregate," 235.
Aikin, Dr. John, 32.
Alcoholic drink in prison, 8, 21-2, 195.
Allen, William, 72.
America, North, Prisons of, 39, 43-4, 94-5, 115, 119, 228; Silent system in, 129; Transportation to, 44, 50, 180.
—— United States of, 30, 115, 177, 250-1; Cellular system in, 217.
Anglican chaplain, 191.
Annapolis, Transportation of Convicts to, 44.
Arundel, Lord, 4.
Asquith, Mr., 219, 220, 224.
Associated Labour advocated by Howard, 37, 89; introduced by Becher, 61; see also *Classification, Silent System.*
Aston Common Gaol (Warwick), 4.
Attfield, Dr., 185.
Auburn, Prison at (New York), 118.
Auburnian System, 118; see also *Silent System.*
Austin, Lieutenant, 164, 169, 171, 173, 174, 175.
Australia, Convict Settlement in Western, 185; Transportation to, 44, 46, 47.
Australasia, Convicts in, 45.

Bailey, J. B., 32, 37.
Baker, Colonel, 185.
Balfour, Jabez S., 181.
Bambridge, —, 21; Prosecution of, 26.
Barclays, The, 72.
Barnes, Prosecution of, 26.
Barnett, M. G., 226.
Barnewell, 80.
Barnstaple, Prison at, 105.
Barrow, T. P., 181.
Basingstoke, New Prison at, 105.
Basket making as prison employment, 226.
Bath and Wells, Bishop of, 38.
Bath City Gaol, 76; Appointment of officers of, 189; Chaplain of, on crank labour, 151; Number of inmates of, 105; Separate system at, 132; Silent system at, 129.

Bathing in prison, 208.
Batley Gaol, 7.
Battersea Park, Site for prison at, 46.
Bayley, Thomas Butterworth, 55, 56.
Bazeley, W., 57.
Becher, Rev. J. T., 47, 48, 60-2, 66, 72, 84, 85, 87.
Becke, L., 45.
Bedford County Gaol, Diet at, 11; Employment at, 198; Howard's reforms at, 34-5; Use of treadwheel at, 98.
Beevor, Sir Thomas, Bart., 55.
Begging by prisoners, 9.
Belgium, 115, 118; Cellular system in, 217; Use of "mask" in prisons of, 189.
Bellows, R. W., 32.
Bennet, Hon. Henry Grey, 64, 69, 70, 72, 101; and Bill to abolish gaolers' fees, 70.
Bentham, Jeremy, 18, 40, 46-9, 67, 68, 97, 110, 217, 233.
Berkshire County Gaol at Reading, Health and overcrowding in, 51; Treadwheel at, 99.
—— Quarter Sessions, Approval of Graham dietary by, 137.
Bermuda, Hulks at, 45.
Bertrand, M. Ernest, 217.
Best, Chief Justice, 80.
Beverley; see *Yorkshire.*
Bideford, Prison at, 105.
Binny, J., 13, 45, 49, 73, 96, 99, 146, 181, 183, 189.
Birmingham, Pin-making at, 88-9.
—— Borough Gaol, 114, 128, 181, 216; Cruelty in, 164, 169-176, 190; Dietary in, 154; Employment at, 150; Governor of, 164-170; Health at, 104; "Mark" system at, 164, 167-8; Royal Commission on, 170-5, 186.
—— Prisoners' Aid Society, 227.
—— Records of, 133.
Birt, Weston, 47.
Black Hole in Calcutta, Prisons like, 18.
Blackstone, Sir William, 38, 39, 40, 59, 66.
Bliss, T., 26.
Blizard, Sir William, 103.
Blount, Mr., 172, 175.
Board of Trade, 198.
Bodmin Gaol, Administration of, 74; Employment at; see also *Cornwall.*
Bookbinding as prison employment, 226.
Books by prisoners, 23, 26, 181, 183, 193, 198, 200, 220, 226.
Borough Compter, The (London), 65; Maladministration of, 106.
Borstal Association, The, 228.

Falmouth, New Prison at, 105.
Farming, The practice of, 5-9, 13-17, 18 ; Advocated by Bentham, 67, 233 ; recommended by Pearson, 163-233.
Farnborough, Lord, 47.
Feeble-mindedness among prisoners, 205, 224, 225, 229, 250-1.
Fees exacted in gaols, 5-8 ; in Houses of Correction, 13-17 ; Abolition of, proposed by Howard, 34 ; regulation of, not enforced, 50, 52 ; Abolition of, 70-1.
Ferri, Enrico, 176.
Feversham, Prison at, 105.
Field, John, 22, 26, 32, 36, 46, 50, 53, 54, 65, 94, 99, 128, 130.
Fielding, Henry, 17, 31.
First Aid Centres, 240.
Fisherton Anger, Wiltshire County Gaol at, 8-9, 54, 56, 103, 105, 109.
Fleet Prison, The, 1, 6, 43, 75 ; Fees at, 71 ; House of Commons Committee on, 21, 25-27, 64 ; Iniquities of, 25, 28-9 ; Number of inmates of, 31 ; Sale of intoxicants at, 8 ; Warden of, 5.
Fletcher, S. W., 181, 220 ; see also *Silent System, Separate System.*
Flogging in prison, 101 ; continuous, at Birmingham, 171 ; at Leicester, 175-6.
Foster, Sir M., 30.
Fothergill, Dr., 46.
France, Prisons of, 94, 97, 115, 181 ; Cellular system in, 217.
Franchise prisons, 3-4, 104-6.
Frost, John, 45.
Fry, Elizabeth, 71-2, 73, 83, 87, 99, 101 ; Reforms due to, 74-5.
—— Katherine, 71.

Galsworthy, John, 223.
Gaol Acts, 73.
Gaol fever, 19-20, 30 ; Absence of abroad, 35 ; Renewed outbreaks of, 51 ; Dying away of, 53.
Gaols, always the King's, 1, 3 ; Multiplicity of owners of, 3, 4 ; Profit-making enterprises, 5-9 ; Character of premises used for, 4 ; Fees in, 5-8 ; Alcoholic drinks in, 8 ; Food in, 8-11.
Gardening as prison employment, 226.
Garnish, 25, 65, 193.
Garotters' Act, 187.
Gauntlet, Running the, 25.
Gay, John, 31.
General Penitentiary Act, 1779, 90.
General Prisons Act, 1835, 72.
General Election 1874, 198, 200 ; of 1892, 219.
Ghent, Prison at, 89, 118.
Gibbs, Eric, 45.
Gibbs of Pentonville, 146.
Gibson, E. C. S., 32.
Gibraltar, Hulks at, 45.
Giltspur Street Prison, 106.
Gladstone, Lord, 220.
Glamorganshire Assizes, 248.

Glass-bead blowing as prison employment, 86.
Gloucestershire, County Gaols of, 48, 74, 76 ; Diet in, 11 ; Employment in, 86 ; Fees in, 50 ; Health and overcrowding in, 51 ; Local Acts re, 40, 53, 58 ; Maladministration of, 57 ; Officials of, 103 ; Solitary system at, 90-91 ; Use of treadwheel at, 97 ;
—— Prisons, 2, 92-3, 40, 103 ; Reform of, 58-60 ; 68 ; Maladministration of, 57.
—— Prisoners' Aid Society, 227.
—— Quarter Sessions Bill, 40, 69.
Godalphin, Earl of, 4.
Goncourt, Edmond de, 179.
Good, Dr. J. M., 8, 66.
Gordon, Charles, 25, 64.
Goring, Charles, 226, 236, 251.
Gosport Prison, 140.
Gover, Dr., 206.
Graham, A., 45.
Graham, Sir James, 114, 134.
—— dietaries, 135-7, 140-1, 143.
Grants in Aid, 190, 234.
Grey, Earl, 45.
Grey, Sir George, 140, 144, 186 ; and Committee on Prison Discipline, 129.
Griffiths, Arthur, 25, 45, 47, 49, 64, 71, 74, 86, 181, 220.
"Groats," 27.
Gurney, J. J., 63, 72-3, 83, 235.

Habeas Corpus Act, 6.
Hales, Dr. Stephen, 30.
Halévy, Elie, 49.
Halifax Prison, Fees at, 4, 193.
Hall, Bishop, 158.
Hall, Captain Basil, 95.
Hanway, Jonas, 12, 21, 32, 55, 90.
Hard labour, Meaning of, 143-4, 181.
Hase, William, 97.
Hay, William, M.P., 26-7.
Haygarth, John, 35.
Hampshire Assizes, 20.
—— County Gaol, 11, 56.
Hatcham, Prison at, 2,.
Headlam, John, 11, 81.
Hereford Prison, 11, 56, 102.
Henderson, Frank, 181, 189.
Hertfordshire County Gaol, Diet at, 11.
Hill, F. Davenport, 74.
Hill, Matthew Davenport, 54, 74, 133, 165, 175.
Hippisley, Sir John Coxe, 99.
Hoare, Samuel, 72, 95.
Hobhouse, Stephen, 115, 118, 231-2.
Hogarth, 12.'
Holford, George Peter, M.P., 48-9, 64, 69, 72, 85, 86, 88, 89 ; Bill introduced by, 69 ; and committee on Transportation, 68 ; and employment of untried prisoners, 81.
Holland, Lord, 69.
Holliday, John, 54, 56.
Holloway Gaol, 198; see also *City of London.*
Home, Bishop, 158.

Royal Commissions on Birmingham and Leicester, 186, 237.
Rug-making as prison employment, 86.
"Rules," The, 6.
Russell, C. E. B., 226.
Russell, Lord John, 114.
Russell, Rev. Whitworth, 88, 119.
Rylands, Peter, 200.

St. Augustine's House of Correction (Kent), 70.
St. Margarets; see *Westminster*.
St. Petersburg, International Penitentiary Congress at, 1889, 32.
Saleilles, R., 230.
Salisbury, Marquis of, 48.
—— Prisons, 105; see *Wiltshire*.
Salvation Army, 185, 218, 242, 247.
San Michele (Rome), Prison of, 116.
Sanctuary, 25.
Sandwich, Prison at, 105.
Savoy Palace, Prison of, 1, 4, 31, 43.
—— Sanctuary at, 25.
Scandals at Birmingham and Leicester, 169-176.
Scougall, F., 181, 220.
Scullard, H. H., 32.
Secondary Punishments, Select committee on, 77, 104, 111.
Secretan, Charles Frederick, 26.
Secretiveness, Policy of, 235-240.
Senior, Nassau, 110.
Separate System, 117-8, 183-5; see also *Silent System, Cellular System*.
Sheffield, Courts of Request at, 194.
—— Prison at, 4.
Sheffield, Sir James, 20.
Shepton Mallet; see *Somerset*.
Sheriff, responsible for gaol, 6, 34, 108-9.
Shoemaking as prison employment, 86, 226.
Shot-drill as prison employment, 155, 156.
Shrewsbury; see also *Shropshire*.
Shropshire County Gaol (Shrewsbury), 6, 25, 40, 51, 132.
Sidmouth, Lord, 73, 88, 107.
Sigerson, G., 200.
Silent System, The, 94-5, 115-8; introduced by Clay and Chesterton, 95-6; at Auburn, 118-9; at Coldbath Fields, 122-5; Adoption of, 127-33, 176-9, 183-5. See also *Cellular System, Separate System*.
Simon, Mr. Sergeant, 206.
Skipton; see also *Yorks, W. Riding*.
Smith, Dr. Edward, 137, 138-9; on the Graham Dietary, 139, 140-1.
Smith, Sydney, on Inspectors, 75; on use of tread-wheel and employment, 81, 88, 96, 99.
Smith, William, M.D., 70, 78.
Smollett, T., 26, 31.
Society of Friends, 115, 242.
Society for the Improvement of Prison Discipline, 2, 68, 72, 5, 79, 83, 88, 97, 98, 99, 102, 104, 105.

Solitary Confinement, 177; see *Separate System, Silent System, Cellular System*.
Somerset, County Bridewell at Taunton, 16.
—— House of Correction (Shepton Mallet), 102.
—— Woollen workers in, 20.
South Molton, New Prison at, 105.
Southwark Prison, 5; see also *London and King's Bench*.
Southwell House of Correction, Classification at, 93-4; Employment at, 80, 84-5; Maladministration at, 60-2; Treatment of untried prisoners at, 80.
Spain, Cellular system in, 217.
Stafford County Gaol, 11, 31, 40, 56, 88-9.
Stamford Prison, 6.
Standing Orders not published, 237.
Steele, Richard, 25.
Stocking-making as prison employment, 83.
Stonebreaking as prison employment, 156.
Stopford, W. J., 202.
Stoughton, John, 32.
Strait-jacket, Improper use of, 170-4.
Stuart, James, 95.
Suffolk, Prisons in, 10, 29, 56, 97; Report of Commissioner in, on dietary of prisoners, 102; see also *Bury St. Edmunds*.
Suicide, at Birmingham, 169; Precautions against, 184; Amount of in prison, 210, 219.
Surrey, Prisons in, 11, 79, 99, 117, 131, 182.
Surveyor-General of Prisons, 114, 117, 146, 178, 187, 202.
Sussex County Gaol, 54, 56, 63, 90, 107; Local Act for, 40.
Swaffham House of Correction, Education at, 157-8.
Swan River, Convict settlement at, 44, 180.
Sweeting, R. D. R., 32, 37.
Swiss Prisons, Solitary sleeping cells in, 89.

Tailoring as prison employment, 83, 86, 226.
Tallack, W., 32, 178, 215.
Tasmania, Convict settlement in, 47.
Taunton Assize, 20.
—— Gaol, 20, 154; see also *Somerset*.
Taylor, T., 32.
Telephone Users, Local Advisory Committees of, 245.
Tewkesbury, New prison at, 105.
Thames, Convict hulks on the, 45.
Thame Bridewell, 17.
Thirsk; see also *N. R. Yorkshire*.
Thistlewood, 1.
Thomson, Sir Basil, 181.
Thumbscrews for prisoners, 10.
Ticket of leave, 180, 182.
Timpson, Thomas, 71.

For Product Safety Concerns and Information please contact our EU
representative GPSR@taylorandfrancis.com
Taylor & Francis Verlag GmbH, Kaufingerstraße 24, 80331 München, Germany

9 780367 110529